11/22 1 X 8/23/15 C 2015

The Reagan Era

THE REAGAN ERA

A History of the 1980s

Doug Rossinow

Columbia University Press
New York

Columbia University Press
Publishers Since 1893
New York   Chichester, West Sussex
cup.columbia.edu
Copyright © 2015 Doug Rossinow
All rights reserved

Library of Congress Cataloging-in-Publication Data
Rossinow, Douglas C. (Douglas Charles)
The Reagan Era : a history of the 1980s / Doug Rossinow.
pages   cm
Includes bibliographical references and index.
ISBN 978-0-231-16988-2 (cloth : alk. paper) — ISBN 978-0-231-53865-7 (electronic)
1. United States—Politics and government—1981–1989.   2. United States—Foreign
relations—1981–1989. 3. Reagan, Ronald.   I. Title.
E876.R676   2015
973.927—dc23
2014011193
⊚
Columbia University Press books are printed on permanent and durable acid-free paper.
This book is printed on paper with recycled content.
Printed in the United States of America
c 10 9 8 7 6 5 4 3 2 1

COVER PHOTO: Courtesy Ronald Reagan Library
COVER DESIGN: Milenda Nan Ok Lee

References to websites (URLs) were accurate at the time of writing. Neither the author nor
Columbia University Press is responsible for URLs that may have expired or changed since the
manuscript was prepared.

This book is dedicated to the class of 1984.

MR. WORLDLY-WISEMAN: How camest thou by thy burden at first?

CHRISTIAN: By reading this Book in my hand.

—John Bunyan, *The Pilgrim's Progress*

Contents

CONTENTS

Acknowledgments

Some of the smartest historians working today read all or much of this book as I wrote it. Robert McMahon, Eric Arnesen, and Rebecca Lowen took extraordinary time and care in reading every word and provided an awesome level of response, as did some anonymous readers. Ken Lipartito, Andrew Preston, Alan Brinkley, Jeanne Grant, and Jon Zimmerman read big pieces and, as the saying goes, rescued me from embarrassment on a number of key points. Geri Thoma represented this project faithfully. Philip Leventhal, my editor at Columbia University Press, showed unwavering enthusiasm and made many very wise suggestions. Philip is that rare thing in intellectual life—a listener, not just a talker. I revised the manuscript in the welcoming embrace of the Institute for Archaeology, Conservation, and History at the University of Oslo, during a splendid semester there as a Fulbright Scholar. My profound thanks go to Professor Tor Egil Førland, head of the department, for the outstanding hospitality he showed me and my family, and to the whole staff and faculty in Oslo. I also owe thanks to students at Metropolitan State University who have taken my course "From Reagan to Obama: America Since 1980." They helped me refine my ideas and express them clearly. Annalisa Zox-Weaver proved a copyeditor nonpareil—she was more knowledgeable about the subject matter than I had a right to expect—and ironed out my maladroit phrasing with diligence and good humor. The entire production process at Columbia was coordinated by the splendid Leslie Kriesel, who, in one especially heroic moment, really saved my bacon.

ACKNOWLEDGMENTS

Words will not express how much better Rebecca Lowen made this book. She was patience itself in her detailed and reflective reading of more drafts of chapters, and then of the whole manuscript, than I can recount. Rebecca went over each chapter with incredible care and thoughtfulness, gently pointing out numerous ways I could strengthen my work. No one else could have done this. This book topic might have been the last one to which she would have chosen to devote so many hours and days, but she did so without a word of complaint. For this, and for more important things, she has my everlasting gratitude as well as my love.

The Reagan Era

Introduction

Common Sense

In 1984, I turned eighteen and voted for Ronald Reagan. I made the same choice as did about six of every ten American voters aged eighteen to twenty-four.[1] Reagan affirmed values that attracted me: unqualified patriotism, national strength, and individual empowerment. I was not very interested in Reagan's specific policy stands. I view many things about Reagan and the 1980s differently today. But now, just as I did then, I see the 1980s as an era of crucial choices for Americans—a time of political transformation and of alterations in social values and ways of life. At the center of these changes—their symbol, their champion—stood Ronald Wilson Reagan.

Reagan is part of a select group of political leaders, including Thomas Jefferson and Woodrow Wilson, whose names became watchwords for political creeds and stances toward society, even toward the world. Judging Reaganism is more important than judging Ronald Reagan as an individual, although any sound guide to the 1980s must also show Reagan for who and what he truly was. Reaganism was a particular variety of American conservatism, and the 1980s were its heyday. None of Reaganism's basic features was new in 1980, and several of them remained prominent in American conservatism after 1990. But in the decade of the 1980s, these elements came together in a specially cohesive and potent way, in response to the era's political and social circumstances, forming a political identity that was also fueled and shaped by Reagan's success.

Reaganism consisted of a few core components: an insistence that unfettered capitalism is both socially beneficial and morally good; a fierce patriotism that waves the flag, demands global military supremacy, and brooks no criticism of the United States; and a vision of society as an arena where individuals win or lose because of their own talents and efforts. On these articles of faith virtually all of Reaganism's adherents agreed. On matters of culture, Reaganism was split down the middle, with the fault line the question of hedonism. Some conservatives in the 1980s reveled in conspicuous consumption, even decadence (a word that took on positive connotations in advertising copy during the 1980s). Others wished to quarantine hedonism in the economic realm, preserving culture and family life as redoubts of warmth, order, and piety against the tides of an individualistic, coarsening world. Both hedonists and traditionalists felt sure that their cultural stance was the authentically Reaganite one, which made Reaganism, on the question of culture, a kind of dual persuasion. But during the 1980s, this rift in conservative ranks was overshadowed by conservative unity on economics and foreign policy.

Reagan often presented himself as an eighteenth-century radical in the style of Thomas Paine, author of *Common Sense*. He was fond of Paine's words of inspiration to the American rebels of 1776, "We have it in our power to begin the world over again." Reagan quoted Paine's words in November 1979, in the speech formally announcing that he was running for the presidency in 1980; he did so again in his address to the Republican National Convention in July 1980, where he was nominated.[2] By 1980, Reagan had been making the same case for nearly thirty years: that the American legacy of liberal idealism, grounded in the dream of individual freedom from tyranny, now had its natural home among conservatives.

In the 1980s, conservatives succeeded in remaking large parts of American life. They reshaped American politics, working an alchemy that transmuted conservative dogma—on the wisdom of low income taxes, the special virtue of entrepreneurs, the parasitic character of government, the need for overwhelming (rather than merely great) military strength, the dependence of social health on proper values, and the nuclear family as the building block of society—into common sense. Reagan and his followers scored many victories, large and small, in the U.S. political system during the 1980s. Along the way, they shifted American political debate onto Reagan's chosen terrain, and Reagan's liberal enemies found themselves permanently on the defensive.

The Reaganite mission to restore popular faith in capitalism and individualism as social norms made substantial headway in the 1980s—gains for American conservatism that liberals have not succeeded in reversing. That these invigorated norms were contradicted by the reality of widespread reliance on government assistance, and not only among the poor, may reveal ambivalence or even hypocrisy on a mass scale. But this contradiction does not erase the victory of political conservatism. Regarding more strictly cultural matters, Reaganism's results in the 1980s were distinctly mixed, as were the sympathies of its supporters. Individualism could not be contained within the sphere of economics. Conservatives hailed the unadulterated individualism known as hedonism in economic life; many liberals and leftists celebrated individuals' expanding choices regarding lifestyle and identity. The less restrained, sometimes crass, culture of the 1980s, featuring casual vulgarity and aggressive displays of sexuality, distressed the avowedly Christian and socially conservative wing of Reaganism. The cultural change that these behaviors reflected extended a process that had begun well before the 1980s. Nonetheless, this continuing cultural transformation was a big part of the Reagan era, one to which some self-styled conservatives and progressives both contributed.[3]

Abroad, America's victory in the Cold War, which began during Reagan's presidency and was completed during the succeeding administration of President George H. W. Bush, is a major legacy of the 1980s. The role of U.S. leadership in the Soviet retreat from superpower military competition remains a matter of controversy.[4] Reagan personally offered unqualified statements of support for liberty and democracy for the peoples living under indirect Soviet rule in Eastern Europe (Bush was more equivocal, at least rhetorically), and, by 1990, this empire had fallen, along with the Berlin Wall that symbolized it. Reagan became president convinced that the USSR had gained a strategic edge over the United States, and he was determined to reverse that trend and put the United States on top through an enormous military buildup. Initially, he showed little interest in diplomacy with the Soviets, but his stance changed dramatically during his second term in office, when Reagan negotiated a breakthrough arms-reduction agreement with a new Soviet leader, Mikhail Gorbachev, a triumph that Gorbachev and Bush followed up at decade's end. The Soviets retrenched at the end of the 1980s in a desperate effort to revive their economy and save their social system. It is not clear that the Reaganite method of enhanced military brawn caused this outcome. Nonetheless, Reagan's goal of securing U.S. primacy was achieved—and the related Reaganite hope of reviving U.S. national pride and self-confidence, widely perceived to have faltered following the Vietnam War, was also realized.

Reaganism met with substantial resistance during the 1980s, but that resistance is not the heart of the era's history as told here. Liberal and moderate opposition to some of Reagan's initiatives was stiff and, indeed, prevented him from completely fulfilling his conservative goals.[5] But liberals had little to cheer about in the 1980s. They found few opportunities to advance their own priorities. They spent their energies parrying powerful conservative thrusts and salvaging what they could of past liberal accomplishments. Some Americans dissented even more sharply than did liberal Democrats from the prevailing political trends of the day. The "front porch politics" of grassroots protest for social justice was vibrant and widespread in the 1980s, as Michael Stewart Foley shows in detail, even if such mobilizing efforts ended more in defeat than in victory.[6] More Americans identified themselves as conservatives than as liberals during the 1980s; however, these proportions did not change over the course of the decade, a fact that should encourage caution in estimating Reaganism's impact. After surveying the evidence, the political scientist Larry M. Bartels concludes, in his 2008 book, *Unequal Democracy*, that "while ideological debate among elected officials and public intellectuals does seem to have shifted to the right over the past 30 years, it is far from obvious that the political views of ordinary citizens have become noticeably more conservative." Fewer Americans in 1990 said that government had too much power than had said so in 1980. This change reflected discontent with the neglect of important public duties by the government in the Reagan era. On the other hand, this shift may suggest satisfaction among Reagan's followers that he had succeeded in curbing government's powers.[7]

Although the evidence concerning the advance of conservative doctrine among the American population as a whole during the 1980s is ambiguous, there can be little doubt that the U.S. political system, ruled—like any such system—by elites, albeit with intermittent popular input, moved dramatically rightward in this decade. Conservatives framed public debate in the 1980s, making the era's politics theirs, as liberals had done in the 1930s and 1960s. The influential and powerful members of the country's major institutions were profoundly affected by Reaganism. Individualism and market forces found more—and more unrestrained—acolytes within academic life in the 1980s. Political sages arrived at a new consensus that America was "naturally" a conservative country.[8] In significant part because of the success of Reaganism in elite circles, Reagan's vision of America carried greater cultural force as a description of objective reality in 1990 than it had in 1980.

For all of its achievements and successes in the 1980s, Reaganism's record was also marred by its limits and defects as a governing ideology. Some of these failings, like Reaganism's accomplishments, were reflected and embodied in Reagan as an individual. Reagan authentically believed that the eighteenth-century radicalism of Paine, who held that "government even in its best state is but a necessary evil," remained relevant to the late twentieth century.[9] But Paine had done more than embrace economic liberty as the wellspring of social health and happiness. He also identified with those who felt the touch of the hangman's noose, and generally protested the cruel treatment of the poor at the hands of the law.[10] Reagan and his most fervent disciples all but scoffed at such sympathies; Reagan's affinity for Paine was highly selective. Indeed, the 1980s was a decade when a long-term project of increased imprisonment in America took off. Money poured into prison construction and local police forces, turning the latter into miniature militaries. The numbers of people held prisoner by the fifty states and the federal government grew dramatically, with the rate climbing from 139 per 100,000 Americans in 1980 to 297 in 1990.[11] This escalation addressed widespread anxiety about violent crime; many took satisfaction from this crusade for incarceration as a policy success, while others came to rue it as excessive, harmful, and unfair. The brunt of this project fell, unsurprisingly, on the poor, and very disproportionately on African American men, a great many of whom were jailed for nonviolent drug-related offenses. Conservatives who said they believed in small government, from Reagan on down, were untroubled by this large exception to their doctrine. They also had a lot of help waging this "war on crime," a large part of it from Democrats.

In the name of freedom, Reaganites declaimed a creed with scant compassion for the disadvantaged. They believed that those lagging in the race of life had no real claim on society and should rely on private acts of beneficence. In the era of the welfare state and progressive taxation, Reaganites viewed the privileged, not the underprivileged, as society's victims. The rich were exploited by the liberal state—they were the proverbial geese who laid the golden eggs. In major instances of widespread suffering during his presidency, Reagan was either an indifferent bystander, as with the deeply traumatic AIDS crisis that exploded in the 1980s, or a contributor to the problem, as with the expansion of homelessness. The hard hand of individualism, albeit gloved in earnest idealism, was placed near the heart of Reaganism.

"What I want to see above all," Reagan said in 1983, "is that this country remains a country where someone can always get rich." With these words, he presented himself as had his namesake, Woodrow Wilson—as the patron of, in Wilson's words, "the men who are on the make, rather than the men who are already made."[12] But in deeds, Reagan showed a special concern for "the men who are already made." Reagan and his followers sought to unburden the rich from taxes and business regulations. Many of his appointees, often drawn from the business world, took a brazen smash-and-grab approach to government service, leading to an astounding array of corrupt practices, scores of criminal indictments, and the largest military procurement scandal in U.S. history. In a well-known affair, Reagan's officials diverted funds meant for low-income housing into projects that enriched favored Republican insiders.[13] Two of Reagan's top three White House advisers during his first term, Edwin Meese and Michael Deaver, ended the decade disgraced over their corruption: Deaver convicted in court for lying under oath about his ill-concealed and prohibited lobbying activities, Meese only escaping criminal indictment for habitually using his government position to benefit himself because, it seemed, the nation's capital had become exhausted by him and simply wanted him to go away. Too pronounced to ignore, this pattern of behavior betrays a deeper pattern of belief. Many Reaganites evidently felt entitled to fleece the public. Honest leadership could hardly defend such abuses of the nation's trust. But Reagan's tendency to ignore inconvenient facts was well known. His warm partisanship for moneyed men, and his impatience with criticism of his appointees' misconduct, no doubt seemed a license for corruption to those with such proclivities. Reagan's disdain for the truth and disregard for the law—revealed most

6

starkly during the Iran-Contra scandal of 1986–1987—ended the interval in American life, corresponding roughly with the presidencies of Gerald Ford and Jimmy Carter, when honesty and probity in high office had been fashionable, even gainful.

Reaganism was also, serious historians must admit, the politics of the white "backlash" against the advance of racial equality. For young people in America's inner cities who experienced depressionlike levels of unemployment and poverty throughout the 1980s, Reaganism was anything but a sunny vision of the future. For them, "Reaganism," in the bitter words of one writer, "was all about tough love and denial and getting used to having nothing."[14] The increasing asperity of the criminal justice system toward the poor and black—which sometimes seemed the main response of the American state to worsening conditions in the nation's cities in the 1980s—informed this view. This perspective from the underside of Reaganism should be neither neglected nor repressed. Anglican Archbishop Desmond Tutu of South Africa, who met with Reagan to protest the president's support for the apartheid white-supremacist government in that country, afterward pronounced Reagan "a racist pure and simple."[15] Reagan's champions have always sharply repelled such charges, arguing that Reagan was personally free from prejudice. His heartfelt anger over antisemitism, for one thing, was well established. In the late 1930s, when Reagan discovered that his Hollywood country club excluded Jews, he confronted the club's leadership and then resigned, joining a new club with a substantial Jewish membership.[16] Later, he forced his sons to endure a home screening of film footage shot in 1945 of liberated Nazi death camps, so concerned was he with the possibility of Holocaust denial.[17] Earlier in life, Reagan's youthful actions suggested he might develop a similar sense of outrage over antiblack racism. As a college student, Reagan hosted two African American football teammates in his family home in downstate Illinois when they were barred from staying at a local hotel on account of their race.

But that was before Reagan became a conservative. His lifelong hatred of antisemitism, reflected in his impulse to challenge and denounce it—to stand shoulder to shoulder with bigotry's victims—only throws into relief the almost total absence of any such feeling regarding racism and African Americans during most of his adult life. The budding pro-black feelings of his youth died early on the vine. Reagan never displayed a speck of support for the civil rights movement in its heyday during the 1960s. He opposed the landmark 1964 Civil Rights Act, which outlawed "Jim Crow" segregation laws, and the Voting Rights Act of 1965. Reagan fell in step with the conservative movement's response to the black struggle, which was to seize on every reason and pretext, no matter how absurd, to denigrate it and deny that it held the moral high ground. It was no wonder that he had no sympathy for the movement against South Africa's apartheid system; he had had none for the fight against America's own version. In the ensuing decades, he never clearly disavowed his anti–civil rights position; it was more that he pretended he had not taken it. As a matter of political history, understanding that Reagan took this stance—and that he reaped great benefits from it—is far more important than plumbing the depths of Ronald Reagan's heart.

Reagan was, perhaps, the most successful white backlash politician in American history. Both Barry Goldwater and George Wallace, who had also fished in these waters, fell short of the presidency. More impressive competition comes from Richard Nixon, who, like Reagan, won the White House twice. Many view Nixon as the pioneer of a fully successful appeal for "law and order," racially coded but not explicitly race-baiting, and Nixon also plied his stance against court-ordered busing of schoolchildren—a policy intended to achieve racial integration—to good (for him) political effect. Reagan was at least Nixon's match on this terrain, and as president his record on civil rights was more negative than Nixon's, his appointees more hostile, his concessions only grudging nods to immovable political realities. Reagan is sometimes judged more generously than Nixon in this matter because, to many, he appears less cynical and calculating, more earnest in his positions. But if, in the words of Reagan's biographer Lou Cannon, "Reagan was simply reluctant to use federal authority in the cause of punishing discrimination of any sort," this conviction is hardly cause for a kind verdict on Reagan's leadership.[18] Reagan's antipathy to federal civil rights laws was sincere, but Reagan was far from guileless in his tactical manipulation of racial division. He left a trail of comments charged with harsh racial connotations but no explicit racial content—as when he warned of a lawless "jungle" arising in the nation's cities, or complained of seeing a "young buck" using food stamps, or confected a story about a "welfare queen" massively defrauding the taxpayers.[19] The alleged offenses Reagan protested had a consistent racial subtext. Yet the care he took in leaving himself room to deny race-baiting intent reflected a discipline on the stump that his opponents often failed to appreciate.

As with America, so with the world. Reagan's belief in the God-given freedom of all the world's peoples was limited—by his version of anti-communism and, perhaps, by his cultural predispositions. Reagan saw America gripped in moral and mortal combat with a global communist enemy who knew no scruples. In waging this fight, he locked arms with violent enemies of human freedom, from Ferdinand Marcos in the Philippines and the military powers of El Salvador to the apartheid regime in South Africa. Democracy and peace would spread to many parts of the world during the 1980s. The United States, under the leadership of Reagan and, even more, under Bush, would stand unmatched in power, the Soviet Union vanquished and near collapse. But the relationship between the march of freedom and the United States in the 1980s was an ambiguous one.

Whatever the flaws of Reagan's vision and the complexities of Reaganism's impact, Ronald Reagan has maintained the aura of the winner, which is the greatest thing anyone can say about an American. As president, his job-approval rating swung wide between highs and lows. But he left office in 1989 a popular president, having emerged as a peacemaker with the Soviets, his last job-approval rating, according to the Gallup Poll, an enviable 63 percent.[20] Yet in 1990, only 16 percent of respondents in one poll called Reagan "highly believable," mainly because he had unconvincingly feigned ignorance about his administration's secret sales of weapons to Iran.[21] In the immediate aftermath of the 1980s, many lamented the toll taken by the driving ideas of the Reagan era, the price America had paid (according to liberals) in decrepitude, fiscal disarray, and moral derangement. Liberals considered the 1980s an era of "moral darkness"; Bill Clinton, the Democrat who unseated Bush in 1992, termed the decade "a gilded age of greed, selfishness, irresponsibility, excess and neglect."[22]

But Reagan's stock rose as time passed. Clinton himself agreed to honor Reagan by renaming National Airport in Washington, DC, after him in 1998. One Republican champion of Reagan's at that time argued that "this man, Ronald Reagan, gave this country dignity, he gave it hope, he gave it optimism."[23] Reagan is now widely considered one of America's great presidents. He has appeared on Gallup's annual list of the ten most admired men at least thirty times—second only to evangelist Billy Graham.[24] This upward revision is due partly to an energetic campaign by conservatives to burnish the image of their greatest modern leader. But it also registers a deeper reality. More than twenty years after the end of the 1980s, to many Americans, Reagan embodies staunch patriotism and national vitality, not overt conservative doctrine. Yet Reagan's true triumph was that in his wake—at least to some—conservatism simply became equated with love of country.

Enough time has passed that we should be able to conduct a sober evaluation of Reagan and the era of American politics that he dominated, an evaluation that is critical but reasoned, fact-based, and not merely partisan. Neither hagiography nor scorn should satisfy us, although, as of this writing, the former is a greater blockage to clear vision than the latter. Reaganite conservatives in the 1980s notched achievements that continue to shape American public life decades later. How we remember Reagan and Reaganism colors our perception of many propositions that powerful Americans continue to proffer, whether concerning economic policy and performance, the place of the United States in the world, or morality and culture. If we wish to understand our contemporary public culture and its origins, to see our collective "common sense" for the construction that it is, and to arrive at sound judgments about the choices our society continues to face, we need to deliver the memory of the 1980s out of the realm of legend.

This is the story of the path that American politics and society traveled between 1980 and 1990. This is also a book primarily, although not wholly, about people favored with power and position; about the things they did; and about how we ought to remember them and their acts. Reagan and many other conservatives said they wanted to remake the world. They did not entirely succeed. Almost no one ever does. Yet their ambitions were not in vain. In only ten years, for Americans as a whole, some doors were closed and others were opened. If a new world did not loom, a changed one did.

One

The Time Is Now

In 1980, the incumbent U.S. president, Democrat Jimmy Carter, was in trouble. Whipsawed politically by price inflation and high unemployment levels—but damaged most of all by the first of these two problems—he was ready for a fall. The person poised to take advantage of this moment was Ronald Reagan, the one-time movie actor and former governor of California who became the Republican nominee for president in 1980. Reagan had harbored presidential ambitions for many years, but his pronounced conservatism had made him seem an unlikely victor to many observers. He skillfully seized the time in 1980, proving such doubters wrong.

Reagan had established himself as a political figure in the 1960s, playing the role of a stern father bringing discipline to unruly children. This early version of Reagan was thin-lipped with a squint and a tight smile, biting off lines of dialogue like the tough-guy villain he had played in his last film, 1964's *The Killers*.[1] He debuted in national politics that year with a televised speech supporting Republican presidential nominee Barry Goldwater, as Goldwater's campaign went down in flames before Democrat Lyndon Johnson's forces. Reagan had delivered this speech hundreds of times to assembled employees of General Electric, the company for which he served as a spokesman in the 1950s. Yet Reagan had begun his adult life as a liberal and a partisan Democrat. He had become an anticommunist in the late 1940s, as many liberals had, when the Cold War with the Soviet Union took shape; at that time he remained a Democrat.[2] Only during the 1950s, with a new corporate employer and a new, conservative wife, Nancy Davis Reagan, did he embrace the hard-right view that the welfare state was the entering wedge of communism in America.[3]

"The Speech," as Reagan's 1964 presentation came to be known, was severe and pessimistic, predicting that America would become an "ant heap of totalitarianism" if the federal government imposed antidiscrimination laws in employment and housing, raised taxes, and imposed new regulations on business. To support Johnson over Goldwater was to invite "a thousand years of darkness," Reagan said, quoting Winston Churchill's words for the prospect of Nazi rule in Europe.[4] Much of "The Speech" could have been lifted from a John Birch Society (JBS) pamphlet. The JBS was a right-wing group founded in 1958, whose members, mainly drawn from middle-class families in rapidly growing areas of the Southwest—like Goldwater's Arizona and Reagan's Southern California— were alarmed by the growing power of state and federal government. JBS members and others on the "new right" protested U.S. Supreme Court decisions barring mandatory prayer in public schools and other signs of a revolution from above against traditional values—but anticommunism was their root passion.[5] The JBS brand of anticommunism was distinguished by its extremism; the group's founder charged that President Dwight Eisenhower was a Soviet agent.

Like Goldwater and Reagan, JBS members tended to oppose antidiscrimination laws, such as California's 1963 Rumford Fair Housing Act or the historic federal Civil Rights Act of 1964, which outlawed southern "Jim Crow" racial segregation. Hostility to civil rights legislation was a passionate cause in that era, both for conservative intellectuals like those associated with the magazine *National Review* and for grassroots conservatives. They believed that the American tradition of freedom required the liberty to dispose of one's property as one liked and to associate only with whom one wished; many overtly shared a commitment to white supremacy. In 1964, the JBS took the Republican Party by storm, winning many delegate seats at the party's national nominating convention in San Francisco. As the columnists Rowland Evans and Robert Novak affirmed at the time, the "unspoken watchword of the 1964 convention" was "the white backlash tactic," an appeal to white voters opposed to racial equality.[6] The black press reported that African American delegates were "shoved, pushed, spat on, and cursed." Jackie Robinson, whose role in integrating major league baseball led him to a career as a Republican newspaper columnist, attended the convention, writing afterward, "I now believe I know how it felt to be a Jew in Hitler's Germany."[7] Four-fifths of Goldwater's Senate Republican colleagues voted for the Civil Rights Act, but Goldwater stood against them and voted nay, siding with the burgeoning conservative movement's cadres, and against the GOP's Washington "establishment."[8] White Southerners gave the Republican nominee unprecedented support in November, winning five Deep South states for the Arizonan. On the epochal issue of civil rights, Reagan stood with Goldwater.

Reagan made a splendid first run for public office in 1966, turning out the incumbent Democratic governor of California, Edmund "Pat" Brown. Reagan, still muscular and athletic in his mid-fifties, was tall, square-shouldered, and square-jawed, with blue-green eyes, thick brown hair, and skin bronzed from time spent outdoors; he was highly photogenic and comfortable with crowds. Tapping into public discomfort with anti-poverty efforts, he criticized government handouts to the indolent, and ran hard against the radical left, then prominent at the University of California (UC) at Berkeley. Brown, a bald-pated, bespectacled deal-maker who lacked charisma, was no radical. He was an ardent big-government liberal, as Reagan had once been, an organization man who had come up through the Democratic Party in San Francisco when it was known as a working-class city, a consensus politician like Lyndon Johnson, committed both to expanding opportunity and to boosting economic growth. But Brown appeared powerless to repress either political subversion or the unrest that erupted among African Americans in the Watts neighborhood of Los Angeles in 1965. Reagan also warned that a new danger—sexual licentiousness, fueled by hallucinogenic drugs—plagued his state. He told one crowd that events in Berkeley were "so bad, so contrary to our standards of decent human behavior, that I cannot recite them to you," although he tried.[9]

In office in Sacramento, Reagan compiled a more moderate record than his JBS supporters likely wished. He signed into law tax increases as well as the California Therapeutic Abortion Act (1967), a measure that legalized the previously outlawed medical procedure if a doctor affirmed that a woman's health was endangered by her pregnancy. (Reagan later said he regretted this decision.) He maintained a steadfast campaign against Berkeley, however. In 1969, Reagan responded to conflict between student radicals, on one side, and university authorities and local law enforcement, on the other, by dispatching thousands of National Guardsmen to occupy the campus; a Guard helicopter dropped tear gas on a protest rally. He tongue-lashed a group of UC faculty members assembled before him, upbraiding them that they should have foreseen that chaos would ensue when they first countenanced the idea of civil disobedience. "All of it began," he said, "the first time some of you who know better, and are old enough to know better, let young people think that they had the right to choose the laws they would obey, as long as they were doing it in the name of social protest." Following this blast of righteous anger, he stood up and exited the meeting.[10] Thus, at one fell swoop, he indicted the civil rights movement and its liberal sympathizers along with new left radicals, who were in some cases avowed enemies of the state. He appealed to the common sense of every parent in the state with his plain-spoken insistence on enforcing rules and hanging tough. Reagan would exclaim in 1970, "If it takes a bloodbath" to restore what he considered law and order on campus, "let's get it over with. No more appeasement."[11] He made a quick, last-minute charge at the Republican presidential nomination in 1968, throwing a scare into Richard Nixon, who ultimately prevailed over all rivals that year. The governor spent the early 1970s waiting for Nixon's expected two terms in the White House to expire.

But Nixon turned the Republican world upside-down when he resigned the presidency in 1974, after revelations of his misconduct in the Watergate scandal made impeachment and removal from office likely. Rather than an open competition for a vacant White House in 1976, Republican and Democratic aspirants faced an unelected Republican incumbent, Nixon's vice president, Gerald Ford. Reagan did not hesitate to run against Ford. He appealed to the proud nationalism of a country still absorbing the shocking images of helicopters pushed into the sea when Communist forces triumphed in Vietnam in 1975. Fewer people on welfare, an end to busing to achieve school integration, more military spending, less negotiation with the Soviet Union, and a rejection of treaties that would cede ownership of the Panama Canal to Panama: America needed these changes, Reagan told his audiences. His remark about the Canal—"We built it. We paid for it. It's ours, and we are going to keep it"—was his biggest applause line on the campaign trail in 1976.[12]

As Goldwater had done in 1964 with the backlash against civil rights, Reagan in 1976 aligned himself with the rising passion of movement conservatives, embracing the pro-life cause—meaning he now opposed keeping abortion legal—and speaking against ratification of the pending Equal Rights Amendment (ERA) to the U.S. Constitution, which the quadrennial GOP convention platform routinely endorsed. Phyllis Schlafly, an indefatigable grassroots activist in the new right, had temporarily departed from her main concern—opposition to détente with the Soviet Union—to lead the campaign against the ERA, which was close to final approval.[13] (Reagan agreed with Schlafly about détente, too.) As an executive, Reagan assembled administrations whose inside circles resembled a men's club, and, in a fashion typical of corporate boardrooms of the 1960s, he sometimes referred to grown women, condescendingly, as girls. However, he betrayed no serious belief in women's inferiority. The rancor that marred Reagan's remarks regarding African Americans was absent from his statements about women and feminism. He had considerable experience with strong women, starting with his mother, Nelle. Many regarded Reagan as the weaker partner in each of his two marriages, a perception that did not seem to bother him.[14] What brought a conservative like Reagan into the anti-ERA camp was not opposition to the idea of equal partnership between men and women, but rather to government-mandated equality in public life. White opponents of civil rights laws often made a similar distinction regarding race relations, but they often betrayed personal discomfort with the notion of social equality with African Americans, and sympathy with institutions that maintained racial inequality. Reagan, who would appoint Sandra Day O'Connor as the first woman to serve on the U.S. Supreme Court in 1981, could more plausibly claim that his opposition to the ERA was based on a principled objection to government management of human relations than he could likewise explain his opposition to laws against racial discrimination.

The pro-life cause, however, entailed a dramatically different view of government's proper role. This cause's adherents, far from wishing to keep government out of social relations, demanded that government insert itself in private affairs. Reagan, like most conservatives, embraced libertarianism on many issues and moral traditionalism, enforced by government's hand, on others. Ford, for his part, favored the ERA and was pro-choice on abortion, both positions that his wife, Betty, declaimed passionately. To movement conservatives, Reagan's positions were obviously better than Ford's. Ford had to rely on the authority and power of the presidency to bring his party in line behind him.

George Wallace, the renegade Democrat who had been the racial backlash candidate par excellence every four years starting in 1964, remained a potent force in presidential politics. Reagan's team in 1976 understood that the Wallace voters of previous election cycles were up for grabs, in both the South and the North. In the Southern primaries—where Reagan, beginning in North Carolina, made a rousing stand—former Wallace voters formed Reagan's base. In the North, Reagan aimed his rhetoric at so-called "white ethnic" voters, mainly Catholic and Jewish, who, often seeing themselves as victims of patrician liberal indulgence toward racial minorities, had toyed with Republican candidates intermittently for many years. "Certainly no one of us would challenge government's right and responsibility to eliminate discrimination in hiring and education," Reagan stated, even though he had spent years challenging exactly this "right and responsibility." He continued, "But in its zeal to accomplish this worthy purpose government orders what is in effect a quota system. . . . If your ancestry is Czechoslovakian, Polish, Italian, or if you are of the Jewish faith, you may find yourself the victim of discrimination."[15] Reagan's effort to stoke white resentment against affirmative action was not sufficiently successful to put him over the top against Ford. But he won among working-class and "ethnic" voters in the 1976 Republican primaries, a harbinger of things to come. In the end, Ford lost a close election to Carter, a former one-term governor of Georgia, and no one thought that Reagan's challenge had helped him.

Economic troubles increasingly dominated American politics in the 1970s. In 1973, the Organization of Petroleum Exporting Countries (OPEC), for both financial and political reasons, cut off its members' flow of oil to the United States, creating shortages and raising prices steeply. Within months, one hundred thousand truck drivers struck in protest against rising gasoline prices; grocery shelves soon showed bare spots, deliveries unmade.[16] The "oil shock" symbolized an economic fall from grace. America had entered an era of uncertain economic progress. Productivity (wealth created per person per hour) increased only 1 percent per year between 1973 and 1980; the figure had been almost three times as high during the previous quarter century.[17] A recession that hit in late 1974 increased joblessness. Unexpectedly, inflation persisted. Recessions usually curb inflation—but not this time. Price inflation during the 1970s would average more than 7 percent per year, whereas it had been only 2.5 percent annually in the 1960s.[18] The term "misery index" came into use as an economic indicator referring to the sum of the unemployment and inflation rates. Ford focused on combating inflation—a classic conservative approach, as banks and other lenders do not wish to be repaid in dollars that are worth less than the ones they have lent. The misery index hovered around 15 percent when Ford lost the presidency to Carter.

Carter began by taking on unemployment, but as the public increasingly deemed inflation the country's most urgent economic problem, he adopted the role of inflation-fighter. As a Democrat, Carter was tied to groups—such as organized labor (despite severe strains in that relationship), African Americans, and advocates for the underprivileged—that were anxious about rising joblessness. Through a variety of measures, Carter helped push the unemployment rate down to the 5–6 percent range by the middle of his term in office. But inflation rose as high as 13.3 percent by the end of 1979, creating a misery index of 19.3 percent.[19] Some Americans stopped worrying about inflation and started enjoying it; they bought cars, vacations, and houses on credit, planning to pay for today's expenses with tomorrow's cheaper dollars. But despite this boon to debtors, inflation made people uneasy. They worried about whether their incomes would rise enough to keep up with everyday costs. In 1978, the cost of meat rose 18 percent.[20] "I used to keep a budget," went the typical lament of one woman in the 1970s. "But it got so discouraging, I gave it up."[21] The problem of "bracket creep," which saw households move into higher income-tax brackets even though their real buying power had not increased, aroused anger. Many Americans actually saw an increase in their net worth in the 1970s because they owned houses whose values rose steeply. But, unless they sold their homes, this enhanced wealth did not help them pay their bills. Their property taxes, based on the assessed value of their homes, went up, and had to be paid each year.[22] In 1979, OPEC sharply raised prices again. Then a revolution overthrew the ruling shah of Iran, long a U.S. ally, and Iranian oil stopped replenishing world markets. Oil prices doubled during 1979, and long lines formed at gas stations for the second time in the 1970s, delivering a potent message about the vulnerability of Americans' accustomed lifestyle. Americans had never seen gasoline priced above one dollar per gallon before.

Under pressure, Carter appointed an orthodox conservative, Paul Volcker, chairman of the Federal Reserve Board ("the Fed"), shored up the strength of the dollar, and worked to reduce the federal government's budget deficit, taking most of the required budget savings from domestic spending programs.[23] He announced a "time of national austerity," recommending, as one historian put it, "the sort of belt-tightening once associated with Republicans like Herbert Hoover."[24] The Fed indirectly pushed interest rates past 15 percent, knowing this response would slow the flow of credit and spending.[25] This new move incensed Democratic constituencies, and inspired Senator Edward Kennedy of Massachusetts, a liberal leader, to challenge Carter for their party's 1980 presidential nomination. By mid-1980 the economy had entered a recession—a brief but severe one—due to Carter's battle against inflation. In March, the volume of housing starts was 42 percent smaller than one year before; idled builders mailed pieces of lumber to the Fed in protest.[26] Huge numbers of "baby-boomers," members of the largest generation in American history, were in their twenties and in the market to buy a first home. The high interest rates they faced provided campaign fodder for Carter's opponents in 1980, first Kennedy and later Reagan.

Carter faced a host of difficulties on the international scene as well, mainly emanating from Southwest Asia. In the fall of 1979, Carter's foreign policy was jolted when radical Iranian students, angry that Carter had admitted the deposed shah into the United States for cancer treatment, occupied the U.S. embassy in Tehran, Iran's capital, taking prisoner more than sixty U.S. personnel.[27] News coverage obsessively counted the days of "America Held Hostage." The hit 1973 song "Tie a Yellow Ribbon 'Round the Old Oak Tree," sung in the voice of a convict who leaves prison and wonders if his love has waited for him, inspired yellow ribbons tied around trees and pinned to clothes. A very long ribbon encircled the football stadium on the day of the 1980 Super Bowl, to signal that the hostages were not forgotten.[28]

In late December 1979, the Soviet Union invaded Afghanistan, desperate to maintain a pro-Soviet regime in power there. Carter stated afterward, "[M]y opinion of the Russians has changed more drastically in the last week than even the previous two and a half years."[29] Racing to the head of a rising anti-Soviet tide of feeling in the country, Carter showed a newly hawkish face, approving a big increase in military procurement— some of it aimed at preparing to fight a "limited" nuclear war. He arranged a boycott of the 1980 Summer Olympics, to be held in Moscow, placed an embargo on U.S. grain sales to the USSR, and introduced adult male registration for a possible military draft. He had already authorized funds for the subvention of the mujahideen, an anticommunist Afghan guerrilla force.[30]

The Middle East was the occasion of Carter's greatest triumph: the peace agreement he brokered in 1978 between Israel and Egypt. His sensitivity toward Arab perspectives helped to make Carter an effective conciliator between these two longtime enemies. But this region also caused him political trouble, as many Jews, an important constituency in Carter's party, came to detect "an unmistakably pro-Arab tilt" to his foreign policy. Carter's brother, Billy, compounded the president's problems by getting entangled with Libya's government, an endeavor he explained by remarking, "The only thing I can say is there is a hell of a lot more Arabians than there is Jews."[31] America's United Nations (UN) representatives also showed unaccustomed sympathy for Palestinian nationalism. The resulting uproar helped Kennedy win the New York Democratic primary. The Kennedy protest vote reached crisis proportions, dealing Carter subsequent defeats in Pennsylvania, Michigan, New Jersey, and California.[32] Carter remained his party's likely nominee, but now it appeared he would be a weakened one.

Carter had bad luck, but some of his problems were of his own making. A devoted Baptist who came to church on Sunday armed with his own Bible, Carter was the first president to advertise himself as an evangelical Christian. His moralism often struck a chord with the public, especially when memories of Nixon's misdeeds remained fresh. But, just as routinely, the appeal of Carter's urgings would fade with time. As his presidency proceeded, this cycle of reactions passed more quickly. Unloved in official Washington, a community that still cherished its peccadilloes in that era, Carter turned sermonic, and delivered a memorable televised speech in July 1979. His manner was dramatic, his delivery intense; he repeatedly clenched his right fist before the camera as he sat at his Oval Office desk. He lamented a waning faith among Americans in their country's future. "For the first time in the history of our country a majority of our people believe that the next 5 years will be worse than the past 5 years," he said. "In a nation that was proud of hard work, strong families, close-knit communities, and our faith in God, too many of us now tend to worship self-indulgence and consumption. Human identity is no longer defined by what one does, but by what one owns."[33] These words became known as the "malaise" speech (even though it was an aide to Carter—not the president himself—who used the word). Initially, the public responded well to Carter's impassioned presentation—but not for long. The 1970s witnessed an enthusiasm for simple living among many Americans, but not enough of them to make Carter's critique of materialism, in the end, a political winner.

The 1978 midterm elections proved tough for liberals, with antitax sentiment, fueled by the anxiety over living standards that Carter appeared to dismiss, on the rise. Property taxes were the target of widespread ire, from liberals as well as conservatives, but a property-tax revolt became the opening wedge of a broader attack on taxes and government spending, an attack that was intrinsically conservative. In June 1978, voters in California passed Proposition 13, insuring low property taxes and making it hard to raise taxes of any kind. Proposition 13 was quickly imitated in Massachusetts (with Proposition 2½) and elsewhere.[34] The fervor spread to income-tax rates, traditionally a target of conservative indignation alone. Before the November elections, the Democratic Congress cut tax rates on capital gains (money from the sale of assets such as real estate or stocks, rather than from wages or salaries). The Senate passed a variation on the 30 percent across-the-board cut in income tax rates proposed by Representative Jack Kemp of New York and Senator William Roth of Delaware, both Republicans, and a joint House-Senate conference committee appeared ready to include the provision in a bill it would report out; but Carter, concerned about deficits, managed to spike the idea, and avoided either signing or vetoing the Kemp-Roth measure. Republicans gained three Senate seats and fifteen in the House in 1978, defeating Democrats like Wendell Anderson of Minnesota; conservative Republicans like William Armstrong of Colorado and Roger Jepsen of Iowa won reelection comfortably.[35] Gaining ground in midterm elections was normal for the nonpresidential party, but more was at work here. The Republicans were moving swiftly with proposals that had caught the wind. Their gains were deep: the number of state governments around the country in which their party held both legislative chambers rose from five to fourteen. Kemp exulted, "We've shifted from the defensive to the offensive. They're now arguing on our turf."[36]

Between 1976 and 1980, Reagan never stopped running. He was the favorite for the Republican nomination to challenge Carter's bid for re-election. Hundreds of radio stations across the country broadcast his commentaries several times a week, stoking the fires of his conservative backers. His comments were conservative boilerplate, expressing outrage at taxes and government waste, at liberals who ignored human-rights abuses in the Soviet Union while railing against those in South Africa, and at welfare giveaways. Reagan complained that the recipients of altruistic U.S. foreign aid were anti-American ingrates. He quoted a Canadian journalist who said, "It is time to speak up for the Americans as the most generous and possibly the least appreciated people in all the earth."[37] Reagan continued this theme in his 1980 campaign. Speaking at a retirement community in Florida, he evoked a fantasy of the past, a time when "even where an American was on business, or on vacation . . . and got caught in some little country that was having a revolution, or got caught in a war, all that the American had to do was pin to his lapel a little American flag and he could walk right through that war and nobody would lay a finger on him."[38]

Reagan had an early scare in his pursuit of the 1980 Republican nomi-nation, as his main adversary, George H. W. Bush, a Yankee by way of Texas with a reputation for party loyalty, prepared carefully and earned a victory in the first meaningful contest, the Iowa caucuses in January. Reagan made adjustments, firing his campaign manager and replacing him with William Casey, a feisty securities lawyer who, decades earlier, had filed the incorporation papers for *National Review*. Reagan's ap-peal to Republican voters proved strong, and he quickly bounced back, trouncing Bush in the New Hampshire primary, and then sailing to the nomination. Starting in late July 1980, Reagan underwent a public trans-formation, now displaying little anger and much sentimentality. Even his voice changed. It was lower in pitch—often called "husky," whereas his delivery in past years had been clipped and somewhat nasal. Reagan's advisers foresaw the usual two-stage procession to the big prize in 1980: first, a campaign for the party faithful in the caucuses and primaries, then a broader appeal to independent and persuadable voters in the fall. But the Reagan team grasped that their man was a special case. His neon-lit record of conservative statements meant that, if Reagan were nominated, Carter surely would paint him as an extremist and warmonger. As his party's summer convention grew near, Reagan was unwilling to call himself a conservative. "I have always deplored labels," he said.[39] In a gesture toward party unity, he chose his vanquished rival, Bush, as his running mate.

The Republican Convention, meeting in Detroit, adopted a conservative platform, to which few besides party activists and close observers of the political scene paid much attention, but which reflected the new power of movement conservatives within the party. For the first time, the Republicans declined to endorse the ERA, instead taking a neutral stance. On abortion, the platform stated, "We will work for the appointment of judges at all levels of the judiciary who respect traditional family values and the sanctity of innocent human life." In a swipe at détente, the foreign policy section called for military "superiority" over the USSR as the wise course. Popular with the attending delegates was the platform's call to repeal the fifty-five-mile-per-hour speed limit on interstate highways, an innovation of the Nixon years.[40]

Reagan's speech accepting his party's nomination served as a smooth launch for his general-election campaign. He quoted Franklin D. Roosevelt, president from 1933 until 1945 and the hero of Reagan's youth, saying that Americans had a "rendezvous with destiny," just as Roosevelt had said at the Democratic Party's convention in 1936. FDR had been defending his New Deal program of government initiatives designed to relieve privation and enhance economic security amid the Great Depression. Reagan described a link between the distress of the 1930s and the problems of 1980, offering himself as a leader whose reassuring confidence in the nation's future could match FDR's. Yet the views of these two men were worlds apart. Roosevelt had identified wealthy businessmen and financiers as a "new industrial dictatorship" thwarting the American people's desire for true freedom. Reagan saw government as a parasite draining away the people's livelihood, stating in exasperation, "We are taxing ourselves into economic exhaustion and stagnation." The national government, he warned, must "do the people's work without dominating their lives." Roosevelt had warned of "a Government frozen in the ice of its own indifference." Reagan looked to "the American spirit of voluntary service, of cooperation, of private and community initiative" to address suffering. His economic ideas echoed not Roosevelt's but those of Calvin Coolidge, a conservative Republican president of the 1920s whose policies Roosevelt repudiated.[41]

If Reagan's appropriation of FDR was striking, so was his invocation of Thomas Paine. Reagan rhetorically flayed the idea that America had entered an age of limits. "They say that the United States has had its day in the sun, that our nation has passed its zenith," he said that night in Detroit. "They expect you to tell your children that the American people no longer have the will to cope with their problems, that the future will be one of sacrifice and few opportunities." He paused briefly before offering his riposte: "I utterly reject that view." In quoting Paine's famous words, "We have it in our power to begin the world over again," Reagan exceeded mere optimism. In the face of national gloom, he embraced the prospect of drastic change as exciting and rejuvenating. This element of Reagan's rhetoric was, indeed, more that of a revolutionary than of a stand-pat conservative.[42]

Reagan's pollster, Richard Wirthlin, who held a leading strategic role in the campaign, had laid out a general-election strategy in a March memorandum. "Specifically," wrote Wirthlin, "we must position the Governor . . . so that he is viewed as less dangerous in the foreign affairs area, more competent in the economic area, more compassionate on the domestic issues and less of a conservative zealot than his opponents and the press now paint him to be." He recommended "a 'peace-oriented' foreign policy position." Reagan had to appear as a safe alternative to the unpopular Carter—a harbor during a storm. The battlegrounds, in Wirthlin's view, were the distressed industrial states of the North, in a band stretching from New York through to Ohio and Michigan. "We must pick up states in the East and heavily in the Midwest to beat Carter."[43] Southern targets were secondary; Reagan's team expected Carter to do well in his home region. The two parties convened in Detroit and New York for good reason; the lone Carter-Reagan debate was staged in Cleveland.

Reagan quickly began revising his own avowed positions on a host of issues. The champion of free markets and fiscal discipline suddenly became friendlier toward federal aid for New York City and the Chrysler Corporation, both of which had needed government bailouts to avert bankruptcy. The committed free-trader intimated that he would consider placing limits on Japanese car imports. Reagan had previously spoken of turning the Social Security old-age pension system into a voluntary insurance plan, a popular idea among conservatives, many of whom dreamt of eliminating this centerpiece of the New Deal. In 1980, however, Reagan backed away from that stance. Although this series of revisions was not lost on the press, the campaign had decided "it's a lot better to be called a sell-out than a nut," as one supporter put it.[44]

Even so, old habits died hard. In the early weeks after the nominating convention, Reagan made numerous comments that provoked widespread criticism. Reagan sent Bush—previously the U.S. envoy to the People's Republic of China (PRC)—on a trip to Beijing, but Reagan simultaneously reiterated his commitment to Taiwan's rival regime, thus undercutting Bush's mission. Speaking to the Veterans of Foreign Wars, Reagan called the Vietnam War "a noble cause," surely a standard view among conservatives, but one that was hazardous for Reagan to express in light of Democratic accusations that, as president, he would prove too ready for war. Reagan repeatedly suggested that the United States should blockade Cuba, reprising the missile crisis of 1962, in response to the Soviet invasion of Afghanistan. These "stumbles" renewed "fears of him as a conservative extremist," as one reporter put it.[45] Before long, Stuart Spencer, a veteran Republican campaign operative, joined Reagan's entourage as a kind of minder, and got Reagan to stick to his scripted talking points.

However, the most incendiary day of the general-election campaign's early phase revolved around not a misstatement but a planned event. Reagan kicked off his postconvention campaign with an appearance on August 3 at the Neshoba County Fair in Philadelphia, Mississippi, a town previously best known as the scene of the murder of three civil rights volunteers in the summer of 1964. Rather than use the venue as an opportunity to transcend his history of opposition to civil rights laws, Reagan told the crowd of ten thousand, "I believe in states' rights," thus making a bold play for "George Wallace inclined voters," as a prominent Republican in the state put it.[46] The term "states' rights" was so firmly linked to segregationism that it had been off-limits to serious presidential candidates for sixteen years. Reagan, like Goldwater, insisted that it referred to an abstract constitutional principle and nothing else. But he could not have chosen a more provocative setting for his remarks. Carter tried to exploit the incident, warning that if Reagan were elected, "Americans might be separated, black from white, Jew from Christian, North from South, rural from urban."[47]

If racial tension was a sore on the body politic, Reagan was willing to poke it more than once. At the outset of the primary season in January, he had made an appearance at Bob Jones University, a fundamentalist school in South Carolina notorious for its ban on interracial dating. Reagan hailed it as a "great institution," and brought his audience to its feet as he denounced what he termed "the evil character of racial quotas."[48] In the fall campaign, Reagan made a pilgrimage to a desolate landscape of empty buildings in the South Bronx—a poor urban area routinely described as looking "bombed-out"—to criticize Carter for having done little to improve the fortunes of local residents, most of them African American or Latino. This visit did not go as planned; Reagan encountered a hostile crowd of residents and got into a shouting match with an African American woman (not for the first time in his career).[49] Although it was surely unintentional, this loss of composure may have helped him with the white voters he aimed to win over.

Reagan also used the late-summer lull in press coverage to appeal to evangelical voters. Born-again Protestants had given Carter, one of their own, a majority of their support in 1976, but many were disillusioned by his support for abortion rights and feminism, and deemed his foreign policy weak. In 1979, the Reverend Jerry Falwell, a conservative Baptist, and others formed Moral Majority, an organization that sought to help elect conservatives to political office. Soon, Moral Majority established a close relationship with the Republican Party at the national level. Reagan, like many Americans, was uncertain whether he was truly an evangelical, and had long neglected church attendance. But in his youth, he had been deeply involved in his mother's Christian Church, also known as the Disciples of Christ. He was familiar with biblical texts and prophecies, and could rival Carter in demonstrations of piety.[50] In August 1980, Reagan appeared on-stage at a large meeting of the conservative Religious Roundtable. Aware that religious groups risked losing their federal tax exemptions if they explicitly supported individual candidates, Reagan said, "I know that you can't endorse me. But I want you to know that I endorse you." Continuing his bid for conservative white support, Reagan blasted Carter for threatening the tax exemptions of Christian schools that excluded black students, shaming this policy response as an effort to "force . . . church schools to abide by affirmative action orders drawn up by—who else?—IRS bureaucrats." Reagan applauded the assembly for working "to protect the American family."[51] He spoke their language.

By tradition, many voters paid little attention to presidential campaigns until Labor Day, at which time the Reagan campaign grasped the opportunity to get back to its general-election strategy. Reagan's fall kickoff event broadcast an image of a vigorous man filled with hope for the future. It also signaled that Reagan would depart from Carter's chastened, modest displays of national pride, which had played well in 1976, in favor of a return to unequivocal flag-waving. The event was staged on the New Jersey coast, with the Statue of Liberty in the background. Winds were stiff, the sky was clear. Reagan's thick hair was tousled; the flags snapped. He appeared in shirtsleeves, several buttons undone, looking a young sixty-nine. The candidate's words were stirring: "I want, more than anything I have ever wanted, to have an administration that will, through its actions at home and in the international arena, let millions of people know that Miss Liberty still lifts her lamp beside the golden door."[52] Reagan deployed the mythology of immigration, powerful in America, as a metaphor for optimism, for a belief that work and determination would bring success in spite of daunting obstacles.

In terms of issues, each candidate's worst political vulnerabilities dictated his opponent's approach. Reagan wanted to talk about Carter's economic record, and Carter wanted to talk about the risk of war with Reagan in the White House. Reagan pitted his optimism and strength against what he charged were Carter's pessimism and weakness, while Carter presented himself as a responsible man of peace and national unity, painting Reagan as a figure of danger and division. Both campaigns were strongly negative, but Carter's was more purely so. His job-approval rating dipped as low as 31 percent in June 1980.[53] He knew his policies were unpopular, so he did not emphasize them. Many voters would have been hard-pressed to name a single proposal for Carter's projected second term. Reagan's intentions were clearer. The centerpiece of his program was the Kemp-Roth proposal for a phased 30-percent cut in federal marginal income-tax rates in all brackets. He also promised a big military buildup, although he exaggerated his differences with Carter on that count.[54]

Reagan found opportunities to mitigate his worst liability, his bellicose image. On the trail at St. Joseph's University, a Catholic school in Pennsylvania, he was heckled by protesters against nuclear weapons, clearly enraged by Reagan's opposition to the second Strategic Arms Limitation Treaty (SALT II), which Carter and Soviet leader Leonid Brezhnev had signed prior to the Afghanistan invasion, but which languished in the Senate, a victim of the new chill in U.S.-Soviet relations. Reagan gave a powerful impromptu response. He said he felt that the protesters were saying "that Christ is betrayed by nuclear weapons," and he asked in reply, "Is there anyone in the world who has not believed that Christ is betrayed anytime we find ourselves embroiled in that greatest of man's stupidities—war against our fellow man?" Reagan then stated that although he was against SALT II, he was not against all arms-limitation treaties, and he would "sit at a table with our adversaries for as long as it took" to hammer out a better agreement.[55]

With the issues and themes of the contest established early on, little of real consequence developed until the only debate between the two major-party nominees, on October 28—one week before Election Day. Reporting on debate night in Cleveland, journalist Elizabeth Drew set the scene: "Carter looks tired . . . his eyes puffed; Reagan looks to be in robust health."[56] Reagan was getting ample sleep, while Carter, thirteen years Reagan's junior at age fifty-six, was working long into the night on frantic efforts to get the Tehran hostages released. (Reagan's campaign feared an "October surprise," in which those efforts would succeed, thereby moving the electorate in Carter's direction. Years later, rumors circulated that top Reagan hands had contacted Iran's government during the campaign to delay a hostage release, on the promise of better relations between the countries under a Reagan administration. This scandalous charge was the subject of numerous investigations, but was never substantiated.[57]) Like many challengers who join incumbents on a debating stage, Reagan found his stature elevated, even though he appeared nervous, his manner halting.[58] He charged that Carter had "accused the people of living too well" and had proposed "that we must share in scarcity." Carter continued to depict Reagan as a threatening figure whose presidency would "lead to a very dangerous arms race." Reagan parried this thrust aimed at his key vulnerability, saying, "I believe with all of my heart that our first priority must be world peace, and that use of force is always and only a last resort. . . . America has never gotten in a war because we were too strong. We can get into a war by letting events get out of hand, as they have in the last three and a half years." Reagan's closing words were direct and forceful. He asked voters, "Are you better off than you were four years ago?" He then struck the desired note on foreign policy when he asked, "Is America as respected throughout the world as it was?"[59] "Reagan dispelled the theory of him being trigger happy," one New Jersey woman told a journalist after the debate. These words were music to Republican ears.[60]

All perceptions of a close race dissolved in the campaign's closing days. The bottom fell out for Carter as the largest number of undecided voters swung to Reagan. The Republican had far more money to spend on advertising in these last days than Carter did, and his campaign used these funds to drive his impending victory toward landslide proportions. Reagan triumphed on election night, besting Carter 50.8 percent to 41 percent in the popular vote, and holding Carter to 49 out of 538 electoral votes. Reagan had swept his targeted battleground states, and more. The industrial North rejected Carter. Carter escaped losing his entire home region only by holding onto Georgia. The Democrat won a mere six states. The congressional districts in which Carter suffered the biggest losses of support between 1976 and 1980 clustered in a clear pattern. Areas experiencing booming population growth and relatively good economic health—in the Southeast, the Southwest, and the Mountain West—were left cold by Carter's talk of reining in expectations.[61] Reagan improved on Ford's performance with several groups, including blue-collar voters, men, and Catholics. The Republican candidate did worse with women than with men (though he won both groups), a reversal from 1976, and a shift that would become a long-term trend.[62] Reagan captured 39 percent of the Jewish vote, the best result ever for a Republican presidential candidate, and a feat which may have cost the incumbent Pennsylvania as well as New York, where turnout was low.[63]

Reagan's big win had coattails. The Republicans gained twelve Senate seats, a huge increase, and took over the upper chamber by a margin of 53–46, the first time their party had controlled either chamber of Congress in almost thirty years. In the process, nine Democratic senators went down in defeat, including liberal heroes such as Frank Church of Idaho and George McGovern of South Dakota. Democrats from conservative states—Idaho, South Dakota, Indiana, Iowa—had won narrow victories in previous election cycles, but the Reagan surge in 1980 tipped them over. The Democrats held onto control of the House of Representatives, but Republicans ousted twenty-eight Democratic incumbents, narrowing the gap between the parties to 243–192.[64] Between thirty and sixty Democratic Representatives were thought to be sympathetic to Reagan's agenda, and they would give his program a good chance of passage. Democrats were shaken. One member of the House majority confided, "For the first time we can *really* see the possibility of losing *our* majority in '82."[65]

Many asserted that the election represented a rejection of Carter more than an embrace of Reagan's conservative agenda. "Ideology is not important to voters," Republican pollster Robert Teeter said flatly.[66] According to a major postelection survey, only 11 percent of those who voted for Reagan said that conservatism moved them to support him on Election Day. Three-and-a-half times as many said it was "time for a change."[67]

This rendition of events was not the whole truth. Voters knew that Reagan was conservative and, in electing him, they were giving conservatives a chance to govern.[68] They had never done so before in the history of the modern conservative movement. Reagan had a mandate for a new direction in economic policy, one that would assign top priority to reducing price inflation—which Carter's 1979–1980 policies had not yet managed to do, despite the pain of the recession. A majority of the voting public had swung behind an economic aim traditionally cherished by the wealthy. This shift in public opinion was the largest factor in electing a conservative candidate president.[69] Reagan's foreign policy instructions were uncertain; voters approved his image of strength, but he had succeeded by blunting the charge of belligerency, not by affirming it. So-called "social issues" such as abortion were dear to the heart of religious conservatives who had gained new champions in Congress, but Reagan had won in spite of the general unpopularity of his positions on those issues.[70]

An era had ended in Washington. Many Democrats had believed that the Nixon-Ford interregnum was just that, an interruption in the normal flow of politics, caused by the turmoil of the late 1960s. Democrats had ruled Congress for almost three decades. Their complacency had run deep. "There was an illusion created at the time of the Democratic

Convention, and continuing through the period of Reagan's mistakes early in the fall, that we were building on the base of the Democrats," said one party insider after the election. "It was an illusion because the base wasn't there."[71] Republicans, on the other hand, found their confidence affirmed. "Ronald Reagan's overwhelming victory hit Washington with such force that overnight the capital became his town," two journalists would recall of the immediate postelection mood.[72] Conservatives eagerly prepared to implement the president-elect's agenda. Like Reagan, their time had come.

TWO

The Agenda

Cutting income taxes for Americans, especially for wealthy Americans, was Reagan's dearest cause and the beating heart of his policy agenda. Beefing up America's military was his second priority. These commitments were the twin pillars of Reagan's 1980 platform. Reducing the federal government's (nonmilitary) spending took a distant third place—although, to gain fiscal credibility, the Reagan team would tackle spending before pushing its tax-cut bill on Capitol Hill. An "alarmist" memorandum on economic policy prepared for the incoming leadership team stressed the need for severe cutbacks in government spending. Its author, David Stockman, a sitting House member from Michigan, was named the new head of the Office of Management and Budget (OMB).[1] Other matters were not deemed worth fighting for. Religious conservatives found that top White House officials treated their demands concerning such issues as abortion and school prayer dismissively. In 1982, Reagan conceded to a journalist that such questions were, to him, "very vital and very important, but they're a periphery to a philosophy."

> QUESTION: "They are not the essence of what you've been crusading about?"
> REAGAN: "No."
> QUESTION: "They are adornments, they are filigree, so to speak?"
> REAGAN: "Yes."[2]

"The president absolutely loathes and despises taxes," remarked Richard Darman, a key White House tactician during Reagan's first term as president.[3] This belief was truly personal for Reagan, as well as a matter of principle. He frequently recounted how, in his Hollywood days in the 1940s, he and his friends "quit working after four pictures and went off to the country," because Washington's stratospheric marginal tax rates would take most of the earnings from any further work. The lesson was clear: high taxes were punitive and self-defeating. To Reagan, taking wealth from creative people—like him—to fund those without his gumption and positive attitude was wrong. He had long socialized with wealthy men from California, like Holmes Tuttle, a car-dealership entrepreneur, Charles Z. Wick, who had made his fortune producing low-budget movies and running for-profit nursing homes, and Justin Dart, the founder of Rexall Drug—men who likewise resented paying taxes. Confiscating large fortunes, which was how wealthy conservatives viewed progressive taxation, was a perversity, a way of bringing society's extraordinary individuals to heel. Like Ayn Rand writing of her hero John Galt in her novel *Atlas Shrugged*, Reagan knew that attempts to tear down great men pointed the way to society's decline.[4]

Reducing the marginal income-tax payments of Americans below the top bracket was the political price to be paid for the administration's true aim: cutting taxes for the rich. Donald Regan, the Wall Street executive who became Reagan's first secretary of the treasury, noted that Reagan's tax-cut proposal "targeted more benefits to those in upper tax brackets, the people most likely to save and invest."[5] In general, Reagan's team showed caution in broadcasting such frank comments. The conservative columnist George Will, whose close association with Reagan's campaign made him a star in the Washington media, acknowledged the calculation. "Kemp-Roth links an emotionally rational [*sic*] act (cutting taxes of the investing class) to a politically palatable act (cutting everyone else's taxes)," as he put it.[6] Some supply-siders were willing to restrict the tax cuts to wealthy Americans only. Reagan, politically more astute, rejected such counsel.

Reagan could afford to do so rather easily, because the tax cuts he proposed for less affluent Americans were small and would not greatly alter the government's finances. Reagan's proposal to cut marginal income-tax rates by 30 percent in all tax brackets (Kemp-Roth) was not always well understood. Kemp-Roth and, later on, the measure ultimately signed by Reagan, the Economic Recovery and Tax Act of 1981 (ERTA)—which cut marginal rates by 23 percent over three years—were routinely described as if they cut individuals' overall tax bills by such whopping figures. The reality was more complicated. First, Reagan did not propose lopping 30 percentage points off these marginal tax rates; rather, he wished to make the rates 30 percent smaller (e.g., a 50 percent rate would drop to 35 percent). Most important, marginal rates described the tax charged not on all income, but, rather, only on those dollars earned above a certain income level. In 1980, the highest marginal tax rate on investment income was 70 percent, and the highest marginal rate for wage and salary income was 50 percent. But the 1 percent of Americans with the largest incomes in 1980 paid, on average, an overall federal income-tax rate of 29.8 percent.[7]

"Supply-side economics" was the term used to argue that lower marginal tax rates on these high earners would strengthen the flow of money into bank accounts and productive investments. This process, in theory, would lead to higher rates of economic growth in the long term. In the 1970s, while conservative ideas in general had gained ground among economists, supply-side theory in particular remained rather peripheral in academia.[8] It was vaulted to *political* prominence, however, by the editorial pages of the *Wall Street Journal*, which served as a "bulletin-board" for conservative ideas.[9] In Washington, supply-side arguments became closely associated with an ebullient coterie of promoters, including Representative Kemp and the wonderfully named Arthur Laffer, a colorful economist—"Short in stature, tall in enthusiasm," according to a fellow supply-sider—who was known for describing a curve purporting to show that if tax rates were cut, the U.S. government would actually see increased tax revenues.[10] This reversal would occur because tax rates, if raised too high, passed a point of negative returns, badly discouraging economic investment. Assuming the United States tax code had passed that point, moving backward on the "Laffer curve" would enhance the incentives to invest so greatly and spur such an explosion of new wealth that the number of dollars taken in by the IRS would go up, even as wealth was taxed at a lower rate.

In fact, no historical evidence supported the notion that the United States lay on the curve's far side.[11] The curve was merely a marketing device used to reassure nervous voters and congressmen that basic arithmetic—which foretold that huge tax cuts and an enormous increase in the Pentagon's budget, with no budget cuts of similar dimensions in prospect, would produce skyrocketing government deficits—could be safely ignored. Reagan, when introduced to the Laffer curve in 1980, was sold; the theory merely confirmed his longstanding conviction that taxes on the rich were too high. At a press conference on February 19, 1981, Reagan explained, "There's still that belief on the part of many people that a cut in tax rates automatically means a cut in revenues. And if they'll only look at history, it doesn't. A cut in tax rates can very often be reflected in an increase in government revenues because of the broadening of the base of the economy."[12] In 1980, the Reagan campaign had assembled a panel of economists, led by Alan Greenspan and Martin Anderson, to assure the press that Reagan's numbers added up. These experts made large but vague promises about economic growth and potential budget cuts in a Reagan administration. (Years later, Greenspan commented with nonchalance, "I believed that if spending was restrained as much as Reagan proposed . . . the plan was credible."[13])

However, the soul of supply-side doctrine was the promise of booming economic growth, not the magical pledge of a balanced budget. The political allure of that promise was clear. From the 1930s through the 1960s, Republicans had preached the gospel of balanced budgets, and it had done them little good politically. "The Republicans' austerity approach to the deficit gave them their image as the party that takes away," wrote Paul Craig Roberts, the top supply-side economist in Reagan's government. Saddled with that commitment, they were a minority party for half a century.[14] But they prided themselves at least on being able to add and subtract, which is why George Bush, campaigning in 1980 against Reagan, had called Reagan's fiscal proposals "voodoo economic policy"; Bush was offended on behalf of Republican orthodoxy.[15] Democrats, meanwhile, since World War II had embraced Keynesianism, the doctrine of economic growth through government spending and tax cuts. Supply-side economics became the GOP answer to Keynesianism. Republicans would use supply-side ideas to free themselves from the shackles of fiscal conservatism and present themselves as champions of "growthmanship."[16]

Criticism of Keynesianism became politically trenchant in the 1970s. Conventional economics held that unemployment and inflation worked against each other; as one index rose, the other fell. However, in the 1970s, the problem of "stagflation," in which growth slows, unemployment increases, and prices rise all at the same time, became pressing. Keynesian doctrine did not seem to provide an adequate response to this situation. At this policy impasse, supply-side advocates sensed they could displace Keynesian dogma in the corridors of government.

Reagan's tax-cut proposal found a warm reception across party lines, in big sections of the country. The South, long a Democratic Party stronghold, was by tradition the home of crackpot financial nostrums that promised something for nothing. Southern Democrats, at the end of the 1970s, offered qualified endorsements of supply-side doctrine. In 1980, Jimmy Carter's top domestic policy advisor said that "economic policy of the 1980s must place *greater emphasis on the supply side of our economy.*"[7] The Joint Economic Committee of Congress, chaired by Democratic senator Lloyd Bentsen of Texas, issued reports in 1979 and 1980 making the supply-side case for cutting tax rates to spur higher rates of growth through enhanced investment, not increased consumer spending. This line of argument amounted to "Reaganomics before Reagan."[18] By 1980, the Southeast had lost pride of place in the tax-cut crusade to the Mountain West and the Southwest. One-third of Senate Republicans from the Southeast cosponsored the upper chamber's 1978 version of Kemp-Roth (sponsored by Sam Nunn, Democrat of Georgia); over half the Southwest's GOP senators did, as did every one of those from the Mountain West.[19] Reagan was their man.

In his distaste for détente—the Nixon-Ford policy of reducing superpower tensions—Reagan also had much company in Washington. In the wake of the Vietnam War, the Democrats were split over whether to continue the Cold War tradition of Harry Truman and John Kennedy. While some reconsidered traditional assumptions about the wholesomeness of U.S. military activities around the world, others joined conservative Republicans in protesting Nixon's strategy of identifying areas of converging interests with Russia and China. Most Southern Democrats, still a large group in Congress, remained strong Cold Warriors. The original foreign policy "neoconservatives" were post-Vietnam associates of Democratic senators Hubert Humphrey of Minnesota and Henry "Scoop" Jackson of Washington, liberals on domestic policy and stalwart foes of communism. Younger torchbearers, led by Richard Perle, a Jackson protégé, and Jeane Kirkpatrick, a Georgetown University professor whose husband,

Evron, had been Humphrey's teacher years before, sought a cross-party alliance against détente starting in the mid-1970s, arguing with some effectiveness that they carried the ark of the Democratic Party's covenant against totalitarianism.

At the same time, advocates of an aggressive anti-Soviet policy conducted operations inside the Republican Party. Gerald Ford and his director of central intelligence (DCI), George Bush, agreed to allow a panel of outside authorities, labeled the B Team or Team B, to conduct an audit of the Central Intelligence Agency's (CIA) alleged insouciance regarding the Soviet military threat against U.S. security. Headed by Harvard University historian Richard Pipes and deriving authority on questions of arms and strategy from Paul Nitze, a gray eminence of America's security establishment, Team B concluded, to no one's surprise, that the Soviets were far more dangerous than the CIA understood.[20] Nitze had begun making his name among strategic thinkers in 1950 by authoring NSC (National Security Council) 68, a key document of the Cold War. NSC 68 argued successfully for placing the nation on a permanent war footing to prevent forceful communist advances around the globe—advances that might leave America the proverbial island of freedom in an ocean of tyranny.

Ultimately, the CIA's more skeptical prognosis about the future health of Soviet Communism proved the more accurate.[21] But during the Carter years, voicing such disbelief seemed, to politicians in Washington, increasingly unwise, as the purported lessons of the Vietnam debacle for American foreign policy shifted from the perils of imperialistic hubris to the cancerous danger of internal dissent and the disastrous consequences of a weakened will to fight in remote places. Carter believed the Soviet system was doomed, and that American values "have a magnetic appeal for people all over the world."[22] Paradoxically, Carter's utter confidence in America's eventual triumph over its adversary was widely construed as a failure of vigilance against the enemies of liberty.

In 1976, the writer Norman Podhoretz, with others including Nitze, Kirkpatrick, Perle, Eugene Rostow (the former dean of Yale Law School and a high official in President Lyndon Johnson's State Department in the 1960s), and William Casey, Reagan's second 1980 campaign manager (who had run clandestine operations in the Office of Strategic Services, forerunner to the CIA, during World War II), revived the name of an old organization, the Committee on the Present Danger (CPD), to press the case for confrontation, not détente. They deemed amoral the "realism" of Henry Kissinger, who had captained foreign policy under both Nixon and Ford. Using language that alluded unsubtly to Britain's effort to make peace with Nazi Germany in 1938 by abandoning Czechoslovakia to German advances, CPD members lamented the "culture of appeasement" that, they claimed, led Americans in the 1970s to value peace over justice.[23] Podhoretz argued that America's cultural elite had grown effete and would let the Soviet bully have its way with its chosen targets.[24] The neoconservative appeal was tailor-made for Reagan, a member of the World War II generation who signed up for the Cold War well before he became a Republican. As Garry Wills observes, even if some found it hysterical, the rhetoric of Team B and the CPD was in keeping with the tone of the Cold War consensus that had reigned in Washington between 1950 and 1970. Reports claiming imminent Soviet strategic superiority had issued from august expert panels throughout the 1950s; indeed, "doomsday scenarios had . . . been the basis of national policy."[25] Only in the years after America's defeat in Vietnam did a major wing of the Washington establishment come to see such "scenarios" as irrational.

Opponents of détente made two different arguments in support of their thesis that the Soviet Union posed a newly potent threat. One was technical, the other easily grasped.

Nitze, Perle, and others testified tirelessly in public about the impressive "throw-weight" that Soviet land-based nuclear missiles represented. If they were correct, size and heft meant strategic power. The USSR had more and heavier intercontinental ballistic missiles (ICBMs) than did the United States. The alarmists warned that this edge brought the superpower relationship out of balance, because it might lead Soviet leaders to contemplate a nuclear first strike against America. In turn, Washington might back down from confrontations for fear of triggering such an apocalyptic attack by an overconfident Soviet Union. The real strategic danger was not that the United States and the USSR would blow up the world, but that nuclear blackmail would embolden Soviet meddling, both political and military, everywhere outside U.S. borders, and that such aggression would succeed in intimidating a frightened America. Many Americans had voiced similar concerns since the 1960s. Democrat John Kennedy had conjured a nonexistent "missile gap" during the 1960 presidential campaign. Conservatives long had warned that a growing Soviet edge in the arms race would empower the Russians to win the fight for world domination "without firing a shot" at the United States—as an oft-heard phrase put it. By 1980, those expressing such fears of Soviet superiority had migrated almost entirely to Reagan's camp. Only in the light of such views did Reagan's comment in his inaugural address— that America wanted peace but that "we will not surrender for it, now or ever"—make sense.[26]

The greater numbers of Soviet ICBMs were counteracted by U.S. superiority in bomber-carried nuclear warheads and a likely technical advantage in submarine-launched missiles. (These three delivery systems were known as the nuclear "triad.") The sea-based nuclear deterrent would be, as all the world's militaries knew, effectively impossible to defend against if used, and was therefore an adequate nuclear deterrent by itself. Even U.S. land-based ICBMs were intentionally made lighter to increase their accuracy, as authorities like Nitze understood full well.[27]

Heated debate about missile arsenals left many Americans scratching their heads, but a simpler argument also was made against détente: world events formed a global U.S.-Soviet struggle, and the Soviet side was making geographic gains. In the late 1970s, charges that the Soviets were stealing a march on the United States focused on events in Africa and Central America, despite the doubtful strategic importance of these areas. Struggles for power developed in Angola and Mozambique after their liberation from Portuguese colonial rule in 1974. Cuba, supported by the Soviet Union, dispatched troops to help leftist revolutionaries win power in Angola; the United States supported other forces diplomatically, fearful of a new Soviet client state. Conservatives adopted Jonas Savimbi, leader of an armed group in Angola, as their favored proxy in the region, hoping to see the United States support him directly. Henry Kissinger, the American face of détente in the 1970s, told Soviet Foreign Minister Andrei Gromyko that "the Soviet Union has nothing to gain in Angola. We have nothing to gain in Angola. Five years from now it will make no difference."[28] Once the Soviets and Cubans were there, however, Kissinger's enemies declared such remote conflicts meaningful simply because the Soviets and Cubans were there. The white-supremacist regime in South Africa, which Reagan and others viewed as a vital anticommunist ally, was determined to intervene militarily in Angola and in Namibia, supporting Savimbi; Pretoria, given cool treatment by Carter, would find a sympathetic ear in Washington with Reagan in power. Meanwhile, in northeastern Africa, the socialist Mengistu Haile Mariam's regime in Ethiopia enlisted extensive Soviet aid in its struggle against aggression from bordering Somalia.

In Central America, leftists also appeared to be on the march. The socialist Sandinista movement displaced Nicaragua's dictator, the longtime U.S. ally Anastasio Somoza Debayle, in 1979. The right-wing government in El Salvador, which also relied on Washington's patronage, faced a guerrilla movement that threatened to duplicate the Sandinistas' feat. Carter tried and failed to keep the Sandinistas hemmed in by a coalition government after Somoza was gone, but he agreed to continue aid to the new government anyway. Carter cut off aid to the Salvadoran government in 1980 after the well-publicized rape and murder of U.S. churchwomen by military forces there (see chapter 4), but restored it when the government seemed endangered by rebel advances. The conservative charge that Nicaragua had become a "second Cuba," and that El Salvador might become a third, was too much to withstand politically. Shooting wars in Central America, more than those in Africa, would become matters for sustained controversy in the United States in the 1980s. But, in the late 1970s, conservatives who argued that détente was a fool's game pointed to expanding zones of Soviet influence and newly declared socialist regimes everywhere on the globe as evidence. As Reagan put the case at his first news conference after taking office, "So far détente's been a one-way street that the Soviet Union has used to pursue its own aims."[29]

Efforts to discredit détente helped to elect Reagan in 1980, and his new conservative foreign policy would take its most definite form in Reagan's command to build a fresh arsenal of missiles, warships, and bombers. Neoconservative rhetoric seemed to recommend confrontation; Washington's willingness to fight, doubtful since Vietnam, had to be reestablished. Yet Reagan had campaigned not on a pledge to fight the Soviets but, rather, by promising to back them down by building up America's strength. As Reagan said at his inauguration, "We will maintain sufficient strength to prevail if need be, knowing that if we do so we have the best chance of never having to use that strength."[30] If one of the superpowers were to be intimidated, it must be the Soviets, not the United States. Carter had already proposed increasing the Department of Defense budget by 4.5 percent annually for five years. Reagan had pledged similar increases, but he and his advisers started upping the ante after the election. As inauguration day approached, Washington was abuzz with talk of large numbers. Carter had forecast a total increase in military spending of $1.2 trillion, and Reagan of $1.6 trillion. But the military's Joint Chiefs of Staff ultimately deduced that a figure between $2.35 trillion and $2.7 trillion was needed to meet Reagan's strategic plans.[31] The numbers were of a scale that soon became meaningless to almost everyone. But all agreed that massive sums of public money soon would flow, through Capitol Hill and the Pentagon, to military contractors. The U.S. military budget would increase by 17.5 percent in both 1981 and 1982, remarkable figures for a country not at war.[32]

Bristling with plans and verve imparted by Reagan's unusually clear governing agenda (both domestic and foreign), movement conservatives streamed to Washington during the pre-inauguration "transition" period, and the Reagan team organized an enormous planning and staffing operation. Congress appropriated $2 million to pay the new administration's transition costs, yet the effort became so big that private donors had to provide another $1.5 million.[33] All perceived that the new men and women were planning to institute a deep change in the executive-branch bureaucracy, placing movement cadres several layers deep in federal agencies. One political scientist noted afterward that "the hostility of many . . . appointees to the programs they would administer was a common characteristic of Reagan's choices for second-level positions. . . . There was achieved in this second round of appointments an uncommon degree of ideological consistency and intensity."[34]

Reaganism's cadres asserted that they were part of a rightward tide sweeping the world, especially English-speaking countries. Margaret Thatcher's Conservative Party had toppled a Labour government in Great Britain in 1979; she would be Reagan's closest ally abroad, and American conservatives admired her bracing, confrontational style of politics. Australia and New Zealand had seen parties relatively friendly to free-market policies take power in 1975. Canada's Liberals, somewhat akin to U.S. Democrats, won the elections in their country in 1980, but their rivals, the Progressive Conservatives, led by Brian Mulroney, a warm Reagan ally, came back to score a breakthrough victory in 1984, gaining over half the national vote. The U.S. Republicans and Reagan's government were more extreme in their pro-business, antiregulatory stance than conservative parties and regimes elsewhere.

Thatcherism and British politics are the most relevant international points of comparison to the American political scene, and the differences were important. Thatcher's government came to a crisis early on because, unlike Reagan's, it tried earnestly to balance its budget, which meant raising taxes on consumers and cutting spending severely amid a bad recession, in order to pay for income-tax cuts. The issue of organized labor and its power figured differently in the two political systems as well. One scholar of Thatcherism summarized Thatcher's agenda as fostering "the free economy" but also "the strong state."[35] Thatcher wanted to show that the British national government still ruled its country, an imperative that was directed at the defiant stance of labor unions, which were very powerful in Britain's Labour Party. The Democratic Party, in contrast, was not a labor party; American unions merely formed one interest among many that jockeyed for influence in it. Unions had little power to curb, and conservatives' hostility to them was an issue of provincial rather than pervasive concern in American politics. Reagan's essential message was antigovernmental—a message he delivered famously in his inauguration speech in January 1981: "In this present crisis, government is not the solution to our problem; government is the problem."[36] Reagan routinely offered exceptions to his doctrine of the weak state; he wanted a stronger military, and embraced a more robust apparatus of law enforcement and incarceration. Yet, unlike Thatcher, Reagan never truly incorporated these exceptions, large as they were, into his governing dogma. He and his cadres professed fidelity to the doctrine of the free economy and the weak state.

To some, Reagan appeared to have a broader agenda than conservatives elsewhere, because of his antipathy to guaranteeing the rights of racial minorities through the national government and, even more, his devotion to conservative religious morals. But the new administration was unwilling to risk precious political capital in public fights over these matters. Reagan contented himself, instead, with altering policy in these areas by curtailing funds to executive-branch agencies and through appointments. His appointees' attitudes, particularly regarding racial inequality and business regulation, were starkly different from those of their predecessors during the 1960s and 1970s, in both Democratic and Republican administrations.

In race matters, Reagan rhetorically hewed to an individualist line, preferring to enforce simple antidiscrimination law but opposing affirmative action, which meant the use of broad patterns (in hiring, promotion, or housing, for example) as evidence of legal wrongdoing and in the formulation of legal redress for discrimination. During the 1980 campaign, Reagan had said, "We must not allow the noble concept of equal opportunity to be distorted into federal guidelines or quotas . . . to be the principal factor in hiring or education."[37] Once elected, he placed William Bradford Reynolds, a critic of affirmative action, at the head of the Civil Rights Division of the Department of Justice and did likewise in naming Clarence Thomas, who pledged to focus narrowly on charges of conscious discrimination against individual plaintiffs, to lead the Equal Employment Opportunity Commission (EEOC). Reagan's judicial appointees also proved hostile to a statistics-based approach to racial discrimination, of the kind that the U.S. Supreme Court had validated in decisions such as the unanimous *Griggs et al. v. Duke Power Co.* (1971)— which ruled that the company, with a history of hiring discrimination, had violated civil rights law by giving job applicants "intelligence tests," on which African Americans scored relatively poorly—and, by a 6–3 vote, in *Fullilove v. Klutznick* (1980)—which found that government "set-aside" programs, guaranteeing a certain proportion of contract business to minority-owned concerns, were legal.[38] By the late 1980s, Republican-appointed judges would reverse precedent in these matters.

Yet Reagan, as president, proved both more politically calculating and more sweepingly unsympathetic toward complaints of discrimination than his campaign rhetoric had suggested he would be. Reagan never launched an assault on affirmative action either through legislative proposals or executive orders, disappointing some conservatives. Members of his own cabinet supported affirmative action, at least in some forms, notably George Shultz, secretary of state beginning in 1982, who had championed the policy in the arena of hiring and promotion during his service as President Nixon's secretary of labor. Faced with disagreement among his cadres, Reagan ducked the issue, handing it to his judicial appointees for future—but potentially far-reaching—action.[39] In early

1982, Reagan signed a twenty-five-year extension of the Voting Rights Act, a law he had opposed in 1965. Southern conservatives favored ending Justice's supervision of their region's elections, which the law required, but Republicans elsewhere showed little zeal for this cause; without GOP unity, Reagan would not wage this fight either. However, his appointees failed to fulfill the promise they offered to safeguard individual rights. Two years into Reagan's presidency, the Justice Department and the EEOC had halved the number of employment discrimination suits they brought forward, and the Department of Housing and Urban Development simply stopped requiring federal contractors to certify that they complied with civil rights laws. There was no drop-off in the volume of housing discrimination complaints in the 1980s, yet the Civil Rights Division, in eight years under Reagan, brought as many cases forward in this area as it had during each year of Carter's presidency.[40] Reagan sometimes showed a remarkably understanding face toward those who engaged in overt racial discrimination. In 1981, at the behest of U.S. Representative Trent Lott, Republican of Mississippi, Reagan instructed Justice and Treasury to relent in the face of a lawsuit brought by Bob Jones University, which sought to keep its tax-exempt status despite its openly segregationist policies. "I think we should" take Bob Jones's side, Reagan wrote. But after the resulting criticism, Reagan's staff got him to back off from his sincere initial move to defend Bob Jones.[41]

Unlike efforts to relax the enforcement of civil rights, aggressive moves to propagate conservative Christian morality through the law were not consistent with the doctrine of the weak state, and such exertions made limited headway in the new government. Reagan supported cutting Medicaid funds that paid for poor women to obtain abortions. Other than this change—important as it was—the religious right mainly got lip service from Reagan. When he nominated Sandra Day O'Connor, a pro-choice, pro-ERA Republican from Arizona, to the Supreme Court in July 1981, religious conservatives felt they had been kicked in the teeth.

Business lobbies, however, knew they now had friends in Washington who would fight to vitiate proconsumer or prolabor statutes and agencies. The best-known case was James Watt, a leader in the corporate fight against the regulation of mining and logging on public lands in the West, who became secretary of the interior, responsible for overseeing public lands. Watt invited controversy and had to resign his position in

1983, but many others with a similar outlook served at the subcabinet level and attracted little public attention. Watt's assistant secretary for natural resources and the environment was a lumber-industry lawyer. Organized labor was an inviting target for a government that catered to business lobbies. Reagan named John Van de Water, previously the head of a prominent "union-busting" law firm, to chair the National Labor Relations Board.[42]

Deregulation of business had become a bipartisan affair in the 1970s, another instance—like cutting capital-gains tax rates—in which Reagan can fairly be said to have extended something Carter and the Democrats started. However, the deregulation of airlines, trucking, and railroads—efforts spearheaded by Democrats before 1981—represented a repudiation of some of the earliest forms of federal regulation that, many believed, were stifling competition and keeping prices high. "Quality of life" regulations, such as the Clean Air Act, were supported staunchly by Democrats. Reagan's deregulatory zeal was more comprehensive. But his ability to legislate a rollback of recent regulatory measures was uncertain. As William Niskanen, an early member of Reagan's Council of Economic Advisers, noted, "The new administration would have substantial support for reducing the traditional forms of economic regulation"—meaning older forms; this would prove true most of all in banking—"but very little support for reducing the newer types of regulation of health, safety, and the environment."[43] Indeed, Congress would not agree to relax pollution controls as a matter of law. Yet Reagan reduced the Environmental Protection Agency's (EPA) budgets for water quality and air quality enforcement by 59 percent and 31 percent, respectively, between 1981 and 1984.[44] He might have gotten further than he did in turning the EPA around, but his top appointees there, Anne Burford and Rita Lavelle, were so bold in their efforts to undermine EPA's mission that, in disgrace, they were forced to lead an extraordinary mass resignation of over twenty EPA appointees in 1983. Congress cited Burford for contempt when she refused to provide documents concerning the "Superfund" toxic-waste clean-up program. Lavelle served time in prison after receiving a conviction for lying in her congressional testimony and obstructing justice in order to protect her former employer—exactly the sort of corporate polluter that Superfund was supposed to hold accountable.[45]

In most cases, the business agenda could be pursued by favorably interpreting existing regulations. In early 1981, a lawyer who worked for industry commented, "None of the lawyers I know can remember anything like the impact the election has had on the regulatory agencies. They're offering me things I wouldn't have dared to ask for before." C. Boyden Gray, who would serve as legal counsel to a new Presidential Task Force on Regulatory Relief, encouraged members of the U.S. Chamber of Commerce in April 1981 to use the task force as a means of circumventing regulatory agencies, which were likely to be stocked with career civil servants not imbued with the new spirit. "If you go to the agency, don't be too pessimistic if they can't solve the problem there. That's what the task force is for."[46] Reagan, after taking office, quickly chilled the prospect of new regulations, issuing orders requiring "cost-benefit analysis" of such proposals.[47] This method was a standard proposal from business lobbyists, who devised dire projections of the economic damage that business regulation would wreak; it left no room for any social good such laws might accomplish that was not a matter of dollars and cents. Whether the issue was curbing television product advertisements aimed at young children, mandating safety standards for car bumpers, or setting more stringent limits on contaminants in drinking water, the administration's approach would follow a pattern: slow things down, require further review, and provide additional opportunities for business corporations to appeal. Where public interest groups such as environmentalists wanted to block private action they deemed harmful, the method was the opposite. Before 1981, those objecting to damage wrought on protected wetlands areas by authorized private development had five appeals they could make, and these could last years. With Reagan and Watt in office, such appeals were cut from five to two, and limited to ninety days.[48]

While Margaret Thatcher and her British followers thought they needed to inject new legitimacy into the pursuit of wealth and profit in a society grown hostile to pecuniary values, American conservatives in the early 1980s felt more confident. In the American conservative view, only liberal snobs derided material pursuits. The problem, as conservatives saw it, was not that money was unloved in America, but rather that cultural elites who exhibited distaste for capitalism had become entrenched in government and other important institutions. At a 1981 convention of

Young Americans for Freedom, a major conservative movement group since its founding in 1960, the assembled activists sang lustily, "God Bless free enterprise,/System divine./Stand beside her, don't deride her,/ Just so long as the profits are mine."[49] Reagan declared in his inaugural address, "It is my intention to curb the size and influence of the Federal government," and averred that the secret to America's wealth was that "here in this land we unleashed the energy and individual genius of man."[50] Private enterprise must be honored and protected. The tax cuts were the heart of Reagan's agenda. But the animating spirit of Reaganism was the drive to liberate the sleeping giants of American wealth and enterprise from the fetters of social obligation, and to make such a flight from obligation unashamed and free from rebuke.

Three

Victory on Capitol Hill

The inaugural festivities of January 1981 were lavish, capturing the new celebration of wealth and contrasting sharply with the modesty of Carter's festivities four years earlier. As the Reagan years dawned, furs, jewels, and stretch limousines inundated Washington. Barry Goldwater, who had passed the conservative torch to Reagan, found it irksome; proud politicians humored themselves that they did not wait at the beck and call of private wealth.[1] Reagan and his retinue found such pretensions misconceived. His friend Charles Wick, whom Reagan appointed head of the U.S. Information Agency, argued that, against a background of economic anxiety created by stagflation, Americans might enjoy the spectacle of high living—just as their parents and grandparents had been delivered from the miseries of the Great Depression by cinematic visions of Manhattan cabaret life. "They loved those glamour pictures showing people driving beautiful cars and women in beautiful gowns," he said.[2] *Time* magazine's White House correspondent, Hugh Sidey, wrote sycophantically, in a rebuke to Carter, "Let's have some class this time around." Frank Sinatra, who had organized the major inaugural gala for John F. Kennedy in 1961, and Efrem Zimbalist Jr., "a second-level leading man" from Hollywood, starred in the show.[3] Lewis Lapham, editor of *Harper's* magazine, discerned a "curious atmosphere of comic opera" in the administration's pageantry. "In somewhat the same way that the Second Empire of Louis Napoleon aped the empire of Napoleon I, the Reagan administration mimics the vigor of President Kennedy's New

Frontier."[4] Amid the merrymaking, liberal intellectuals could do little more than take solace in such arcane put-downs.

Nancy Reagan discovered, however, that the opulence could go too far and could linger too long past inauguration day. She raised eyebrows by accepting gifts of dresses and jewelry worth tens of thousands of dollars from luxury designers and then by dissembling when confronted on the matter. In California, she had been used to accepting such largesse from wealthy friends.[5] She claimed she planned to return the clothes or donate them to museums and that, therefore, they were loans, not gifts. In 1982, she swore off the practice of accepting these items, but she continued taking them nonetheless, sometimes keeping them and failing to report them on financial disclosure forms. The value of her free wardrobe over eight years likely exceeded $1 million, and featured between sixty and eighty outfits from one designer alone.[6] Nancy Thompson, an officer of the Republican Women's Task Force, called the First Lady's practices "outrageous." But the designer Bill Blass gallantly rose to defend the president's wife, saying, "I don't think there's been anyone in the White House since Jacqueline Kennedy Onassis who has her flair."[7] Despite Nancy Reagan's popularity with couturiers, the criticism intensified as she led an entourage befitting a Hollywood star when she attended the wedding of Britain's Prince Charles to Diana Spencer in July 1981, and as news spread of further generous "donations" that helped redecorate the presidential living quarters, including ornate formal dinnerware—all amid a worsening recession. Yet she won the affections of the Washington press with a satiric performance, dressed as a homeless woman, of the old song "Second-Hand Rose," at the annual Gridiron Dinner, an important social event in Washington, in 1982.

Such appearance-focused distractions from grave matters of government policy perpetuated a pattern from the campaign, presaging Reagan's successes in his first year as president. When Reagan took office, a majority of the Congress, including numerous Democrats representing areas where Reagan had polled well, were champing at the bit to pass his spending cuts, tax cuts, and military buildup. Reagan's public support was strong. Democratic leaders later allowed that in late 1980 and early 1981 their constituent mail ran heavily in favor of Reagan's agenda.[8] Prominent Democrats made little effort to talk down Reagan's chances on Capitol Hill. Representative David Obey of Wisconsin, a blunt liberal, said in February, "I personally think it would be a political mistake if we don't give the administration an opportunity to test its views. There is a mandate for the administration to proceed with significant budget cuts and significant tax cuts."[9] "Mandate" was a word that seemed to be on everyone's lips. The Speaker of the House, Thomas "Tip" O'Neill of Massachusetts—as famous for his red nose, white hair, and protruding middle as he was for his unabashed big-government liberalism—violated Washington decorum when, at an early meeting with Reagan, he condescendingly remarked that, in contrast to Reagan's years as California governor, "you're in the big leagues now."[10] Such bluster was out of step—and ineffective. A friend of O'Neill acknowledged that Democrats feared being labeled "obstructionists" if they refused all compromise with Reagan.[11] The Speaker controls the schedule of business considered on the House floor, yet O'Neill relinquished this weapon when he agreed not to delay bringing Reagan's budget and tax bills forward.

The political parties were a study in contrast. The Republicans were united. The incoming Senate majority leader, Howard Baker, offered, "We are a team, the president is the quarterback and we are his blockers and we can't say now we don't like the plays."[12] Representative Willis Gradison of Ohio, an old Washington hand and no conservative firebrand, described the feeling in the Republican caucus, saying Reagan "had not only defeated an incumbent Democratic president but brought in a Republican Senate and a working majority in the House. There was a sense of euphoria that at first translated into almost automatic support."[13] On the other side of the aisle, Southern Democrats who had seen their constituents vote heavily for Reagan prepared to abandon ship, sometimes for good. Early in 1981, the Democrats' Senate leader, Robert Byrd of West Virginia, made clear his intention to vote for Reagan's proposed budget, not for the one emerging from his own party's ranks.[14] The lead sponsor for Reagan's budget in the House was Phil Gramm, a Democrat from Texas, which was the happiest hunting ground for Republicans rounding up Democratic votes in 1981 and 1982. Reagan had won the state by a margin of six hundred thousand votes. In 1983, Gramm would switch parties.

Carter had become known for his aloofness from Washington's elite social life, and Reagan, a man as gregarious at a party as he was remote in private, would not make that error. The journalist Lou Cannon, who parlayed his reporting on Reagan in Sacramento into a career as Reagan's leading biographer, perceptively noted the continuity in Reagan's career: "He realized that Washington was a company town, and he had been a company man since his Hollywood days."[15] Reagan made three trips to Washington during the transition period to socialize with those who could help defeat or advance his program. The best-known of the exclusive dinners honoring him during this phase was given by Katharine Graham, in her youth a liberal who romanced a radical longshoreman, now the empress publisher of the *Washington Post*, the capital's leading newspaper.[16] Reagan made a rare faux pas when he broke his commitment to attend a December 1980 banquet celebrating the twenty-fifth anniversary of the founding of *National Review*. The magazine had publicized Reagan's scheduled appearance; the event was to be a celebration of the conservative movement's empowerment. Some took Reagan's cancellation as a signal that his old movement friends now embarrassed him and that, once in office, he would moderate his agenda.[17] More truly, the schedule change showed Reagan's adeptness at the power game. Before his victory, he had cultivated those who would help get him nominated and elected; now, he focused on those who would help him succeed as president.

The top White House staff under Reagan performed impressively in the early going, when taxing and spending were the top priorities. Reagan, who well understood how much responsibility he wanted to delegate, chose James Baker—whom he knew only by observing him as the leader of Bush's 1980 campaign—for his White House chief of staff. Reagan pushed aside Ed Meese, his most loyal retainer and a true comrade, who wanted the job and whom movement conservatives expected to uphold their standard. This unexpected choice reflected the force of the president's desire for calm and order. Reagan had doubts about Meese, in spite of the two men's closeness. Shortly before the 1980 election, the candidate had confided to Stuart Spencer, "Ed cannot be chief of staff. He's not organized."[18] Indeed, the chaos inside Meese's briefcase became something of a Washington legend. Administration economist William Niskanen called Meese "the most conspicuously mediocre man in American public life . . . a terrible manager."[19] Baker, in contrast, was trim and controlled in both look and manner, a buttoned-down sort who spoke softly where others might yell, fastidious but not fussy. Such men appealed strongly to Reagan. As consolation, Meese received the title of counselor to the president, with oversight of both the NSC and the Domestic Policy Council—and, informally, membership in the famed "troika" of Baker, Meese, and Michael Deaver that sat atop the White House power structure.

Baker easily outmaneuvered Meese. Both men signed an unusual memorandum, Baker's handiwork, explicitly dividing their responsibilities. Baker ceded policy development to Meese, securing for himself "coordination and control of all in and out paper flow to the President and of presidential schedule and appointments," as well as "hiring and firing authority over all elements of White House Staff."[20] Baker asserted control over White House communications and maintained a chokehold over access to the Oval Office. Reagan occasionally evaded this control to meet with unauthorized outsiders, but White House personnel did not get time with the president unless Baker permitted it. Meese could walk into the Oval Office, but the memorandum stated that Baker could join them at such moments; thus, Meese was rarely alone with his longtime boss.[21] Baker's name soon became linked with the phrase "levers of power."[22] Meanwhile, according to Niskanen, Meese "would often be speaking to some 4-H club at a time an important issue was being resolved."[23] Cabinet "councils," cutting across departments, were established to coordinate policy, but they proved a series of cul-de-sacs. "Decisions would get made in the cabinet councils and unmade by the Baker team," one council chair noted bitterly.[24]

Deaver, disdained as a mere valet by some, and seen by many—perhaps even himself—as a hick from Bakersfield, was the maestro of President Reagan's public appearances, and was therefore crucial to Reagan's successes. He did far more than tend to the backgrounds and camera angles for Reagan's television performances. He claimed wide-ranging authority, and did not hesitate to press hard for the ouster of high-ranking officials when he thought they were hurting the president. Deaver, who may have considered Meese an ideologue not up to the top staff job, had promoted Baker for chief behind the scene. Baker cemented the alliance with Deaver, isolating Meese and benefiting from Deaver's personal relationship with the Reagans—something Baker lacked. Baker handed Deaver control over Ronald Reagan's schedule. With Deaver choreographing Reagan's movements, and Baker controlling what and whom the president saw during meetings, they were—in truth—a duo, not two parts of a troika, at the center of power. Nancy Reagan trusted Deaver as a pure Reagan loyalist of long tenure. His portfolio included mollifying her concerns that "Ronnie" was at times ill-served by his subordinates and sustaining her influential and sometimes shrewd messages in the inner councils of a White House that soon acquired the ambience of a royal court.

Two essential meetings became the alpha and omega of White House politics. Each morning at 8:15, Baker, his protégé, Darman, communications director David Gergen, and the presidential press spokesman met to decide on the "line of the day" that White House statements and presidential appearances were to convey.[25] The Legislative Strategy Group (LSG), which ran the Pennsylvania Avenue campaigns to get the White House agenda through Congress, met on late afternoons, in Baker's office, to make key decisions on legislative proposals and dealings with Congress. Baker and Meese officially cochaired the LSG, but Baker, with aggressive support from Darman, controlled it. Baker's adroit manipulations were on full display in May 1981, when Reagan endorsed a proposal to reduce Social Security payments substantially for Americans who chose to retire and begin taking benefits from the system early—at age sixty-two instead of sixty-five. Baker, upon learning of the president's decision, recognized it as a relapse into a politically lethal enthusiasm of Reagan's. During the 1976 campaign, Reagan had spoken of making Social Security a voluntary system. Baker had worked that year for Ford's team, which had pounced on Reagan after this blunder. Now Baker called a snap meeting of the LSG, in which he asserted his right as chief of staff to determine how the proposal would be made public. He insisted that the secretary of health and human services (HHS), Richard Schweiker, and not Reagan, announce it, and that Schweiker do so at the HHS building, not the White House. "The Schweiker plan" was dead on arrival on Capitol Hill. Eight days after the announcement, the Senate, at the prodding of Daniel Patrick Moynihan, Democrat of New York, voted 96–0 for a resolution stating the upper chamber would reject any bill that would "precipitously and unfairly penalize early retirees."[26] Reagan disowned the plan he had embraced in private.

The wunderkind who had helped temporarily persuade Reagan to cut early-retiree benefits was David Stockman, the chain-smoking budget director, sometimes called ascetic but more accurately described as obsessive. Stockman, aged thirty-four with salt-and-pepper hair that he wore a bit long, was determined to show he was the smartest person in the government and could work the longest hours. Stockman was the walking nerve center of the administration's assault on government spending, often seen hugging a huge black folder or a stack of books as he walked from one meeting or hearing to the next, the picture of an overgrown pupil burdened with his obscure treasure. His legend rose in the early days of the administration. This former divinity student spoke easily of his zeal for "revolution" against big government, and he seemed to know more about budget arcana than anyone else.

During the transition, Stockman won the Office of Management and Budget (OMB) job, in part by playing Jimmy Carter effectively in Reagan's rehearsals for his 1980 debate with the incumbent. Quickly perceiving the vacuum in economic policy leadership in the incoming government, Stockman inserted himself in it. He started generating binders filled with specific recommendations. Baker understood that Stockman was ready to move and agreed that time was of the essence—so he let out the reins on Stockman. The budget director was not, in most administrations, the central economic policy maker. But as Reagan's team settled in, Stockman was soon recognized as the key person on all spending decisions. Reagan understood virtually nothing of federal government budget processes and little of the budget's contents. "The fiscal and economic illiteracy among the core White House group," Stockman reflected later, allowed him to assert leadership on the nuts and bolts of the "Reagan Revolution," and to outline significant and wide-ranging spending reductions.[27]

Stockman served his boss's purposes well, but was too proud of his own cleverness and proved politically naïve. Ultimately, he failed to shrink the government, instead merely making it more parsimonious toward society's unfortunates. Throughout his tenure at OMB, he was a tool of those who wished to set the table for a feast of tax cuts for the wealthy. He was powerless to limit the fantastic new military spending that mocked his dream of a smaller government, or to hold back the stampede of wealthy interests who gorged themselves in Reagan's Washington. "The hogs were really feeding," he would say.[28] In the end, the joke was on Stockman. A leading player in the political dramas that consumed Washington in 1981, he was barely, if ever, recalled in the capital by the time Reagan left office.

On January 30, Stockman met with Caspar Weinberger, the new secretary of defense, only realizing later how badly Weinberger had beaten him at the numbers game. Weinberger had served as Reagan's budget director in Sacramento—ably, in Reagan's view. Then he had been deputy to George Shultz at OMB in the Nixon administration, before taking over the top slot there when Shultz moved to a Cabinet post. His sanguinary nickname, "Cap the Knife," referred to his willingness to implement unpopular economies while at OMB. But Stockman's hope that he would have an ally at Defense was wrongheaded. Weinberger, who never impressed with his knowledge of weapons systems or military affairs, became, with Reagan's strong support, an implacable proponent of the highest possible increases in Defense spending at every turn. Colleagues underestimated Weinberger because his maximalist arguments often lacked reason; he protected every extra dollar in his budget by echoing Reagan's own insistence that (in the president's words) "what we're doing in defense must be seen as different than Carter. It must be a symbol of a change of climate as regards defense."[29]

Therefore, as Stockman understood, politically, the 5 percent per year increase in the military budget that Reagan had advocated during the campaign was now not enough. Carter had left the incoming administration with the gift of his own call for a 4.5 percent increase. On January 30, Stockman and Weinberger agreed arbitrarily on 7 percent growth per year through 1986, which represented a compromise. Weinberger grumbled that this was "a pretty lean ration." Stockman, at the end of a very long day, somehow agreed to calculate the increases from the baseline of the fiscal year 1982 budget—not the 1980 budget, the original target of Reagan's campaign criticism. "When I finally took a hard look at [the numbers] several weeks later, I nearly had a heart attack," he recalled, adding:

> We had taken an already-raised defense budget and raised that by 7 percent. Instead of starting from a defense budget of $142 billion, we'd started with one of $222 billion. And by raising that by 7 percent— and compounding it over five years—we had ended up increasing the real growth rate of the United States defense budget by *10 percent* per

year between 1980 and 1986. That was double what candidate Ronald
Reagan had promised in his campaign budget plan.[30]

Stockman then spent months trying to undo what he considered a
mere arithmetic error, with Weinberger treating their January agreement
as holy scripture. Finally, they took their dispute over Defense spending
to Reagan, which was the kind of thing Reagan hated. Stockman described
the fiscal calamity that would result if the current agreement held. Weinberger responded with a series of charts and pictures: images of Soviet
weapons factories and aging U.S. weapons (whose replacements Stockman was not threatening), and, as a pièce de résistance, cartoons that
represented the different proposed budgets as different soldiers. Weinberger's soldier was big and strong, Stockman's, weak and small. Reagan
chose Weinberger's. "If it comes down to balancing the budget or defense, the balanced budget will have to give way," the president had said
only days before. In the end, Stockman secured a measly $15 billion in
reductions from the planned five-year military buildup of $1.46 trillion.
"It was so intellectually disreputable, so demeaning," Stockman wrote
later with bitterness, "that I could hardly bring myself to believe that a
Harvard-educated cabinet officer could have brought this to the President of the United States. Did he think the White House was on Sesame
Street?"[31]

Another episode in the comedy of Stockman's disillusionment came
on February 7, when he, Murray Weidenbaum, the chair of the Council
of Economic Advisors, and Treasury Department officials came to terms
over the administration's economic forecast for late 1981 and 1982. Their
estimates would influence how members of Congress viewed spending
and tax proposals. Wishful thinking is always involved in such a patently
political exercise, but this forecast was so outlandish that many in Washington mocked it as the "rosy scenario." Different factions favored different predictions, with the supply-siders projecting magical levels of
economic growth. The group settled on a figure of 5.2 percent growth
for 1982—and, as with military spending, this high figure was a compromise (there was a recession instead, and a growth rate of −1.9 percent in
1982). They also agreed to predict a still-high inflation rate of 7.7 percent
for 1982, partly because this number would both produce a high level of
tax receipts for the government—the supposedly evil "bracket creep" at

work—and reduce the size of the budget deficit.[32] It was easy for Stockman to come up with whatever numbers he needed. He just rigged OMB's computers, changing the assumptions in its program. The huge deficits produced by initial computations then simply disappeared.[33]

Stockman and his administration allies intermittently worried about their credibility on Capitol Hill. At first, Republicans on the Senate Budget Committee "choked on" the deficit projections that the Congressional Budget Office (CBO)—a kind of competitor to OMB in the forecasting department—reported would ensue if the Reagan program went through. But Stockman mollified them with the device of the "magic asterisk," as Howard Baker named it: this asterisk popped up in OMB's budget proposals to denote "future savings to be identified," which, again, made the deficits disappear—at least long enough for the committee to overcome its episode of honesty and vote through Stockman's budget.[34]

The outlines of a proposed government spending budget started in the House of Representatives. O'Neill and his chief subordinate, House Majority Leader Jim Wright of Texas, worried immediately after the 1980 election that Southern House Democrats (known as "boll weevils"), including Charles Stenholm, Kent Hance, and Phil Gramm, all from Texas, would fail to heed the call of party solidarity. The real boll weevil had devastated cotton crops in the South, yet some claimed this event had paved the way to a healthier, more diversified economy in that region; Alabama built a monument honoring the pest. "We may not have a monument erected in our honor," Stenholm commented, with dark humor, suggesting that Southerners organized in the Conservative Democratic Forum (CDF), in which he was a leader, might have to destroy in order to bring positive change.[35]

The Democratic majority in the House was, in effect, illusory. Reagan worked hard to get the votes to defeat the Democrats on the budget, continually meeting with House members in small groups, calling them on the telephone, and sending them telegrams. He repeated his broad, by then familiar, economic proposals in a speech to a joint session of Congress on February 18 and was well received. On June 4, Reagan met with a group of Southern Democrats and pledged that he would not personally assist their Republican opponents in the 1982 election campaigns if they voted with him now. "I couldn't look myself in the mirror if I went out and campaigned against you," he told them. He placed his program's success over the aspirations of House Republicans to take over the lower chamber.[36]

Reagan was moving toward victory on the budget when John Hinckley Jr. sought to enter history, on March 30. Reagan spoke that day to the Building Trades Council of the AFL-CIO at the Washington Hilton hotel, close to busy DuPont Circle in northwestern Washington. After the speech, with the presidential limousine door open, Reagan raised his left arm to wave to a woman in the gathered crowd. Hinckley, a deranged man who hoped to impress the movie actress Jodie Foster with his reprise of Robert DeNiro's violent role in the 1976 film *Taxi Driver*—which had featured Foster playing a child prostitute and DeNiro as her self-appointed protector—fired six shots from a cheap .22 caliber pistol, hitting five men, before he was subdued. One of these small bullets bounced off the car's rear panel, flattened into a disk, and penetrated Reagan's chest under his left armpit, slicing a narrow entry slit. Reagan had not seen Hinckley and did not know he had been shot.[37] A Secret Service officer pushed him down on the rear floor of the limousine and landed on him hard, at which point Reagan felt great pain. "You son of a bitch, you broke my ribs," he shouted in a moment of pique.[38] Confusion reigned for a time at the White House and among the press and public. Reagan's press secretary, James Brady, lay on the sidewalk, shot in the head.

By the time Reagan arrived at George Washington University hospital, he had gathered himself and delivered a superb performance under hairraising circumstances. He staggered with assistance from his car to the hospital door; then, as one witness recounted, his "eyes rolled upward, and his head went back, his knees buckled and he started to collapse."[39] The flattened bullet had tumbled end over end inside his chest, cutting a dime-sized path. A lung had caved in, and Reagan's chest was filling with blood. As the medical staff began working on him, Reagan was conscious but had great difficulty breathing, as he repeatedly told them. "I feel so bad," he said.[40] But he managed to joke, "Please tell me you're Republicans," before he was anesthetized. "Today, Mr. President, we are all Republicans," said the vascular surgeon in charge of the operating room.[41] The assassinations of the 1960s were not distant memories. Television newsmen appeared anguished. A major theme of Reagan's postelection period had been that the nation could not afford another failed presidency. As the hours passed on March 30, Reagan was transformed into a symbol of precisely what he had invoked as the frame for his conservative economic program: the resilient American spirit. The president suddenly embodied the drama of the nation's recent setbacks and its struggle for renewed vitality.

As Reagan recovered from a successful surgery, his surrogates kept his budget plans moving through the House. In a hospital room or convalescing in the White House residence, the wounded president hovered as a constant political presence. On April 6, Tip O'Neill visited Reagan in his hospital room; clearly moved, he took Reagan's hand, kissed his head, and knelt at his bedside as he and the president together recited the words of the Bible's Twenty-Third Psalm.[42] On April 28, a mere four weeks after the shooting, Reagan spoke to the entire Congress, looking strong and receiving a conquering general's thunderous welcome. His message was little different in substance from that of his February 18 address. In their hearts, O'Neill, Wright, and other Democratic leaders in the House may have known then that their fight was over. Television networks refused the Democrats airtime to respond to the president.[43] His ordeal had sanctified his agenda as something to be treated with respect bordering on genuflection, like a wartime leader's order of battle.

A majority of CDF members voted for the budget known as Gramm-Latta (after Gramm and Republican Del Latta of Ohio) instead of any proposed by Democrats. Observers thought the official Democratic budget proposal, crafted by Budget Committee Chairman Jim Jones of Oklahoma, offered "roughly 75%" of what Reagan demanded in spending cuts, tax cuts, and new military spending, but would open a smaller budget deficit and would aim the tax cuts at middle-income taxpayers.[44] Jones failed to hold his fellow Democrats. On May 7, the first crucial budget vote, establishing rough budget guidelines, went 253–176 for Gramm-Latta, with sixty-three Democrats in support, including thiry-eight of forty-seven CDF members.[45] But then, according to established budget procedure, various House committees, controlled by Democrats, drew up spending plans in their bailiwicks, determined to exceed the limits outlined in Gramm-Latta. Stockman wanted to avoid debates and votes in the full House on these separate committee recommendations. He persuaded Reagan to endorse an aggressive maneuver, short-circuiting the normal budget process by forcing the House into a binding up-or-down vote on the whole Gramm-Latta budget. In a chaotic scene on June 26, the House approved the bill, 232–193. The historic legislation members had voted to adopt had been assembled frantically overnight, and hardly anyone knew most of what was in it.[46] It was stuffed with special favors to House members whose votes Reagan, Stockman, and Baker thought they needed. It wrote into law changes in about 200 different government programs, virtually without floor debate on the specific reductions.

The substance of the budget gave the lie to Stockman's pretensions. He had started out hoping to take an ax to what he deemed unworthy subsidies for business interests, such as loans from the Export-Import Bank to some of the biggest names in U.S. manufacturing, to reduce estimated future outlays from Social Security by trimming benefits in various ways, and to keep expected increases in the Pentagon budget within some limits. "The defense budgets in the out-years won't be nearly as high as we are showing now, in my judgment," he had predicted.[47] But Stockman failed to meet all of these goals. "We are interested in curtailing weak claims rather than weak clients" of the government, he had said. "We have to show that we are willing to attack powerful clients with weak claims."[48] Otherwise, the budget cuts would simply punish the weak to help finance tax cuts aimed largely at the wealthy.

Precisely Stockman's worst fear came to pass. The largest pieces of the budget—"entitlements" like Social Security, Medicare (health care for the elderly), and veterans' benefits—were exempted from cuts, and Defense got a huge increase. This left only 17 percent of the budget to absorb all the needed reductions. Moreover, Stockman pitched in to help buy votes in the House and the Senate with the very pork-barrel projects he derided, which came out of that 17 percent. There were railway funds for Northerners, subsidies for synthetic fuel development for Charlie Wilson, Democrat of Texas, money for a troubled nuclear "breeder" reactor project in Tennessee for Howard Baker, and new quotas on sugar imports for Representative John Breaux, Democrat of Louisiana, who said, "They're not buying my vote, only renting it."[49]

This scheme set up the remaining programs—those without powerful "clients"—for what analysts termed "staggering" cuts.[50] When Reagan, in August, signed the resulting Omnibus Budget Reconciliation Act of 1981 (OBRA)—at the same ceremony, held at his California home, Rancho del Cielo, where he signed his tax-cut bill into law—at least four hundred thousand families of the working poor would lose all their welfare benefits, and another three hundred thousand would lose some, because they worked.[51] A million people would be pushed out of the food-stamp program. School breakfast and lunch programs would lose money. About $1 billion in grants to state governments to cover Medicaid costs would vanish; aid to workers whose jobs were lost due to foreign imports would dwindle. All this and more was due to take effect in October, even as a new recession had officially begun during the summer. To make matters more extreme, everyone knew, as Gramm-Latta was adopted, that tax cuts—favoring the wealthy most of all—were barreling down the tracks.

The Dickensian aspect of the 1981 Reagan budget satisfied movement conservatives who thought the poor needed to be kicked into moral wakefulness. Alan Greenspan, whom Reagan would appoint to replace Paul Volcker at the Fed, embraced this philosophy and felt that Reagan shared it, too. Years later, he reflected, "Reagan's kind of conservatism was to say that tough love is good for the individual and good for society. . . . it implies much less government support for the downtrodden. Yet mainstream Republicans were conflicted about thinking or"—Greenspan noted carefully—"talking in such terms, because they seemed contrary to Judeo-Christian values. Not Reagan."[52]

All the detailed work—at OMB and on Capitol Hill—that had gone into the budget cuts was, as already noted, intended to set the table for the tax cuts Reagan had promised. Slashing discretionary spending, although congenial to all conservatives, had not been a central thrust of Reagan's campaign. The pledge of income-tax cuts had been, in contrast, essential and highly specific (see chapter 2). Passing the tax cuts in Congress was relatively easy; most members preferred, in effect, giving to taking away. Serious qualms over the deficits that the tax cuts would produce proved easy to sweep aside legislatively. Ironically, the most dangerous fiscal conservative, from the administration's viewpoint, lurked within the citadel walls. David Stockman was worried.

It did not take long for supply-side advocates to suspect the truth: Stockman hoped to scale back or delay the tax cuts, because Congress had not cut as much spending as he had wished. They had cut about $35 billion for 1982, with reductions projected to reach $140 billion over the coming three years—a figure Stockman said was, to a great extent, "composed of promises and paper savings." He had wanted a minimum of $225 billion in cuts for 1982–1984.[53] The tax cuts, if Reagan got what he wanted, would amount to far more than that.

Ultimately, Reagan did agree to scale back the tax cuts modestly. The first yearly installment in the three-year rate shrinkage was 5 percent (not the initially proposed 10 percent), followed by 10 percent in 1982 and 10 percent in 1983. (The actual average total rate cut was 23 percent.)[54] Reagan had always wanted to cut the top marginal tax rate of 70 percent, which applied only to "unearned" or investment income, straight down to 50 percent. In February, Reagan reluctantly agreed to give up that provision.[55] Representative Dan Rostenkowski, Democrat of Illinois and Chair of the House Ways and Means Committee, fashioned a bill featuring a two-year, 15 percent cut in marginal rates, and other tax cuts aimed at those earning between $15,000 and $50,000 per year. In trying to compete with Reagan for conservative support, Rostenkowski also chose to start a bidding war of giveaways to the wealthy and the corporate sector, and he put the 70-to-50 drop back on the table. Thus, this provision ended up in the Economic Recovery and Tax Act (ERTA). Stockman later explained that the 70-to-50 issue was the really important one as far as supply-siders were concerned, because they were focused on big investors. "The rest of it is a secondary matter," he said. "The original argument was that the top bracket was too high, and that's having the most devastating effect on the economy." For the benefit of those who still did not understand, he added, "In order to make this palatable as a political matter, you had to bring down all the brackets. But, I mean, Kemp-Roth was always a Trojan horse to bring down the top rate."[56]

Reagan asked for network television time on July 27, two days before the major votes on the tax cuts were expected in both the House and the Senate, and pushed on the open door. "Are you entitled to the fruits of your own labor or does government have some presumptive right to spend and spend and spend?" he asked, reprising familiar campaign rhetoric. There could only be one answer to this question. It was as if the impending multiyear Pentagon spending binge were nonexistent. On July 29, the Senate voted 89–11 for Reagan's bill. The key House vote was 238–195, with 48 Democrats in support. It cut the capital gains tax from 28 percent to 20 percent, and made it easier for Americans to circumvent the IRS when passing their wealth to their heirs, more than tripling the wealth threshold needed to trigger estate taxes and raising the ceilings on tax-exempt gifts by a similar factor.[57] Stockman asked William Greider, the liberal journalist who had become his confidant, "Do you realize the greed that came to the forefront?"[58]

Washington hailed Reagan's triumph, and Reagan basked in the glory of his victories. But Stockman knew what the picture of exploding deficits would look like down the road. In 1986, when he published his memoir, *The Triumph of Politics*, he wrote, "The overall bottom line is this. . . . The tax revenue giveaway implemented by the Reagan Administration has amounted to *four times more* than the spending takeaway."[59] ERTA cost the U.S. Treasury three-quarters of a trillion dollars in revenue from 1982 through 1986.[60] Stockman waged a campaign in the fall of 1981 to get a second round of spending cuts through Congress, but now resistance was stiff. When he met with GOP House members, Trent Lott exclaimed that any more talk about cutting Social Security benefits was "dead in the water. That's like in: No way! Period! End of discussion! Not a prayer!" Representative Richard Cheney of Wyoming, who decades later would become vice president under President George W. Bush (son of Reagan's vice president), said, "You can't go back to the well over and over. . . . The deficit isn't the worst thing that could happen."[61]

In late 1981, Reagan proposed a new round of spending cuts, but they went nowhere. With this option gone, the White House staff began the agonizing process of convincing Reagan to take back some of the tax breaks he had celebrated at Rancho del Cielo. Reagan was incredulous, even outraged, at first. "Well, damn it, Dave," he told Stockman, "we came here to attack *deficit spending*, not put more taxes on the people."[62] Eventually, he agreed to authorize a real negotiating process with Democratic leaders over some tax increases. They were labeled "revenue enhancements" to spare Reagan embarrassment.

In September 1982, Reagan signed the Tax Equity and Fiscal Responsibility Act (TEFRA), raising $98 billion in taxes over three years. By one calculation, it took back about 17 percent of the value of the tax breaks corporations had received in ERTA. A generous new formula for tax write-offs of business expenses, also instituted by ERTA, was reversed. The effective corporate tax rate, which had been slashed from 33 percent to 4.7 percent for 1981, settled at 15.8 percent after TEFRA's enactment. The law also doubled the federal cigarette tax, tripled the federal telephone tax, and raised taxes on air travel. It did not come close to corral-ling the huge budget deficits—which passed the $100 billion mark for the first time in 1982 and exceeded $200 billion in 1983. However, it may have served to assure Wall Street investors that the gaping fiscal deficits that lay ahead would not be exacerbated.[63]

By 1983, Reagan could be satisfied that his policies had contributed to the outcomes he had desired. All American taxpayers saw their federal tax bills decline. But these effective declines were far from the equal across-the-board reductions that Reagan's campaign rhetoric had sug-gested. The bottom three-quarters of the population in terms of income saw small federal tax reductions, amounting to tens or hundreds of dol-lars. Meanwhile, the percentage of income the top 1 percent paid in fed-eral taxes dropped from 29.8 percent to 24.8 percent. Moreover, wealthy Americans got a larger share of national wealth, both before and after paying taxes—a result of both the recession of 1981–1983 (see chapter 5) and Reagan's tax policies. A CBO analysis that divided taxpayers into de-scending income groups of the top 1 percent, the next-highest 4 percent, the highest 20 percent after that, then the third quartile, and, finally, most of the bottom half of the taxpaying population, found dramatic changes between 1980 and 1983, changes weighted heavily in favor of the highest-income Americans (see table 3.1).[64]

Reagan would raise taxes several times more during his presidency. These tax hikes would be regressive ones, like many in TEFRA, hitting less affluent Americans harder than the wealthy. Government policy moved in the direction Reagan favored: letting the wealthiest keep more of their money.

Leaving private wealth more nearly whole and hoping this boon to the rich would eventually benefit society was an old idea. One of the names long attached to this theory was the disdainful label "trickle-down eco-nomics" (a term widely associated with the ideas of Andrew Mellon, U.S. treasury secretary in the 1920s). "Trickle-down" was what liberal Demo-crats called the Reagan tax proposals. Republicans insisted that supply-side economics was new and different: more dynamic, more growth-oriented. So, when the December 1981 issue of the *Atlantic Monthly* magazine made news by running a long article, "The Education of David Stockman," by Greider, based on secret meetings he had held with Stock-man throughout the budget and tax-cut struggles, the most newsworthy

TABLE 3.1
Change in Percentage of Income Going to
Federal Taxes, Top to Bottom Income Groups,
1980–1983

1st percent:	−5.0 percent
2nd–5th percent:	−3.4 percent
6th–25th percent:	−2.1 percent
26th–50th percent:	−1.4 percent
51st–95th percent:	−0.5 percent

Change in After-Tax Income

1st percent:	+22.7 percent
2nd–5th percent:	+5.6 percent
6th–25th percent:	+0.3 percent
26th–50th percent:	−0.3 percent
51st–95th percent:	−2.8 percent

quotation concerned the difference between trickle-down and supply-side. "It's kind of hard to sell 'trickle down,'" Stockman admitted, "so the supply-side formula was the only way to get a tax policy that was really 'trickle down.' Supply side is 'trickle down' theory."[65]

After Stockman's year in Washington's sun, topped off by this sensational article, he faded into obscurity. Stockman had thought to use Greider to convince liberal intellectuals of the integrity of his fiscal program. Instead, Greider charted Stockman's disaffection with Reagan and the Republican Party. The article was studded with candid, cutting remarks from Stockman, even as it highlighted his ability to rationalize all of his setbacks and compromises. To Republicans, he appeared immature and disloyal, while Democrats claimed he had confirmed their charge that Reagan cared only for the rich. James Baker wanted to keep Stockman at OMB; they had become allies. Baker devised the story that Reagan took Stockman to the "woodshed" in a private meeting, and that, with due contrition, Stockman was forgiven his trespasses. In truth, Stockman and Reagan met, but Reagan was gentle; he suggested Stockman had been taken in by a wily reporter who twisted Stockman's words. Stockman stayed on through the end of Reagan's first term, his revolutionary ambitions shriveled. He was first forgiven, and then almost forgotten.

Reagan had mastered Washington—partly due to his and his team's political skills. His success was, more fundamentally, the result of the November 1980 election returns, which made his program's passage certain in the Senate and likely in the House. The demoralization, division, programmatic exhaustion, and mediocre leadership of the Democratic Party played a role, too. But it must be noted that, despite Stockman's hopes, Reagan, in his triumphal first year as president, did not ask Congress to take a hard path. No powerful interests opposed his program. Reagan looked like a world-beater. But he did so primarily by asking Congress to take politically attractive actions—voting huge new military expenditures and cutting taxes for everyone, most of all for the wealthy and powerful. The most controversial and least popular of his efforts had been the spending cuts, aimed mainly at the needy. There was scant evidence of a clamor for slicing away at programs that assisted the poor; Reagan, with a shrewd sense of public opinion, had made few, if any, such specific promises in 1980, despite his criticisms of the welfare system. However, with these programs serving "weak clients," in Stockman's phrase, the only real obstacle blocking the budget cuts was the conscience of the nation's lawmakers, and Reagan and his team got around this. Reagan had triumphed with the voters in 1980; he did so with lawmakers in 1981. His essential campaign goals were secure. He had won.

Four

An Aggressive Foreign Policy

In 1980, in Ronald Reagan's mind, communism and terrorism were the organically linked plagues of the age, and he had little time to lose in turning back this raging double-sided blight. American politicians had long referred to Communists as terrorists, and Reagan declared a "war on terror" during his presidency. He viewed the enemy structure as a coordinated worldwide menace that tied nonstate groups such as the Palestine Liberation Organization (PLO) and the African National Congress (ANC) to rogue governments, most of them socialist, in Nicaragua, Libya, Ethiopia, and elsewhere. And, as he saw it, the Kremlin's hand was ultimately pulling the strings behind this consortium. Conservative analysts described strategic "crescents" that served to link conflicts separated by thousands of miles. (One left-wing wag called this "the croissant approach to geopolitics."[1]) Reagan sought to confront the Communist-terrorist combine most aggressively on strategically peripheral fronts. He paid special attention to Central America throughout his presidency, working to prevent revolution in El Salvador and waging a barely covert war against the Sandinista regime in Nicaragua.

On the strategically central issue of U.S.-USSR relations, Reagan put diplomacy in a deep freeze, instead making a U.S. military buildup his essential Soviet policy. He had run for the presidency in 1976 and 1980 arguing that the United States had become "number two" to the Soviet Union in military might and that he would make the United States number one.[2] Paradoxically, Reagan viewed the Soviet Union as both militarily superior and doomed to ultimate failure. Like Carter, Reagan saw communism as an unnatural, immoral system that suppressed human desires for freedom and that would eventually collapse. However, there is no evidence of any master plan on Reagan's part to topple the Soviet regime. Richard Pipes, the Harvard historian who had led Team B during the 1970s (see chapter 2) and who worked at the NSC in 1981 and 1982, wrote privately, in March 1981, "*We must put the Soviet Union on the defensive.*"[3] But Pipes explained to an audience in 1982, "Now no responsible persons can have any illusions that it is in the power of the West to alter the Soviet system or to 'bring the Soviet economy to its knees.'"[4] The most that Pipes, one of the administration's hardliners on Soviet policy, hoped for was to encourage reform, not revolution. The idea was not to engineer the downfall of the Soviet state, but rather to increase stress on the Soviet system and slow its ascendancy, giving the United States time to regain its onetime strategic dominance.[5]

Aside from building up U.S. arms, Reagan's focus regarding the Soviet Union was a revivified propaganda offensive, designed to reassert the moral illegitimacy of state communism. The denial of freedom in Eastern Europe was the target of some of Reagan's most powerful rhetoric. In June 1982, he spoke to British parliamentarians in Westminster Palace. "From Stettin on the Baltic to Varna on the Black Sea," he observed, "the regimes planted by totalitarianism have had more than 30 years to establish their legitimacy. But none—not one regime—has yet been able to risk free elections." Turning a Marxist catchphrase on its head, Reagan predicted that "the march of freedom and democracy . . . will leave Marxism-Leninism on the ashheap of history."[6] From Britain, he traveled to West Germany; he visited West Berlin, and said of the Berlin Wall, "It's as ugly as the idea behind it."[7]

In the most controversial element of Reagan's rearmament program, the installation of new nuclear-armed missiles in Western Europe, he was merely fulfilling a pledge Carter had made to North Atlantic Treaty Organization (NATO) allies, one that would counter a new generation of missiles the USSR had placed in Eastern Europe. This planned deployment of Pershing II ICBMs and Tomahawk "cruise" missiles became a subject of sharp conflict in West Germany only after Reagan's election. Both the Social Democratic and Christian Democratic governments that ruled in Bonn in the early 1980s wanted the new missiles, but Reagan's bellicose image and apparent lack of interest in arms-control talks with

Moscow made it harder to welcome them. Richard Perle, assistant secretary of defense for international security affairs, devised the "zero option," under which the United States would not deploy its new missiles if the Soviets would remove theirs. Perle thought arms-control agreements with the Soviet Union were folly, and the U.S. proposal was widely perceived as an effort to prevent serious talks from getting off the ground. No one thought the Russians would withdraw expensive new weapons. Reagan declared himself in favor of arms *reductions*, not arms control. However, he would consider reductions only in areas where, according to the administration, the Soviets held the advantage.

Reagan's arms buildup was indiscriminate, ranging from the goal of a six-hundred-ship navy and the deployment of newly developed MX intercontinental nuclear-armed missiles to the revival of the previously scrapped B-1 bomber, which was only rescued from congressional skepticism when the air force spread related subcontracts more widely across representatives' districts. Defense analysts noted that Reagan and Weinberger were setting exotically ambitious military planning goals, some of them incompatible or unrealistic. For instance, they sought the capability to attack Soviet ports. Any such scenario would require an enormous armada and prodigious air support, given the losses to be expected from Soviet homeland defenses, and would run a high risk of triggering a Soviet nuclear attack, an event that much of U.S. strategy was intended to prevent.[8] Despite the multiplication of weapons programs underway, at the end of March 1982, Reagan continued to state, "The truth of the matter is that on balance the Soviet Union does have a definite margin of superiority."[9]

Despite the supposed urgency of the huge buildup, political considerations sometimes trumped strategic ones, as the MX affair showed. Approved by Carter, this ICBM was to carry ten warheads and was to be mobile in order to thwart Soviet countermeasures. This design would close the "window of vulnerability" of which Reagan had warned. Yet Reagan was unwilling to locate the new missiles, as Carter had planned, in the deserts of Utah and Nevada—strong Republican states where opposition to the idea was fierce. Reagan eventually decided to put 50 of the missiles, at $320 million apiece, in existing, stationary missile silos, which negated the MX's purpose. The Soviets would have had to commit 9,200 missiles to destroy the 200 mobile MX missiles Carter had intended to deploy; they would need only hundreds to target the smaller, immobile MX fleet.[10]

In spite of the strategic incoherence evident in some components of Reagan's buildup, many in America and elsewhere became concerned that Reagan was genuinely willing to fight a nuclear war. In early 1981, the *Bulletin of the Atomic Scientists* moved its famous "doomsday clock" from 11:53 to 11:56 p.m., reflecting heightened fears of superpower confrontation.[11] As if to confirm such apprehensions, Eugene Rostow, nominated to head the Arms Control and Disarmament Agency, testified at his confirmation hearings that Japan "not only survived but flourished after the nuclear attack." A nuclear exchange in 1981 would be incomparably more destructive than the unilateral detonation of two fission bombs in 1945 had been. But Rostow remained sanguine. "The human race is very resilient," he said. Early in 1982, Deputy Secretary of Defense Thomas Jones made himself infamous with his comments that American civilization could recover a semblance of normalcy within four years after an all-out nuclear war. Americans would need to "dig a hole, cover it with a couple of doors and then throw three feet of dirt on top. It's the dirt that does it," he said.[12] In May 1982, Weinberger's first "Defense Guidance," summarizing the administration's military strategy, was completed. It called for preparations to fight a "protracted" nuclear war with the USSR.[13]

The public was appalled by such statements. Courting nuclear holocaust was not what those who had voted for a strengthened defense posture in 1980 had had in mind. Disarmament activists seized the opening they saw and launched a movement for a bilateral nuclear "freeze"—a halt to the deployment of new nuclear weapons by both superpowers. The notion had broad appeal. About one million people—in the largest political protest in U.S. history—massed in New York City in June 1982 to express support for the freeze and opposition to Reagan. During the summer, the pollster Louis Harris remarked on the "urgent hunger for peace" that his findings detected in the American public. The freeze proposal picked up momentum in the political mainstream: scores of U.S. senators and representatives endorsed it, as did city governments around the country. A freeze resolution seemed to have some chance of passage in the House. On Election Day in November 1982, pro-freeze resolutions were on the ballot in ten states and thirty-seven cities and counties around the country, and these succeeded almost everywhere, garnering 60 percent of the votes overall in what was, arguably, the "largest referendum on a single issue in American history, covering about a third of the U.S. electorate." In May 1983, a freeze resolution passed in the House, 278–149, but failed in the Senate. The White House, alarmed, organized a concerted effort to derogate the freeze as irresponsible policy. The president initially responded to the freeze movement by charging that unnamed persons "who want the weakening of America and so are manipulating honest people" were driving it forward. But this tactic proved ineffective. So Reagan shifted course and, in mid-1982, began to affirm that "a nuclear war cannot be won and must never be fought."[14] Echoing the dynamics of the 1980 campaign, Reagan disarmed critics of his foreign policy more easily by professing his own desire for peace than by accusing them of disloyalty or stupidity.

Public relations aside, U.S. foreign policy was a shambles, the scene of debilitating closed-door infighting that Reagan showed little interest in stopping. While the president offered a determined face to the public, in private his top officials often found him uncommunicative or inconstant. One observer lamented, "Whoever gets in the back door to see the president can get the decision made his way."[15] Only Director of Central Intelligence (DCI) William Casey truly enjoyed Reagan's confidence, and this relationship of trust was cause for alarm. Casey's mumbling and Reagan's poor hearing, Casey's inclination to cut corners, which he would display in Lebanon (see chapter 10), and Reagan's susceptibility to Casey's dramatic schemes and interpretations of world events, were a recipe for disaster. Secretary of State Alexander Haig, warmly recommended for the post by his former boss Richard Nixon, was rebuffed in his efforts to gain presidential approval for the State Department's dominion over foreign policy. Haig's requests to see Reagan sometimes went unanswered. Frustrated, he mused aloud near the end of his eighteen-month tenure, "What am I, a leper?"[16] Haig failed to appear statesmanlike. At one point, he expressed his willingness to turn Cuba into "a fucking parking lot," a statement that may have heartened some on the right but did not appear to win Reagan's confidence.[17] The secretary's excitable temperament caused the president to withdraw. Pipes reflected the general view of Haig in the White House when he described him as "sinister, aggressive, a kind of Iago (except that [Reagan] would not play Othello, ignoring him completely)."[18] Barely two months on the job, when Reagan was shot and almost killed in April 1981 (see chapter 3), Haig damaged himself by making a breathless, disquieting appearance in the White House, telling the assembled press corps, "As of now, I am in charge here, in the White House, pending the return of the Vice President," who was on a plane.[19] As for the NSC, Reagan chose Richard V. Allen, an obscure Californian, to coordinate the body as national security adviser and denied him, too, regular Oval Office access. Within a year, Allen resigned, embarrassed over murky ties to Japanese business and political figures. Reagan would appoint five more men to Allen's position during his two terms in office.[20]

Haig, at his first press conference after his confirmation, had made a bid to garner authority by echoing the conservative view that terrorism and world communism worked hand in glove. Terrorism should be the top priority of U.S. foreign policy, he said, replacing Carter's concern for human rights. The Soviet Union was guilty of "training, funding and equipping" terrorist groups, said the secretary. The *Economist* reported, shortly afterward, that "the state department and the somewhat startled intelligence agencies have been scrambling"—in vain, it turned out—"to provide evidence to support this new policy."[21] The links among terrorist groups were real, but the guiding hand of Moscow was imaginary. Haig had read galley proofs of *The Terror Network*, a new book by Claire Sterling, an independent journalist, which boldly made the argument for Soviet control of world terrorism. Haig, like Casey, preferred it to the findings of his own professional analysts.[22]

In 1980 and 1981, Claire Sterling was all the rage. *The Terror Network* was rushed into print by her publisher. The *New York Times Magazine* ran an excerpt in March 1981, following a *Washington Post* opinion piece in January in which Sterling summarized her argument.[23] Sterling claimed that rising terrorist groups in countries across the world were all linked through training camps and arms suppliers who were, in turn, cat's-paws of the Soviet Union. The middlemen were Cubans, Palestinians, and Libyans, who ran training camps in remote locales such as Soviet-allied South Yemen. Thus, the contemporaneous rise of violent groups as disparate politically as the West German Red Army Faction, the "Provisional" Irish Republican Army, Basque separatists, and others, was not a coincidence. This rising terrorist tide was a product of the USSR's policy to demoralize "the West," according to Sterling. Pipes agreed with Sterling that evidence of a Soviet master plan to seed the free world with terrorism was elusive. But they brushed this detail aside. Terrorism simply looked, to them, like something Communists would orchestrate.[24]

In April 1981, a new Republican U.S. senator, Jeremiah Denton of Alabama—who had spent almost eight years as a prisoner of war in North Vietnam—convened hearings of a new Subcommittee on Security and Terrorism. The opening roster of witnesses consisted of Sterling, former DCI William Colby, and the writers Arnaud de Borchgrave and Michael Ledeen. With the exception of Colby, who distanced himself from the more lurid theories abounding, these were publicists with a flair for drama, suddenly elevated by circumstance into the company of national-security experts. When critics assailed Sterling's casual way with evidence, she complained, "I'm naked and alone out there in the middle and the stray shot is getting at me."[25] Ledeen, with a special interest in Iran, often wrote for newspapers about the Middle East. De Borchgrave, a former *Newsweek* war reporter, had switched to writing novels detailing the western media's suppression of news that incriminated Soviet misdeeds.[26] This notion was fantasy, as de Borchgrave's turn to fiction suggested. But he had his defenders. The *New Republic*, long a liberal public-affairs journal, under the leadership of publisher Martin Peretz gave both Ledeen and de Borchgrave a platform. To Peretz, what mattered was that de Borchgrave's "version of international reality is more true than that of the Institute for Policy Studies," a left-wing outfit sharply critical of U.S. foreign policy, "by far."[27] In 1986, de Borchgrave would resurface as editor-in-chief of the *Washington Times*, a newspaper created in 1982 by the Unification Church of the Reverend Sun Myung Moon, who wished to offer movement conservatives in the nation's capital a reliable alternative to the establishmentarian *Post*. Such figures circulated only in the movement-conservative social orbit outside the administration. Yet the president, like Haig and Casey, agreed with their view that Third World anti-Americanism was the respectable bedfellow of both Soviet intrigue and terrorist mayhem.

Reagan sought a "rollback" of socialist revolution in the Third World, a longstanding conservative position. To him, the Nicaraguan "Contra" forces, whom the United States funded and helped organize with the aim of overthrowing the socialist Sandinistas, were like the Hungarian rebels who, left to their own devices by the United States, had been crushed by a Soviet invasion in 1956. Reagan would say of the Contras, "God bless them" for being counterrevolutionaries. He shared their convictions, and that, he said, "makes me a contra, too."[28] Reagan, partly in reaction to what he saw as rampant anti-Americanism in the Third World, took a series of actions as president that proclaimed a new U.S. unilateralism. He withdrew U.S. support for a treaty on the Law of the Sea, long in the making. The U.S. delegate to the World Health Organization cast the only dissenting vote from a new global code governing the marketing of infant formula. In 1984, Reagan removed the United States from UNESCO, the UN cultural organization.[29] He made Jeane Kirkpatrick—the least diplomatic of his diplomats—his ambassador to the United Nations. She had made a career of arguing that the United States should rely on rightist dictatorships in its Latin American policy. She gave this preference a moral gloss in a 1979 article, "Dictatorships and Double Standards," in which she argued that "authoritarian" states might reform themselves in the direction of liberal democracy—and thus were suitable clients—but that "totalitarian" states, by which she meant Marxist-Leninist ones, could not.[30]

Reagan's stance toward the Third World proved a consolation to his conservative supporters, disappointed at the lack of progress on abortion and school prayer. Evangelical Protestant missionaries fanned out across Central America in the 1980s, bringing aid and Bibles to people caught up in civil wars. They embraced far-right politicians such as the Salvadoran Roberto D'Aubuisson, whom the administration thought too blood-stained to be a suitable public leader, but whom television evangelist Pat Robertson called a "very nice fellow."[31] Members of Young Americans for Freedom chaperoned D'Aubuisson when he visited Washington; they wore t-shirts bearing the acronym of his political party, ARENA, which was closely linked to the "death squad" killings in his country.[32] In a weird echo of the guerrilla romanticism of the 1960s left, young Republican cadres traveled to Angola to have their pictures taken, guns aloft, with soldiers and leaders of UNITA, the right-wing army that was fighting, with funding from Washington, alongside South African forces against Cubans. Jimmy Swaggart, another television preacher, traveled to Chile to praise Augusto Pinochet's dictatorship and involved himself in southern Africa, where Mozambique's leftist government accused him of aiding the rightist RENAMO guerrillas in that country.[33]

Conservative activists might go further than Reagan would in some of these proxy battles of the Cold War, but Reagan showed that he was willing to pick a fight if the right opponent presented itself. If Reagan were looking for a regime that embodied all the dangers he saw posed to America from the Third World, he found it in the Libyan state, avowedly socialist (and officially Islamic), run by Moammar Qaddafi. For almost ten years, the United States had accused Qaddafi of exporting revolution to other African countries and of training and arming terrorist groups. Libya also had become a major buyer of Soviet arms. In March 1981, after reports attributed the killing of a Libyan opposition figure in Chicago to Qaddafi's government, Reagan broke diplomatic ties with Qaddafi, and subsequently ordered aggressive overt and covert tactics against Libya. Reagan dispatched navy ships and planes to the Gulf of Sidra, in waters that Libya declared its own—a claim honored by few others. He knew that international law would be on his side if Libya sought to defend its broad claim of sovereignty with force against a U.S. challenge. On August 19, 1981, an encounter unfolded that could not have turned out better for Reagan if Hollywood had scripted it. Two U.S. jets engaged their Libyan counterparts in the air; one of the Libyan jets fired a missile at one of the U.S. jets, missing its target; the U.S. planes turned and destroyed both Libyan aircraft.[34] Reagan, who had approved the rules of engagement before the incident, greeted his staff the following morning by playacting the role of an Old West gunman, unholstering and firing imaginary pistols from his hips. Later that day, he appeared on board the USS *Constellation* and stated, "This is the rule that has to be followed—if our men are fired on, they're going to fire."[35] Subsequently, word leaked to the press that the White House believed Qaddafi had dispatched assassination teams inside the United States, targeting Reagan, Bush, and other White House officials. "The mystery of the assassination teams" deepened as Reagan's men then stated that Qaddafi had called off the threat; privately, U.S. intelligence judged the initial reports unreliable.[36] The administration urged that U.S. citizens leave Libya, and the United States forbade the purchase of Libyan oil. To Americans, Qaddafi would remain a menacing figure hovering behind the threat of terrorism.

The administration's perspective on the Middle East in general mingled concern over terrorism and Soviet influence. In September and October, the White House fought a grueling battle to keep the Senate from blocking the U.S. sale of advanced radar-equipped planes—dubbed AWACS—to Saudi Arabia, which Reagan and Haig viewed as a potential regional counterweight to Iran and Syria. American officials viewed Syria as a Soviet client state and saw both Iran and Syria as backers of international terrorism. Reagan had to overcome the opposition of pro-Israel groups and of Israeli Prime Minister Menachem Begin, to whom the Saudis were a hostile regional power. Reagan was viewed as staunchly pro-Israel; in 1977, he had echoed the claim, long made by some Israeli leaders, that, historically, "there was no nation called Palestine" whose rights could be violated. Thus, he surprised some with his determination regarding AWACS.[37] "The President would have done almost anything to avoid defeat on this," James Baker commented. Reagan clawed back commitments to vote against the arms sales from one Republican senator after another. He framed the issue as a test of his power over foreign affairs, telling them, "Vote against me and you will cut me off at the knees." After he prevailed, Reagan said the experience had been "like shitting a pineapple," an expression he favored for describing painful ordeals.[38]

Events in the Middle East were spiraling out of Washington's control. In October 1981, Egyptian President Anwar al-Sadat was murdered by religious extremists enraged by his peacemaking with Israel. In December, Israel officially annexed the Golan Heights, territory it had occupied since wresting it from Syria in the "Six-Day War" of 1967. In June 1982, Israel invaded Lebanon. Reagan and Haig defended Israel's initial stated goal of venturing only forty kilometers into Lebanon, to eliminate PLO positions that could launch attacks against Israeli territory. Israeli Minister of Defense Ariel Sharon had made preparations and briefed Washington. Begin told his cabinet, "The hour of decision has arrived. . . . The alternative to fighting is Treblinka," citing a Nazi death camp, "and we have resolved that there would be no more Treblinkas."[39] When the Israel Defense Forces (IDF) expanded their attacks to target Syrian forces in Lebanon, shooting down twenty-three Soviet-made MiG jets without losing a single plane, few in Washington shed any tears. But when the IDF then raced more than eighty kilometers north of Israel's border, laying siege to Beirut and aiming to oust the PLO from its stronghold, Reagan was surprised and upset.

An extraordinary series of exchanges between the two countries' leaders ensued. In July, the IDF cut Beirut's flow of electricity and fresh water. Reagan protested to Begin, and the water and power came back on. At one point, Sharon ordered heavy bombing that killed three hundred Lebanese. Footage of Israeli bombardment in and around Beirut damaged Israel's cause in the court of world opinion. Reagan phoned Begin and said, "Menachem, this is a holocaust." "Mr. President, I think I know what a holocaust is," came the inevitable reply. The bombing ceased for the moment.[40] Despite these behind-the-scenes strains, in strategic terms, Begin prevailed: the United States negotiated an evacuation of PLO forces by boat to Tunisia; Israel occupied a swath of southern Lebanon; and Israel's Lebanese allies in the Christian Phalange, a military-political movement with an avowed affinity for fascist ideology, gained the upper hand in Lebanon. The bloody drama was not finished before the Phalange, enraged over the killing of its leader, Bashir Gemayel, murdered between seven hundred and two thousand Palestinian refugees between September 16 and 18. The IDF, in control of the area, facilitated the carnage, letting the Phalange into the refugee camps, called Sabra and Shatila, and launching illumination flares overhead during the two nights of the massacre.

Many thought Haig had encouraged Sharon carelessly before the invasion, and the Lebanon mess of 1982 helped cost Haig his job. It was just a matter of when Reagan would fire him, which the president did in July. In April, Haig had lost a political battle after exerting himself in an effort to avert war over the South Atlantic islands that the Argentines called Las Malvinas and the British called their colony (the Falklands). Kirkpatrick, for her part, raised eyebrows by associating herself publicly with the Argentines as war approached. She viewed U.S. alliances with Latin American strongmen as more valuable than the "special relationship" with Britain. But Reagan felt a personal bond with Margaret Thatcher, who sent warships steaming toward the Falklands. Reagan did not share Kirkpatrick's Argentine partisanship. Nor did he forcefully support Haig's diplomacy. When the shooting started, Reagan got off the fence and supported Britain. The Argentines were used to torturing students and labor activists, not to fighting a well-equipped, modern navy, and lost the war quickly.

The Argentines had mistakenly thought they could count on Washington to stay neutral, as Haig had appeared to want, particularly because the two governments had been collaborating quietly on a project of some importance to President Reagan. Military juntas and guerrilla movements had been waging asymmetric warfare for years across Latin America. In the 1960s and 1970s, conditions for the poor peasant majority in Latin America had worsened, as land ownership became even more concentrated in fewer hands. In Central America, the landless peasantry tripled in size in these decades.[41] Guerrilla movements sprang up almost everywhere from Guatemala to Chile; rightist *golpes* displaced wobbly civilian governments. The phenomenon of *los desaparecidos*, "the disappeared," followed: governments arrested, tortured, and murdered tens of thousands of actual and potential dissidents. All opponents of rightist regimes were targeted for elimination; all were labeled "subversives" or "communists." As the governor of Buenos Aires province summed up the Argentine junta's vision, "*First we will kill all the subversives, then we will kill their collaborators, then . . . their sympathizers, then . . . those who remain indifferent; and finally we will kill the timid.*"[42] The Argentines saw themselves in the vanguard of the "dirty war" against the left, and took it as their mission to export their sanguinary methods to other lands. After Somoza's fall, the Argentine government brought defeated Nicaraguan soldiers to Buenos Aires for training in the hope of ousting the Sandinistas.

When William Casey took charge at the CIA, he learned of the Argentine-Nicaraguan operation and offered funding. "It takes relatively few people and little support to disrupt the internal peace and economic stability of a small country," he once remarked.[43] U.S. personnel would be two steps removed from the effort to bring down the Sandinistas. Carter had authorized modest covert funding for Nicaraguan opposition groups before he left office. By 1981, Nicaraguan and Cuban exiles were working together in military training camps in Florida, advertising for soldiers on Miami radio stations.[44] Now the U.S. government wished to begin funding a counterrevolutionary or Contra army. On March 9, 1981, Reagan signed a classified "finding"—a presidential directive authorizing a covert operation—which sanctioned bolder action in Central America.[45]

Further documents followed, expanding the scope of these activities. Casey felt little obligation to share the truth with the House and Senate Intelligence Committees, openly disdaining "those assholes on the Hill," as he called Congress. Shambling to the witness table to testify before the committees, unkempt wisps of white hair trailing behind him, sometimes speaking inaudibly, Casey was an unsettling spectacle. He told them that the money he requested to equip and train an exile Nicaraguan force was intended to interdict arms from the Sandinistas to leftist rebels in El Salvador. Congress granted $19 million in December.

Kirkpatrick said, "I believe Central America is the most important place in the world for the U.S. today."[46] Haig called the land bridge between continents a "strategic choke point" where Soviet influence was impermissible, but had difficulty explaining what of importance would be choked off there. He came closer to the point when he reportedly told Reagan, speaking of El Salvador, "Mr. President, this is one you can win."[47] The administration insisted El Salvador would not become another South Vietnam. "In no sense are we speaking of participation in combat by American forces," said Reagan. But El Salvador's attraction as a venue for U.S. intervention was precisely that it might replay the Vietnam War with a successful ending. The Christian Democrat José Napoleón Duarte was serving as a respectable figurehead for the Salvadoran government, while the military and security forces maintained links to assassination groups, or death squads, which murdered opposition activists with great brutality. Government forces routinely used rape as a method of terror. Corpses littered the roads and were piled at dumping grounds near the Pacific coast. In October 1980, security forces kidnapped en masse the leaders of the aboveground, democratic left, murdering over half of them. During the presidential transition period in Washington, the rebels of the Farabundo Martí National Liberation Front (FMLN) launched an offensive aimed at destroying the right-wing junta, but fell short. In Washington, Democrats and Republicans alike were frantic to prevent a socialist revolution. In January 1981, this ceased to be Carter's problem and became Reagan's. The Salvadoran right was overjoyed. "I knew Reagan was one of us," said one death-squad figure.[48] "I think the degree of commitment to moderation and democratic institutions within the Salvadoran military is very frequently underestimated in this country," remarked Kirkpatrick.[49]

In December 1980, the worst happened, from the perspective of a *norteamericano* government intent on supporting the Salvadoran regime. Three U.S. Catholic nuns and one lay worker—Ita Ford, Maura Clark, Dorothy Kazel, and Jean Donovan—became civilian casualties of war. These women, inspired by "liberation theology," worked among the poor, teaching them to read and supporting them in their demands on their government for the bare necessities of life. This solidarity with the poor marked the women as communists in the eyes of the military establishment, and the National Guard decided to make examples of them. A guard squad, dressed in civilian clothing as ordered, stopped the van in which the four Americans were driving home from the airport in the capital, San Salvador. They took the women into the surrounding countryside, raped them, shot them, and buried them in shallow graves, where they were soon found. The killings sparked a storm of outrage. "'This time they won't get away with it,' Robert White"—Carter's ambassador to El Salvador—"was reported to have said as he watched the bodies of the four American women dragged from their common grave," wrote the author Joan Didion, "but they did, and White was brought home."[50]

The new administration in Washington defended the Salvadoran regime as best it could—by, it seemed, blaming the victims. Haig, answering questions about the churchwomen's murders, said, "I would like to suggest to you that some of the investigations would lead one to believe that perhaps the vehicle the nuns were riding in may have tried to run a roadblock or may have accidentally been perceived to have been doing so, and there had been an exchange of fire, and perhaps those who inflicted the casualties sought to cover it up."[51] Haig subsequently backed away from this utter fiction. "My heavens, no," he told the Senate Foreign Relations Committee the next day when asked if he was claiming the women had engaged in some kind of battle with Salvadoran security forces.[52] The embarrassment he caused the administration did not stop a key House appropriations subcommittee from voting, 8–7, to give a supplemental $5 million in military aid to the Salvadorans mere days later. Two Democrats, Jamie Whitten of Mississippi and Charles Wilson of Texas, joined the committee's six Republicans to approve the funds, foretelling the future of such aid requests. Mail to the state department ran 10-to-1 against the aid, and members of Congress reported similar imbalances.[53] Unpopular as the aid might be, few officeholders wished to be held responsible if another Central American country "went red." El Salvador would receive $744 million in U.S. military aid between 1981 and 1983. Its counterinsurgency campaign would continue for ten years, with U.S. funding averaging more than $1 million per day, for a total of more than $3.5 billion.[54]

El Salvador policy threatened to come apart on January 27, 1982, when explosive stories appeared in both the *Washington Post* and the *New York Times* relating eyewitness accounts of a massacre, six weeks earlier, of several hundred civilians by Salvadoran troops—by a battalion specially trained by the U.S. Army, no less—in Morazán province, near the Honduran border. On March 3, Assistant Secretary of State Thomas Enders testified to Congress that he had no evidence of such a deliberate slaughter. Behind the scenes, the U.S. embassy in San Salvador knew more than Enders revealed. Reagan, to comply with the toothless conditions placed by Congress on Salvadoran aid, "certified" that San Salvador was making "adequate progress" in the field of human rights. Evidence to the contrary made no difference.[55] The journalists who had revealed the Morazán killings, Alma Guillermoprieto for the *Post* and Raymond Bonner of the *Times*, became targets of conservative criticism in the United States for "bias" against administration policy. The *Times* editor, A. M. Rosenthal, sympathetic to Reagan's policy, eventually recalled Bonner to New York, whereupon Bonner quit the paper, creating a small cause célèbre.

Some opponents of Reagan's policy began to build a continental network of resistance. Residents of Tucson, shocked to find that the U.S. government was deporting Salvadorans who had fled the horror of their homeland—sending them back to likely torture and murder—began to smuggle Salvadorans, and sometimes Guatemalans, across the border and to shelter the refugees in their homes. The government welcomed with open arms Cubans and others fleeing Communist regimes, while the Salvadorans had escaped a violent government for which Washington bore some responsibility. "Initially, I disbelieved our refugee's stories of personal peril, bestial treatment by the army, rampant murder of villagers, and persecution of family," one participant in the movement said. "It was too incredible to me. Eventually, I realized he was telling the truth.... It was very disturbing." Another said, "The crucifixion has taken on new meaning for me: it is through suffering, I have learned from the refugees, that we learn compassion."[56] Churches of many denominations became involved in hiding refugees and helping them settle in the United States. Los Angeles and New Mexico declared themselves "sanctuaries," where authorities would not cooperate with federal efforts to find and deport Salvadoran refugees; over two hundred other state and local governments eventually followed suit. Organized groups began traveling to Central America, sometimes placing themselves in war zones in Nicaragua in the hope of preventing Contra attacks.

If official Washington regarded such citizen activities with derision, a succession of U.S. ambassadors on the scene in San Salvador found it impossible to ignore the violence of the government there. Reagan's first appointee to the post, Deane Hinton, gave a blistering speech in October 1982 before a prominent business gathering in San Salvador. He asserted that, in the civil war, perhaps thirty thousand Salvadorans had been "murdered, not killed in battle, murdered!" He denounced the "eloquent silence" of Salvadoran elites about the bloodbath and called the death squads a "Mafia." He intoned, "The gorillas of this Mafia, every bit as much as the guerrillas of Morazán and Chalatenango, are destroying El Salvador." Hinton's audience was shocked. He had cleared his speech with his superiors at the State Department, where George Shultz had replaced Haig (see chapter 6), but not with the White House. The internecine strife over foreign policy–making in the administration continued. Hinton was silenced. Two months later, Reagan himself made a trip to Guatemala; it was considered unsafe for him to travel to El Salvador. While there, he said the Salvadoran government's human rights record was improving and that his Guatemalan host, the recently installed strongman Efraín Ríos Montt, was "a man of great personal integrity" whose regime was getting "a bum rap" from human rights groups. Organizations such as Amnesty International condemned the Guatemalan government for its violence against its own people, so massive that many called it genocide.[57]

Shultz was still new on his job and, for the moment, the NSC was in the ascendant. Haig's former deputy at State, William Clark, a close confidant of Reagan, had been called to replace Richard Allen as national security adviser, even though Clark conceded that he knew little of foreign affairs.[58] In late 1982, Clark, Casey, and Kirkpatrick appeared to control policy-making. They urged intensified efforts at counterinsurgency in El Salvador and insurgency in Nicaragua.

Several Contra forces were moving against the Sandinistas by this time. Casey elevated Duane Clarridge, a man of action, to command his Directorate of Operations' Latin America division. Miskitu Indians on the isolated Atlantic coast of Nicaragua, long estranged from the government in Managua and experiencing political repression at the new regime's hands, were ripe for recruitment; the CIA had done similar work with the Hmong in Laos. The major Contra forces operated from Honduras, which shared a long border with Nicaragua to the latter country's north. Someone was blowing up oil storage facilities and coffee mills in Nicaragua. Clarridge denied responsibility for the attacks. "Not ours. Checked it. Not ours," he told the committees on Capitol Hill.[59]

In December 1982, Democrats in the House threatened to cut off Contra aid. As a compromise, the House unanimously passed an appropriations bill amendment, authored by the chair of the Intelligence Committee, Edward Boland, Democrat of Massachusetts. This "Boland Amendment" stated that U.S. government funds could not be used "for the purpose of overthrowing the government of Nicaragua." Arms interdiction remained a legitimate purpose of U.S. policy. The administration continued along its path as if nothing had changed.

In Reagan's first two years as president, he succeeded in resetting U.S. foreign policy on a newly aggressively rightward course. Carter had become more hawkish in his last year as president, but his support for the global right had been tempered by human rights concerns. Reagan, instead, almost embraced a no-enemies-to-the-right stance. Violent and ethically compromised regimes traditionally allied with the United States received fresh and unqualified support. After Reagan became president, his first state visit was from Chun Doo Hwan, president of the Republic of Korea (ROK, or South Korea), a key bastion of U.S. military power, home to about forty thousand U.S. troops. The ROK soon received new fighter aircraft from the United States, despite Chun's seizure of power in 1979–1980 and the spectacular wave of killings perpetrated by Korean security forces against protesters in the city of Kwangju in May 1980.[60] Reagan would nearly double the level of U.S. aid to Ferdinand Marcos, who had suspended democracy in the Philippines in 1972 and ruled as a dictator since then. Reagan did not continue Carter's carping about Marcos's record of violence. In 1981, Reagan dispatched Bush to Manila, where Bush spoke of Marcos's "adherence to democratic principles."[61] Reagan traveled to New York in 1981 to visit Imelda Marcos, the Filipino first lady, who was on an American shopping trip. Ronald and Nancy Reagan both felt personally committed to the Marcoses. Gestures like these, both substantive and symbolic, combined with the Reagan administration's unwavering commitment to its indirect warfare against the Sandinistas and to massive aid to the Salvadoran government, made it clear in Washington and to the world that there was a new sheriff in town. Relations with the Soviet Union also had become frostier. Yet, by late 1982, there were indications already that Reagan realized he might have to temper his tone regarding superpower relations in light of popular anxiety over nuclear brinkmanship. In November of that year, Leonid Brezhnev, the longtime general secretary of the Soviet Communist Party and thus the head of state in the USSR, died and was replaced by Yuri Andropov. This rare change in leadership in Moscow raised modest hopes around the world that an opportunity now existed for a shift to mellower U.S.–USSR relations. Where the Third World was concerned, however, Reagan's hand reached for sharp swords.

The Purge

The recession of 1981–1982 was a watershed in America's social history. High interest rates and a strong U.S. dollar devastated the economy's manufacturing sector and turned the "Rust Belt," a region stretching from New York to Wisconsin, a deep garnet. Americans became familiar with the awkward term "deindustrialization," as a plague of shuttered manufacturing plants, facilities once associated with the nation's economic might, spread across the Great Lakes region. Communities where, since World War II, young men had expected to take high-paying union jobs "on the line" in automobile plants and other mass-production factories found this security gone. The U.S. economy lost about 1.9 million jobs during the Reagan recession.[1] In 1982, the nation's unemployment rate reached the 10 percent mark for the first time since the Great Depression of the 1930s. In cities like Detroit and Flint, Toledo and Gary, Youngstown and Milwaukee, the recession seemed endless. The jolting shifts of these years marked a turn to an economy weighted more toward sales, finance, and other services, and less toward the production of tangible goods. It would be an economy in which households relied more than before on debt, dual incomes, and cheap imports to maintain or improve their standards of living.

These were long-term trends—the plant closings, for example, erased more than 5 million jobs between 1979 and 1984, and had started earlier—but they took on a new, more severe aspect after Reagan became president.[2] Reagan's recession was the intended result of a conscious policy, driven by the decisions of the Federal Reserve and supported without stint by the White House. Carter and the Democrats, in the 1970s, had had little idea what to do about deindustrialization, and Carter appointed Volcker, who orchestrated both the Carter and Reagan recessions, to lead the Fed.[3] But Carter's ambivalence about Volcker's harsh medicine was replaced, under Reagan, by a deep faith in the treatment. With President Reagan, the government's unresponsiveness to economic turmoil and transformation was a matter of principle. To conservatives, this was nature at work and must proceed.

The Reaganites, who stood and watched as wealth drained from the economy under a withering regime of high interest rates, were ideologically committed to rejecting pleas for government aid to the distressed. And they went further. Reagan's administration took steps, in its historic first budget, to curtail assistance to the poor and jobless. In 1982, when the recession was at its worst, only about 45 percent of jobless Americans received unemployment insurance (UI), because the administration had toughened the eligibility rules. In 1975, a comparable recession year, the proportion receiving UI had been 76 percent. Terminations of benefits from Social Security Disability Insurance quadrupled between 1980 and 1982, as government employees pored over the rolls for recipients newly defined as undeserving.[4] The official poverty rate rose from 11.7 percent to 15 percent during the recession; about half the increase was due to Reagan's cutbacks in aid to the poor.[5] In the decades since the New Deal had established a role for the federal government in maintaining a social safety net, the government had never actually reduced assistance to the needy during a major recession.

Just as the recession was beginning to bite, early in August 1981, President Reagan intervened personally in a labor conflict national in scope, and his action landed like a thunderbolt. His stance toward labor-management relations would forever afterward be linked to the acronym PATCO (for the Professional Air Traffic Controllers Organization). Ironically, PATCO had been one of the only unions to endorse Reagan's candidacy in 1980. As U.S. government employees, they were forbidden by law to go on strike, or to bargain collectively over wages. Reagan's team quietly consented to the latter of these forbidden practices, offering the controllers more money. But PATCO's militancy, the result of a decade's discontent over pay and working conditions, overrode any temptation to accept these new terms, and a strike commenced. Exclaimed one controller, "Fuck the president. We've done it. Let's stand by it. Let's see what the outcome is." Leaders of other labor unions were disconcerted by PATCO's maximalism. "This could do massive damage to the labor movement," warned Douglas Fraser, leader of the United Automobile Workers.[6]

Reagan gave the controllers two days to end the walkout. When, on August 5, these forty-eight hours ran out, the president decreed that the more than eleven thousand of PATCO's members who had failed to return to work had quit their jobs. Taking questions from reporters at the signing ceremony for his budget and tax-cut laws in California on August 13, Reagan commented, "There is no strike. There is a law that Federal unions cannot strike against their employers, their employers being the people of the United States." In his view, the air-traffic controllers "terminate[d] their own employment by quitting. . . . And I just don't see any way that it could be expected that we could now just go back and pretend that they weren't breaking the law or breaking their oath."[7] Supervisors and others would fill in for the fired controllers on an emergency basis. Months later, the administration officially decertified PATCO as the controllers' representative; Secretary of Transportation Drew Lewis, who had tried to avert the showdown, asserted, "There is no PATCO." Reagan never allowed any of the controllers back to work for the Federal Aviation Administration (FAA), whose chief summed up the mood in the administration—and among a majority of the American public—when he said, "They made their bed and they can sleep in it."[8]

Lane Kirkland, head of the nation's main labor federation, denounced the firings as "massive, vindictive, brutal."[9] However, the public, reacting to what had become a dramatic confrontation between Reagan and the controllers, sympathized more with the president. Many saw PATCO as a group of well-paid professionals with secure jobs in a time of rising insecurity for most American workers. The White House initially received thirteen phone calls supporting Reagan's action for every one against it. In the month following the firings, the FAA received more than one hundred thousand applications from those eager to replace the old controllers.[10] Most Americans took this episode as the harbinger of a new era, even though Reagan presented the affair in narrow terms, carefully affirming the right of private-sector workers to strike. Many brushed aside such distinctions. One corporate lawyer needed to explain to his overeager clients, who felt inspired by Reagan's example, that they could not simply do as the president had done—no law forbade their employees to go on strike. Donald Rumsfeld, once Gerald Ford's secretary of defense and, in the early 1980s, the head of the G. D. Searle pharmaceutical company, later remarked of Reagan's action, "It struck me as singular. . . . It showed a decisiveness and an ease with his instincts" that Rumsfeld clearly admired.[11]

In fact, a new day was dawning in American labor relations. In the 1980s, a decision to strike was, increasingly, tantamount to forsaking a job—and an entire industry, as strikers were easily tracked and blacklisted—just as it had been for PATCO members. The legal specialty of union-busting expanded in the early 1980s, as did the use of strikebreakers, who were now called, euphemistically, "replacement workers." "In the 1980s, prominent employers saw strikes not as conflicts to be avoided, but as opportunities to break or tame unions," observes labor historian Joseph McCartin. The same drama played out in one conflict after another: with Phelps Dodge copper miners in Arizona in 1983, with Greyhound bus drivers that same year, with Hormel meatpacking workers in Minnesota in 1985–1986. In each instance, strikes turned out disastrously for unionized workers. Automation, eager replacement workers, and newly flexible supply chains and production networks made corporations realize that they did not need to woo strikers back to the bargaining table. Companies pressed government forces into service on their behalf, as state governments in Arizona and Minnesota—under Democratic governors Bruce Babbitt and Rudy Perpich, respectively—dispatched the National Guard to keep workplaces open and operating with skeleton crews. These trends lasted well beyond the return of national prosperity, as the new ensemble of strikebreaking techniques and the bipartisan hostility of political elites toward labor militancy made for a permanent change in workplace dynamics. Workers absorbed the lesson: striking meant quitting. From the early 1980s onward, as McCartin writes, "The United States never again saw the annual number of major work stoppages reach even one-third of pre-PATCO levels."[12]

The broad meaning that many Americans assigned to the PATCO drama in its immediate aftermath reflected the nation's darkening economic picture. By November 1981, the Fed's "Red Book" or "Beige Book," which summarized observations from the twelve regional Reserve Banks around the country, noted, "Chicago indicates the demand for workers may be at the lowest level since the 1930's, and many employers are seeking substantial concessions when renewing labor contracts."[13] By March 1982, "In response to widespread layoffs and reduced job opportunities, unionized workers have been increasingly willing to grant concessions."[14] Macroeconomic conditions produced union flexibility. The phenomenon of givebacks, in which unions agreed to wage freezes, to shifting health-care costs from employers to workers, to the elimination of vacation and other benefits, and to the introduction of new, lower wage scales for new workers, began to spread. This trend extended from troubled manufacturing enterprises into the relatively healthy service sector, even after the recession ended. Management had become newly assertive, and unions were scared and dispirited. By 1983, Reagan appointees to the NLRB—for the first time comprising a majority of the Board—affirmed business tactics previously in question, such as closing unionized factories and moving production to nonunion locales while a collective bargaining agreement was in effect. The Board allowed its case backlog to increase from four hundred in 1981 to seventeen hundred three years later.[15]

Although no serious candidate for elected office would dare endorse the policy of recession in the heat of a campaign, Reagan understood and accepted it. In 1978, he predicted, "I'm afraid this country is just going to have to suffer two, three years of hard times to pay for the binge we've been on." In 1980, he ran against Carter as the candidate of optimism, and kept such comments out of his campaign speeches. Yet close advisers knew that Reagan, schooled in economics by conservative professors at Eureka College and then by his mentors at General Electric in the 1950s, responded positively to the idea that good times could become too good and must then be followed by a lean winter. As David Stockman put it, "The purgatory view of inflation was out of sight, but not out of mind."[16] Reagan stubbornly resisted acknowledging that recessionary policy had caused a recession. In a radio address in September 1982, he labeled "the most cynical form of demagoguery" the charge that anti-inflationary policy and rising unemployment were linked.[17] But he knew better. As Paul Craig Roberts, the supply-side economist, noted in disillusion after he left the government, "The Republican establishment . . . believes in fighting inflation with unemployment. . . . In principle the administration was supply-side, but in practice its faith still rested in the traditional pain-and-suffering approach to the economy."[18]

Reagan's mind was a rag-bag filled with pieces of conservative wisdom acquired over the years. Intellectual coherence or consistency was no particular virtue to him, although, paradoxically, he could be highly dogmatic. There were many kinds of economic conservatism; they often conflicted. Reagan could, under the right circumstances, embrace any of them wholeheartedly. When, as president, he first met with Volcker, Reagan astounded the Fed chairman by asking why the nation needed a Federal Reserve Bank at all. Hostility to the Fed's existence found a home in certain quarters of both the right and the left, and someone who read *Human Events* as regularly as Reagan did—this magazine, a favorite of Reagan's, offered a conservatism so severe that Baker and Deaver conducted a running battle with the president to try to keep it out of his hands—would not have been shocked by the question. Reagan also believed in the wisdom of returning the U.S. dollar to the gold standard and sometimes derided his country's currency as worthless fiat money. When Volcker recovered his composure and gave a brief defense of the institution he led, Reagan dropped the matter and subsequently assured Volcker that he enjoyed the president's confidence.[19]

In 1981, Volcker resumed the squeeze on the economy that the Fed had begun in 1979 but had relaxed in 1980. Traditionally, the Fed set the pattern for short-term interest rates in the economy by adjusting its own lending rate to banks (the Discount rate) and by indirectly manipulating the rate banks charged one another for overnight transfers (the Federal Funds rate). But in October 1979, Volcker steered the Fed into an experiment in monetarism, setting money-supply targets instead of interest-rate targets. If the money supply shrank, interest rates would rise; interest is the price of borrowing money, and if there is less money, those who have it will command a higher price for it. The new method merely put the Fed one step further back from responsibility for its impact on interest rates. "The rhetoric of monetarism cast an obscurantist cloak over the harsh reality: we were 'targeting monetary aggregates,'" economist Paul Krugman describes this episode, "not throwing people out of work so that those still holding jobs would reduce their wage demands."[20]

Although rising interest rates, by making it harder for businesses to borrow and invest, would indeed throw people out of work by inducing a recession, this was the policy's intention and its effect. In May 1981, the targeted money supply dropped by more than 11 percent, and short-term interest rates jumped from the April level of 13.7 percent to 16.3 percent. Meanwhile, long-term interest rates, which are set in the bond market, were climbing higher, past 13.5 percent and toward the 15 percent range.[21] Reagan's expansive fiscal program, which might fuel inflation by pumping money into the economy, was making investors uneasy—exactly the opposite of what the supply-siders had predicted. "No one wants to buy bonds yet," said one banker. "There is a buyers' strike because investors don't like the outlook on inflation."[22] Inflation is good for borrowers, because they can pay back loans in dollars that are more plentiful and cheaper than the ones they borrowed, but equally bad for lenders—like bond investors. Long-term interest rates indicated what lenders charged borrowers, and lenders demanded a high enough rate that even substantial inflation would leave them with healthy returns.

Choking off businesses' access to credit worked wonders. In July 1981, the recession began, ending the briefest period of economic expansion in post–World War II American history, one of only twelve months' duration.[23] In October 1981, the inflation rate dropped like a stone, from 13.2 percent to 4.8 percent, a level not seen since Nixon's presidency. The unemployment rate—always a "lagging indicator," in economists' parlance—climbed to 8 percent, modestly higher than the 7 percent range it had occupied for seventeen months. The jobless rate would climb past 9 percent by March 1982, and above 10 percent in September 1982—where it would stay for ten excruciating months. Inflation was licked, reaching negative territory in March and remaining in the 3–4 percent range on a yearly basis in the mid-1980s. The bond market finally responded to this enduring trend, bringing long-term interest rates down to the 10–12 percent range in late 1982 and 1983. Sustained economic expansion began in late 1982. But the unemployment rate did not dip below 8 percent until February 1984, fifteen months, by economists' reckoning, after the recovery began. Layoffs and plant closings in manufacturing continued.[24]

The Fed's Beige Books in 1981 and 1982 told the story of an economy whose industrial sector was suffering, and whose scarce bright spots— due to oil wells and military contracts—were concentrated in the South, the Southwest, the Boston area, and some parts of the West Coast. *September 1981*: "Boston attributes the weakness in manufacturing to the strong U.S. dollar making U.S. goods uncompetitive overseas. Minne-apolis, St. Louis, Atlanta, and San Francisco attribute the weakness to the soft homebuilding industry. . . . Cleveland and New York attribute it to cutbacks in capital spending; St. Louis attributes it to poor auto sales; and Chicago attributes it to both of these developments. Oil field equip-ment is the only product that has enjoyed strong orders and production." *November 1981*: "Deteriorating economic conditions appear to be spread-ing." *December 1981*: "No improvement in automobile sales was evident, and dealers in cleveland were prepared for one of the worst months ever." *January 1982*: "Retail sales . . . have sagged again, and prospects for a quick recovery are not widely perceived. . . . In the manufacturing sec-tor . . . unwanted stock piles up and leads to production cutbacks. Finally, reports from the agricultural sector indicate falling commodity prices, with farmland prices dropping too, as many farmers find it impossible to stay in business." "The residential housing market is universally de-pressed. . . . Only houses in the highest price brackets are selling." *March 1982*: "Price inflation continues to slow. With a downturn developing in oil and gas development, defense procurement becomes the principal expanding sector. . . . The Chicago and Cleveland districts with their em-phasis on hard goods continue to present the blackest pictures. . . . Layoffs in the Fourth District included workers from the last auto passenger tire plant in Akron. . . . Richmond reports a rise in demand for cigarettes."[25] Surely this last item was a sign of grim and stressful times, particularly for working-class Americans.

The political climate began to sour for the president as early as Sep-tember 1981. His budget cuts coincided with the worsening recession, sparking outrage.[26] The issue that broke through to public conscious-ness was the effect of reduced federal funding for the National School Lunch Program (NSLP). This program had defrayed the cost of meals since 1946; 90 percent of America's schools participated, and its positive impact on child nutrition had been significant. Reagan cut the funding by 40 percent, saying that children of comfortable families were having their meals subsidized needlessly. One effect of the reduction was to limit the caloric goal for all children served from one-third of a recommended daily intake to 18 percent at most. Milk servings would shrink from six ounces to four. To allow schools to put the best face on the new regime, the Agriculture Department would let them count tomato ketchup and pickle relish as vegetables. Eggs used in cakes could be counted as meat substitutes, cookies as bread.[27]

The ridicule was vehement. Columnist Russell Baker wrote, "This is an idea by one of Oliver Twist's workhouse bullies, isn't it? Sure it is. No fellow who smiles so easily and likes jellybeans would tell a moppet that two ounces of milk make him a welfare bum."[28] (News stories about the White House regularly noted the presence of a jar of jellybeans on the table at cabinet meetings.) Senate Democrats publicly sat down to meals "consisting of a meat-and-soybean patty, a slice of bread, a few French fries, ketchup, and a partially filled glass of milk." Senator John Heinz, Republican of Pennsylvania, heir to a gigantic ketchup-and-relish fortune, affirmed, "Ketchup is a condiment."[29] This fracas gave added impetus to the "Solidarity Day" rally, planned for September 19 by labor leaders and others to protest Reagan's budget and tax policies. This mammoth gathering, whose name was intended to evoke comparisons to Poland's labor-based Solidarity movement, drew about a quarter-million people, roughly the size of the famous 1963 March on Washington for Jobs and Freedom. Lane Kirkland (a staunch supporter of anticommunist trade unions like Polish Solidarity) assured the crowd, "If you do not embrace the proposition that this president has a mandate to destroy the programs that feed the roots of a decent society, look about you. You are not alone."[30] Although it would be little remembered, as such huge political assemblies had become more common since the 1960s, 1981's Solidarity Day was a sign of a shifting mood. Richard Cohen of the *Washington Post* wrote scornfully, "The spirit of Marie Antoinette infuses the administration of Ronald Reagan. The president wears $1,000 cowboy boots. His wife sets the table with china worth over $200,000. The . . . secretary of Health and Human Services poses for a magazine cover in white tie, tails and moronic grin. He is shown sitting down at a banquet table the same week the administration says that the size of school lunches will be shrunk and condiments will now be considered vegetables."[31]

Reagan backpedaled on NSLP, but he aggravated matters by denying responsibility. "I don't know whether it represented bureaucratic sabotage or not," he told reporters, mysteriously. "This is a regulation change that was made or advocated . . . by departmental [employees] we didn't know about, and I've canceled it." These remarks angered Secretary of Agriculture John Block, who knew Reagan's explanation was not true.

The new regulations were Reagan's policies at work. At Block's insistence, a White House spokesman later that day stated, "It's safe to say he [Reagan] no longer feels it was sabotage." Reagan still justified the scale of the cuts. "There are programs that are being abused by people, who . . . are getting benefits they are not entitled to," he said.[32] But, as the *New York Times* pointed out in an editorial, the NSLP was intended to help the nation's children as a whole. Reagan wished to make the program "a welfare project, and a badly funded one at that," the paper charged. Ketchup would not be labeled a vegetable, but some funding cuts remained in place.[33]

Reagan, stung by the new criticism, became less visible, but he could not remain out of the public eye forever. In March 1982, with the country seven months into the recession, he again showed a face his advisers would have preferred to keep private. Joblessness had reached an official rate of 8.8 percent in February, and the number of part-time employees was higher than ever. The unemployment rate among African Americans was 17.3 percent.[34] Reagan sat for an interview with reporters from the *Daily Oklahoman*, known for its conservative editorial policy. Perhaps at ease in supportive company, the president complained about the attention paid to spiking unemployment levels. News reports on such matters were "entertainment" rather than serious news, Reagan said, suggesting that television reporters and producers were interested in the sensational rather than the informative. "Is it news," he asked, "that some fellow out in South Succotash someplace has just been laid off, that he should be interviewed nationwide?"[35]

With his impatience regarding stories of misfortune, Reagan was in danger of forfeiting the healthy level of blue-collar backing he had won in 1980. His job-approval rating dropped sharply, into the mid–40 percent range, from a high of two-thirds in April 1981 (after Hinckley shot him), and his support among unionized households tracked that overall trend closely.[36] A majority of Americans favored canceling the last 10-percent installment of Reagan's signature tax-rate reductions (although, interestingly, those with less income were more likely to favor going through with the rate cut).[37] During the 1980 campaign, and in Reagan's early legislative successes as president, some critics had lamented that he seemed coated with "Teflon," a nonstick surface for cooking pans.[38] His gaffes had seemed to do him little harm. But by the spring of 1982, the

Teflon had worn thin. Howell Raines of the *New York Times* wrote that Republicans detected "a general antipathy to what one consultant called 'the regal Presidency,'" and he reported critically on Reagan's trip to Fort Wayne, Indiana, a city besieged by river flooding and by a 13.7 percent unemployment rate. Raines portrayed a president out of touch with general conditions and awkward with the residents of a working-class city. The only aid Reagan offered Fort Wayne was "a rambling anecdote about a speech he once made as a company spokesman in a General Electric Company plant.... The connecting link in Mr. Reagan's mind was the fact that in the G.E. plant and in the flood victims' shelter, he spoke from atop a cafeteria table."[39]

Opposition to Reagan's leadership found a new voice, in April 1982, when the CBS television network aired a one-hour evening news special hosted by Bill Moyers, once a press secretary to President Lyndon Johnson. The program, called *People Like Us*, showcased the stories of individuals hurt by Reagan's budget cuts. Larry Ham was afflicted with cerebral palsy, but new eligibility standards pushed him off government assistance. Cathy Dixon, with a disabled daughter, suffered reduced Medicaid payments and felt compelled to institutionalize her child for fear that she could not afford to care for her at home. Frances Dorta, despite her poverty, lost her federal welfare benefits under the new rules because she had a job; when her son needed back surgery that she could not afford on her wages, she quit her job in order to reacquire Medicaid assistance. Moyers's narration charged that Reagan's budget "falls most heavily on the poor" and "the weak."[40] The program's title served to rebuke a perception that liberals feared was rampant among the general public: that those dependent on government spending were not "like us," meaning that their attitudes or values were defective. Conversations about whether the poor and dependent were or were not "like us" also carried a tense racial undertone. The White House criticized the show as distorted and merely anecdotal. The irony was lost on few: these adjectives often described Ronald Reagan's speeches.

In the attenuated political discourse of the era, the question of Reagan's attitude toward the distressed became known as "the fairness issue." The issue was, indeed, fairness to those lacking social advantages, and it had a cutting edge. Descriptions like the one cultural critic Mark

Crispin Miller offered of "those unremarkable men, like Caspar Weinberger and Donald Regan, who simply look like Republicans, i.e., as if
their one desire in life is to repossess your house," found a readier audience now that home foreclosures and business failures were rising to
painful levels.[41] Twenty-four thousand American businesses vanished
in 1982, the biggest number since 1933.[42] Yet Americans learned to talk
about the spreading heartbreak of the early 1980s as one from a menu of
political "issues." This classified it as not a national crisis but, rather, the
concern of a sector of the electorate with a special interest in such matters. The language of political consultants, which operated at one remove
from social reality, had infiltrated civic life in general.

Still, the president's political capital, as 1981 gave way to 1982, was
much diluted. The next full budget Reagan sent to Congress, in the spring
of 1982, was notable, remarks historian Gareth Davies, for "how *little* the
administration changed course in response to [the] deterioration in its
political standing." This new budget proposal "placed the principal burden for deficit reduction on a fresh round of cuts in Medicaid, AFDC
[Aid to Families with Dependent Children, the country's main welfare
program], and the food stamps program."[43] Republican senator Robert
Dole of Kansas, sensitive to "the fairness issue," said that "somebody else
is going to have to start taking a hit besides welfare recipients." Senator
David Durenberger, Republican of Minnesota, asked plaintively, "Does
this administration—does my party—care about the poor?" This was
"the big question of this election year," he declared.[44] "More and more of
us are starting to think it's every man for himself," remarked one House
Republican, dismayed over the White House's apparent lack of concern
about the backlash that GOP congressional candidates might suffer over
Reagan's new proposed spending reductions.[45] However, when Reagan
shifted course and switched from more spending cuts to new tax increases as his way of showing fiscal discipline, in TEFRA (see chapter 3),
he split Republican ranks in Congress, as he enraged conservatives, who
voted against the measure. Reagan needed both Democratic and Republican votes to pass TEFRA.

Reagan sought to placate conservatives, unhappy about TEFRA's tax
increases, by supporting efforts, led by Senator Jesse Helms of North Carolina, to strengthen restrictions on government support for abortions and

to strip the U.S. Supreme Court of its right to review state and local laws permitting prayer in public schools. But these efforts ruptured the president's party anew, as a passel of Republican senators who had supported Reagan's economic program opposed this "new right" social agenda. Successful filibusters against these measures were led not by Democrats but by Republicans Lowell Weicker of Connecticut and Bob Packwood of Oregon (who headed the Republican Senate Campaign Committee). Barry Goldwater's constitutional scruples led him to side with them. "I don't like being called New Right," the Arizonan said. "I'm just an old, old son of a bitch. I am a conservative."[46] Helms, hailed by one Christian conservative activist as "the generalissimo of our movement," was a firebrand who excelled in raising money for conservative candidates. But he earned a reputation for untrustworthiness among his Senate colleagues and proved unskilled at parliamentary procedure.[47] The filibusters against Helms's measures lasted from August 16 to September 23, and even conservative Republicans such as Dan Quayle of Indiana and S. I. Hayakawa of California tired of the battle and finally abandoned him.

Many questioned how strongly Reagan pushed for Helms's proposals. Reagan made a series of public statements about abortion and sent a letter to wavering senators urging they support the antiabortion proposal as a "responsible statutory approach to one of the most sensitive problems our society faces—the taking of the life of an unborn child." But the White House proclaimed itself neutral on the school-prayer measure, which the Justice Department considered unconstitutional, and preferred a constitutional amendment, which had no chance of passage.[48] "My view is Reagan doesn't have his heart in it," Democratic senator Max Baucus of Montana said. "It is a token appeasement of the right wing."[49]

The Democrats enjoyed a happy Election Day in November 1982. They expanded their U.S. House majority by twenty-six seats, running on the slogan, "It's not fair, it's Republican," and emphasizing Republican efforts to trim Social Security outlays. The Democrats increased their majority of the nation's governorships by seven and netted control of nine additional state legislative chambers. Five gubernatorial swings to the Democrats came in the country's hard-hit north-central tier: Ohio, Michigan, Wisconsin, Minnesota, and Nebraska.[50] Reagan's party showed little of the strength in the Southeast that his performance there in 1980 had seemed to portend. The president made a point of campaigning against five Democratic House incumbents in North Carolina who had declined to support his economic program, but all five won, and two Republican incumbents in the state were ousted.[51] The unemployment figure for September, 10.1 percent, was released the Friday before the election, and evening news broadcasts emphasized it.[52] Some Democrats who had supported the Republican slate in 1980 "came home." One unemployed Baltimore man, James Willders, had appeared as a Democrat in a Republican campaign commercial in 1980. In 1982, he was featured in a Democratic advertisement. "Remember me?" he asked. "I'm a Democrat, but I voted Republican once—and it's a mistake I'll never make again."[53]

However, despite Democratic euphoria, the returns, in light of the recession's severity, easily could have been more punishing for the GOP. Since 1900, the average loss of House seats for the party that, two years before, had taken control of the White House was twenty-five, almost exactly the 1982 figure. Yet, when the economic conditions and the president's job-approval ratings of 1982 were considered in historical perspective, close students of such matters would have predicted a Republican loss of perhaps twice as many House seats.[54] In the Senate, the Republican majority was unchanged, at 54–46.

Perhaps most important in buoying Republicans in 1982, as the political scientists Thomas Mann and Norman Ornstein explained, was the reality that "the predicted referendum on President Reagan was clouded by the public's confusion and uncertainty over which party to blame for and how best to deal with the nation's economic problems." In one Election Day poll, 53 percent of voters said they thought Reagan's economic program would eventually lead to prosperity, and the Democrats received a bigger share of blame for the nation's economic ills than the president did.[55] While Democrats believed economic concerns now worked in their favor, research in political science indicates they were wrong about this assumption. The GOP enjoyed an advantage in voters' minds on such questions, an advantage damaged only partially and temporarily by the pain of the recession. The conservative economic perspective that had triumphed in 1980, emphasizing tax cuts and battling inflation, remained powerful.[56] By some measures, Reagan's job-approval rating, while not robust, had stabilized before the 1982 elections. The last 10-percent installment of the marginal tax-rate reductions came into effect on July 1, enhancing voters' disposable income in the months before the election, always a help to incumbents.[57]

The Democrats' new stance as champions of deficit reduction was not particularly alluring to voters. They had won tactical victories by letting Republicans take the lead on the 1982 tax increases. But the tax increases were not popular—they were aimed to please Wall Street, not Main Street—and the Democratic leadership supported them. Democrats had helped divert Reagan from his tax-cutting agenda of 1981. But in doing so, they began to pitch their tent on the hard ground of fiscal austerity, even as they struggled to protect social welfare spending from the budget ax. Still, the Republican losses in the House were enough to prevent the return of the conservative working majority the White House had enjoyed in 1981, in part because the Democrats' emerging fiscal conservatism helped to bring the conservative members of their caucus back into the party fold.

Some Americans were doing well. The costs of the recession were far from equally shared. The financial sector enjoyed high profits during the recession, as creditors collected on high–interest rate loans with dollars that became ever more valuable as the inflation rate fell. Large banks, according to the Fed, enjoyed a return on their equity of 13.66 percent in 1981—"a banner year . . . far better than anything the major banks had enjoyed in the 1950s or 1960s."[58] Older Americans who depended on investments earned nice returns; between 1980 and 1984, the disposable income of families headed by those sixty-five and older rose 9.5 percent, almost triple the average increase for all American families across that period.[59] Unemployment remained high, as did *real* interest rates, which was good for lenders. By 1983, *nominal* rates had dropped by about one-third from their peak. But inflation had plummeted, decreasing by about two-thirds. Therefore, real interest rates—nominal rates minus inflation—were actually higher once the recession ended.[60] Lenders continued to collect hefty premiums.

If the numbers still were not good for many in 1983, the direction of the trends was better. Americans increasingly felt they had touched bottom. Contrary to supply-side theory, the blossoming recovery was led by consumer demand, not by enhanced capital investment. In March, the Fed's Beige Book reported, "In most areas the recovery is being led, in many cases exclusively, by personal consumption expenditures and residential real estate sales and construction." However, "Capital goods . . . remain severely depressed in most areas." In December, "The 1983 Christmas season looks to be the best for retailers since 1978. . . . With striking uniformity the twelve Federal Reserve Districts report very strong growth in retail sales. Apparel, home furnishings, and home appliances are most frequently mentioned as the fastest moving items, and automobile sales continue to increase," aided by low gasoline prices caused by increases in global petroleum supplies. Yet, as late as March 1984, the Fed reported that "unemployment remains disturbingly high, especially north of the Ohio [R]iver. Cleveland reports that cautious employers are increasing use of overtime and part-time help in preference to permanent increases in force." In the capital goods sector, "Investment is frequently oriented toward controlling costs and enhancing productivity, rather than adding to capacity."[61]

The country's manufacturing heartland remained a trauma zone, a terrain of despair memorialized in popular culture through the songs of Bruce Springsteen's uncompromising album of 1982, *Nebraska*. It was populated with characters like "Johnny 99," a laid-off automobile-plant employee who, after drunkenly killing a store clerk, asks the judge at his trial to sentence him to die, and with the doomed losers of "Atlantic City," desperate for a piece of the action in a rebuilt casino town whose new patina of glamour did not conceal the seediness beneath. In earlier recordings, Springsteen had made himself a working-class champion of immediate gratification and youthful male self-assertion, celebrating the joy of romance in a New Jersey landscape of motorcycles and epic partying. He became known as "the Boss," an ironic nickname for a singer who railed against social authority. "I hate bosses," he once said.[62] Now, with his back-up band gone, accompanying himself almost solely with an acoustic guitar and harmonica, singing in a narrow vocal range marked by repetitious, mirthless rhythms and guttural shouts, Springsteen painted a scene of blasted hopes and stacked decks. Some of his songs referred to possibilities of rebirth and perseverance, but the overall tone of the record made these refrains sound foolish or sarcastic. A sense of entitlement to a happy, fulfilled life had died inside blue-collar America.[63]

The irony of the Reagan recession was profound. Ronald Reagan had castigated Jimmy Carter in 1980 for, Reagan charged, telling Americans they were living too well. Yet this was exactly what Reagan thought about many Americans. When he spoke of the purge that would have to follow the "binge" of high living and big spending that supposedly had occurred during the years of liberal ascendancy, he did not mean that everyone had lived too well or that all need suffer. Reagan subscribed to the classically conservative view that if the poor and the working class lived too well, inflation would run riot. Generous government spending on the poor worsened the problem. Just as clearly, he believed that what was good for creditors and investors in the short term would strengthen the economy in the long term and thus benefit all social classes. It is often said that Reagan changed American conservatism by bringing to it a sunny, optimistic visage. Reagan's economic conservatism, however, was in truth deeply traditional and administered harsh medicine—but not to all.

Six

1983: The World at the Brink

In 1983, humans lived in the greatest peril of nuclear war since the Cuban Missile Crisis of 1962. Ronald Reagan was convinced that his confrontational foreign policy would prepare the way for a strategic balance of global forces favorable to America. But the road that Reagan chose to travel in foreign affairs proved rocky and dangerous, and 1983 was the year when events got undeniably out of his—or anyone's—control. The result was worldwide fear and tension of a kind that Americans aged twenty and younger had never before witnessed. This was a year of turmoil, featuring a cascade of dramatic, sometimes violent, events on many fronts.

Reagan took his most aggressive actions in the Caribbean basin, reflecting his preoccupation with the spread of revolution in that region. In February, U.S. and Honduran forces conducted large military exercises called Big Pine, and the United States built up the military infrastructure in Honduras that the Contras used to launch forays into Nicaragua.[1] In March and April, the president made a series of speeches declaring that the United States faced urgent security risks in the region. On March 10, Reagan spoke to the National Association of Manufacturers, warning of the revolutionary government of the tiny island nation of Grenada. Critics had belittled Reagan's focus on a country whose main export was nutmeg. The president retorted, "It isn't nutmeg that's at stake in the Caribbean and Central America. It is the United States' national security." But, he went on to ask rhetorically, in response to a widespread concern, "Are we going to send American soldiers into combat? And the answer to that is a flat no."[2]

On April 26, 1983, President Reagan delivered a televised evening address to a joint session of Congress, asking for $600 million in aid to Central American governments. Seeking to convince a skeptical public of the importance of this region, the president suggested that, in the event of a world war, hostile powers with a presence in the area could interrupt the flow of oil to the United States. "If the United States cannot respond to a threat near our own borders, why should Europeans or Asians believe that we're seriously concerned about threats to them?" he asked. This still, however, begged the question of exactly what threat existed south of the border. (Few took the oil issue seriously.) Reagan again raised the issue of Grenada, lamenting that Cuban personnel were helping to build a long runway at the airport there. He praised El Salvador's recent parliamentary elections and described the FMLN guerrillas as terrorists who tried to coerce *campesinos* out of voting. Reagan expressed puzzlement that "the Government of Nicaragua has treated us as an enemy" and "rejected our repeated peace efforts." The president mocked the Sandinistas' contention that they "are . . . being attacked by forces based in Honduras," although this was plainly true.[3]

Senator Christopher Dodd of Connecticut, influenced in his view of the Caribbean basin by his youthful experience as a Peace Corps volunteer in the Dominican Republic, issued a searing response to Reagan's speech for the Democrats. Of El Salvador, he said, "I have been to that country and I know about the morticians who travel the streets each morning to collect the bodies of those summarily dispatched the night before by Salvadoran security forces—gangland style—the victim of bended knee, thumbs wired behind the back, a bullet through the brain." He denounced "our association with criminals such as these" as "not America's tradition."[4] Joan Didion, who traveled to El Salvador in 1982, published a chilling report in March 1983. She described a bloodletting unimaginable to most North Americans:

> The dead and pieces of the dead turn up in El Salvador everywhere, every day, as taken for granted as in a nightmare, or a horror movie. . . . Bodies turn up in the brush of vacant lots, in the garbage thrown down ravines in the richest districts, in public rest rooms, in bus stations. Some are dropped in Lake Ilopango, a few miles east of the city, and

wash up near the lakeside cottages and clubs frequented by what remains in San Salvador of the sporting bourgeoisie.[5]

Yet Reagan got his way, accounts like Didion's notwithstanding. After Reagan's speech, in spite of Dodd's response, House Foreign Affairs
Committee Chair Clement Zablocki, Democrat of Wisconsin, said, "I
certainly don't want to be accused of losing El Salvador by voting against
more aid." His committee then reversed a recent vote and approved
some of the aid Reagan was seeking for San Salvador. Reagan was convincing a majority in Congress, if not the U.S. public, to support his Central America policy.[6]

By this time, George Shultz, on the job as Haig's successor for almost
nine months, was, in his slow, determined way, settling in for bureaucratic trench warfare in his bid to wrest control over U.S. foreign policy
from Defense, the NSC, and the CIA. Shultz long had been viewed, for
obscure reasons, in Republican Party circles as a highly suitable secretary of state. He had an impressive resume: secretary of labor, secretary
of the treasury, and budget director under President Nixon; before that,
dean of the University of Chicago's business school; and, after Nixon's
presidency ended, chief executive officer of the Bechtel Corporation, an
engineering and construction company with "global reach," as Shultz
put it.[7] But conspicuously missing from his government background was
extensive or deep experience in foreign affairs. Nonetheless, Shultz, like
James Baker, attracted admirers with his temperament, which seemed
emollient after Haig. Shultz was composed, even stolid. This demeanor,
combined with his impassive face, thick frame, and egglike shape, earned
him a description as "Buddha-like." After Shultz's installation, in the
historian Garry Wills's wry appraisal, "There were no longer five or six
foreign policies, as in the first years of the Reagan administration—more
like two or three."[8]

The Shultz-Weinberger power struggle was a saga in itself. The two
men had long been associates, with Weinberger playing the subordinate
role. He had been Shultz's deputy at OMB under Nixon, then corporation
counsel to Bechtel when Shultz was chief executive. Now Weinberger
had his own massive power center at the Pentagon and could square
off against Shultz as an equal. Whereas Shultz projected steadiness and

chose his moments of personal conflict carefully, Weinberger was pugnacious and tireless, ever ready for argument. Intensely proud of his army service during World War II, Weinberger often spoke of his reverence for Winston Churchill and flattered both himself and President Reagan by suggesting they followed in the wartime leader's footsteps, this time confronting Communist rather than fascist totalitarianism. No matter the setting, when addressing others, he often acted as if he were speaking in Parliament, his phrasing dramatic and rather pompous. Shultz's and Weinberger's inclinations on foreign policy, like their manners, differed sharply. Shultz wanted to nudge Reagan toward arms-control negotiations with Soviet leaders, while Weinberger and Richard Perle, an assistant secretary of defense who took a leading role on questions of strategic weaponry, sought to block such moves at every turn. But regarding the use of force, Shultz played the hawk, advocating military action in Lebanon and the Caribbean, while Weinberger piled argument upon argument against waging war, placed numerous restrictions on U.S. troops in war zones, and eventually offered his own "doctrine" that would make U.S. warfare a rare circumstance.[9] Conflicts and rivalries within the administration laced every foreign policy issue with a web of intrigue.

As the internal struggle over U.S. foreign policy escalated in mid-1983, Central America became the bone of contention. In April, Shultz learned, while traveling abroad, that William Clark, the national security adviser, was trying to interfere in Latin America policy, and fired off a message to the president. Shultz said he was "disturbed," and believed that Clark's maneuverings would effectively "remov[e] the direction of the policy from my supervision. I do not see . . . how a secretary of state could continue to serve under such circumstances."[10] Characteristically, Reagan professed ignorance, but sought to mollify Shultz (as he had not with Haig), assuring him that State would run Central America policy. As a compromise gesture toward hardliners, Shultz agreed to move Assistant Secretary of State for Latin America Thomas Enders and Ambassador to El Salvador Deane Hinton out of their roles; others had attacked them as too critical of U.S. allies in the region or too inclined to negotiate settlements to civil wars.[11]

Then, on July 15, Reagan approved another set of military exercises in Central America, Big Pine II, the biggest ever in the region, involving twenty thousand U.S. personnel. Marines would land on beaches, U.S.

jets would simulate bombing runs, and battleships would steam off-shore, all around Nicaragua's borders. The planning for Big Pine II, which would run through the end of the year, came from the Pentagon with support from the NSC. No one consulted Shultz about it; he learned of the exercises through news reports.[12] "Deeply disturbed," Shultz wrote later, "I now realized that I could not trust the answers I got from the White House staff." He blamed the provocative display of force for the temporary defeat of a Contra-aid bill in the House later that month. On July 25, Shultz met with Reagan, insisting that Vice President Bush, Clark, Baker, and Meese also be present. Perhaps the president should replace him, Shultz suggested. "Bill Clark seems to want the job." Nothing changed immediately.[13]

Later in 1983, Shultz began to exert control over the administration's foreign policy in general, but his impact on Central America policy remained uncertain in light of the president's aggressive proclivities in the region. In November, the new U.S. ambassador in San Salvador, Thomas Pickering, felt encouraged to tell Salvadoran president Alvaro Magaña to dismiss a small number of army officers linked to the death squads. Magaña did nothing. Pickering, echoing Hinton, then gave his own speech in San Salvador, saying, "No one wants to live in a country where no efforts are made to find who dumps bodies in gas stations and parking lots."[14] On another occasion, Pickering called Colonel Nicolas Carranza, the commander of El Salvador's Treasury Police and reportedly a key figure in setting up the death squads in 1979 and 1980, a "fascist." One U.S. official said, "There's no way the government can purge itself. Too many people have blood on their hands. The government itself is a rightwing death squad."[15]

Reagan responded to these displays of distress from his State Department by personally reaffirming the hard line on Central America. He undermined Pickering's efforts when, in November, he pocket-vetoed a bill that would have extended for another year the human rights certification requirements regarding aid to El Salvador. Considering how light a burden these requirements were, this action sent a clear message that the administration would tolerate few obstacles in its chosen path in Central America. Appearing before an assembly of high school students on December 2, Reagan was asked about El Salvador. He conceded, grudgingly, that there were "so-called death squads" operating in the country.

Then he said, "I'm going to voice a suspicion I've never said aloud before. I wonder if all this is rightwing, or if those guerrilla forces have not realized that . . . they can get away with these violent acts, helping to try to bring down the government, and the rightwing will be blamed for it."[16] There is no reason to think this was anything but a fanciful storyline that Reagan devised in a desperate effort to explain away ugly realities. Those in the U.S. government inclined toward violent action in the region took their lead from the top. In October, after CIA contract employees raided and destroyed the oil depot in the Nicaraguan port of Corinto, Casey, proud of his work, took photographs of the scene straight to the president. Some within the CIA questioned this operation, which amounted to covert warfare. They were rebuffed by Duane Clarridge, Casey's point man on Latin America, who reportedly said, "That's what the President wants. He knows and that's what he likes."[17]

Despite Central America's importance to Reagan, the region receded into the shadows of public perception as 1983 wore on. As the months passed, the most important and dangerous of all U.S. relationships—that with the Soviet Union—hurtled into newly treacherous territory. Reagan gave two speeches in March, in which he shared his views on the USSR and how America should cope with it. On March 8, the president spoke to the National Association of Evangelicals (NAE), the nation's largest umbrella organization of evangelical Protestant churches, in Orlando, Florida. Most of his presentation concerned the social-policy agenda of the Christian right. Only when Reagan came to his "final points" did he bring up foreign policy. His purpose was to denounce the campaign for a nuclear freeze, which had attracted substantial clerical support. He warned his audience to beware that evildoers "sometimes speak in soothing tones of brotherhood and peace," perhaps alluding darkly to the endtime belief, common among his audience, that Antichrist would come disguised as a man of peace. The freeze was "a very dangerous fraud," he said, for it would lock in place the strategic advantage Reagan still thought the Soviets enjoyed. He implored the crowd, "So, in your discussion of the nuclear freeze proposals, I urge you to beware the temptation of pride—the temptation of blithely declaring yourselves above it all and label [sic] both sides equally at fault, to ignore the facts of history and the aggressive impulses of an evil empire." The president then added that he still wished to "negotiate real and verifiable reductions in the world's nuclear arsenals and one day, with God's help, their total elimination." This expression of hope for the abolition of nuclear weapons was remarkable, and basically unprecedented in Reagan's public statements. But almost the only things anyone later remembered about Reagan's speech were the phrases "focus of evil in the modern world"—which, Reagan said, lay in the Kremlin—and "evil empire."[18]

Even so, Reagan was not the first to call the USSR an "evil empire," and the NAE speech might have faded in historical memory if not for the crisis atmosphere that worsened with Reagan's next big speech, fifteen days later.[19] This would become known as the "Star Wars" speech. On March 21, Shultz received a message from Robert "Bud" McFarlane, Clark's deputy at the NSC, stating that the president would give a televised speech in two days' time, in which he would announce "a high-tech strategic defense system that can protect us against ballistic missiles." The Joint Chiefs had persuaded Reagan to announce this missile-defense program, Shultz was told. Reagan had kept the secret from both Shultz and Weinberger until the last possible minute, nurturing the missile-defense proposal with a small group of military and scientific boosters, and bypassing what there was of a regular policy-development process in the executive branch.

Most of the March 23 speech, delivered in the Oval Office and televised to the nation, consisted of familiar refrains, but these remarks were prelude to a big surprise. Reagan said, as he had to the NAE, that the freeze proposal "would reward the Soviets for their massive military buildup" and would keep the United States in a strategically inferior position. But then, said the president, "Let me share with you a vision of the future which offers hope." He reflected that "to rely on the specter of retaliation, on mutual threat" to keep the nuclear peace was "a sad commentary on the human condition." Instead, what if "we could intercept and destroy strategic ballistic missiles before they reached our own soil or that of our allies"? Reagan claimed that "current technology has attained a level of sophistication where it's reasonable for us to begin this effort." That was as far back as Shultz's last-minute pleas had been able to push the president's initially planned statement of exuberant technological optimism. Reagan added that his proposed research program, which would be named the Strategic Defense Initiative (SDI), would be "consistent with our obligations of the ABM [Anti–Ballistic Missile] treaty" of 1972, which it seemed rather obviously not to be.[20]

Space-based lasers and other esoteric technology able to identify and destroy the hundreds or thousands of incoming ballistic missiles that would comprise a Soviet attack were the stuff of fantasy. Yet such visions had a history. They had circulated on the political right for years. In 1965, Phyllis Schlafly and Chester Ward had published a book titled *Strike from Space* that envisioned the orbital realm as a new arena for weaponry.[21] Ironically, Reagan also echoed old Soviet rhetoric in labeling antimissile technology "defensive," in contrast to "offensive" strategic nuclear weapons. U.S. negotiators had had to overcome *Soviet* insistence on the moral superiority of missile defense in order to forge the ABM Treaty.[22] Since the late 1970s, Reagan had voiced his discomfort with the strategic concept of "mutual assured destruction," which entailed U.S. vulnerability to a nuclear attack, as a means of keeping the peace. Like many others, he called the acronym MAD (for "mutual assured destruction") ironically appropriate. If, instead of relying on deterrence, nations could make a hypothetical nuclear attack ineffective, people would be safe, and these weapons would become obsolete. This seemed, to him, a better way of preventing war.

Reagan's thinking was confused and ill-informed. The missile-defense system he described was impossible, as a series of failed or rigged tests of developmental components of SDI would demonstrate.[23] Even if a flying object or a laser could hit a ballistic missile in flight, it would be relatively easy for a superpower to overwhelm such a system by increasing the number of missiles launched, including "dummy" missiles without warheads. Technical feasibility aside, the destabilizing impact of even a belief in the viability of antimissile systems was clear. If superpower A merely believed, even incorrectly, that it was safe from nuclear attack, it might feel it could launch a nuclear first strike with impunity. By this same logic, if superpower B feared that A was nearing the successful development of such an antimissile shield (or a deluded belief to that effect), then B might feel driven to launch a preventive first strike. Moreover, if any missile-defense system became real rather than imaginary, it would take years to develop and deploy it, and that "window" would be an extended period of peril during which the enemy would feel sorely tempted to attack rather than await proof of its arsenal's obsolescence and its own vulnerability.

The most basic problem in Reagan's strategic thinking was his belief that MAD was a doctrine that could be embraced or rejected—instead of an existential "condition," as the journalist J. Peter Scoblic aptly puts it, created by the technical capacities of the two superpowers.[24] In 1976, Reagan sorrowfully described nuclear deterrence as "two men pointing cocked and loaded pistols at each other."[25] This was no way to keep the peace, he suggested—and he implied that there must be an alternative. In his error, Reagan had been encouraged by Paul Nitze and others in the Committee on the Present Danger (see chapter 2), who mocked the concept of MAD because it was linked to the idea of strategic parity between the United States and the USSR. Henry Kissinger had remarked, "Military superiority has no practical significance . . . under circumstances in which both sides have the capability to annihilate one another."[26] But Reagan, like Nitze, insisted that strategic superiority was still possible for one superpower or the other. Reagan believed the Soviets had achieved it, and he wanted it back for the United States. He hoped to revive a Pax Americana that, in his view, had prevailed when America had been the sole atomic power. To Reagan, U.S. supremacy equaled peace and was in the whole world's interest. In 1980, he reminisced "that peace was never more certain than . . . when we had the mightiest mil[itary] force in the world and a monopoly on nuclear weapons."[27] In 1983, facing criticism that he was a warmonger who considered a nuclear conflict winnable, Reagan painted his longstanding interest in missile defense with new colors of visionary statesmanship and peace.

Critics almost immediately ridiculed Reagan's proposal as a childish dream, dubbing it "Star Wars" to stick it with the label of science fiction, not science. World leaders reacted to Reagan's speech with shock. While Soviet leader Yuri Andropov had called the evil empire speech "lunatic," he labeled the SDI speech "insane."[28] America's NATO allies saw Reagan's notion of a shield protecting the U.S. population against incoming missiles as either ludicrous or dangerous, or both. After the speech, Margaret Thatcher was beside herself. She joined the chorus of those who thought Reagan's idea absurd. "As a chemist," Thatcher told Reagan, she knew the science was impossible. (She had earned her undergraduate degree in chemistry at Oxford.) But if Reagan merely believed SDI was feasible, the danger loomed that U.S. security policy, if it were to shift toward the concept of an impregnable homeland defense, might become "uncoupled" from that of Western Europe.[29]

The scientific implausibility of SDI did not prevent Congress from voting to spend a great deal of money on SDI research (almost 90 percent of it, in 1983 and 1984, going to ten large military contractors).[30] Still, month by month and year by year, administration officials were compelled to modify their claims for the technology's promise. Military commanders shifted to describing SDI as a technology to protect U.S. strategic weapons from destruction, rather than a system that would insulate the entire country from attack. But Reagan never made this pivot in describing SDI, and continued to talk as if it were a plan for population defense.[31]

By the spring and summer of 1983, people around the globe feared the superpowers were moving toward a clash. Despite administration efforts to stop them, the National Conference of Catholic Bishops in early May voted, 238–9, to adopt a pastoral letter on nuclear weapons that effectively denounced nuclear warfare and nearly endorsed the freeze movement. "The whole world must summon the moral courage and technical means to say 'no' to nuclear conflict, 'no' to weapons of mass destruction, 'no' to an arms race which robs the poor and the vulnerable, and 'no' to the moral danger of a nuclear age," read the 150-page document.[32] The next evening, the House adopted a freeze resolution, 60 Republicans joining 218 Democrats, contributing to a sense of snowballing opposition to Reagan's stance.[33] Later that month, almost 250 Catholic and Protestant antinuclear protesters were arrested as they knelt to pray in protest in the Capitol rotunda in Washington.[34]

Witnessing this tide of criticism, Reagan made a private appeal signaling his desire to ease international pressures. On July 11, he composed a letter to Andropov, with Shultz's approval, in reply to a letter Andropov had sent him. Reagan wrote, "Let me assure you the government & the people of the United States are dedicated to, 'the course of peace' and 'the elimination of the nuclear threat,'" quoting phrases from Andropov's missive.[35] The ultimate goal of eliminating nuclear weapons had been a staple of Soviet rhetoric for decades. Few in America had taken it seriously. In 1977, however, Jimmy Carter, in his inaugural address, pledged his support for this idea. Now, Reagan was beginning to echo this call. He had first done so clearly in his "evil empire" speech, but it was almost an afterthought on that occasion. Haltingly, in the course of 1983, Reagan began to embrace the concept of a nuclear weapons–free world more tightly, fending off critics of his bellicosity. For the first time, he truly contemplated the only policy that could convert his distaste for nuclear deterrence from a pointless rejection of realities into an actual program for change. The only way to escape the world of nuclear deterrence would be to take the radical step of eliminating nuclear weapons, and now Reagan began to take this idea seriously.[36] He continued to advocate his concept of SDI as well, arguing that it was a pathway toward nuclear abolition.

Even if, in private correspondence, Andropov and Reagan were groping for ways to reverse the escalation of fear and danger, the violent events of 1983 had the opposite effect. In the summer of 1982, U.S. Marines had joined French and Italian troops to form a Multi-National Force (MNF) in Beirut as part of a plan to remove PLO forces from the city. After the Lebanese Phalange perpetrated the massacres at Sabra and Shatila, with Israeli support (see chapter 4), the MNF took on a new role, trying to buy Lebanese forces time to gain control of the area. The MNF was routinely called a peacekeeping force, but that is not the way it appeared to many Lebanese. Lebanon's government had a partisan, Christian basis and was allied with Israel. Thus, writes historian David Crist, "As the United States strengthened the Lebanese army, it chipped away at the perception of American neutrality."[37] On April 18, 1983, a new instrument of asymmetric warfare made its imprint on the American consciousness. A suicide truck-bomber, possibly in the employ of Syrian intelligence and perhaps linked to the Lebanese Shia group Hizbollah (Army of God), drove into the U.S. embassy in Beirut, hard by the Mediterranean. The bomber killed sixty-three people, including seventeen Americans, including both the CIA station chief and Robert Ames, the CIA's top Middle East analyst. In the following months, local forces targeted mortar fire on U.S. troops stationed at the Beirut airport. In response, the battleship USS *New Jersey* hurled its enormous shells onto the nearby heights. American officials watched the Lebanese situation uneasily through the summer of 1983, as the marines took casualties and American retaliation exacted a large toll on Lebanese civilians.

On September 1, Reagan's team, along with the rest of the world, were jolted by another shock—one of the great tragedies of the late Cold War. A Soviet jet fighter shot down a Korean Air Lines 747, flight KAL007, on the edge of Soviet airspace near the military airfield on Sakhalin Island. Two hundred sixty-nine people were dead; their plane, which had gone badly off course, had plunged into the North Pacific, embedding itself in the ocean floor. Those onboard included sixty-one Americans, one of them U.S. Representative Larry McDonald, Democrat of Georgia, the president of the John Birch Society. Months before, the Soviet government had adopted a new law mandating violent action against aircraft that encroached into the country's territory. When Soviet pilots, flying at night in pursuit of the passenger airliner, could not identify it as such and could not establish communications with it, the law gave them little discretion, in spite of the doubts expressed by some officers involved.[38]

The new law had come after two years of aggressive U.S. military probes along the edges of Soviet territorial waters and airspace. Starting in 1981, the Pentagon had embarked on a program to discover the strengths and weaknesses of Soviet defenses. But these probes, in the air and at sea, together with a series of simulated air attacks, were also designed as psychological warfare operations, intended to keep Soviet leaders guessing about U.S. military intentions. This "psyops" program worked all too well. "It really got to them," said William Schneider, undersecretary of state for military assistance and technology at the time. "They didn't know what it all meant. A squadron would fly straight at Soviet airspace. . . . Then at the last minute the squadron would peel off and return home."[39] The Soviets had put their global intelligence apparatus on alert for signs of an impending nuclear first strike by the United States and its allies. This program, known by the acronym RYAN, created an atmosphere of readiness to respond to attack—preemptively, if possible—among Soviet leaders.[40]

Unsurprisingly, when KAL007 went down, U.S. officials made no mention of their psyops program. The public statements of the president and secretary of state were unsparing. "The United States reacts with revulsion to this attack," said Shultz. "We can see no excuse whatsoever for this appalling act."[41] Andropov and other Soviet officials first denied that the incident had occurred at all, and then shifted to insisting on the fiction that the airliner was a spy plane working in cooperation with the United States government. Reagan gave the horrifying incident the broadest interpretation. Speaking live on television from the White House on the evening of September 5, he called it a "massacre" and a "crime against humanity." It was proof of the moral degeneracy of the entire Soviet political system, said Reagan, "an act of barbarism, born of a society which wantonly disregards individual rights and the value of human life." Going the distance with his claims for the salience of totalitarianism, the president went on, "Memories come back of Czechoslovakia, Hungary, Poland, the gassing of villages in Afghanistan." Yet Reagan's harsh words were not matched by actions. He finished his Oval Office statement by declining to discontinue arms-control talks, saying, "We are more determined than ever to reduce and, if possible, eliminate the threat hanging over mankind."[42]

The danger of an almost unthinkable conflict erupting between the superpowers remained frighteningly real. Politburo members continued to search intelligence reports for signs of imminent U.S. war plans. On September 26, the USSR's missile warning system reported an ICBM incoming from the United States. Luckily for the entire world, Soviet lieutenant colonel Stanislav Petrov, on duty in the USSR's nuclear-attack early-warning and response center, correctly identified this as an error; a first strike would have involved thousands of missiles. He also disregarded four further mistaken reports of incoming missiles.[43]

In mid-October, at a turbulent moment, Clark left the NSC to take James Watt's vacated job at the Interior Department. The First Lady had become Clark's enemy, believing his prominence was making the president appear bellicose. His resignation was announced on October 13. Jeane Kirkpatrick, stationed at the UN, wanted to replace him as national security adviser. "She had her heart set on the job and told me so," Reagan wrote later. But Shultz thought her "not well suited to the job . . . not at all the dispassionate broker and faithful representative of divergent positions" that the position required.[44] If Clark's image was that of a provincial ideologue, Kirkpatrick's was merely that of a worldly one. Baker and Deaver made an audacious power play: they proposed to the president that Baker take the helm at NSC, and that Deaver move up to become chief of staff. With Shultz's support, Reagan agreed. But when the president informed Clark of these plans, Clark corralled Meese, Casey, and Weinberger, who together objected strongly, and Reagan backed off. Instead, McFarlane, a compromise candidate who was not expected to make a deep imprint on policy, was announced as the new national security adviser on October 17. "This job is way beyond me," he confided to a friend.[45]

On October 19, amid this flux in Washington, the situation in Grenada—which had become "an obsession" for Reagan, according to one administration official—became volatile.[46] Prime Minister Maurice Bishop was murdered in a coup by a rival faction in his government. Some eight hundred American medical students were on Grenada, enrolled at the St. George's School of Medicine. The need to evacuate them and prevent a hostage crisis like that which had helped destroy Carter's presidency became the linchpin for a U.S. plan to invade the island and dislodge the coup leaders. At the same time, Reagan long had described the prospect of a Cuban–Soviet air base on the island as a threat to the United States, and the students' safety was widely seen as a pretext for the invasion. Now, informal U.S. inquiries prompted a request for intervention from the Organization of Eastern Caribbean States, and by Saturday, October 22, Reagan moved the invasion planning to the starting gate.[47]

Then another blow came in news from the Middle East. In the early morning hours of October 23, word reached Shultz and Reagan that a truck loaded with explosives had penetrated the defenses around the marine barracks in Beirut. When this mobile bomb detonated, it caused what was thought to be the largest nonnuclear explosion on record. The digits "241" formed an iconic number, stenciled on the memory of a generation: the number of marines dead in the rubble of what had been the barracks. Minutes later, another bomber struck the French paratroop headquarters only two miles away, killing fifty-eight. Now Reagan's policy was widely questioned. Weinberger and the Joint Chiefs had warned that the marines were simply targets without a coherent mission in Beirut, implying that withdrawal of U.S. forces was the sensible course. However, to leave under fire seemed, to others, inconceivable; on October 24, Shultz met with members of Congress and told them, "The president is not about to be driven out of Lebanon by this kind of terrorist attack."[48] Nonetheless, months later, Reagan removed the marines.

On the evening of October 24, Reagan ordered the invasion of Grenada. Code-named Urgent Fury, the attack began the next day. Cuban troops and workers put up strong resistance with limited firepower. Two

U.S. helicopters were lost and nineteen personnel killed. But the invasion had gone ahead, in no small part, because it was a sure thing. Almost one hundred Cubans were killed or injured; the United States quietly ferried the remainder, more than seven hundred, back to their home country. The American medical students were brought home, where the first one on the tarmac after their plane landed in the United States knelt and kissed the ground. The U.S. public supported the invasion with gusto. A giant had swatted a gnat. But America's mood in 1983 was such that the Grenada victory was occasioned by outsized pride.

Three days after ordering the invasion, Reagan spoke from the Oval Office in a televised speech, explaining that "events in Lebanon and Grenada, though oceans apart, are closely related." Reprising Claire Sterling's theory, he stated that the Soviets supported "the violence in both countries . . . through a network of surrogates and terrorists."[49] Some in high places saw in the invasion of Grenada a valuable demonstration of Reagan's willingness to make war. On the night of Reagan's address, William Casey dined at home with the journalist Bob Woodward as his guest. Casey said the invasion had sent a strong message to the USSR and to Cuba about U.S. intentions in the Caribbean basin. "'That we might strike in Nicaragua,' he stated," Woodward wrote in his account. "The word 'strike' was given strong emphasis."[50]

In November, international peril mounted further, although the peoples of the world did not know the half of it. Between November 2 and 11, NATO forces conducted an unprecedented war-games exercise, code-named Able Archer 83. It simulated the beginning of a nuclear war with the Soviets; high officials, including Thatcher and West German chancellor Helmut Kohl, participated. The RYAN program had put Soviet leaders on the lookout for signs of an imminent U.S. assault. In this environment, the Soviets, it seems, were prepared to believe the war games were a ruse: a real attack designed as a simulation. NATO was using communication codes never seen before, and allied forces moved all the way to "DEFCON 1," the state of imminent readiness for war. The Soviets responded by placing some of their nuclear forces on high alert, readied for use. They sent nuclear-armed submarines speeding out of the Arctic Ocean toward the United States. This "war scare," unknown to the public, dissipated by the time the exercise was over. Oleg Gordievsky, the KGB station chief in London, was secretly working for British intelligence and, in alarm, relayed the Soviet perceptions to his controllers. Casey hurried to London and met with Gordievsky.[51]

The war scare, it appears, further encouraged Reagan to reconsider his course regarding superpower relations and nuclear weapons. In mid-October, he commented to Shultz, "If things get hotter and hotter and arms control remains an issue, maybe I should go see Andropov and propose eliminating all nuclear weapons."[52] On November 18, he mused in his diary that the Soviets were "paranoid about being attacked," and considered, "We ought to tell them no one here has any intention of doing anything like that."[53] That same month, Reagan traveled to Asia and, in a speech to the Japanese Diet, endorsed the goal of nuclear disarmament in public with greater clarity and emphasis than ever before. "I say our dream is to see the day when nuclear weapons will be banished from the face of the Earth. . . . We want significant reductions and we're willing to compromise."[54] On December 17, Reagan noted to Shultz with excitement that two days earlier Soviet Defense Minister Dimitri Ustinov had called for the elimination of all nuclear weapons.[55] Still, Reagan sent mixed signals about his seriousness. In August, he joked on the radio (unaware that his words were being broadcast) about launching a nuclear strike against the USSR.[56] His awareness of Soviet fears and his interest in disarmament grew with time, but not without missteps or backsliding.

As 1983 drew near to its close, Reagan's private musings remained just that—private—and the public scene was more grim and pessimistic regarding international affairs than at any other point in his presidency. Reagan's Japanese message received little notice at home. On November 20, the ABC television network broadcast an original movie, *The Day After*, which depicted a nuclear war from the perspective of Lawrence, Kansas. ICBMs were launched into the air from their prairie silos, as incoming Soviet missiles sailed, simultaneously and inexorably, toward the American heartland. After the bombs killed uncounted thousands and obliterated most built structures, the walking wounded staggered like zombies through a hellscape of starvation, radiation sickness, and severed human connections. The president had had an advance preview in the White House, and noted in his diary that it "left me greatly depressed."[57] The planned deployments of U.S. nuclear weapons in Europe were unaffected, however. On November 23, the first Pershing missiles arrived in West Germany, and the Soviet Union marked the occasion by exiting from the ongoing negotiations on medium-range nuclear missiles.

Popular culture was sprinkled with harbingers of disaster. The German singer known as Nena scored a big hit record in West Germany in 1983, and then in the United States the following year, with her musical tale of a bunch of red balloons mistaken for an incoming nuclear missile, "99 Luftballons (99 Red Balloons)." Her song portrayed military men as all too ready, even eager, to confront their enemies.[58] Hollywood produced a popular film, *WarGames*, in 1983, a story of a hair-trigger U.S. military establishment moving to within an inch of the apocalypse, this time due to misperceptions of games played by a brainy teenager who gains access to the computers supposedly in control of U.S. nuclear forces. The movie ends, Armageddon averted, with a giant computer screen displaying the words, "The only winning move is not to play." Reagan watched the film in the White House and seemed to enjoy it.[59]

Amid public anxiety that rivaled any previous fears of nuclear war—and with Reagan bearing the brunt of global criticism over the rising tension—he resolved to deliver, in January 1984, a major speech on U.S.-Soviet relations, one that could set those relations on a less dangerous course. Reagan pronounced himself satisfied with the results of his military buildup. "I believe that 1984 finds the United States in the strongest position in years to establish a constructive and realistic working relationship with the Soviet Union," said the president. This was the "position of strength" Reagan had always said he wanted as a starting point for arms-reduction negotiations. "We've come a long way since the decade of the seventies," said Reagan, "years when the United States seemed filled with self-doubt and neglected its defenses."[60] Some dismissed Reagan's speech as "a curtain raiser of sorts on the presidential political campaign." Andrei Gromyko, the USSR's foreign minister, called it a "hackneyed ploy."[61] Andropov died soon afterward. His successor, Konstantin Chernenko, quickly expressed skepticism about Reagan's intentions.[62]

For the time being, words were all that Reagan was offering, but with repetition they became more powerful. In September 1984, his new interest in diplomacy reached a rhetorical peak when he spoke before the UN General Assembly in New York. Here he reiterated, "America has repaired its strength," and therefore, "We are ready for constructive negotiations with the Soviet Union." Reagan continued, "For the sake of a peaceful world . . . let us approach each other with ten-fold trust and thousand-fold affection."[63] Reagan surely hoped to burnish his image as a man of peace in advance of the presidential election, fewer than two months away. Just as certainly, the world hungered for any evidence that the superpowers were edging away from the precipice.

Seven

The High Eighties

Some Americans would remember the 1980s as the time of their lives. Wall Street buccaneers, young conservative activists, art-scene denizens, club-hoppers, rich kids, and rising stars of academe may have thought they had little in common. But they all lived large at the high tide of Reaganism, alternately affecting ennui and pursuing vivid sensation. The cultural temperature ran hot and cool at the same time. Postmodernism, postpunk, and post-postmaterialism—all trends of the era—bore family resemblances. Adherents of each loved shiny surfaces and slummed amid gritty realities. As the big party proceeded, the ascendancy of hedonism, embraced with a full-throated roar by the new apostles of unbridled capitalism, posed a moral quandary for the conservative movement.

Americans experimented with different ways of acting rich in the 1980s. Loving evocations of interwar Anglo-American refinement proliferated, from *Chariots of Fire*, a drama of British Olympic athletes that won the 1981 Academy Award for best picture, to the fashions of clothing designer Ralph Lauren (*né* Lifshitz), which epitomized an enormously popular preppie look of sweater sets, boat shoes, and Oxford-cloth button-down or short-sleeved polo shirts, thought to evoke life among the West Egg or Eton set.[1] Lauren had designed the men's costumes for a 1974 film version of *The Great Gatsby*; he named his clothing line simply "Polo."[2] *The Official Preppy Handbook*, a gentle, affectionate satire that promoted the upper-crust lifestyle it outlined, became a bestseller in 1980.[3] (Young women who eschewed the preppie look sported blouses with ballooning sleeves, in a gesture toward conservative dresses associated with bygone pioneer days, or business suits with thick, jutting shoulder pads, conveying with great obviousness a new sense of business-world empowerment.) Polyester was almost banished from the apparel business, displaced by a rage for cotton and wool. The literature scholar Paul Fussell, in his withering 1983 book, *Class*, cited "the organic-materials principle": "materials are classier the more they consist of anything that was once alive." Nancy Reagan brought the modest portions and light flavors of *nouvelle cuisine* to the White House. Fussell classed the Reagans as parvenus, with splendid condescension labeling the president's style "Los Angeles (or even Orange) County Wasp-Chutzpah."[4] A riot of bright-colored, wide suspenders and expensive cigars erupted among bond traders and stockbrokers, while the middle class found new satisfaction in small indulgences like flavored vinegars and higher-fat ice cream. One popular poster of the era showed a man decked out in traditional horse-country attire, complete with riding crop, posed in front of a Bentley, an old name in luxury cars, toasting the good life with a glass of champagne; the words above the photograph read, "Poverty Sucks." If poverty sucked, wealth ruled. It was important to say it and show it—whether through displays of excess or attempts at tastefulness so overt they were ostentatious. *Lifestyles of the Rich and Famous*, a weekly syndicated television program that reverently showcased sumptuous celebrity habitats, premiered in 1984.[5]

While old and new money both made out well in the 1980s, the latter rather than the former reigned supreme culturally. Looking like old money (or looking like what people thought old money looked like) was good, but it was even better if one maintained the quicker passions of the arriviste. In the 1981 film comedy *Arthur*, the third–biggest earning movie of the year, the title character, a wealthy drunkard, is asked at one point, "How does it feel to have all that money?" Arthur pauses, and then replies, "It feels great."[6] It always feels great to be free of material cares. But only in some eras do people feel it necessary to say so. The spirit of the 1980s retained, as a kind of hangover from the 1970s, a stubborn grievance against the antimaterialist or postmaterialist values that had been prominent in that earlier time. Arthur rescues his working-class love from economic worry, in an age-old fantasy: poor girl wins lottery by catching rich man's eye. Yet this narrative was an old formula with a new twist. Arthur emits a constant stream of insults, but he is meant to be funny—except to those who are, like him, rich, but, unlike him, stiff and conceited. The film's working-class characters, including Arthur's servants and a group of prostitutes, take to him warmly. Arthur is a mean, rich drunk with the common touch: a hero for a new era. His wealth is inherited but he behaves like a stereotypical nouveau riche, which enhances the legitimacy of his privilege. Arthur is very rich and not very nice, but he is not stuck-up.

If the fast life of the in-crowd at the dawn of the Reagan era had a headquarters, it was Studio 54, the famous discothèque that opened in Manhattan in 1977. Celebrities like rock star Mick Jagger and his wife, Bianca, clothing designer Calvin Klein, and lawyer Roy Cohn, famous from his work for Senator Joseph McCarthy in the 1950s and well known in both gay and political circles, mingled beneath its glitter-ball.[7] Former antiwar radical Jerry Rubin also showed up there. Having embraced capitalism, Rubin organized what he called a "success salon," a gathering place for high-aspiring individuals who could do one another good turns.[8] The art impresario Andy Warhol (*né* Warholka) held court at Studio 54. Like Rubin, Warhol had embraced conservatism. In 1981, he attended the Reagan inaugural and announced he had "become a Republican."[9] "Money is the moment to me," he said. "Money is my mood."[10] Art critic Robert Hughes pinned him to the wall in 1982. "In politics, *Interview*"—Warhol's magazine—"has one main object of veneration: the Reagans, around whose elderly flame the magazine flutters like a moth . . . hoping for invitations to White House dinners or, even better, an official portrait commission for Warhol." Hughes found the president and the artist "both obsessed with serving the interests of privilege," and wrote that "they signify a new moment: the age of supply-side aesthetics." A master of aphorism, Warhol said, "If you want to know all about Andy Warhol, just look at the surface of my paintings and films and me, and there I am. There's nothing behind it."[11]

Cocaine fueled the speed behind both the excitements of high life and the urgencies of low life. Television star Johnny Carson, hosting the 1981 Academy Awards broadcast, joked about cocaine's prevalence in the film industry, saying that most of the Oscars were due to Columbia: "not the studio—*the country!*"[12] Everywhere there was money, there was cocaine, it seemed. In the early and mid-1980s, it was widely used among professional baseball players— most notoriously among the New York Mets (winners of the 1986 World Series). Keith Hernandez, the Mets' star first baseman, testified in court that the drug had been "a demon in me."[13] The laid-back subculture of marijuana smoking, still foregrounded and presented as rather benign in the popular 1982 film comedy *Fast Times at Ridgemont High*, was being displaced by the ravening world of cocaine.[14] In 1983, director Brian De Palma's remake of the 1930s gangster film *Scarface* hit movie screens, with the action updated to Cuban and Columbian immigrant cocaine suppliers in contemporary Miami; De Palma's film immortalized the crass excess associated with the era's new rich.[15] By 1984, the battle against drug kingpins in and around Miami became the basis for a television drama, *Miami Vice*, which featured an interracial duo of undercover cops who dressed like fashion models. The show's style resembled a music video.

In 1982, the Reagan administration commenced a new "war on drugs," one that downplayed the drug-treatment component that had been front-and-center in an earlier version of this war, under Richard Nixon's presidency.[16] Reagan focused on the cross-border trade in powder cocaine and the violent crime that attended it, as well as on marijuana use. Cocaine was streaming into the Florida peninsula in boats and planes from Columbia and Bolivia. A new South Florida Task Force, under Vice President Bush's authority, coordinated an interdiction effort by multiple government agencies. Reagan involved the navy and coast guard and had to suspend the old law of *posse comitatus* to allow this militarization of domestic law enforcement. The Task Force intercepted smugglers, seized contraband, and made arrests in steeply increasing numbers. Yet the volume of cocaine imports and consumption continued to rise. The demand seemed insatiable, and smugglers shifted their deliveries to other parts of the border. Also in 1982, Nancy Reagan began promoting an antidrug message directed at the nation's children, urging them to refuse enticements from pushers of marijuana, "angel dust" (phencyclidine), and other illicit substances. The campaign's slogan, "Just Say No," soon became a ubiquitous phrase. Similarly, in 1983, a program called Drug Abuse Resistance Education, commonly known by the acronym DARE, brought local police officers into public schools to teach a "zero tolerance" message concerning illegal drug use. The program spread rapidly in the ensuing years, although its effectiveness was disputed.[17]

By 1984, a new form of cocaine, crack, had begun an epidemic of addiction, one that reached far beyond the playgrounds of the rich. Crack was an adulterated form of the rocklike "freebase" cocaine distilled from the familiar powder, cocaine hydrochloride. It was fairly easy for those with access to powder cocaine to make either freebase or crack—and the supply of powder inside the United States grew rapidly in the 1980s; the crystal then could be broken up to produce a large number of doses, to be smoked using small pipes, from a relatively small amount of starter powder. Ricky Ross, an enterprising drug dealer in Los Angeles, was often credited as the pioneer purveyor of crack as a down-market drug. Ross would say later, "When I started getting involved with cocaine, no blacks were involved with it. . . . They felt they couldn't afford it. . . . One of the things that I felt I did was I made it affordable for minorities."[18] Ross may have sold as much as $3 million worth of cocaine per day by 1982, and he soon established a far-flung distribution network across the United States. However, some accounts contend that, with few impediments to entry into the business, crack was spread by many small operators, whose vicious competition over territory and market share likely caused the frequent murders that the crack trade seemed to entail, at least in its early years.[19] (The decline of this violence in the 1990s may have been due, in part, to the consolidation of the commerce in the hands of larger organizations.) Crack produced a swift and powerful high, as inhaling it in vaporous form allowed for efficient absorption of the drug into the vascular system through the lungs, but it also brought on nightmarish and paranoid hallucinations, often involving insects or other creatures crawling under one's skin. It was, at least for some users, very addictive. But even if one rock was easily affordable at a cost of $10—and still falling, by the later 1980s—addicts' savings and lives were easily wrecked by the terrible, endless compulsion for more.

Middle-class America became aware of crack starting in 1986, when media portraits of the inner-city trade and its destructive social consequences began to appear. The best-known was a CBS television news special, "48 Hours on Crack Street," which set a sensational tone that persisted in frightening claims that a generation of "crack babies," addicted in utero, born to poor urban mothers, then often to be abandoned to a hobbled future, lay in store.[20] Crack was a major problem, particularly among the urban poor. In 1990, police drug testing of arrestees in seven of America's eight biggest cities showed that an eye-popping 49 percent tested positive for cocaine, and the largest component of this was almost surely due to crack.[21] Stories of grandparents, sometimes grandmothers alone, taking in and raising children of their own crack-addicted children became commonplace. At the same time, some found the attention lavished on crack excessive, suggesting either that the long-term impact of early exposure to crack was uncertain, or that the economic and political abandonment of America's inner cities (for liberals) or family breakdown (for conservatives), rather than crack, was the main source of urban social ills. Critics from the left, as well as libertarians, would come to see the preoccupation with crack as a pretext for an unwarranted escalation of police activity.[22] Community leaders in America's poorest urban areas, however, generally saw crack as a real emergency.

Judges and legislators swung into action against the drug scourge, sometimes taking steps with broad consequence. The U.S. Supreme Court loosened restrictions on police searches and on the ability of prosecutors to use evidence gained improperly. In *Illinois v. Gates* (1983), the Court, by a vote of 6–3, made the "totality of the circumstances" the criterion for judging whether a warrant truly described the "probable cause" needed for a search, dispensing with more specific requirements. In *United States v. Leon* (1984), the same six justices held that even if a search warrant did not show probable cause under the new rule, evidence resulting from the search in question still might be admitted into court, so long as the police officer who wielded the warrant plausibly showed "good faith" that he believed the warrant was valid. This ruling, by placing great legal weight on the policeman's word, weakened the so-called exclusionary rule, long a mainstay of protection against police authorities under the Constitution's Fourth Amendment. Democrats and Republicans in Washington worked together to pass the Bail Reform Act of 1984, the U.S. Sentencing Reform Act of 1984, the Anti–Drug Abuse Act of 1986, and other tough-on-crime measures. These laws established mandatory minimum prison sentences for crimes of drug possession and distribution. The "mandatory minimums" punished crack offenses far more harshly than those involving powder cocaine, a difference in treatment that produced huge disparities in prison time between black and white drug felons. At the time, these new sentencing requirements were supported by about half the members of the Congressional Black Caucus, frantic over the effects of crack in their urban districts.[23]

Cocaine, in one form or another, became a fixture in the recreations of many young Wall Street professionals, riding high in the new era of swashbuckling finance. Tom Wolfe satirized them as Masters of the Universe (the brand name of a line of children's action toys) in his 1987 novel, *The Bonfire of the Vanities*.[24] Journalist Michael Lewis, who spent time working on Wall Street, reported that bond traders called themselves Big Swinging Dicks.[25] After spending the 1970s in the doldrums, the stock market was coming on like gangbusters. Capitalism, subjected to moral and cultural criticism in the 1960s and 1970s by a generation longing for a simpler and more ethical life, received a fresh blessing from the highest levels of American leadership in the 1980s. A celebration of finance and its captains gripped America's media with an intensity unmatched since the 1920s. Dealmakers like Donald Trump, T. Boone Pickens, and Carl Icahn became culture heroes, appearing on the covers of news magazines and publishing bestsellers under their names. Ivy League graduates clamored for jobs at investment banks and management-consulting firms. Ivan Boesky, a prominent risk arbitrageur—really just a stock speculator—who craved acceptance in polite society, reached his pinnacle when he was invited to speak at the commencement ceremonies at the University of California at Berkeley in 1986. Here was the consummate triumph of American capitalism, capturing what had been the stronghold of the radical left. Only a couple of lines from Boesky's remarks were remembered. "Greed is all right, by the way," he said. "I want you to know that. I think greed is healthy. You can be greedy and still feel good about yourself." Despite the references Reaganites frequently made to Adam Smith, their invocation of unbounded selfishness as a social good owed more to Ayn Rand. A 1981 statement by a Texas group calling itself the Institute for Christian Economics was typical: "The man who makes the highest profit is the man who is best serving the public."[26]

Boesky had strong ties to the world of mergers and acquisitions (M&A), which was where much of the real action was in finance during the 1980s. Twenty-nine percent of the biggest 500 companies in the country in 1980—144 corporations—were targeted for acquisition in the 1980s, and 125 of these efforts succeeded. The Reagan administration was friendly to the new takeover wave. The Securities and Exchange Commission signaled its relaxed vigilance; the Justice Department dropped a long-running antitrust suit against International Business Machines (IBM) when Reagan took office.[27] M&A specialists ran up stock prices as they bought shares. Needing to raise huge sums to buy stock, the takeover engineers bypassed traditional commercial banks by going to investment banks, who underwrote bonds purchased by lenders. The new owners might then split up multidivisional companies and sell the pieces for a higher total value than the conglomerate had fetched. Often the liquidation of assets was required to pay off the creditors who had financed the takeovers. By the end of the decade, about one-third of the corporations that had existed in 1980 had vanished.[28] The big fees and commissions to be had from M&As, no matter their ultimate outcome, gave everyone in the financial sector an incentive to promote takeovers. Some viewed the takeover artists negatively. Participants in the annual conference staged by Drexel Burnham Lambert, the firm powered by Michael Milken, known as the "king" of the new realm of finance, called it "the predators' ball," reveling in their image as brigands. But many hailed the movement, saying it forced efficiency on lazy companies. Milken was an innovator. He raised prodigious sums for his clients by floating high-yield or junk bonds, meaning they promised a high interest rate to purchasers because the risk of default by the issuing company was also high. But Milken persuaded a growing audience that the risk was far lower than the ratings agencies thought. As the sums he brokered grew ever larger, so did his power in the financial markets. He grew able to bribe and coerce his customers into buying his bonds. He could make or break companies.

However, admiration for the wealthy coexisted with resentment toward them. This ambivalence was true not only of the stupendously wealthy like Boesky or Trump, a real estate developer preoccupied with his own celebrity. These mixed feelings also applied to the broader ranks of successful professionals who snapped up depressed urban real estate and drove European cars through dilapidated streets to and from their law offices, medical practices, and brokerages. These were the "yuppies," a term that came into wide use in the early 1980s, shorthand for "young upwardly mobile professional" or "young urban professional." Yuppies drew sharp anger from the start over their conspicuously high-end consumption, their sense of entitlement, and their real estate incursions into urban neighborhoods with "texture" and "potential"—from Boston's

South End to Brooklyn's Park Slope to Manhattan's Lower East Side to Chicago's Hyde Park, and on to Seattle, San Francisco, and points between. Coastal living, however, was strongly favored. It was hard to be a proper yuppie in Cincinnati or Omaha. Yuppies drove up rents and drove out poorer tenants, whether older people in "white ethnic" neighborhoods, African Americans, or university students. Old industrial lofts, once associated with penurious artists, were gutted to make way for refinished wood floors and modern bathroom fixtures (with brick walls left exposed). Other buildings were demolished, and luxury condominiums built in their place. *Newsweek* declared 1984 the "year of the yuppie."[29] But by decade's end, the caustic, only partly ironic cry of "Die, yuppie scum!" became a familiar refrain. Such protests struck glancing blows, at most, to yuppie self-esteem, however. Middle-class multitudes still aspired to yuppiedom.

For others as well, the 1980s were a great party. These included young conservative activists who, bankrolled by generous donors, started right-wing publications at elite universities. Their favorite targets were affirmative action, white antiracism, and curricular innovations that moved higher education away from the familiar names known sweepingly as "dead white men." All these things were degradations of the higher learning, according to the young movement cadres. The best known training ground for conservative publicists was the *Dartmouth Review*, begun in 1980. Under Dinesh D'Souza's editorship, the *Review* published a satirical piece in 1982 entitled "Dis Sho Ain't No Jive, Bro," intended to mimic the speech of supposedly illiterate African American students. In a lame imitation of black urban dialect, the author wrote, "Dese boys be sayin' that we be comin' here to Dartmut an' not takin' the classics. You know, Homa, Shakesphere; but I hea' dey all be co'd in da ground, six feet unda, and whatchu be askin' us to learn from dem?"[30] The young provocateurs postured as brave souls willing to speak truths others preferred to keep hidden. The *Review*'s notoriety bought its staff tickets to the big game. D'Souza went to work for the White House in 1987; the author of "Dis Sho Ain't No Jive, Bro" became a speechwriter for Reagan's secretary of education, William Bennett. Another *Review* figure, Laura Ingraham, later clerked for a Supreme Court justice.[31] Ingraham and other young conservatives like David Brock, who arrived in Washington from Berkeley in 1986 to work at a magazine produced by the *Washington Times*, had a grand time. They caroused long into the Washington night and were feted at salons. The capital was their sandbox.

Conservative moralism was not for them. The traditional values they claimed to defend against the intellectual left were those of high culture and American patriotism, not those of private life. Only a few notable thinkers, like George Gilder, tried to reconcile the unbridled pursuit of wealth and individual happiness with moral traditionalism. The author of *Sexual Suicide* (1973) and *Wealth and Poverty* (1981), Gilder was an eccentric whose enthusiasms shifted abruptly every few years. Yet he was the best that the conservative movement could do in merging laissez-faire with Leviticus.[32] In fact, a number of well-known Washington conservatives were gay and not really closeted, a reality that ill comported with the Reaganite refrain of "traditional values," a phrase that certainly denoted compulsory heterosexuality. Highly placed gay conservatives, who could be rather openly gay so long as they stayed in Washington, included Brock, Terry Dolan, founder of the National Conservative Political Action Committee, and Robert K. Gray, a cochairman of Reagan's first inauguration and one of the country's most powerful public-relations operatives.[33] Some gay conservatives, like Marvin Liebman, a key longtime organizer who came out in the early 1990s, tended toward libertarianism; others, like Dolan, whose brother was a White House speechwriter and a vocal advocate for conservative Catholicism, simply lived a contradiction. The most cited defense of the Western "canon" in higher education, *The Closing of the American Mind*, published in 1987, made its author, the University of Chicago philosophy professor Allan Bloom, a surprise celebrity on the lecture circuit. Bloom also was gay, as his friend, the novelist Saul Bellow, revealed to the public after Bloom's death, in a book whose lead character was based on Bloom.[34] An impassioned defender of ancient Greek philosophy who had sought to cleanse Plato's writings of the encrustation of later Christian ideas, Bloom was a hero suited to the pagan ambience of some of movement conservatism's inside circles in Reaganism's heyday. Gay conservatives and many of Reaganism's intellectual cadres, whatever their sexuality, were linked by their alienation from the small-town ways that Reagan and many of his Christian followers championed.

Bellow also disclosed, in his novel, *Ravelstein*, that Bloom had died from the consequences of Acquired Immunodeficiency Syndrome (AIDS).[35] The quickening whirlwind of the AIDS tragedy intensified the pathos of gay conservatism in the 1980s, pushing the conservative inner conflict between individualism and traditionalism perilously close to the surface of public discussion. AIDS killed Dolan in late 1986. It killed Roy Cohn the next year. Terry Dolan's brother, Anthony, protested vigorously when the *Washington Post*, after Terry's death, wrote of Terry's homosexuality.[36] Pat Buchanan, another conservative Catholic who had replaced David Gergen as White House communications director in 1985, mourned Dolan. Yet Buchanan had commented, in a 1983 newspaper piece, "The poor homosexuals—they have declared war on nature, and now nature is exacting an awful retribution."[37] Many conservatives viewed the AIDS epidemic—whose first signs appeared in America in 1981 in New York City and San Francisco—as the wages of sin. Edmund Morris, President Reagan's official biographer, reported that he witnessed Reagan make jokes about AIDS "as late as December 1986, and five months after that wax biblical in his opinion that 'maybe the Lord brought down this plague'" to bring Americans back to the straight and narrow path.[38] William F. Buckley Jr., the most respected conservative intellectual in the country, said in 1986, "Everyone detected with AIDS should be tattooed in the upper forearm, to protect common-needle users, and on the buttocks, to prevent the victimization of other homosexuals."[39] Gay conservatives, for the most part, simply endured this condemnation silently. Conservatives shrouded in silence the suffering of gay AIDS victims who were fellow movement cadres. When Terry Dolan was alive, the playwright and gay activist Larry Kramer chanced upon him at a Washington party in 1984 and threw a drink in his face. "You take the best from our world and then do all those hateful things against us," Kramer upbraided Dolan. "You should be ashamed."[40]

If fiscal irresponsibility was the great open secret of Reaganism in policy terms, hedonism was conservatism's open secret in the realm of culture and values. Only when discussing economic theory would conservatives, in the 1980s, propagate the doctrine of the individual's liberation from society's mores. Hedonism was, of course, the exclusive property of no one sexual community. Yet conservatives sometimes talked as if it were; moral traditionalists often identified gay life in particular with sexual chaos and cultural decay. They feared the social and moral effects of any sexuality detached from the imperative to reproduce—a fear they sometimes applied to heterosexual life, criticizing sexual liberation in general—but they saw homosexuality as a pure expression of this supposedly cataclysmic tendency. What they defined as gay decadence was, evidently, the only variety of hedonism they felt totally free to condemn in tones that approached those of genuine hate. Traditionalists drew a hetero-normative lesson from the AIDS plague, one they sometimes delivered, as in Buckley's and Buchanan's comments, with terrible scorn and a striking lack of sympathy for human suffering. It was as if the conservative moralists displaced onto gay men their anguish over the all-embracing hedonism with which they, the traditionalists, had made their political bed. If someone had to pay for the strategically crucial entente between traditionalism and hedonism, that someone would be gay.

The symptomatology of AIDS became clear to scientists fairly quickly, after an initial period of alarmed perplexity. At first the disease went by a series of names, including "gay cancer." Among the early signs of the syndrome was a spike in cases of a previously exotic skin cancer, Kaposi's sarcoma, which produced tell-tale purple lesions. Gradually, researchers concluded that something, probably an infectious agent like a virus, was disabling the immune systems of victims, almost all of them intravenous (IV) drug users or gay men with prodigious sexual histories. (This thesis was soon confirmed, with the virus ultimately named the Human Immunodeficiency Virus, or HIV.) A horrible set of ailments struck those afflicted, often starting with chronic diarrhea and recurrent pneumonias, progressing to utter bodily breakdown. "It's the worst way I've ever seen anyone go," said one doctor. "I've seen young people die of cancer. But this is total body rot."[41] The incubation period for HIV turned out to be as long as ten years, and epidemiologists feared that early death tolls from AIDS offered only a hint of a far darker future. AIDS felled over nine hundred Americans in 1982, almost five thousand in 1984, almost twelve thousand in 1986, and more than eighteen thousand in 1988. By the end of the 1980s, the total fatalities numbered over one hundred thousand.[42] Most Americans were insulated from HIV. But among gay men—and, as time passed, among IV drug users and those intimate with them—AIDS became a veritable holocaust. Only medieval plagues and modern geno-cides approximated the environment of radical depopulation inhabited by at-risk groups, and these became the most common metaphors used to describe the experience.

Gay men's widespread commitment to sexual liberation, a legacy of the opprobrium and repression they had experienced all their lives, spelled disaster once HIV was loosed. As more gay Americans had moved out of the closet during the 1970s, Christian conservatives had mobilized against them, charging that gay men and women had designs on straight America's children. Slandered as pederasts and grotesques, some gay men, specifically in New York City and San Francisco—the great centers of gay life (about 20 percent of San Franciscans were gay in 1980)—cre-ated pleasure domes where they could do openly what they and those who shared their sexuality had had to do secretly.[43] To many, the ideology of gay liberation (as with more general ideas of sexual liberation) meant freedom from bourgeois ideas about monogamy and sexual self-control. Gay activists who called for changes in sexual practices found themselves labeled reactionaries, even "sexual Nazis."[44] Larry Kramer, who sounded the alarm early in New York, became an outcast for his denunciations of gay (and straight) insouciance. Gay bathhouses, venues for anonymous sexual encounters, were big financial contributors to gay organizations and were not about to close up shop; they intimidated public-health offi-cials from moving against them. Gay organizations first denied the reality of the problem, and then fixated on the menacing possibility that those with AIDS might be rounded up and put in concentration camps. This idea was only a horrible nightmare, not a real possibility—although a *Los Angeles Times* poll of 1985 suggested that half of Americans would support a quarantine of AIDS sufferers.[45] In 1984, the publisher of the *New York Native*, an important gay newspaper, asked James Curran, the top AIDS official at the U.S. Centers for Disease Control, "Now that you've suc-ceeded in closing down the baths"—which neither Curran nor anyone else had done—"are you preparing the boxcars for relocation?"[46] How-ever, despite the denial and political obstructionism of some outspoken activists, as early as 1983 gay men's culture showed signs of change, as condom use gained popularity and long-term monogamy acquired new allure.[47]

Medical science outpaced political will where AIDS was concerned. Most public officials were completely irresponsible. Mayor Dianne Feinstein of San Francisco distinguished herself by supporting obvious public-health measures, even when her public-health officials refused to act. By mid-1983, San Francisco had appropriated as much money to spend on AIDS, mainly on hospital care and outpatient services, as the National Institutes of Health had spent on AIDS research.[48] But New York City, where the biggest number of AIDS cases appeared, was burdened with a leader, Mayor Edward Koch, who seemed terrified that serious action on his part would refresh rumors about his own sexuality.[49] New York City did nothing about the disease until well past mid-decade. In Washington, Reagan refused to speak of AIDS and well-intentioned officials within the national public-health bureaucracy were hamstrung by White House coldness on the issue. AIDS researchers were desperate. Reagan was an old man; his apparent discomfort with any subject linked to gay sex was unsurprising and did not make him stand out. Journalists and newspaper editors proved squeamish about printing words like "semen" and "anal intercourse," thus encouraging public misunderstanding. The euphemism "bodily fluids" led some to think, incorrectly, that people could get AIDS through saliva or sweat. News outlets were reluctant even to say that the disease was primarily killing gay men. One gathering of several thousand gay men to protest public inaction in 1983 was described in the *New York Times* simply as "mostly male."[50] An editor at *Advertising Age* wrote, in a 1985 cri de coeur:

> I am tired of compiling lists of the dead. They are actors and writers and designers and dancers and editors and retailers and decorators and sometimes when you see their names in the obituary pages of the *Times* you think, yes, I knew that fellow. . . . The dead are homosexuals who have contracted and will perish from AIDS. Almost everyone who knew them knows this, but there is a gentle, loving conspiracy of silence to deny reality. . . . Men are dying and we in the press cough politely and draw curtains of discretion across the truth.[51]

Public debate shifted abruptly in July 1985, when the news media reported that Rock Hudson (a friend of the Reagans) was being treated for AIDS in Paris. Suddenly U.S. Representative Henry Waxman, Democrat of California, who had been among the most aggressive members of Congress in seeking to press additional funds upon the administration for AIDS research, found that a Sunday-morning television news show wanted him as a guest to talk about the issue. The show's producer warned Waxman, however, "Of course, if it turns out that Rock Hudson doesn't have AIDS, we're going to cancel the show."[52] Hudson did die of AIDS, in October, and the rush of news outlets to cover the story was ferocious. Hudson was a household name with a longstanding image of heterosexual virility, notwithstanding the sudden revelation of his homosexuality. The magic of celebrity made straight Americans feel that AIDS had killed someone they knew or liked, and the news media lost its fear of covering the story's basic realities. The new course of public discussion was not wholly positive. Most Americans were at low risk of contracting HIV. The refrain that AIDS "could strike anyone," which some AIDS activists encouraged for the empathy it inspired with AIDS sufferers, received new impetus and may have worsened the public hysteria about how easily transmissible HIV was.

In spite of the dawning sympathy many felt for AIDS sufferers, the panic seemed to peak in 1986 and 1987. In June 1986, the U.S. Supreme Court, in *Bowers v. Hardwick*, upheld the conviction of a Georgia man under a state antisodomy law. A police officer had entered the man's home and then his bedroom, found him in flagrante delicto with another man, and arrested them both. At the time of *Bowers*, over twenty states had similar laws in place, virtually never enforced. The laws generally outlawed some opposite-sex activity as well as same-sex acts, but the five justices who supported *Bowers* basically ignored this point and focused on gay sex, which they asserted enjoyed no protection under the canopy of privacy rights. Americans had no "fundamental right to engage in homosexual sodomy," wrote Justice Byron White, the decision's author. Chief Justice Warren Burger, in a concurring opinion, cited "millennia of moral teaching" to support his position and quoted the view of the eighteenth-century legal authority William Blackstone that sodomy was "an infamous crime against nature." In response to this festival of verbal gay-bashing from the nation's High Court, Justice Harry Blackmun read part of his dissent from the bench, decrying the majority's "almost obsessive focus on homosexual activity."[53] The simultaneous, rampant fear of AIDS may have been mere coincidence—but, then again, perhaps not. The fear extended to all those with HIV. Perhaps the most notorious incident concerned the Ray family of Arcadia, Florida, whose three sons, hemophiliacs who had contracted the virus through blood transfusions, were expelled from their local public school in the fall of 1986. When the Rays successfully petitioned the courts for permission to send their sons back to school, other parents organized a boycott, which kept about half the district's pupils home out of fear of catching HIV. The drama culminated when someone set the Rays' home afire, driving them out of the area.[54] Almost all Americans were appalled at this violence—and commentary did not fail to mention that these boys were "innocent" victims of HIV—but many quietly empathized with those who were terrified of contact with HIV carriers.

Those who saw the conservative movement as their sworn enemy—including most gay Americans, African Americans, and feminists—perceived the 1980s as a dark time politically and socially. This perspective was also shared by many academics in the nation's universities, institutions that were, in the 1980s, rather hospitable both to many members of these largely oppositional groups and to far-reaching social criticism. Yet it was, perhaps paradoxically, an exciting time as well for many academic professionals. These were the salad days of "theory," a general term used to refer to the wave of difficult literary and interpretive concepts that had migrated belatedly to America from France, bringing a new charge of energy to the humanities. The ideas most often discussed were deconstruction and postmodernism. Such theories exposed hidden instabilities and contradictions in what had seemed expressive and metaphysical certainties. Language was cast as arbitrary and evasive, signifying no deeper and firmer reality. The very idea of the stable subject, the idea of "I," essential to the entire Enlightenment project of emancipating the individual and achieving freedom, was now, for some thinkers, a pretender to be unmasked, its deceptions revealed. Authenticity and originality were just conjuring tricks; the truth was that all selves were "performative," and all performance a pastiche of "dead styles," as Frederic Jameson put it.[55] To some, the writings of Don DeLillo reflected the cool postmodernism of American fiction in the 1980s, conveying minimalist style and emotional detachment. *White Noise*, his 1985 novel, updated the well-worn genre of the liberal arts college comedy. Its protagonist, Jack Gladney, is an academic entrepreneur who founds the field of Hitler Studies, in a parody that soon would seem only too plausible. A mysterious airborne cloud of toxic chemicals hovers over the action, creating a sense of dread anxiety over sickness and pollution.[56] Postmodernism was a stance and mood that had made its peace with the unattainability of moral integrity; no more heroic defeat, no more angst. Many postmodernists styled themselves radicals, but they were radicals who deemed the political left—bound to the Enlightenment tradition—part of the problem, not the solution.[57]

The ambiguous radicalism of postmodernism was underlined by the sympathy with which some young female intellectuals viewed it, at a time when the feminist movement confronted the challenge of generational change. Postmodernism, with a crazy-quilt emphasis on borrowings from disparate sources and surprising juxtapositions, gleefully tore down the hierarchy of high versus popular arts. But postmodernism also dissolved conventional ideas of oppression and freedom. Some younger women were drawn to a creed that made sport of male-dominated traditions of high art and politics. But it was more postfeminist than feminist, because the feminist tradition itself was rooted in Enlightenment ideals. The postfeminist moment found young women suspended between rebelliousness and disillusionment. In the low-budget but influential 1983 film *Liquid Sky*, the protagonist, Margaret—raped and otherwise abused in the drug-saturated downtown Manhattan fashion scene—takes revenge on predatory men as space aliens begin to kill her sexual partners when they experience orgasm. Margaret finally delivers a memorable postfeminist soliloquy:

> So I was taught that I should come to New York, become an independent woman. And my prince would come, and he would be an agent, and he would get me a role, and I would make my living waiting on tables. I would wait—till thirty, till forty, till fifty. And I was taught that to be an actress, one should be fashionable, and to be fashionable is to be androgynous. And I am androgynous not less than David Bowie himself. And they call me beautiful, and I kill with my cunt. Isn't it fashionable?[58]

The edgy and irreverent qualities of postmodernism made it seem, to some, like a natural fit with the newer forms of academic progressivism.

But progressivism, in the end, made no sense if one found the concept of progress ridiculous.

The themes of performance and pastiche led the 1980s culturally, but not without artistic originality. While Bruce Springsteen strove for authenticity with his anthems and dirges of American losers yearning for comfort, the other performers who equaled or exceeded his success in the decade were the avatars of performance—Michael Jackson, Madonna, and Prince. All three were born in 1958. Each built a powerful retail brand. Madonna Ciccone and Prince Nelson simply went by their first names. They were the pure examples, masters of stage personae who toyed with gender roles in public and forthrightly rejected the racial divide that long had structured American music, like so much else in American life. In 1980 one music critic remarked, "Seldom in pop-music history has there been a larger gap between what black and white audiences are listening to than there is right now." African Americans were becoming more interested in rap, while many young whites were absorbed in European technopop–influenced New Wave bands like Talking Heads and Devo.[59] No informed observer could describe such a division in 1990. The music industry in the 1980s moved toward blockbuster albums that generated multiple hit singles, and the leading artists in this trend either were African American or drew white and black audiences together, or both.

Madonna, with a series of dance hits from her self-titled debut album of 1983 and her distinctive personal style, showcased in MTV (Music Television, a cable channel that started broadcasting in 1981) videos, instantly became a postfeminist icon. Her funky, layered look, "thrift store chic" (also popularized, with different inflections, by Cyndi Lauper and the Go-Go's, other white female acts), spread like wildfire among teenage girls.[60] With her second album, *Like a Virgin* (1984), Madonna became controversial and revealed herself as a quick-change artist. For cultural conservatives, the title track's flagrant sexuality was a sign of decadence; for feminists, the notion that a woman, presumably experienced in sex, would long to feel *like* a virgin was reactionary. Liberals and conservatives alike were also irritated by the other big hit from the album, "Material Girl," in which the singer explains that she sees men as meal tickets. The video for the song was an homage to the Marilyn Monroe dance number "Diamonds Are a Girl's Best Friend," from the 1953 comedy *Gentlemen Prefer Blondes*.[61] In 1989, the title song of a new album, *Like a Prayer*, and its accompanying video, showed an artist interested in continuing to tweak the conventions of many Americans—and with a social awareness previously hidden from view. In the video, Madonna prays to and loves a black man who appears alternately as a wooden saint and as a flesh-and-blood innocent victimized by an implicitly racist criminal-justice system. The Detroit-area native sings and dances joyfully with an African American gospel choir and stands dramatically in front of a range of burning crosses. Conservative Christians and those uncomfortable with interracial crossover—particularly between a white woman and a black man—were unhappy.[62] At the video's end, red stage curtains descend and the performers take a bow. It is just a show.

The extremely prolific Prince seemed a walking encyclopedia of musical styles, rapidly producing albums, starting in the late 1970s, that integrated funk, heavy metal guitar, psychedelic rock, electronica, and other styles into what was known, for a time, as "the Minneapolis Sound" (named for his hometown). Prince worked with a large, often changing, and usually racially diverse ensemble—known, until 1986, as the Revolution—that recalled the influence of Sly and the Family Stone and George Clinton's Parliament-Funkadelic. His 1982 album, 1999, was his breakthrough to the mass market, but the 1984 soundtrack album to his feature movie vehicle, *Purple Rain*, was part of a bigger, multimedia blitz. Prince always put himself front-and-center, posing in one overtly artistic stance after another on his album covers. His songs consistently earned "explicit" ratings for their sexual content, and he was daring in his sexual self-presentation. Prince took this tendency furthest in his nude pose on the cover of 1988's *Lovesexy*, sitting among hugely enlarged images of flower petals. His musically conjured couplings always seemed to be heterosexual; his goal, it seemed, was to confound stereotyped images of male heterosexuality. Eventually, he would change his name legally to an unpronounceable "Love Symbol," as he called it, created, according to some, by combining signs representing male and female.[63]

But Michael Jackson was the biggest star of the 1980s, his career at its meteoric, unsurpassed height between his smash album *Thriller* (1982) and his follow-up, *Bad* (1987).[64] He became known as "the King of Pop" and was celebrated by presidents. In 1984, Jackson came to the White House garbed in a bright blue tuxedo jacket festooned with gold epaulets, braid, and sash, his right hand alone gloved in white, and accepted an award for his donations to drug- and alcohol-addiction rehabilitation centers. *Thriller* was a true phenomenon. "[I]t became a hydra-headed monster . . . begetting seven top 10 singles, and, at one point, luring one million buyers a week." It remains the biggest-selling album ever.[65] Jackson's dance performances and the videos he released to accompany his singles were inseparable from the album's success. The videos for *Thriller* were the first to bring feature-film production values to the form. The first one, for "Billie Jean," shows Jackson as an otherworldly being, dancing alone on the edges of an unreal, blighted city, the sidewalk squares lighting up when his feet touch them, the pavement a magic hopscotch course. The song's beat is steady and insistent, an immediately infectious dance rhythm. Synchronized with the visuals and music are Jackson's remarkably precise dance steps and vocals. His voice was emotionally intense and assertive as never before. Few commented on the song's lyrics, in which Jackson angrily rejects a woman's paternity claims. Jackson debuted what became his trademark move, the moonwalk—in which he seemed to glide, frictionless, backward over a stage while moving in a forward stride—in a much-remembered performance in 1983 in a televised celebration of Motown Studios' twenty-fifth anniversary.

Jackson's riches, and the excess of his lifestyle, became as famous as his music. In his 1984 White House appearance, he looked the part of a head of state visiting from a fantasy realm. Four years later, he purchased a large tract of land in California where he would build his "Neverland Ranch," named for the magical place in *Peter Pan* where children never grow up. Soon his changing appearance—his skin grew paler, his nose smaller and sharper, and a dimple appeared in his chin—led to rumors of plastic surgery designed to make Jackson look less stereotypically African American. He was less a master of postmodern culture than its living embodiment, a prisoner of the masks he wore, unable to switch them endlessly. What the shimmering surface covered, if anything, was unclear—and it was immaterial to his stardom. The inner life of wealth and celebrity sometimes appeared a void. There was nothing new about the search for exhilaration and satisfaction. But in the 1980s, that quest took forms shaped by Reaganism's celebration of money, power, and fame. By the decade's later years, the era's quest for gratification had burned through its initial giddiness. Whether American society as a whole was ready to turn to other pursuits was not clear. But the thrill was gone.

Days of Fear

Reaganism as a creed expressed a fierce national pride and promised an American revival, both domestically and internationally. Yet behind these positive and optimistic messages, making them matters of national urgency, lay fear—fear of national decline, of enemies abroad, of dangerous classes at home. The foreign threats, in the Reaganite view, were Communists and terrorists. Domestic fears often focused on the perceived and actual dangers of city life. But the fears swirling through American life in the 1980s also encompassed panic over predators who hunted children, sometimes far from the city. Dread of "sick" behavior and social chaos sometimes seemed vague or broadly inspired, and easily shifted from one object to another. However, at other moments the atmosphere of apprehension fixed quite consistently on specific fears. Anxieties over violence, violation, and disorder were often strongly racialized. Americans were frightened of violent crime. White Americans generally associated this threat closely with cities and with black Americans. Cities like Baltimore, Newark, Detroit, New Orleans, and Oakland seemed, to many whites, like a land that time forgot, a postindustrial stalking ground of idle, dangerous youth. Many African Americans, and sometimes members of other racial minority groups, in turn, lived in dread of violence from government authorities and vigilantes, sometimes randomly visited in efforts to bring supposedly unruly social elements to heel.

America's political elites, from Ronald Reagan downward, did not create the climate of racial fear and tension in the 1980s. The tendency to racialize social problems, especially those of social class, was the product of deep cultural dysfunctions in American life, ones with long historical roots, and this proclivity intersected with a very real crime wave that stretched from the 1960s through the 1980s. But those elites did little to stem the toxic tides of fear and anger, and probably contributed to them by responding crudely and opportunistically—sometimes on a strongly bipartisan basis—to public concerns about crime and disorder. Reagan and other conservatives in particular did give unqualified political expression to popular frustration with crime and perceived social chaos in the inner city, and to the punitive mood that fear often breeds. They also showed little interest in the wrongs committed against the poor and unlucky in the name of "getting tough." In 1981, *Time* magazine asserted that violent crime was "more brutal, more irrational, more random" than ever before; U.S. Supreme Court Chief Justice Warren Burger described a "reign of terror in American cities." In 1984, President Reagan remarked that "the American people have lost patience with liberal leniency and pseudo-intellectual apologies for crime."[1] Fear of crime was well founded in the 1980s. Yet fear and anger tend to simplify and distort perceptions of social reality, and these destructive emotions threatened to overtake American life.

Many African Americans in the 1980s felt besieged, catching the blunt end of both social disorder and the coercive efforts to curb it. This decade was "the worst period in racial relations since the 1890s," one black writer claimed.[2] Remarks like this one, if they did not offer a nuanced or reliable history lesson, nonetheless spoke the truth about the relations between Reaganism and African Americans in the 1980s. Those relations were extremely hostile. "We do not admire their president," wrote Alice Walker, the African American novelist, in 1984. "We know why the White House is white."[3] Walker did not invent the notion that Reagan—the candidate who, in 1980, initiated a tradition of Republican presidential contenders making a pilgrimage to the segregationist Bob Jones University—was a president for white America. The sociologist Andrew Hacker concluded when the 1980s were over, "One of the two major parties—the Republicans—has all but explicitly stated that it is willing to have itself regarded as a white party, prepared to represent white Americans and defend their interests."[4]

The social experience of African Americans as a whole in the 1980s was complex. Black Americans were undergoing stark class differentiation, with some sinking into immiseration and others achieving marked upward mobility. Overall, African Americans were becoming less urban. The suburban proportion of the black population in some large metropolitan areas increased markedly during the twenty years between 1970 and 1990—from 27 percent to 61 percent in the Washington, DC, area, from 25 percent to 64 percent in and around Atlanta.[5] The 1990 Census revealed that in the New York City borough of Queens, a kind of inner-ring suburb inside a huge city, and historically home to those entering the middle class, the average income of two-parent black families slightly exceeded that of married white households. The percentage of black Queensians with college degrees rose from 30 to 52 in the 1980s, and the black poverty rate for the borough fell from 13 percent to only 3 percent.[6]

A new black elite was increasingly visible. The onward march of African American politicians into elective and appointive positions, most of all in local office, continued, as the raw numbers of black public officials grew in the 1980s by approximately the same figures as in the 1970s. The total numbers rose from 1,469 to 4,607 in the 1970s, on to 7,335 in the 1980s.[7] Black mayors held office in New York, Los Angeles, Chicago, and Philadelphia in the 1980s—four of the country's five biggest cities. In 1989, Virginia, once a stronghold of segregationism, became the first state to elect a black governor, the Democrat Douglas Wilder. That same year, the writer Trey Ellis contended, "For the first time in our history we"—meaning African Americans—"are producing a critical mass of college graduates who are children of college graduates themselves." They were, he said, "the ones in the bookstore wearing little, round glasses and short, neat dreads."[8]

Even Americans who did not understand the broader class dynamics in play knew about Bill Cosby. He starred in *The Cosby Show*, a television series depicting the lives of an affluent African American physician and his family, the Huxtables, which became the nation's most watched program during its run between 1984 and 1992. The show presented itself as a kind of televised how-to manual for buppies, the popular term for black yuppies, its characters didactically venturing on outings to tasteful and expensive leisure venues. Many observers took satisfaction from the success of this depiction of wholesome and highly successful black family life. Surely it would combat negative stereotypes of African Americans. Yet, ironically, the leading study of *The Cosby Show*'s impact on white viewers concluded that it reinforced harsh racial attitudes. "The Huxta-bles proved that black people can succeed"—without the help of noisy civil rights advocates or nosy government officials—wrote the authors. "In so doing they also prove the inferiority of black people in general (who have, in comparison with whites, failed)."[9]

However, alongside the new black middle class, poverty and racial in-equality remained deep problems for African Americans, in both suburbs and inner cities. Blacks inherited older suburbs abandoned by whites in favor of newer, bigger homes built on former farmland.[10] While average incomes for African Americans, especially for married couples, contin-ued to rise as more people moved into salaried positions, in some ways this progress was stalling. The racial earnings gap between black and white men actually widened within particular occupational categories in the 1980s.[11] Single parents, most of them women, faced hard going eco-nomically, and they made up a far larger share of black families than of others. While single women headed 11 percent of white households in 1980 and 12.8 percent in 1990, they headed 37.1 percent of black house-holds in 1980 and 43.9 percent in 1990.[12]

In the cities, poverty was most concentrated and in some ways the most harrowing for those who experienced it, as negative trends of the 1970s worsened. Life in the ghetto was becoming more violent. Sanyika Shakur, a.k.a. Monster Kody Scott, would recall that clashes between Los Ange-les gangs became progressively more violent during the 1980s. Shakur turned seventeen in 1980 and was a member of the Eight Tray Gangster Crips. "Because back then," he said, referring to his early years, "if you saw somebody from an enemy set, chances are you'd just fight with 'em. . . . Whereas now—it's gunplay."[13] In 1981, Chicago's mayor, Jane Byrne, earned headlines when she and her husband lived for three weeks in an apartment in the Cabrini-Green public-housing complex. The episode only spotlighted the projects' unfitness for human life, as the Byrnes re-quired extraordinary police protection for their sojourn—protection un-available to permanent residents.[14] There, as at the Robert Taylor Homes, another huge Chicago public-housing facility, conditions were scandal-ous. Soviet urban planners had visited the Taylor Homes when they were being built in the 1950s and were shocked by the prisonlike austerity of the cinder-block walls. By the 1980s, gangs were pervasive, police were a rare sight, garbage overflowed trash chutes, plumbing facilities did not work, and children's lives were often short. In one scandalous incident that underlined official incompetence, a sea of new kitchen appliances sat rusting in water in a locked basement, ruined, animal carcasses rotting inside them, as residents made do without working stoves.[15]

Observers routinely added to their tales of decline sad commentary on the social pathologies of the long-term poor. Many conservatives—and some liberals—called this a "culture of poverty," which they blamed for the frustration of attempts to help the poor. Liberals and social democrats had first popularized the idea of a culture of poverty during President Lyndon Johnson's "War on Poverty" in the 1960s, but they had seen it as an adaptation by the poor to a long-term lack of economic opportunity, not as poverty's cause.[16] In fact, antipoverty programs and economic growth had combined to halve the official poverty rate, from 22 percent in 1960 to 11 percent in 1973. But that trend had slowed, along with economic expansion, in the mid-1970s.[17] In the 1980s, the official unemployment rate among African Americans never fell below 11 percent and rose as high as 19.5 percent in 1983.[18] In the early 1980s, amid the new conservative mood, policy debate focused on the intractability of many of the poor, who now were called an "underclass"—prolific, resentful, sometimes violent. The reporter Ken Auletta, in a series of articles published in *The New Yorker* in 1981, popularized this term and made the concept safe for liberals.[19] In 1984, Charles Murray's book *Losing Ground* captured the cultural moment. He identified Aid to Families with Dependent Children (AFDC), the joint federal/state welfare program, as the cause of an increase in family breakdown among the poor. According to Murray, welfare gave poor mothers an incentive to stay unmarried and jobless, and basically kept them poor.[20]

Murray's argument was flawed, and not only because of the actual successes of the War on Poverty. The use of AFDC, indeed, had expanded among the poor starting in the 1960s. But the decreasing presence of two-parent households among the poor, which Murray and others explained as a response to the increasing allure of welfare, continued to advance throughout the 1970s, even as the real value of welfare benefits fell. The decline of the two-parent family also appeared among the nonpoor, suggesting a noneconomic explanation. Many white Americans thought of poor welfare recipients as black, and perhaps increasingly so. While African Americans were disproportionately poor, they accounted for the same share of America's poor in 1967 and 1988; in both years, about seven of ten poor Americans were nonblack.[21] The spike in the incidence of out-of-wedlock births among black women (from 23 percent in 1960 to 62 percent in 1987) was often misunderstood. The birth rate among unmarried black women did not almost triple, as some people thought from a glance at these numbers. Instead, these figures represented an increasing proportion of all African American births to unmarried women, which was chiefly the result of a steeply declining birth rate among married black women.[22] Moreover, states with more generous welfare benefits did not have higher levels of poverty, one-parent households, or illegitimate births, which they should have if Murray's picture of the urban poor as rational calculators of economic advantage, calibrating the effects of their behavior on their income, had been true.[23]

Both critics and defenders of the welfare state, and of the poor, often slighted the perspective of poor black women, who found themselves described either as devious spongers or as botched mothers stuck in a deep cultural pit. In this regard, many African American rap music performers and black commentators like the essayist Stanley Crouch sounded like scholars funded by the conservative Manhattan Institute. The historian Tera Hunter noted in 1989 that rappers like Public Enemy (PE), in their song "She Watch Channel Zero?!," portrayed a black woman as "a self-centered zombie" who lets her children run wild in the streets while she watches television. At the same time, paradoxically, a process of class stratification by gender among African Americans produced a resentful, corrosive theme in urban culture of upwardly mobile black women as race traitors. As of 1990, almost two-thirds of all black professionals and 55 percent of black managers were women. "Now she wants a sucker but with an attaché/And if you ain't got it, she'll turn you away/You can smile with style but you lost your trial/Cause you got a gold tooth, she thinks you're wild," PE rapped in "Sophisticated Bitch."[24] White Americans, for their part, were largely oblivious to these tensions and conflicts among African Americans.

It gradually became difficult for Americans of any race to see the urban poor solely as a black underclass, however, as pedestrians in urban downtowns encountered a growing number of homeless people, a diverse group in terms of race and other factors. Individuals—and, in many fewer, but still striking, cases, parents with children—camped alongside city streets became a common sight in the 1980s. Many homeless individuals showed signs of drug addiction or mental illness. Their ranks had grown in part because somewhat radical moves toward deinstitutionalizing mental patients, begun in the 1970s, were not accompanied by public financing for the outpatient services that were necessary to make such a change of treatment regime really successful.[25] However, the proliferating homeless included some who were just too poor to pay rent, or who found the grim, sometimes dangerous housing they could afford worse than sleeping in a homeless shelter, in an abandoned building, in a train station, or out in the open. President Reagan appeared callous when he remarked in 1984 that the homeless were homeless, "you might say, by their own choice."[26] If this claim was literally true of at least some of those who were not deranged, this was because the options available to the poor in the 1980s were too often abysmal. It was absurd to think that anyone not seriously mentally ill actually wished to live on the streets. It was not the case, as some claimed, that Reagan had reduced federal funds for affordable housing. But many state governments failed to make adequate provision for the poor during the recession of the early 1980s, pushing some toward homelessness; and some Reagan administration initiatives—as when it threw hundreds of thousands of Americans off Social Security Disability Insurance—also worsened the problem.[27]

Scholars and activists debated, sometimes acrimoniously, the scale of homelessness in America during the 1980s. Estimates of the number of those without a home to call their own on a given night during the 1980s ranged from 250,000 to 2 million. Many people were homeless only for a traumatic interval of days or weeks, or else intermittently, and the composition of the total homeless population changed rapidly. It is likely, even using some of the lower figures for specific points in time, that several million Americans were homeless at some time during the 1980s. No one seriously doubted that the problem had gotten much worse. The sociologist Christopher Jencks, who made some liberals unhappy with his skeptical stance toward the larger numbers, ventured that the nation's homeless had increased from about 100,000 in 1980 to about 400,000 by 1988.[28]

By the late 1980s, a genre of social protest literature appeared, expressing outrage over the spectacle of growing homelessness in an age when wealth and acquisitiveness seemed to hold places of cultural honor. Books like *Rachel and Her Children* by Jonathan Kozol (1988) reflected widespread indignation at the plight of the homeless, focusing on the minority of the homeless with whom most Americans might most readily identify—families and those tipped into dire straits by economic circumstances.[29] Yet the public did not like encountering the homeless, most of whom were single men who sometimes panhandled aggressively and, not surprisingly, took up residence in public parks, making these places to avoid for many others. Local governments took increasingly coercive action to push panhandlers off sidewalks and to clear parks of the homeless. Los Angeles, in advance of the Summer Olympics, held in that city in 1984, did so in a particularly big offensive.[30] Americans found the problem of worsening homelessness distressing and thought it said something alarming about their society—even if they could not entirely agree about either the phenomenon's causes or its likely remedies.

The homeless found a champion in Mitch Snyder, a superb showman who led the Center for Creative Non-Violence (CCNV) in downtown Washington, DC. Early in Reagan's presidency, Snyder helped establish a tent city for homeless people in Lafayette Park, across the street from the White House. He made himself a nuisance at the highest levels, scaling the fences around the presidential residence and staging hunger strikes to bend government officials to his will. In 1984, the CCNV commandeered an abandoned U.S. government building in Washington and started using it as a homeless shelter, demanding that Reagan bless their occupation. Days before the election, Reagan did so, pledging to make the building a "model." But after his reelection, the president reneged on his promise. In 1986, Snyder, who had been influenced by radical Catholicism, publicly burned a copy of Reagan's proposed 1987 budget and smeared the ashes on the foreheads of homeless people. Snyder ultimately prevailed in this battle, as Republican senator Mark Hatfield of Oregon, a devout Christian and chairman of the Senate Appropriations Committee, produced funds to rehabilitate the downtown building. The CCNV continued to do battle with the Metro, the capital's subway system, tearing down barriers built to keep the homeless from finding protection from winter nights inside the stations.[31]

The despair of the urban poor found an analogue in the American countryside, where "towns began to resemble ghettos with boarded-up stores and abandoned buildings," as an economic crisis of debt and foreclosure sealed the fates of fast-growing numbers of family farms starting in the early 1980s.[32] Overproduction, spurred by growing world markets in the 1970s, had led to a bust; farmers had borrowed against inflated land values to expand their cultivation. The end of high inflation made it harder to earn the dollars needed to make loan payments, and continued high real interest rates gave no quarter. Farmers in the Upper Midwest started looking back to the agrarian organizing of the 1930s and earlier for political inspiration. In 1985, a group of music headliners, including country, folk, and rock acts, performed at the first Farm Aid concert, in Champaign, Illinois, to raise money and awareness for indebted farmers; Farm Aid became an annual event as well as an organization that lobbied, with modest success, for legislative relief.[33] Hollywood showed more interest in depicting the stout virtues of (white) farm families battling the forces of far-off capital—in films like *Country* and *The River* (both 1984)—than in bringing sympathetic presentations of inner-city life to the big screen. The political ferment in the Great Plains provided some unsteady moments for conservative Republicans in the farm belt in the 1980s. President Reagan showed little interest in farm policy; he considered *Country* "blatant propaganda" against his administration.[34] But he believed in free markets, and a free market, at least in land and finance, was what was killing the family farm.

With little political relief on the horizon, some in the countryside shifted hard to the right, embracing white-supremacist, survivalist politics, in groups known by the names Posse Comitatus, Aryan Nations, and Christian Identity. Occasionally, they turned to violence, as in the case of Gordon Kahl, a North Dakota man killed by federal marshals in 1983. Kahl, influenced in his youth by *The International Jew*, Henry Ford's potted version of Russian antisemitic theories of Jewish world domination, believed the U.S. government was Jew-controlled and resolved to wage an insurrection. Kahl and his son killed two marshals when they came for him at his home and then fled across the Plains, receiving shelter from a string of sympathizers before dying a fiery death in a battle in Arkansas.[35]

The anger of dispossessed farmers in the 1980s was geographically concentrated. In contrast, the intensifying fear of violent criminals who menaced the nation's children was pervasive, spreading like a powerful wave through suburbs and cities alike. In 1980, a panic spread among African Americans over a wave of kidnappings and killings of black youths in Atlanta. Many of the disappearances were likely unconnected, but the idea of a single man—or a ring of predators—stalking black boys and teenagers extended a powerful grip. Many black Americans, including the renowned author James Baldwin, speculated in macabre terms about conspiracies behind the Atlanta killings, perhaps involving government agencies.[36] A book titled *Michelle Remembers* was published in 1980, a shocking account of Satanic sexual abuse recounted from the author's childhood on the basis of "recovered" memories, previously repressed due to emotional trauma. As the years passed, a series of explosive criminal investigations captured in their nets scores of individuals, often associated with daycare facilities, accused of engaging in hundreds of rapes and ritual murders of young children—all attracting no notice until surviving children, coached by suggestive therapists, verified these fantastic stories. Several convictions occurred, resulting in long prison sentences, based on this child testimony. Americans proved willing to believe claims that tens of thousands of children per year were kidnapped, usually raped and murdered, "like garbage," said one supposed expert, even though no evidence supported such statements. Television news shows aired sensational segments with titles like *Devil Worship: Exposing Satan's Underground*. In 1984, President Reagan officiated at the opening of the National Center for Missing and Exploited Children, a private organization chartered by the government.[37]

Yet perhaps most widespread of all was Americans' fear of a violent underclass, pressing at the boundaries of its desolate urban habitat. The incidence of violent crime—murder, assault, rape, and robbery—had risen sharply, starting in the 1960s. Sociologist David Garland wrote, "From the mid-1960s onwards, rates of property and violent crime that were double and treble those of pre-war rates increasingly became an acknowledged and commonplace feature of social experience. By the early 1990s, despite some leveling off, the recorded rates were as much as ten times those of forty years before."[38] This phenomenon resulted partly from the entry of a large generation of men into the age range—roughly fifteen to twenty-five—always responsible for much of society's mayhem. But other factors, including an amorphous but widely felt decline in adult supervision of youth in the Cold War era, also contributed to the mounting violence. Many Americans viewed the famous U.S. Supreme Court decisions of the 1960s that stiffened the rights of criminal defendants, such as the *Miranda* decision of 1966, familiar to any viewer of television crime dramas, as a hindrance to police seeking to hold back a tide of barbarism. Crime rates began to drop in the early 1980s, but violence spiked one last time in the decade's second half, an upsurge widely linked to the spread of crack. Perceptions of the threat of crime became acute by the late 1970s—and stayed that way.

Always present in the minds of white Americans was the awareness that young African American men committed a disproportionately high share of violent crimes. Black men, comprising about 12 percent of American males, committed over half of all murders and about one-quarter of all rapes, according to the Census Bureau's victimization surveys.[39] The fact that blacks were the victims in most of these crimes—by 1990 young black men were murdered at seven times the rate of young white men; for black males aged fifteen to nineteen, the incidence of gunshot deaths rose an appalling 300 percent between 1984 and 1990—did little to dispel white fears of black men.[40] Many whites came to view inner cities as arenas of unremitting violence, lethal no-go zones unimaginable as settings for normal life. They wanted the police and government to push back against the crime wave.

Conservatives had advocated such a push since the 1960s. By the 1980s, public opinion had become strongly receptive to their calls.[41] Government authorities snapped into action in the 1980s, nowhere more forcefully than against black men. While African Americans may have committed about 25 percent of rapes in 1989, they accounted for about 43 percent of those arrested for this crime in that year.[42] One study, in 1989, calculated that 23 percent of all black men in their twenties were entangled in the criminal justice system—meaning that they were imprisoned, on parole, or on probation—likely several times the rate for their peers of other races.[43] Another analysis found that the proportion of black males aged eighteen to twenty-nine without high school degrees who were incarcerated almost tripled between 1980 and 1989, rising from 7.4 percent to 20.1 percent—strong evidence of a sharp police offensive directed at young black men in the 1980s specifically.[44]

City government was on the front line of the new war on crime, and in the 1980s, urban politics was racial politics. Harold Washington entered a chaotic fray in Chicago in 1983 and became that city's first black mayor; many of Chicago's white politicians deserted the Democratic Party in a desperate, failed effort to stop him. African Americans topped out at about 40 percent of Chicago's population, and Washington secured power by sealing a coalition with the city's Latino voters. But, after he died in office in 1987, the black-brown entente fell apart, and a new white-brown coalition ascended to power, giving the junior Richard Daley his father's old job.[45] In New York, the Anglo portion of the city's population fell below 50 percent during the 1980s, marking a change in the fortunes of Mayor Edward Koch.[46] For most of the decade, Koch, first elected in 1977, was king of the city, running as the nominee of both major parties when he was reelected in 1981 with 75 percent of the vote.[47] Koch had started as a liberal reform Democrat in the 1960s; but, as mayor, he was the tribune of white New York. Attending Washington's funeral in Chicago in 1987, Koch put his head in his hands and wept with abandon. It was as if he were mourning all his own spoiled promise. Eventually, many New Yorkers who had welcomed Koch's law-and-order reign threw him over in 1989 for an alternative, David Dinkins, the city's first black mayor and a politician with a style more soothing than Koch's.

Much further south, in May 1980, the Liberty City district of Miami, home to many poor black residents, witnessed the first major race riot since the late 1960s after an all-white jury acquitted five policemen who evidently had beaten a black motorcyclist, Arthur McDuffie, to death with flashlights or clubs. An eyewitness testified of the police, "They looked like animals fighting for meat." The defendants, showing an eerie confidence that they would escape punishment, incriminated each other in court, but got off clean.[48] Rioters attacked whites and Latinos, and eighteen people died; white Miamians armed themselves for battle. "Black Miami is isolated," wrote one reporter. "Walls of superhighway separate it from prosperous white Miami, where Latin tourists peel $100 notes from rolls of bills to make purchases at the expensive Omni Hotel and shoppers visit the Rolls Royce showroom on Biscayne Boulevard."[49] Latinos outnumbered African Americans by more than two to one in Dade County, where Miami was located, and blacks feared Latinos were passing them by economically. One black schoolteacher railed, "You have to be bilingual to get a decent job. Bilingual. We blacks were born and raised here. We laid every brick in this city. But if you don't speak Spanish, you can't get a job. Bilingual—!"[50]

It is hard to say whether police violence against African Americans escalated during the 1980s, although some argued that it did.[51] It was a sign of both desperation and determination among black Americans—and others disturbed by what they perceived as a newly punitive environment for people of color—that several killings of blacks by whites, not all of them police killings, became occasions for sharp protest. In 1983, Michael Stewart, a black graffiti artist or "tagger," was set upon by a group of transit police as he was tagging a wall in a lower Manhattan subway station. What some called art, most called defacing public property; many had cited the inability of city authorities to keep subway cars free of graffiti as a signal failure of authority, "a symbol that we have lost control," in the words of Richard Ravitch, the New York City transit chief.[52] The police delivered Stewart, unconscious and badly beaten, to a hospital, where he died after thirteen days in a coma. In 1985, an all-white jury acquitted the policemen of all charges.[53] Artists including the singer Michelle Shocked and the painter Keith Haring, both habitués of New York's contemporary bohemia, expressed deep anger, memorializing Stewart's killing in stark works recalling intellectuals' reactions to infamous court cases of the 1920s and 1930s. In 1988, Shocked released "Graffiti Limbo," a powerful blues rendition of the Stewart case.[54]

In 1982, an Asian American became the object of a notorious hate crime, when a white Chrysler plant superintendent, Ronald Ebens, and his stepson followed Vincent Chin through the dark streets of Highland Park, Michigan, and beat him to death with a baseball bat. They thought Chin, a Chinese American, looked Japanese; the woes of the U.S. automobile industry were often laid at the feet of the Japanese manufacturers who had gained market share in the United States and around the world. The killers escaped jail by pleading guilty to manslaughter. The sentencing judge explained that, in his view, "These weren't the kind of men you send to jail." In a later jury trial brought by the U.S. Department of Justice on civil rights charges, the two men won acquittal, shocking Asian Americans. Among those who took note was the Reverend Jesse Jackson, who appealed to Asian Americans as well as blacks and Latinos when he ran for president in 1984 and spoke of forming a "Rainbow Coalition" for social justice. He discussed the Chin case on several occasions, suggesting after the initial verdict that "it would have been a fairer trial if all the politicians, all the corporate executives, the union leaders, and the journalists who have told the American people to 'blame it on the Japanese' had stood trial with those two auto workers."[55]

The Chin killing disgusted most Americans when they learned of its details, but reactions were less united around an infamous case stemming from an incident on a New York subway car on an afternoon in December 1984. Four African American men, all aged eighteen or nineteen, approached Bernhard Goetz, a white man, tall but slightly built, with a withdrawn manner, and demanded five dollars. In 1981, Goetz had been attacked and robbed by a group of black men. On this occasion, Goetz took out a gun and shot all four of his would-be assailants. One of them, Darrell Cabey, sat slumped on a seat, doubtless stunned by the turn of events, as Goetz shot him, severing Cabey's spinal cord, leaving him paralyzed for life from the waist down. Goetz fled but turned himself in to police in New Hampshire a week later, on New Year's Eve. Goetz became a symbol—to some, a sign of frightful and probably racist vigilantism, to others, a righteous avenger of crime victims. "There is a broad sense of frustration and anger over the state of the criminal justice system, and right now people don't seem to care about the facts or whether or not Goetz used appropriate force," one television host observed.[56] Goetz stated, "I wanted to kill those guys. I wanted to maim them. I wanted to make them suffer as much as possible"—a sentiment that went far past the idea of self-defense.[57] One woman said she had heard Goetz say at a community meeting from the time before the shootings, "The only way we're going to clean up this street is to get rid of the spics and niggers."[58] In June 1987, a jury of ten whites and two Hispanics acquitted Goetz of attempted murder but convicted him of illegal gun possession, and he served eight months in prison.[59] Outside the courtroom following the verdict, white spectators held up signs reading "CONGRATULATIONS! GOETZ WINS ONE FOR THE GOOD GUYS!" A black man on the scene shouted, "Goetz is a Nazi!"[60]

Public opinion was split along racial lines, but not as severely as these incendiary comments suggested. A newspaper poll found that while 83 percent of white New Yorkers surveyed and 78 percent of Hispanic city residents supported the jury's verdict, so did 45 percent of African Americans, as against 42 percent who said the verdict was wrong—a clear racial divide, but a divide among blacks as well as between African

Americans and others. More black women than black men supported the verdict. One African American woman simply said, of Goetz, "He shot out of being scared. There were four of them against him. I would have done the same thing." It emerged that six of the twelve jurors had been victims of street crime in the past.[61] Most New Yorkers concluded that Goetz had had little responsibility to guess what degree of weaponry his presumed attackers bore before striking preemptively with anything he possessed.[62]

Koch had criticized public enthusiasm for Goetz, seeking to draw a bright line between vigilante violence and actions by his city's police, which he invariably supported. New York's mayor again denounced private-sector violence against black New Yorkers in December 1986, two years after the subway shootings. Late at night, three black men left a broken-down car on an isolated causeway that ran among sheltered channels and bays on the south side of Queens and Brooklyn. They made their way to Howard Beach, a heavily Italian American enclave, not far from John F. Kennedy International Airport. There, while the three ate at a local pizzeria, a group of white men gathered. The outsiders left the restaurant, and the small mob chased them, shouting racial epithets, catching and beating two of them. One of the victims, Michael Griffith, broke free, but was trapped between his tormentors and the Belt Parkway. He took his chances on the highway, where a car struck and killed him.[63] One week later, a protest gathering of more than five thousand protesters, led by the Reverend Al Sharpton, marched through Howard Beach, chanting, "This is not Johannesburg!"[64] Sharpton cut a startling figure for a political activist, often appearing in a polyester track suit pulled taut over his huge belly, his long tresses straightened and then gently curled and highlighted. To some, he was a reliable defender of African American interests in an era when many urban blacks felt abandoned by "established" civil rights leadership; others derided him as a clownish provocateur. He began to work closely with two lawyers, C. Vernon Mason and Alton Maddox, who represented the interests of the dead man's family. Elected officials expressed outrage at the killing. Koch called it a "lynching."[65] In 1987 and 1988, three men were convicted of manslaughter and sentenced to minimum prison terms ranging from five to ten years.[66]

If Griffith's killing made the very name Howard Beach a byword for violent racism, uniting most Americans in horror, Mason and Maddox ruined their reputations—and Sharpton did his own serious damage—with their actions in the case of Tawana Brawley, which shocked the nation. By 1987, the racially themed violence of New York had become a national media sensation, the talk of the country. The horrified fascination with these New York stories escalated further in November of that year when Brawley, a fifteen-year-old African American from the town of Wappingers Falls in Dutchess County, a largely white area of the Hudson Valley, was discovered in a shocking state: inside a plastic garbage bag, her clothes torn and burnt, smeared with excrement; someone had written KKK, NIGGER, and other slurs on her skin. Brawley was alive, but the evidence seemed to show she had been through a horrible ordeal. She had been missing for four days. She recounted that she had been kidnapped and raped by a group of white men, one of whom had a policeman's badge. Sharpton, Mason, and Maddox soon became advisors to Brawley's family. Anger over the teenager's violation and suffering then turned to confusion, as questions tumbled forth about her story. Medical examination produced no evidence of sexual assault, and Brawley had not, in fact, suffered any discernible physical injury. Brawley turned secretive about her ordeal. Her family refused to let her cooperate with investigators and repeatedly changed their version of her story. At least one witness had seen her get into the bag herself, unassisted. Journalists ultimately concluded that she had staged the entire episode, possibly as a way of escaping punishment at the hands of her mother's boyfriend after an unexplained absence from home.[67] But many African Americans had invested heavily in her story and reacted with indignation to the rising skepticism. Sharpton and his confederates pulled farcical stunts and made groundless accusations of official misconduct to distract from the truth that many people, themselves perhaps included, had been taken in.

The civic fabric, badly frayed, started to come apart, at least in New York, in the heat of 1988's summer—but now the rising specter was one of class war, not racial strife. Late one August night, 450 police officers assaulted an encampment of the homeless, rowdy music fans, drug dealers, and activists in historic Tompkins Square Park, in the then-none-too-safe Alphabet City district, east of Greenwich Village. Local residents had complained about the noise and dirt in the park. But Mayor Koch started to lose white middle-class support when the police used gross and indiscriminate violence. The attack continued into the next day. It was like a scene out of the Gilded Age. Ironically, in 1874, the city police had attacked workers and the unemployed gathered in the same park for a political rally; as if to enhance the antique aspect of the violence, in 1988, police charged into the park on horseback like Cossacks. One man whom the police beat and dragged pointed out that they had not read him his rights. "When I asked them about that, they said, 'You have no rights.'"[68] Some of those assaulted by the police responded by breaking into the lobby of a nearby condominium development, shouting, "Die, yuppie scum!" But some of the "scum" expressed misgivings about the social dynamics in which they were enmeshed. One local activist observed, "The streets were full of people who I see coming out of their houses every morning with briefcases . . . I mean people who work on Wall Street, and they're standing in the street screaming 'Kill the pigs!'"[69] The problem of maintaining public order and urban livability when the homeless had nowhere to go except public spaces lingered.

Only the resumption of gruesome crime dramas with prominent racial themes diverted attention from the saga of class reorganization that was remaking city life in America. On an April night in 1989, Trish Meili, aged twenty-eight, went running in New York's Central Park. She was attacked, raped, and beaten so badly that her skull cracked open, her brain was traumatized, and one eye came loose from its socket. Doctors were surprised that she lived. When she awoke, she had no memory of the assault. That same night saw numerous reports of roving groups of male teenagers, black and Hispanic, attacking walkers and bicyclists in the park, in a violent spree that was labeled "wilding." The police swept up about thirty black and brown youths, and five of them—all African Americans, aged fourteen to sixteen—confessed to raping Meili, who was white. The furor was tremendous. Linda Fairstein, an assistant district attorney who headed a successful sex-crimes unit, employed questionable tactics, concealing the discovery that DNA analysis of the semen taken from Meili ruled out the "Central Park Five" as the rapists. The confessions were products of high-pressure police methods. The five defendants were convicted and imprisoned. Only many years later, after another man confessed to the rape and said he had acted alone—and after the genetic evidence was shown to match his DNA and to have come from only one man—were the prisoners freed and the convictions vacated.[70] Those who remembered the atmosphere surrounding the crime in 1989 recalled it as almost like a fever, a delirium of fear and anger.[71]

The era's roiling racial discord received a lasting memento in June 1989 with the premiere of *Do the Right Thing*, a feature film directed by a young African American auteur named Spike Lee. The excited response from critics and audiences reflected the resonance of the material presented in a flawed, sometimes crude picture. *Do the Right Thing* renders a tableau of Bedford-Stuyvesant, a poor, black Brooklyn neighborhood, at the center of which stands a pizzeria run by Sal, an Italian American, and his family. Sal sees himself as a benign padrone, but many of his customers and his employee, Mookie, see him as an alien, exploitative presence. Sal's son, Pino, expresses his visceral hatred for the black neighborhood and its residents with an explicitness rarely given voice on the screen. The film culminates in a demonstration against Sal's that ends in violence: the police strangle a young black man in a clear reference to Michael Stewart, and Mookie (played by Lee) leads the mob in destroying the restaurant where he works. They shout "Howard Beach! Howard Beach!" At the end of a scene in which Mookie warns his unbelieving sister that Sal's attentions to her are sinister, the characters exit the screen, revealing a bitter graffito spray-painted on a brick wall: "TAWANA TOLD THE TRUTH!"[72]

The film's soundtrack featured a new song, "Fight the Power," by Public Enemy, whose growing celebrity marked a coming-of-age for rap music. Few could have predicted that rap music, part of a broader urban hip-hop milieu, would prove the era's most enduring and influential cultural form. Most radio stations long resisted giving rap much airtime; MTV all but refused to broadcast rap videos until 1988.[73] But its spreading popularity was unstoppable. The hip-hop world began in diversity, a mix of styles devised by African Americans, Jamaican immigrants, and Puerto Ricans, its seedbed the South Bronx. But as rap took off commercially, its blended origins were often forgotten. By the late 1980s, hip hop had shifted from its early emphasis on good times to an angry register, increasingly providing an outlet for expressions of alienation by young (usually male) African Americans.

PE, who followed up their first album, *Yo! Bum Rush the Show* (1987), with 1988's *It Takes a Nation of Millions to Hold Us Back*, made plain its admiration for the Reverend Louis Farrakhan, the leader of the black-nationalist Nation of Islam and a perfectly controversial figure, routinely accused of antisemitism, not without good reason. Yet PE's music was powerful, and white and black critics and fans alike gave it a positive verdict. Never before had a rap group had a charismatic front man like Chuck D, PE's lead singer. His deep, booming, rapid-fire delivery, with police sirens in the background, made PE's music riveting. The group had a talent for phrasemaking; not only "Fight the Power" but also "Don't Believe the Hype," and other song titles took on life outside their original contexts. In the late 1980s, when urban black youth perceived in Farrakhan one of the few leaders unashamed to be seen in their company, PE succeeded more because of its embrace of him than in spite of it. This association served to verify their "street cred," which was important in light of PE's many Jewish friends and backers as well as Chuck D's middle-class upbringing in Long Island's (segregated) suburbs. His sidekick, Flavor Flav, played jester, expressing serious truth from beneath a comic appearance. At the close of "Bring the Noise," a track from *It Takes a Nation of Millions*, Flav says, "Yo, we ain't goin' out like that." Here was a defiant vow for a generation of young men of color who saw themselves marked for an early demise.

But PE's politicized rap did not maintain its prime position for long. Gangsta rap, born of the black districts of Los Angeles and soon known as West Coast rap, seized the hip-hop baton in 1988 with the release of *Straight Outta Compton* by Niggaz With Attitude, or NWA, the group's very name a ceaseless provocation.[74] With blunt titles like "Fuck tha Police," the group issued gut-level responses to their era. Rappers like Ice Cube and Eazy-E intensified rap's portrayal of women as mere sexual accessories to an outlaw lifestyle. At the same time, they told the story of deindustrialization and presented criminal activities as the only viable path to self-sufficiency and self-respect for many of their peers. "Fuck flippin' burgers/I deserve a 9-to-5 I can be proud of," sang Dr. Dre.[75] This new guard had witnessed the rise of a high-technology surveillance regime pioneered by the Los Angeles police and the State of California. By the late 1980s, West Coast units of government had deployed sophisticated databases, arresting thousands of black and brown youths for their alleged conformity to a "gang profile," which might mean wearing the wrong clothes or having the wrong hairstyle. Those detained were often released, but their data was now in the system, smoothing the path for future arrests, convictions, and harsh sentencing.[76]

African Americans in the nation's cities felt pressed, on one side, by a hostile white society and police forces that often acted like occupying armies and, on the other, by new immigrant groups that were reclaiming urban turf from economic bleakness and were hailed by many whites as proof that America's promise remained bright. This was a low-wattage form of gentrification—reclamation of land not by wealthy yuppies but by members of "buffer" races and ethnicities, not black but also not white. Black Americans saw praises sung to the virtues of Korean shopkeepers as an implicit rebuke to them; the immigrants had the right values, it was said, and therefore they thrived, at least in relative terms. Koreans and other immigrants also often arrived in the United States with at least modest capital in hand, and were known for pooling their resources in communal loan arrangements.[77]

The 1980s saw the biggest wave of immigrants arrive in the United States since the 1910s and would push the foreign-born share of the U.S. population to almost 8 percent by decade's end, a level not seen since the 1940s.[78] The United States had first relaxed a previously restrictive immigration law in 1965, but not until at least a decade after that change did very large numbers of migrants once again begin entering the country from abroad. They were a heterogeneous group, mainly from Latin America, the Caribbean, and East Asia and the Pacific. The Latin American and Caribbean share of the country's foreign-born population rose from 33 percent to 44 percent during the 1980s, the Asian share from 19 percent to 26 percent. Some immigrants were quite poor and were considered a burden by the natives. The lion's share of these came from Mexico, the origin of about 22 percent of foreign-born U.S. residents in 1990, by far the biggest single national group (Filipinos were second, with 5 percent).[79] Mexicans, Salvadorans, and Guatemalans accounted for a majority of L.A.'s immigrants. Similarly, Cubans, Haitians, and Nicaraguans dominated Miami's immigrant life. New York City's immigrants were more diverse; Dominicans (who were quite poor), Chinese, Jamaicans, and Italians were the only four national groups accounting for more than 100,000 each of the city's foreign-born population in 1990, and together they comprised only a bit under 30 percent of the total.[80] By official classification, only 50 percent of the foreign-born were white in 1990, while 90 percent had been in 1970 (when the foreign-born population was far smaller).[81]

Despite concerns among the native-born over public expenditures on poor newcomers, college degrees were common among the immigrants. Often the U.S. government bestowed visas on immigrants to fill high-skill occupational niches. Sixty-five percent of Indian immigrants were college graduates in 1990, and about 20 percent of immigrants overall, the same proportion as among the native-born.[82] Between 1982 and 1988, more than half the top sixty winners of the famed Westinghouse science competition for high school students were immigrants or their children.[83] Some Americans, unsettled by this turn of events, seemed unable to decide whether immigrants were stealing their taxes or eating their lunch. Iranian physicians filled hospital staffs in Los Angeles; Chinese and Filipino businesspeople populated California's valleys; Cubans continued to flock to Florida but also to New Jersey; Vietnamese and Hmong streamed to the New Orleans delta, Orange County, and Eau Claire, Wisconsin. In California's Southland, "great waves of Chinese, Korean, and Armenian middle class immigrants, augmented by Israelis, Iranians, and others," in Mike Davis's judgment, "made Los Angeles the most dynamic center of ethnic family capitalism on the planet."[84]

Countries that had close political links to the United States sent large numbers there, while economic dislocation in farm villages, spurred in part by U.S. investment and laissez-faire policies pressed by Washington officials, caused an outflow of migrants from south of the Rio Grande as never before.[85] Many conservatives, fearing for their country's identity, hoped that President Reagan would support efforts to limit immigration. But nativism left Reagan cold. His sentimental view of immigration, disclosed in his repeated association of himself with the Statue of Liberty, was clear. He gave the restrictionists no help, and ultimately signed the Immigration Reform and Control Act of 1986, which included a toothless set of penalties for employers who knowingly hired those in the country illegally. The law included provision for the largest amnesty of such immigrants ever; about two million took up the U.S. government's offer.[86]

New cultural forces, pointing to a possible departure from the climate of fear, were afoot. Those who came of age in the 1980s passed through a time marked by hateful conflicts over turf, but also an era that, in the end, bore in on its tide a new complexity of identity and culture. The unexpected breakthrough hit of 1988 was Tracy Chapman's "Fast Car," a spare, desperate song, performed in the voice of a woman living in a homeless shelter and dreaming of a different life.[87] The American public's enthusiasm for this somber ballad from a young black woman, narrating the underside of the Reagan years, showed an openness among young Americans to social criticism and offered a small hint of an alternative vision in which race might not divide and distract, in which the call to redeem those excluded from the era's wealth would be a source of adhesion and mobilization. However, Chapman's success was, in these terms, exceptional. Such prophecies of a different America remained fugitive visions in the 1980s, an era when harsh and divisive emotions were ugly companions to the decade's bright celebrations of American pride.

Nine

The Winner

By late 1983, as the nation directed its attention toward the elections of the following year, the public mood was turning in Ronald Reagan's favor. The international scene was turbulent, but even in this realm, anxiety about violence in Beirut, conflict in Central America, and the chill in U.S.-Soviet relations was mixed with pride over the flexing of American muscle in Grenada (see chapter 6). Meanwhile, the domestic outlook was growing sunnier. Joblessness remained a terrible problem in some places, but the national unemployment rate was moving downward. Reagan's gigantic military budgets were sending money coursing through the nation's financial arteries, consumer spending was pulling the economy into a period of growth, and inflation remained low following the deep recession of 1981–1982. The narrative of national resuscitation, advanced relentlessly by the White House, was taking hold. Many Americans cheered on that theme of revival and better days. "All together shout it now/There's no one/Who can doubt it now," Vanessa Williams, Miss New York, sang out in Atlantic City in September 1983. "So let's tell the world about it now/Happy days are here again." Performing a slow, lounge-style rendition of "Happy Days Are Here Again," Franklin Roosevelt's 1932 campaign theme song, Williams became the first African American woman to win the Miss America Pageant, confirming that for black Americans the 1980s was a period of new breakthroughs as well as great trials. Williams and the pageant judges, of course, were not working for Reagan's reelection team. But they could not have scripted a better kickoff to the president's effort if they had been. The theme of happier days, featuring a restored national pride, communicated in a media campaign of unsurpassed smoothness, would constitute almost the entirety of Reagan's campaign.

In political terms, the White House devoted 1983 and early 1984 not, primarily, to advancing conservative causes, but rather to methodically removing obstacles from the path to the president's reelection. The most important was conflict over Social Security. In 1981, Reagan had appointed a commission, led by Alan Greenspan, to examine the system's future, but it received little attention until after the 1982 elections. "By the time the November [1982] election was over, Baker, Darman and that crowd were in charge of the issue," recalled one lobbyist. "It was clear that they would take their own grandmothers off Social Security to get a deal with the Democrats. They were in the trough of a depression, the President's popularity was at bottom, they had lost their [effective] House majority, and they wanted it *done*, behind them!"[1] In early 1983, the commission delivered recommendations to strengthen the system's long-term finances. Congress embraced them by passing a series of amendments to the Social Security Act, followed by Reagan's signature. In the most important change, the retirement age would rise from sixty-five to sixty-seven by the year 2027. As well, some benefits to high-income households would be taxed for the first time. The commission's report repudiated views long held by many on the political right, including Reagan. It stated, "The National Commission considered, but rejected, proposals to make the Social Security program a voluntary program, or to transform it into a program under which benefits are a product exclusively of the contributions paid."[2] Social Security was neutralized as a political issue for the foreseeable future.

The Reagan camp still needed to cool the smoldering perception of the president's indifference toward the disadvantaged. The alienation of African Americans—disproportionately hurt by Reagan's cuts to social-welfare programs—offered a rallying point for all of his enemies. Reagan could afford to do badly with black voters. But ignoring white voters concerned over "the fairness issue" and racial tension was unwise. In May 1983, Reagan inflamed civil rights groups anew when he appointed to the U.S. Commission on Civil Rights a set of neoconservatives, who opposed most forms of affirmative action. In August, a coalition of civil rights groups, labor unions, peace activists, and feminist organizations duplicated the feat of the 1963 March on Washington—and of 1981's Solidarity Day (see chapter 5)—by gathering another crowd of a quarter-million in the nation's capital to mark the twenty-year anniversary of the peaceful protest where Martin Luther King Jr. had delivered his "I Have a Dream" speech. Benjamin Hooks, leader of the National Association for the Advancement of Colored People (NAACP), the nation's foremost civil rights organization, made the point of the 1983 protest clear, leading the assembled in a cry of "Reagan No More in '84!" He proclaimed that the crowd was "committed to the elimination of Reaganism from the face of the earth." Coretta Scott King, Martin King's widow, linked domestic concerns to U.S. foreign policy. "We must demand justice in Harlem and in the Bronx . . . but also in the Philippines. We must demand justice in the barrios of Los Angeles . . . but also in El Salvador."[3]

The issue that offered Reagan the opportunity to show, albeit reluctantly, that he was not retrograde on racial issues was the continuing agitation for a national holiday honoring Martin King. Civil rights groups mounted a concerted lobbying effort, funded in part by the musician Stevie Wonder. The Democratic House leadership swung behind a bill that would create the holiday in 1983, and it passed by a veto-proof majority, 338–90. Conservative Republicans such as Newt Gingrich of Georgia and Jack Kemp spoke in favor of the measure. It faced a tougher test in the Senate, where Jesse Helms, who had castigated King and his associates as Communist tools during the 1960s, filibustered it. Helms recycled old charges that King was a dangerous subversive, and supplied his colleagues with a binder filled with material collected by the Federal Bureau of Investigation (FBI), whose former director J. Edgar Hoover had hounded and spied on King. Tempers rose. Daniel Moynihan called Helms's binder "a packet of filth" and dramatically threw it on the Senate floor. On October 19, a supermajority of seventy-eight senators voted for the bill, breaking the filibuster, with Republicans voting aye two to one.[4]

Reagan, heeding rising pleas from Republicans, dropped his longstanding opposition to the holiday and signed the bill. His previous statements had, at least at some moments, revealed a view of King little different from those of Helms or Hoover. A former governor of New Hampshire, Meldrim Thomson Jr., a member of the John Birch Society, released an exchange of letters with the president in which Thomson called King "a man of immoral character." Reagan replied, "I have the reservations you have" about the proposed holiday and lamented that admiration for King was "based on an image, not reality."[5] On the day of Senate passage, Reagan held a press conference where he said of the holiday's advocates that "since they seem bent on . . . it," he would not try to block it. At the signing ceremony, on November 2, Reagan's peevish, faintly disgusted tone was gone. "Dr. King . . . awakened something strong and true," Reagan said, "a sense that true justice must be colorblind, and that among white and black Americans, as he put it, 'Their destiny is tied up with our destiny, and their freedom is inextricably bound to our freedom; we cannot walk alone.'"[6] Even here, the mention of King's "colorblind" legacy was, in 1983, a rhetorical sop to neoconservatives who opposed the race-conscious government policies advocated by liberals. But, by agreeing to create the holiday, Reagan moderated his image on racial issues, helping himself politically.

Reagan also made deals with Congress to clean up a messy budget process in Washington. After the 1982 elections and as a result of a painstaking consensus-building effort within the Democratic caucus, conservative Democrats, starting in 1983, worked with their party, not with the White House. Deficit reduction became the glue now holding the Democrats together. In March 1984, the Democratic-controlled House Budget Committee voted to approve a "pay as you go" budget for fiscal year 1985. The House GOP, aware of growing opposition to Reagan's fiscal priorities, would not even introduce the president's proposed budget. Timothy Wirth, Democrat of Colorado, insisted on doing so in order to put them on the spot. Only Kemp voted for Reagan's budget, with 401 voting nay. The process dragged on; the budget was well overdue. In July 1984, Reagan at last signed the Deficit Reduction Act, which raised $50 million in new government revenue by eliminating shelters and loopholes and increasing telephone and liquor taxes—continuing Reagan's pattern of raising taxes of various kinds while keeping sacrosanct the lowered income-tax rates he had won in 1981.[7]

A last liability of the president was the continuing stream of corruption scandals and allegations surrounding his appointees. Richard Allen, Reagan's first national security adviser, had had to resign because of petty gifts from foreigners, and Secretary of Labor Raymond Donovan faced a lengthy investigation over charges that he had links to organized-crime figures in New Jersey. More than ten other administration officials were also under official scrutiny for wrongdoing.[8] A fresh crisis emerged when Reagan rewarded Edwin Meese for his long service by nominating him for the position of U.S. attorney general. Confirmation hearings commenced in March 1984. Democrats lifted the rock covering Meese's personal finances, and what they found was not pretty. One California businessman had contributed $70,000 (a loan never repaid) toward the purchase of one of Meese's two houses by another man, which eased Meese's financial strain, and then this benefactor became a deputy secretary of the interior. Meese's accountant "arranged" $60,000 in loans to Meese and received an appointment to the Postal Service Board. A savings-and-loan in San Diego let Meese stay behind in payments on his $420,000 mortgage loan for more than a year without penalty; its chairman and vice president both got jobs in the Reagan administration.[9] After a month of such reports, Reagan announced he would suspend Meese's nomination, and he named an independent counsel to investigate these matters.

For all the compromises Reagan made in advance of the 1984 campaign, on one matter he would not relent, his hand stayed only by congressional force. This was the continuing war against Nicaragua. Late in 1983, Reagan approved a CIA proposal to mine Nicaragua's harbors, in the hope that damage to international shipping would impair Nicaragua's foreign trade. During a Senate debate over a proposed Contra-aid bill, in April 1984, Barry Goldwater, a Senate Intelligence Committee member, discovered a memorandum offering details of the operation. Shocked, Goldwater began reading the document into the record, causing a ruckus. Meanwhile, the news media reported damage to ships from the mines, and Nicaragua announced it would bring a case against the United States in the International Court of Justice. The Reagan administration replied that, contrary to U.S. treaty law, it would not recognize the court's judgment. Intelligence Committee members expressed outrage, embarrassed by their own lack of inquisitiveness. "I feel like such a fool," said Goldwater. David Durenberger, also on the committee, said, "There is no use in our meeting with Bill Casey. None of us believe[s] him." Soon Casey agreed in writing to provide the committee with all new presidential findings and other details of covert operations "prior to the implementation of the actual activity." The Senate and House both voted strongly to condemn the harbor mining. Of these resolutions, Reagan said, rather defiantly, "If it is not binding, I can live with it."[10]

In May, the International Court ruled in favor of Nicaragua, stating that the United States must stop "military or paramilitary activities which are prohibited by principles of international law." Only the U.S. judge dissented. The State Department argued that U.S. actions against Nicaragua were legitimate because they were really a defense of U.S. ally El Salvador. Few were persuaded. Even one administration official said of this argument, "Unfortunately, it's bullshit." The House voted against the pending request for Contra aid, and the Senate voted for it, creating an impasse. In October, the House leadership—more committed to their position than their Senate counterparts to theirs—prevailed. The airtight language that the House had adopted, drafted—like the earlier, less effective provision of 1982—by Edward Boland (see chapter 4), became law for fiscal year 1985. This second Boland Amendment stated that "no funds available to the Central Intelligence Agency, the Department of Defense, *or any other* agency or entity of the United States involved in intelligence activities may be obligated or expended for the purpose *or which would have the effect* of supporting, *directly or indirectly*, military or paramilitary operations in Nicaragua *by any* nation, group, organization, movement, or individual."[11] The U.S. government, quite simply, now could do nothing for the Contras. On this issue in 1984, Reagan had been uniquely disinclined toward compromise. This defeat would lead Reagan down the road toward the Iran-Contra scandal (see chapter 10), with powerful consequences for his presidency in his second term. It had no effect on the 1984 election, as most voters had other things on their minds.

The Democrats were playing a weak hand in 1984, although some of them were slow to realize it. Even if they had an opening against Reagan on the issues of economic fairness and the prospects for peace in the world, their party was adrift in terms of policy, without confidence in the popularity of big-government liberalism and lacking unity around anything more appealing. Following the 1982 elections, many Democrats had felt that public opinion had turned against Reaganism. Unemployment remained high, despite signs of economic recovery. Their complacency solidified support behind Walter Mondale, a familiar face from his time as Jimmy Carter's vice president, as their next presidential nominee. William Galston, a young political scientist, was less sanguine about the prospects for his party's tried-and-true lunch-pail appeal in 1984. "The standard Democratic line was Reagan was [Herbert] Hoover and all we have to do is a credible recreation of FDR and we're off to the races," he recalled later.[12] Such a view, Galston feared, failed to take account of the Democrats' lack of credibility as a ruling party among large sections of the voting public. It also ignored the possibility of a further improved economy.

Mondale, a pastor's son who had grown up in poverty and believed in both government assistance to the needy and fiscal rectitude, was an up-through-the-ranks politician who seemed formed in a pre-television era. He appeared to have no personal detractors at all, a rare thing in his line of work. But he was a slightly awkward speaker and generally lacked magnetism. Mondale was challenged for the Democratic nomination with surprising force by Senator Gary Hart of Colorado and the Reverend Jesse Jackson, a longtime civil rights activist and the most formidable African American presidential candidate to that point in U.S. history.

Hart, aged forty-seven, was only nine years younger than Mondale, but the two men belonged to different generations. One was shaped by the Great Depression and World War II, the other by the Vietnam War. Hart, opportunistic and poised, ruggedly handsome with ample, slightly unruly brown hair, proclaimed himself the herald of "new ideas." He had said of his own rising generation of Democrats, "We are not a bunch of little Hubert Humphreys," deriding Mondale's mentor.[13] In some ways, Hart was more liberal than he wished voters to think; in 1982, the American Civil Liberties Union (ACLU) gave him the highest score of any senator, 96 percent.[14] Hart suggested Mondale was too wedded to big-government domestic policy, while criticizing him from the left on foreign affairs. Mondale charged that Hart paid too little heed to "the excesses of the extreme left," seemingly a reference to Hart's alleged softness on the issue of communism abroad.[15] Hart stunned Mondale with a ten-point victory in the New Hampshire primary. But then Mondale gradually overwhelmed Hart by questioning the younger man's liberal commitments and depicting Hart as little more than a pretty face. Mondale did not have much style, but his earnestness wore well against Hart's vanity.

Jackson, like Hart a talented but egotistical man, had no chance to win the nomination, but he posed a grave threat to Mondale's fortunes in a general-election campaign. Jackson's bid spotlighted the Democrats' dependence on African American votes—a political connection, it was widely felt, that made some white Americans reluctant to support Democrats. Previously, Jackson had flirted with elements of the political right and left, influenced by black nationalism, which tended to defy those categories. But in 1984, Jackson campaigned as a voice for liberal anger at Reaganism.[16] He proved the most charismatic figure of the political opposition in the 1980s. In certain ways, he was like a younger version of Reagan, albeit with a different style—tall and broad-chested, physically imposing and a thunderous orator with a telegenic smile, personally charming when he wanted to be, often unconcerned with details. Jackson long had forged ties with Third World nationalists abroad, and he raised his profile in January by traveling to Damascus and gaining the release of a U.S. Navy officer, Robert Goodman, whose plane had been shot down while flying over Syrian-held territory in Lebanon.[17] But Jackson narrowed his slim prospects further by showing, very unwisely, that he retained unsavory elements from his black-nationalist background, thus blemishing his new image. Bodyguards from the Nation of Islam, a black separatist group tainted with antisemitism, formed part of his entourage. In February, an uproar resulted when the *Washington Post* reported that Jackson had referred to Jews as "Hymie" and to New York as "Hymietown." Yet, in several state primaries, Jackson trounced Mondale in the contest for African American support—support that Mondale needed badly in order to vanquish Hart. Jackson won at least 75 percent of the black vote in each of Illinois, Pennsylvania, and New York.[18] With Jackson pressing him, Mondale had to appeal to black officials and activists more publicly and urgently than he probably wished. Aided by his party's establishment, Mondale won the nomination through a process that gave him 49 percent of all delegates with 39 percent of votes cast.[19]

Mondale realized, by this time, that he faced long odds against Reagan. Needing to shake up the race, he rolled the dice and chose as his running mate Geraldine Ferraro, a third-term U.S. House member from New York, the first female major-party vice-presidential nominee in American history. Little known outside of the Congress, Ferraro was a former prosecutor with a brisk, businesslike manner. "She's a woman, she's ethnic, she's Catholic," a Mondale aide remarked hopefully. "We have broken the barrier. She will energize, not just women, but a lot of men who have fallen away from the Democrats."[20] But Mondale's selection process was slipshod and failed to unearth unseemly details about the finances of Ferraro and her husband, a wealthy businessman. When journalists revealed these matters, they proved a serious distraction from Mondale's campaign themes of honesty, integrity, and concern for the disadvantaged.

Mondale's campaign came to seem amateurish, in technical terms, when compared to the tremendously skilled Reagan reelection effort. The strategic savvy and media wizardry of the Reagan juggernaut in 1984 compensated for the thin content of this last campaign by a candidate who, in earlier contests, had emphasized policy issues. The White House surely wished to protect Reagan's tax cuts and deregulation against possible reversals under a Democratic president, and the election was a referendum on whether to stay with the course Reagan had set. Nonetheless, the absence of new proposals from Reagan was striking. Stuart Spencer, a trusted Reagan campaign aide, concluded, "The . . . administration fired all its bullets very early and very successfully in the first two years." He realized, he said (switching his metaphor), "that they don't have a goddamn thing in the pipeline."[21]

Reagan ran for a second term less as a guardian of conservative policies than as a suitable champion of national pride and rebirth, almost as a figure above politics. His campaign showcased a speech Reagan delivered in June on the cliffs of Normandy commemorating the D-Day invasion of Europe in 1944, and tied him closely to the 1984 Summer Olympics in Los Angeles. Reagan urged Americans to "go for the gold" and stick with him. The president officiated at the opening ceremonies of the Olympics in late July. The U.S. boycott of the 1980 Olympics, held in Moscow, was echoed four years later with the abstention of the USSR and all of its Warsaw Pact allies except Romania, as well as Cuba. In these circumstances, the strong U.S. team won the most gold medals and the most medals overall by wide margins. Keyed by the feats of track-and-field star Carl Lewis and the all-around women's gymnastics champion Mary Lou Retton—whose bodysuit was, essentially, an American flag—the Los Angeles Olympics became a festival of surging American patriotism. Enormous crowds of spectators filled the huge spaces of the Olympic events with chants of "U.S.A.! U.S.A.! U.S.A.!" Even Bruce Springsteen's hit album, *Born in the U.S.A.*, which topped the record charts throughout the month of July, seemed, to many, to amplify the flag-waving mood (despite the fact that most of its songs were "about laid-off workers and towns shutting down").[22]

Reagan's television commercials were strikingly different from his sober messages of 1980 and displayed production values never before seen in political advertising. They were like thirty-second or one-minute Hollywood movies, or like advertisements for national brands of orange juice or fast-food chains, full of smiling actors filmed in a gauzy style, complete with background music that swelled at the intended emotional climax. The campaign's signature commercial showed a small town "bathed in butterscotch morning light," a young couple's marriage, an old man raising the country's flag, and smiling children of diverse races.[23] The narrator explained the economic successes of Reagan's leadership— inflation and nominal interest rates down, and employment rising—and said, "It's morning again in America."

Reagan needed little meat on his campaign's bones, not just because his commercials were so good and his campaign so successful at keeping him above the fray, but also because he worked from a sound electoral strategy, one based in the Southeast and the West. In 1980, Reagan's team, planning to run against a southern incumbent, had targeted a band of cold industrial states running from New York to the Mississippi River as the battlegrounds. His strong showing in the Southeast provided the icing on Reagan's cake. His reelection campaign would reverse these priorities. In early 1983, a young, hyperactive White House political aide, Lee Atwater, who had won his spurs as a successful manager of local and state Republican campaigns in South Carolina with his attention to detail and his taste for rough tactics, assembled a memorandum, "The South in 1984," that helped win him a top spot in Reagan's reelection campaign. Atwater argued for a race-based Republican strategy in the South and cast a class-based strategy by the Democrats as the threat to GOP dominance in Dixie. Atwater urged that the Reagan campaign "must remember the fundamentals of Southern politics." In his view, the "fundamental" elements were "country clubbers," affluent whites who identified strongly with the Republicans; "populists," who were "usually Democratic," but "will swing to the GOP under the right circumstances"; and African Americans, who were solidly Democratic. "In 1984 we must assemble coalitions in every Southern state largely based on the country clubbers and the populists," he wrote. "We must stave off Democratic attempts to forge a strong coalition of populists and blacks." Later that year, he wrote another missive, "Building an Electoral Fortress in 1984," in which he argued, "If our campaign can get the South firmly in tow before the general election . . . few states will remain beyond our grasp." Atwater identified Florida, Texas, and California as the three "anchors" of Reagan's reelection strategy.[24] In Florida, between 1980 and 1984, new Republicans registered at almost twice the rate of new Democrats.[25] With James Baker supervising from the White House, Atwater's office became a nerve-center for campaign operations.

The Democrats' convention, held in San Francisco in July, came too early to let Mondale borrow any of the Olympics' patriotic glow, and he chose a message of austerity in accepting his party's nomination, seeking vainly to escape accusations that he pandered to his party's liberals. Mondale had considered promoting an "industrial policy" of government aid to selected manufacturing enterprises, but prominent young economists had helped derail that policy in Democratic circles, calling it fools' gold.[26] Instead, he quoted Harry Truman's comment that a "President . . . has to be able to say yes and no, but mostly no." Mondale denounced Reagan's record on deficits, Social Security, nuclear arms, civil rights, and the environment, and his "assault" on "the poor, the sick, and the disabled." He called Reagan's government one "of the rich, by the rich, and for the rich." But midway through his speech, Mondale turned from this tone of economic populism toward talk of fiscal rectitude. He announced, "Let's tell the truth. Mr. Reagan will raise taxes, and so will I. He won't tell you. I just did." Concerning the federal budget he said, "We must cut spending and pay as we go."[27]

Mondale had tacked left to become his party's nominee, and now he tacked right to try to win the general election, but he got the worst of both worlds. First, in the nomination fight, he had alienated moderates by seeking and gaining endorsements from liberal groups, such as the National Organization of Women (NOW) and the labor unions, which conservatives termed "special" interests. "This whole special-interest, over-promising thing, our polls show," said Robert Teeter, one of Reagan's survey analysts, "has hurt Mondale a lot."[28] Then, at the convention, Mondale left his liberal base cold with his new focus on budget-balancing. One journalist, reflecting widespread opinion, later pronounced Mondale's taxing and spending plan "one of the most carefully considered

and detailed budget blueprints ever offered during a presidential campaign."[29] But Mondale's emphasis on fiscal conservatism won him few
supporters.

One month later, less than two weeks after the Olympics ended, Republicans gathered at their convention in Dallas to see the president
present his case for another term in office. Now stepping into the fray,
Reagan delivered a speech longer than Mondale's and more sustained in
its attack on the opposing party. Flinging criticism of his fiscal indisci-
pline back at Mondale, Reagan said, "You know, we could say they spend
money like drunken sailors, but that would be unfair to drunken sailors."
Interrupted by cheers of "Four more years! Four more years!" Reagan finished his joke: "I was going to say, it would be unfair, because the sailors
are spending their own money."[30] In an ideologically charged flashback
to his 1964 speech, "A Time for Choosing," Reagan warned of the progres-
sion from "the welfare state to statism, to more and more government
largesse accompanied always by more government authority, less individual liberty and, ultimately, totalitarianism, always advanced as for our
own good." Rebounding from that jolting passage, his peroration was patriotic and sentimental, narrating the travels of the Olympic torch across
America to Los Angeles and linking it to the torch upheld by the Statue of
Liberty, at that time undergoing repairs. "We can be forgiven for thinking
that maybe it was just worn out from lighting the way to freedom for 17 million new Americans," he said. "Her heart is full; her door is still golden,
her future bright. She has arms big enough to comfort and strong enough
to support, for the strength in her arms is the strength of her people. She
will carry on in the eighties unafraid, unashamed, and unsurpassed."[31]

This convention, like the Los Angeles Olympics, was a nationalist
pageant for television viewing. It was a success as an extended campaign
commercial, but it lacked drama. "Watching it all on TV was like being
trapped for four days in Lobotomyville," the television critic Tom Shales
wrote irreverently.[32] The climax to the festivities was the appearance on
stage of the singer Ray Charles, who delivered his distinctive, brilliant
version of "America the Beautiful," and afterward posed with Ronald and
Nancy Reagan. Charles and Reagan were, in a way, a perfect pairing: two
master showmen, their performances marked by impeccable phrasing,
every word practiced.

The fall campaign was the opposite of suspenseful. Surveys after the election would show that almost half of voters had made up their minds about whom to support by early 1984, and another 20 percent did so by Labor Day.[33] During the course of 1984, 101 major polls matched Reagan and Mondale; Mondale won only one, by a margin of two points, conducted immediately after the Democratic convention.[34] An air of inevitability hung over the contest, but the nominees soldiered on. Mondale and Ferraro, almost universally expected to lose, received sympathetic press coverage. Attention to Reagan was more critical. His running mate, Vice President Bush, was depicted most unflatteringly, particularly after his crude remark, following his obligatory debate with Ferraro, that he had "kicked a little ass."[35] Reagan and Mondale debated twice. At the first meeting, Reagan seemed addled, unable to answer questions; he sweated heavily, his hands holding his podium tightly. Mondale did well, but what he saw unnerved him. "The President's not all there," he told an aide immediately afterward. "His eyes were wandering, he seemed shaky. The President is out to lunch." At the second debate, Reagan said, in response to an inevitable question about his fitness for office, "I will not make age an issue of this campaign. I am not going to exploit, for political purposes, my opponent's youth and inexperience." The laughter that filled the debate hall reflected relief from an audience suddenly in need of reassurance.[36] Perhaps a nimble, aggressive, and youthful candidate, like Hart, might have succeeded in exploiting the sudden fear of the president's senility. But Mondale proved unable to take advantage, and Reagan's moment of vulnerability quickly passed.

On Election Day, Reagan substantially increased his share of the national vote from 1980, securing 58.8 percent against 40.6 percent for Mondale, who won only his home state of Minnesota (and Reagan came within about four thousand votes of winning there). In soundly defeating Mondale, Reagan showed strength among almost all sectors of the electorate. The biggest chunk of his gains over his 1980 showing came from white Southerners who had stuck with Carter in the earlier contest.[37] Reagan won two-thirds of white voters in 1984, a year in which they accounted for some 85 percent of all voters. Despite the presence of a Catholic on the Democratic ticket, Reagan won a majority of Catholic votes, getting the highest percentage of this group by any Republican nominee since Calvin Coolidge in 1924.[38] Reagan's support among men was far higher than among women, but (again, despite Mondale's selection of Ferraro) he handily won a majority of each group. This was a "gender gap" that Republicans could live with. Much attention was paid to Reagan's strong pull among young voters as well, with good reason. He won the vote among those aged eighteen to twenty-nine by a 58–41 margin, after losing this group narrowly to Carter in 1980. However, in terms of age, Reagan's strongest support came from the oldest voters. Mondale's share of the sixty-and-over vote was only 36 percent—the lowest figure for a Democrat since George McGovern in 1972.[39] Nonetheless, Reagan was forging a new generation of Republicans. In August 1984, the youngest adults polled by Gallup were those who affirmed in the largest numbers—as if in reply to the question Reagan had asked in 1980—that they were better off than they had been four years earlier.[40]

The Democrats, for their part, were becoming what many middle-class and white voters perceived them to be: a party of the poor and disadvantaged. The journalist Thomas Edsall emphasized that, in terms of party identification, the highest-earning 10 percent of Americans in 1984 gave the GOP an advantage of 33 percentage points, while comparably large majorities called themselves Democrats only among the poorest 30 percent. Almost exclusively among especially impoverished groups, such as African Americans, did Reagan fare really badly in 1984.[41]

Postelection analyses revealed a corrosive racial current running through the electorate's continuing distaste for Democratic leadership. In 1965, after Democratic president Lyndon Johnson had signed the Voting Rights Act—ending local practices that long had disenfranchised black Southerners—he had remarked, "We just delivered the South to the Republican party for a long time to come."[42] But Johnson's prediction had been too geographically restrictive. Many white voters in post-1965 America, in both the North and the South, identified liberal policies on a broad range of issues with advocacy for African Americans, and white Americans proved unwilling to give a majority of their ballots to any Democrat running for president (with the result that the only Democrat elected president between 1964 and 1992 was Carter in 1976, which could be dismissed as a fluke produced by the Watergate crisis).[43] By nominating a proud liberal in 1984, the Democrats invited disaster. In 1985, the Democratic pollster Stanley Greenberg conducted a set of focus groups in white working-class suburbs of Detroit; his findings would haunt his party's candidates and strategists for years. In Michigan, a state that had suffered badly during Reagan's first term, Reagan received a full 10 percentage points more of the vote in 1984 than he had in 1980. Greenberg thought he had found the explanation. "For these white suburban residents," he wrote, "the term 'blacks' and Detroit are interchangeable: Detroit is just 'one big ghetto.' For them, blacks mean 'crime,' above all, but also 'dirty' and 'corrupt.'" He read to the focus-group participants a statement made by Robert Kennedy in the 1960s, asserting that American society owed a debt to African Americans because of the history of black enslavement and discrimination at white hands. "The participants rejected the concept without qualification and without hesitation: 'That's bull—.' 'No wonder they killed him.'" The white interviewees, one-time Democrats, saw government efforts to help black Americans as harmful to people like them. They "believe government has personally intervened to block their opportunities. Appeals to fairness, opportunity, etc. are now defined in racial terms that have been stripped of any progressive content."[44] After the election, the Democratic National Committee (DNC) conducted its own study and came to similar conclusions. DNC Chairman Paul Kirk reportedly was so alarmed that he ordered the relevant documents destroyed.[45]

Mondale, with no real chance of winning, had little to lose in the 1984 campaign by speaking from his heart, which he sometimes did. On September 25, he gave his doomed campaign's most memorable speech, at George Washington University in Washington, DC. There, he railed against the trivialization of politics and described the choice facing voters as a moral one. He said, "I won't permit this crowd to steal the future from our children without a fight. I won't let them put ice in our soul without a struggle. They have a right to ask for your vote. But I'll be damned if I'll let them take away our conscience."[46] If Mondale had given this same speech every day between his nomination and the November election, he still would have lost, but he hardly could have finished worse than he did. Even Mondale's intermittent moral critique of Reaganism may have proved too much for Reagan to stomach. The president was ungracious on election night; he deemed Mondale's concession speech too defiant and refused to offer his vanquished rival the customary compliment on a race well run.[47]

"I wish the President had proposed a serious program in that campaign," said one conservative after the election. "He might have ended up carrying 42 instead of 49 states, but at least he would have had a mandate."[48] In contrast to 1980, there was little, if any, talk of a mandate after Reagan's smashing 1984 win. Reagan was personally popular, but his job-approval ratings had been unimpressive for most of his first term compared to those of his recent predecessors. On many policy issues, Americans saw themselves disagreeing with the president. "People who gave Reagan only a C grade overall tended to vote for him" in 1984 "by a ratio of better than 2 to 1," remarked one journalist.[49] The salient question on each issue was whether voters preferred Mondale to Reagan. On the question of "keeping peace in the world," an area of particular concern to the president's team, by late 1984, polls showed that Reagan, benefiting from his newly conciliatory tone toward the Soviet Union (see chapter 6), was favored strongly over the Democrat.[50]

All surveys concurred that economic matters were most pressing at election time, and these turned in Reagan's favor. But it was not just an economic rebound that gave Reagan an advantage on what the Democrats had hoped would be "their" issue. While the economy was improving, the pain of the recession was hardly forgotten—indeed, it lingered in some areas. Even as deindustrialization remained an ongoing ordeal, the conservative economic appeal of 1980 proved durable. Reagan got credit for whipping inflation. "I liked what he did to hold down inflation," one *Democratic* activist in Iowa said in October 1984. "Although it was painful, he took the proper measures to keep it down."[51] This remark perfectly summarized Reagan's conservative economic wisdom. In a time when even foot-soldiers in Democratic campaigns showed sympathy for conservative arguments, voters in general, faced with a choice between a conservative Republican and a liberal Democrat, chose the former. Mondale merely compounded his troubles by promising tax increases.

Reagan and his entourage staged another grand party to mark his second inaugural in early 1985, but the stage was now set for political stalemate in Washington. Reagan had modest coattails; his party had gained fourteen seats in the House but lost two in the Senate. Perhaps, if the political mood of the country and the capital had been the same in 1985 as four years earlier, this result would have allowed Reagan to reassemble the conservative majority he had commanded in the House in 1981.

But conservative Democrats had cast their lot with their party, as it had chosen to embrace fiscal discipline as its signature issue. Tip O'Neill, who had let it be known that he planned to serve only one more term as House Speaker before retiring, still had to quash a brewing challenge to his leadership of the Democratic caucus in December 1984, before the new Congress convened. His manner of doing so was telling. O'Neill was contrite, saying, "The truth of the matter is that for many years we paid no attention to one group in that Caucus, the conservatives. We felt that there was no need for them; there were always 25 or 35 Republicans who would vote along with us."[52] But that political math was a thing of the past. Moderate Republicans could no longer be expected to break ranks. Now liberal Democratic leaders needed to court the votes of their own party's conservatives, mainly white Southerners. They succeeded. Measures of "key votes" showed an upward trend in Democratic concord on Capitol Hill. While the high point of Republican solidarity in Congress during the 1980s had come in 1981, Democrats would reach that point in 1988.[53] Conservative Democrats, emboldened, formed the Democratic Leadership Council in 1985, a launching pad onto the national stage for Senator Charles Robb of Virginia, Governor Bill Clinton of Arkansas, and others.[54] Their prospects brightening inside their own party, they found fewer reasons than before to do Reagan's bidding.

In both domestic and foreign policy, Reagan's second-term administration soon reflected mediocrity and presidential disengagement. Baker, the highly effective White House chief of staff, and Regan, the treasury secretary, decided on their own to switch jobs soon after the 1984 election. This episode signaled Reagan's weakening interest in domestic policy.[55] In a dismal coda to the campaign, Meese finally got the job Reagan had promised him—attorney general—in 1985.[56] Meese had had to wait out the election and an independent counsel's report. The counsel did not recommend indictment, but he documented numerous instances of Meese's corruption. Meese had taken money improperly from Reagan's 1980–1981 transition funds. Far more serious, he had, in effect, sold government offices from his perch in the White House in exchange for financial assistance. The Senate, with a Republican majority, ultimately was unable to refuse Reagan's wishes and approved Meese (with thirty-one senators dissenting).[57] Even many of the senators who sustained his confirmation doubtless found the appointment unfortunate, and the feeling that the revamped administration would be less than formidable grew stronger.

Congress turned its attention to stemming the tide of government debt it had helped Reagan generate. In September 1985, Senators Phil Gramm of Texas and Warren Rudman of New Hampshire, both Republicans, proposed a draconian law that would trigger automatic across-the-board cuts in federal spending, bringing the deficit down to zero by fiscal year 1991, if the Congress could not reach an agreement to reduce the deficits through the normal budget process. This proposal, which became known as Gramm-Rudman, drew wide support in a frustrated Senate, quickly passing by a vote of 75-24. The House Democratic leadership signed on—with certain conditions.[58] Gramm-Rudman would work as intended, forcing the White House to come to terms with a Congress in which Democrats (after the 1986 elections) would control both chambers, and producing budgets that repeatedly trimmed spending and raised assorted taxes.

With the White House empty of legislative "bullets," the main Capitol Hill accomplishment of 1986 was a borrowed Democratic initiative, the Tax Reform Act. It reduced the number of personal income-tax brackets, lowered the top marginal rate for personal income tax to 28 percent, strengthened the earned-income tax credit—a kind of "negative income tax," whereby the government reduced tax bills for the working poor—and closed loopholes that had allowed large corporations to elude taxation.[59] It had something in it to please almost everyone; the idea came from Richard Gephardt in the House and Bill Bradley in the Senate, both Democrats. Reagan embraced it for lack of any legislative agenda of his own.

Despite Reagan's dwindling power over domestic policy in general, conservatives could feel satisfied that one conservative project remained very much alive: the rightward transformation of the federal judiciary. Reagan would name about half of all federal judges, partly because Congress created many new judgeships in 1984. Reagan's judges were notably whiter and richer than those of previous and later presidents. He nominated only seven black judges in his eight years as president and twenty-eight women (out of 372 appointments).[60] Reagan's Supreme Court nominations were conservative, but he never had the chance to exchange a Democratic-appointed justice for one of his own. Sandra Day O'Connor replaced Potter Stewart in 1981, and Anthony Kennedy replaced Lewis Powell Jr. in 1988, two careful conservatives taking seats from two others. Republican activists were more pleased when, between O'Connor and Kennedy, in 1986, Reagan swapped the retiring Chief Justice Warren Burger, a lackluster right-leaning judge, for Antonin Scalia, fiery and deeply conservative. On the hot-button issue of abortion rights, O'Connor and Kennedy would allow states greater leeway to restrict abortion, but they (unlike Scalia) would shrink from overturning *Roe v. Wade*. They showed less restraint elsewhere, in O'Connor's case, for example, on racial matters. One analysis in 1998 revealed that, in forty-one close decisions involving race that had come before the Court since O'Connor joined it, she voted against the minority plaintiff thirty-nine times; she became a leader on the Court in restricting affirmative action.[61] Reagan also won a somewhat tough fight to replace Burger as chief justice with Associate Justice William Rehnquist, the most conservative member of the Court, despite revelations that Rehnquist had begun his political career in Arizona by appearing at polling places to challenge the right of African Americans to vote.[62]

Eventually Reagan, as his second term progressed, would forsake domestic policy to focus on foreign affairs, and would leave a lasting achievement in superpower relations by doing so. But in 1985 and 1986, much of his foreign policy displayed a tin ear, and a jarring sympathy for far-right political forces abroad, that recalled his first years as president. Reagan became embroiled in controversy in April 1985 over his plans to lay a wreath at a military cemetery in Bitburg, West Germany, at the invitation of Chancellor Helmut Kohl, a valued ally. But the graveyard contained bodies of men who had served in the Waffen SS, members of a Nazi political order notorious for their war crimes. Kohl, needing to guard his own right flank, implored Reagan not to back out. Reagan claimed, falsely, that all the men buried at Bitburg had been conscripts, and threw fuel on the fire when he asserted (echoing Kohl), "They were victims, just as surely as the victims in the concentration camps." The Senate voted, 82–0, to urge Reagan not to go. To mollify his critics, the president stopped at the site of the Bergen-Belsen concentration camp before proceeding to Bitburg. However, this revision of the president's schedule did not undo the damage his image suffered—indeed, it may have made things worse, since it seemed like an effort to strike a balance between honoring dead victims and perpetrators of the Holocaust, as if these two groups were moral equivalents—so soon after his installation for a new term.[63]

Reagan's moral standing in the realm of foreign policy suffered a further setback when, in 1986, Congress forced a change in his gentle treatment of South Africa's apartheid government. Grassroots pressure, on college campuses and elsewhere, had been building for years to oppose U.S. government support for Pretoria and to press units of government to divest themselves of stock holdings in corporations that did business in South Africa.[64] Reagan's government maintained that, far from supporting apartheid, it pursued a policy of "constructive engagement," by which it quietly persuaded South Africa to reform its policies. Civil rights groups rejected this notion, instead seeing Reagan as effectively pro-apartheid. Between June and September, the U.S. House and Senate agreed on a sanctions bill, prohibiting new investment by U.S. corporations in South Africa until the government there met a host of conditions—among them, freeing political prisoners including Nelson Mandela. Reagan vetoed the bill. In early October, both houses of Congress overrode Reagan's veto and the Comprehensive Anti-Apartheid Act of 1986 became law.[65]

As with many second-term presidents, Reagan would continue to pursue his agenda through appointments and within foreign policy, despite congressional efforts to interfere in both. He could do little else, because his triumphant reelection was largely a personal vindication and a rejection of liberalism, and only in a very limited way an acclamation of conservatism. The public's aversion to inflation had been the prime factor in gaining Reagan his first term as president, and inflation's defeat—despite the severity of the method used to achieve it—was the one element in Reagan's conservative record that the public clearly affirmed in reelecting him. Otherwise, his mandate was uncertain at best. A largely content-free reelection campaign had not set the stage for further conservative breakthroughs. As Reagan's second term advanced, public dissatisfaction with Reaganite prescriptions for a wide range of social problems would grow sharper.

Arms and the Man

"Good News!" wrote President Reagan on a note to his national security adviser, Robert McFarlane. It was May 1984, and Reagan had reason to feel happy. McFarlane had been on a private aid mission to see Saudi Arabia's ambassador to the United States, Prince Bandar bin Sultan. The Nicaraguan Contras were in trouble, McFarlane told Bandar. Congress might cut off their U.S. government funding. Bandar took the hint. Soon he assured McFarlane that the Saudi royal family would deposit $1 million per month in an account for the Contras' use. McFarlane kept the State Department and the Pentagon in the dark concerning this development, repeating the pattern set with the gestation of SDI ("Star Wars" to its harshest critics; see chapter 6). He informed Reagan of the Saudi commitment by inserting a card into the president's morning briefing papers. The president returned the card to McFarlane, with his enthusiastic response on it.[1] The president and the NSC were running a foreign policy on the sly—a course of policy that would remain secret for a time from the State and Defense Departments, and, for much longer, secret from Congress. President Reagan had started down an illegal path, and at the path's end lay a potential constitutional crisis.

When Reagan's top foreign policy advisers first discussed the mere possibility that Reagan might do what he and McFarlane—unbeknownst to the others—were already doing, Secretary of State Shultz warned that it would be "an impeachable offense." He made this attention-grabbing statement on June 25, 1984, at a key meeting of the National Security Planning Group (NSPG), convened to discuss how to advance Reagan's

Central America policies if Congress should disallow Contra aid (as it soon did; see chapter 9). The meeting featured an intense debate over the legality of soliciting other governments to support the Contras if U.S. funds were banned. Shultz claimed that he had discussed this idea with White House chief of staff James Baker (who was absent) and that Baker had said "it is an impeachable offense." William Casey shot back, "I am entitled to complete the record," and asserted that Baker had changed his mind after further discussion. But Shultz continued to press his view, saying, "Jim Baker's argument is that the US Government may raise and spend funds only through an appropriation of the Congress," implying that a program of third-country support for the Contras would be an illegal effort by the executive branch to spend money by proxy.[2] Reagan and McFarlane sat and listened to this dispute, neither of them revealing that they had already secured Saudi money. "If such a story gets out, we'll all be hanging by our thumbs in front of the White House," said Reagan in bringing the meeting to a close.[3]

Vice President Bush weighed in near the meeting's end. "The only problem that might come up," he said, "is if the United States were to promise to give these third parties something in return so that some people could interpret this as some kind of an exchange."[4] Years later, as part of the legal proceedings against NSC staffer Oliver North, the U.S. government would "stipulate" a lengthy itemization of the many such "quid pro quos" with the governments of Honduras, Saudi Arabia, Israel, Brunei, and others—arrangements in which those countries furnished support to the Contras in exchange for various favors from Washington.[5] North led the efforts by U.S. government officials to prompt and coordinate this third-party aid. Others involved included Reagan, Bush, and Assistant Secretary of State Elliott Abrams. North talked regularly with Casey, who viewed the brash marine lieutenant colonel as something of a protégé. McFarlane would say, for his part, that he viewed North as "like a son of mine."[6]

North sat at the center of what became known, starting in late 1986, as the Iran-Contra scandal. He was the point man both in Reagan's policy of offering arms, sold to Iran's government, to gain the release of American hostages taken captive in Lebanon, and in the president's underground effort to sustain the Contras during the period of the second Boland Amendment. North overcharged the Iranians for weapons and gave some of the proceeds to the Contras, thus linking the two initiatives.[7] North worked at the NSC, a body that coordinated presidential decision-making and sometimes developed foreign policy. But it had no business, by law or custom, instigating or running operations abroad, in the name of the U.S. government or otherwise. That is, however, exactly what North and others did, with Reagan's knowledge and encouragement: they ran foreign operations where there were supposed to be none, in order to pursue plainly illegal policies.[8] In the eyes of the American public, the effort to trade arms for hostages—by selling weapons to a government labeled a terrorist state by the United States—was the worst element in the scandal. Yet the Iran-Contra affair had its deepest roots in Reagan's determination to continue the war against Nicaragua. The allure of money for the Contras impelled North to advocate selling weapons to Iran well past the time when most sensible observers would have concluded that doing so was sheer stupidity.

"Ollie was about thirty to fifty percent bullshit," said a fellow NSC employee, voicing a widely held opinion. "Too much flash," remarked a colleague in the marines, the military service branch where North had made his career, which included distinguished service in Vietnam.[9] North was smart, creative, and energetic, and often excelled in his assignments, but he was known as terribly ambitious and sycophantic. A vigorous man, thirty-eight when first detailed to the NSC in 1981, North was smooth-skinned and trim with a ready, wide, gap-toothed grin, a character who charmed people even when they doubted his word. He rose quickly amid the chaos of Reagan's NSC, acquiring a reputation as a can-do operative, and was an early adopter of computer technology. In 1974, following North's Vietnam experience, he had received psychiatric treatment after threatening suicide when his wife, tired of his neglect, initiated a separation.[10] He saved his marriage, converted to evangelical Christianity, and by the 1980s seemed to have overcome whatever depression he had experienced. Yet his inexhaustibly dynamic job performance at the NSC may have owed something to a manic tendency. He did not have the Oval Office access he sometimes claimed—partly because Michael Deaver worked to keep him away from the president. North would "fly to Beirut, be back twenty-four hours later, and brief the president," said Deaver. "Reagan loved him, the style."[11] As the face of the scandal, North, testifying at length at congressional hearings in the summer of 1987, polarized public opinion; some thought him a hero, others, a villain. The central role of the president, and the extensive knowledge of the vice president, remained obscure to many. Reagan was shielded by the conclusion, reached by the Special Review Board, headed by Senator John Tower of Texas (thus often called the Tower Commission), which Reagan authorized to investigate the affair when it became public, that the president's hands-off "management style" had allowed the NSC to go astray. Shultz and Weinberger were vehemently against the arms sales to Iran, but they proved powerless to stop them before the scandal broke. Stanley Sporkin, counsel at CIA, jibed, "Weinberger was Dr. No, and Shultz was Dr. I Don't Want to Know."[12] Many Americans did not realize, or did not wish to know, how deeply the president had been enmeshed in the operations.

The CIA was the lead agency in funding and organizing the Contras from 1981 into 1984. In the spring and summer of 1984, Casey, warily eyeing growing congressional sentiment for ending this program, arranged for North, who had worked on Central America policy at NSC, to take over primary responsibility for maintaining contact between the Contras and the U.S. government.[13] As the second Boland Amendment went into effect, North began coordinating private efforts to replace aid previously supplied by the CIA and the U.S. military. He turned to retired CIA and military men who had experience running covert operations. Central to his plans was Richard Secord, a former general who for three years in the 1970s had been the top U.S. Air Force official in Iran. Felix Rodriguez, an ex-CIA employee with ties to Donald Gregg, Vice President Bush's national security adviser, was recruited to oversee the receiving end of the supply operation in El Salvador. Rodriguez advertised his closeness to Bush, and met with him repeatedly; the agenda for one meeting included "resupply of the contras."[14] Secord established a set of corporations that he called "the Enterprise," which could deliver arms to the Contras if funds were available. North approached the governments of South Africa and Israel unsuccessfully, although earlier, Israel had delivered arms it had captured from the PLO for the Contras' use.[15] Abrams, North's ally in the Nicaraguan cause, successfully obtained a pledge of $10 billion from the sultan of Brunei.[16] North also helped raise funds from wealthy Americans with which to purchase arms, meeting with prospective donors—which the president occasionally did as well.[17] The issue of money was forever pressing. NSC and CIA personnel knew of the Contras' use of Enterprise planes to ferry cocaine into the United States, a rich source of revenue. In his voluminous notebooks, North jotted notes such as, "Want aircraft to pick up 1,500 kilos" and "aircraft to go to Bolivia to pick up paste."[18] When these matters became public, in 1987, widespread alarm arose in the press, Congress, and the public over the possibility that North, at Casey's behest, had coordinated a shadow covert-operations force. It would be, in North's words, "self-financing, independent of appropriated monies," and able to pursue policies forbidden by law and unknown to Congress.[19]

Reagan was directly involved in the fight to keep the Contras alive "body and soul," as he described the NSC's mission to McFarlane.[20] On February 19, 1985, Reagan signed a directive ordering steps to ensure that the government of Honduras would, in McFarlane's words, "persist in aiding the freedom fighters." The directive stated that a "special emissary" would personally deliver a signed letter from Reagan to President Roberto Suazo Córdova, and that the emissary would "very privately explain our criteria for the expedited economic support, security assistance deliveries, and enhanced CIA support" that Washington could provide his country. In March, Bush traveled to Tegucigalpa and met with Suazo, assuring him of swift military and economic aid. Within another month, however, the Hondurans had gotten cold feet, and intervened to stop the delivery of arms to the Contras by the Enterprise on their territory. Reagan telephoned President Suazo. The U.S. president noted afterward that the arms were to be released, and that Suazo had requested further U.S. aid to his country.[21]

The administration persisted in lobbying for a resumption of Contra aid. The White House launched a somewhat effective "public diplomacy" communications effort aimed at completely ruining the Sandinistas' standing in Washington. The president denounced socialist Nicaragua as a "totalitarian dungeon" in 1984, reflecting this renewed political offensive.[22] With the Contra-aid program operating out of sight, the debate in Congress shifted away from the Contras' well-documented misdeeds—violence against civilians, what the president dismissively called "so-called atrocities"—and onto those of the Sandinistas. In June 1985, the administration persuaded Congress to refrain from extending the Boland Amendment into the coming fiscal year. The House joined the Senate in supporting "nonlethal" aid to the Contras, administered through the State Department. (North would hijack this program for his own purposes, installing one of his operatives, Robert Owen, in the "humanitarian" aid office—a convenient cover for Owen's travels to Nicaragua to deliver illicit money to the Contras.) Conservative Democrats in the House, including John Murtha of Pennsylvania and Dave McCurdy of Oklahoma, broke ranks with their leadership to vote through this assistance. "I am very, very upset with [Murtha]," said Tip O'Neill, whose aunt had been one of the founders of the Maryknoll order of Catholic nuns and who harbored deep feelings about Central America. "And McCurdy, he put the knife in us."[23] The policy debate was swinging back in Reagan's direction. But his men's activities during the time that the second Boland Amendment had been in effect—only one fiscal year—would come back to haunt him.

Capitol Hill reacted sharply when, in June, July, and August 1985, the *Miami Herald*, the *Washington Post*, and the *New York Times* reported on NSC activities in support of the Contras.[24] Congressional committees requested documentation relating to North's recent contacts with the Contras. A cover-up at the NSC commenced immediately. McFarlane ordered North to falsify a set of NSC documents that would reveal clear violations of the law.[25] On September 12, McFarlane replied in writing to House and Senate committees. In these letters, initially written by North for his superior's signature, McFarlane committed himself to a course of public mendacity. "None of us has solicited funds," he wrote of NSC staff, "facilitated contacts for prospective potential donors, or otherwise organized or coordinated the military or paramilitary efforts of the resistance."[26] This was actually a good description of North's work with the Contras, and North was not alone. McFarlane's assurances worked to fend off congressional inquiries.

As sensational as they would be, future revelations of illegal Contra aid would prove less outrageous to the American public than the "Iran" part of Iran-Contra. Reagan had flailed about in his search for a successful policy toward the Middle East, where the United States had become engrossed in regional conflicts, including the Lebanese civil war—leading to the highly lethal truck-bombing of the U.S. embassy and the U.S. Marine compound near Beirut (see chapter 6). Ill-considered U.S. policy excited a burst of anti-American terrorism, including hostage taking, which in turn prompted unsteady and ineffective American responses. Arab nationalists and extremists saw America as taking sides in local matters. In December 1983, al-Dawa, a Shia Muslim group based in Iran, bombed the U.S. embassy in Kuwait City, killing six and injuring many others. The Kuwaiti authorities convicted and imprisoned seventeen people for the crime; they became known as the al-Dawa prisoners. In March 1984, Hizbollah members or allies kidnapped William Buckley, the new CIA station chief in Beirut. There would be many other kidnap victims in Beirut, but Buckley was the most valuable one. He would die at his captors' hands. In September 1984, another car-bomber struck an annex of the new U.S. embassy in Beirut, killing twenty-four.

The United States started hitting back in 1985, but—far from quelling terrorism—this response seemed to fuel it further. Casey authorized a bombing in the Beirut neighborhood of Bir al Abed in March, intending to kill the Hizbollah leader Mohammed Hussein Fadlallah. The bomb missed its target; Fadlallah was unhurt, but eighty people in the crowded vicinity were killed. Hizbollah fighters hung a large banner at the site of the explosion that read, "MADE IN THE USA."[27] On June 14, Palestinian militants hijacked Trans World Airlines flight 847, en route from Athens to Rome. The hijackers screamed "New Jersey!" and "Marines!" at the bewildered passengers. The armed men were referring to the shelling, in 1983 and 1984, of the Lebanese heights by the U.S. battleship *New Jersey*, which had killed numerous civilians. They forced the pilot to shuttle the plane back and forth between Beirut and Algiers. Identifying one passenger, Robert Stethem, as a U.S. Navy officer, they beat him and killed him, then threw his body onto the tarmac in Beirut. When a Lebanese air-traffic controller questioned their brutality, they retorted, "Did you forget the Bir al Abed massacre?" They released most of the passengers, but held back a group of Americans. Behind the scenes, Syrian president Hafez al-Assad and Iranian president Ali Rafsanjani reportedly worked to gain their release. The hijackers demanded that Israel release seven hundred Lebanese whom it had imprisoned during its occupation. The Israelis agreed, and the Americans came home. Reagan greeted Stethem's body upon its arrival in the United States, and vowed "that America will never make concessions to terrorists—to do so would only invite more terrorism. . . . Once we head down that path there would be no end to it."

The president also stated, without mentioning Bir al Abed, that a military reprisal targeting terrorists amid civilian areas, if it killed innocents, would constitute "an act of terrorism itself."[28]

There seemed no respite from lethal terrorist attacks. In October, Palestinian extremists pulled off a spectacular job, hijacking an Italian cruise ship, the *Achille Lauro*, at sea in the Mediterranean. They demanded the release of their jailed countrymen. To the world's horror, they chose one passenger, an elderly, wheelchair-bound American named Leon Klinghoffer, and murdered him, dumping his body overboard—perhaps thinking this act of awful cruelty would demonstrate their seriousness. The hijackers put ashore in Egypt and boarded a plane bound for a friendly destination. But U.S. intelligence intercepted private communications by Egyptian President Hosni Mubarak revealing the location of the plane, and U.S. planes forced it down in Sicily. After a standoff with the Americans, Italian authorities took the criminals into custody.[29] In December, bombs exploded at the desks of the Israeli airline El Al in the Vienna and Rome airports on the same day, killing twenty, including five Americans. Reagan had made it clear he thought any U.S. president must respond forcefully to such outrages—but he found no way to do so effectively. He also showed no understanding of the links between terrorist tactics in the Middle East and American policy there. In particular, U.S. intervention in Lebanon on behalf of Israeli and Lebanese Christian goals—regardless of Reagan's forceful private dealings with Menachem Begin—reinforced the longstanding view among many Arabs that the United States was a powerful anti-Arab force in the region.

Public awareness of the hostage-taking in Beirut was becoming intense, and Reagan became anxious to do something about it. The family of one captive, the Catholic priest Father Lawrence Jenco, deployed an ·effective media campaign to publicize his plight. In June 1985, they succeeded in cornering the president in a highly unusual personal meeting in an Illinois high school gymnasium; the confrontation, far from the friendly surroundings of the White House, left Reagan dazed, and soon he began pressing his aides continually about any news regarding "the hostages," as they became simply known.[30] According to Weinberger, in December Reagan told his top advisers that the American public simply would not understand if "big strong President Reagan passed up a chance to free hostages."[31] If Reagan's rendering of his own public image was crude, it was accurate.

Reagan became receptive even to audacious and astounding ideas—like bribing Iran to help win the captives' freedom. This notion came to Washington from Israel, even though the regime in Tehran regularly denounced Israel as an illegitimate "Zionist entity." Before the shah's fall in 1979, Israel had had warm relations with Iran. Later on, the United States, along with right-wing Sunni regimes in Saudi Arabia, Kuwait, and elsewhere in the Persian Gulf region, favored Iraq's cause in the protracted war that began in 1980 when Iraq attacked Iranian territory. They saw Iraq's dictator, Saddam Hussein, holding the line against the spread of Iran's antimonarchical Shia revolution into the Arab world. Some in Israel viewed things differently. A quiet resumption of their old alliance with Iran would match the one forged by Israel with the government of Turkey, following the Israeli "doctrine of the periphery," a strategy designed to outflank Israel's Arab enemies.[32] U.S. strategy in the Middle East had foundered since the shah's ouster; no other country had replaced Iran as the pillar of U.S. security in the region. Iran, in short, seemed a great prize to those who viewed Southwest Asia as a grand chessboard. Journalists later reported that, as early as 1981, the United States approved Israel's secret sale of arms to Iran. (Israel had bought these weapons from the United States, so the Arms Export Control Act required U.S. approval for their resale.)[33]

In May 1985, Michael Ledeen, who—like other foreign policy neoconservatives—had talked himself into a position at NSC, traveled to Israel as McFarlane's emissary and met with Prime Minister Shimon Peres. Ledeen had gained McFarlane's blessing for discussions of a secret U.S.-Israeli diplomatic approach to Iran.[34] In June, McFarlane's staff produced a draft National Security Decision Directive that advocated a diplomatic opening to Iran, featuring arms sales. The idea withered under ridicule from Weinberger, who seemed relatively unaffected by the hostage issue and therefore had no sympathy for the thin strategic rationalization covering the arms-for-hostages gambit. On July 8, President Reagan delivered a speech in which he identified Iran as part of a network of terrorist-sponsoring states akin to "Murder Incorporated." These governments, including Nicaragua's, were "run by the strangest collection of misfits, looney tunes, and squalid criminals since the advent of the Third Reich," said the president.[35] But McFarlane, still hopeful, had met on July 3 with David Kimche, director-general of Israel's foreign ministry. Kimche told McFarlane that Israel had promising Iranian contacts who might work to gain the release of Americans held by Shia groups in Lebanon. But one hand must wash the other. The Iranians would want to gain something in return for such action, if the way were to be paved for better relations between Washington and Tehran. Iran wanted U.S. weaponry. McFarlane summarized this discussion for the president.[36] This briefing may have been the first time that Reagan was privy to any discussion of furnishing arms to Iran in indirect exchange for the release of hostages in Lebanon.

When Reagan was hospitalized in mid-July to have cancerous tissue removed from his colon, McFarlane mentioned the Iranians' specific interest in obtaining advanced U.S. antitank TOW missiles.[37] On August 6, McFarlane relayed to Reagan a request by Israel for permission to sell one hundred TOWs to Iran. The United States then would sell Israel new TOWs to replace those sent to Iran. Bush, Shultz, Weinberger, and Reagan witnessed this conversation. At that time, Reagan neither approved nor rejected the proposition; Weinberger said bluntly, "I don't think it's legal." McFarlane later stated that Reagan telephoned him after several days to give the go-ahead. Perhaps Reagan had wanted to mull things over; perhaps he worried that his top officials would scotch the idea if he expressed open enthusiasm. Israel shipped ninety-six TOWs to Iran on August 19. But no hostages were freed.[38]

Less than one month later, a new delivery of 408 TOW missiles arrived in Iran from Israel. The Iranians had promised that, in exchange for this delivery, they would work to free one American captive. That same day the Reverend Benjamin Weir, held prisoner in Lebanon for more than a year, was released. Congressional investigators later concluded that the president had advance knowledge of this second missile delivery. Reagan's official biographer, Edmund Morris, mentioned Weir's release to Reagan at the time. "Six more to go," the president replied.[39] But more hostages were quickly taken in Beirut, negating the apparent gains of the arms deals.

Ledeen once again pushed the endeavor forward, meeting, in Europe, with Iranians and Israelis to discuss further transactions. Soon afterward, Israeli Defense Minister Yitzhak Rabin told McFarlane that Israel planned to send a battery of Hawk antiaircraft missiles to Iran, and reminded McFarlane that the U.S. government had pledged to replenish Israel's stock of weapons after the shipments to Iran. McFarlane relayed the message to Reagan. North involved the Enterprise in getting this shipment through. North turned to Richard Secord, whose past service in Iran no doubt made him seem like the perfect man to get this job done. The same private network used to supply the Contras was "involved in every NSC-connected shipment of weapons to Iran" after this point.[40] Cash from the Iran deals and money intended for the Contras started passing through the same accounts. Within days, at a summit meeting in Geneva, Switzerland, between Reagan and the new Soviet leader, Mikhail Gorbachev, McFarlane briefed the president on the arms delivery. Two years later, Reagan would state that, upon learning of this matter in Geneva, he had been so outraged that he ordered the arms sent back to Israel. That claim was wholly imaginary.[41]

On December 5, 1985, the president signed a finding authorizing arms sales to Iran.[42] This finding was extraordinary in two respects. First, although findings are supposed to be produced before the covert action they authorize begins operation, this one was retroactive. It stated blandly, "All prior actions taken by U.S. Government officials in furtherance of this effort are hereby ratified." Specifically, this finding was meant to cover the November shipment of Hawk missiles by Israel. High officials at the CIA had insisted upon the finding once they learned that North had involved CIA official Duane Clarridge in North's activities when obstacles arose during that arms shipment. Second, the finding instructed executive-branch employees to keep the finding itself secret from the congressional intelligence committees. The law required that the president share findings with these committees. Yet the draft finding stated, "Because of the extreme sensitivity of these operations, in the exercise of the President's constitutional authorities, I direct the Director of Central Intelligence not to brief the Congress of the United States as provided for in Section 501 of the National Security Act of 1947, as amended, until such time as I may direct otherwise."[43] Sporkin, the CIA's counsel, deemed this legally questionable finding better than none at all. John Poindexter, McFarlane's top deputy at the NSC, took over as national security adviser when McFarlane resigned, almost exactly to the day when Reagan signed this finding; Poindexter, ultimately reconsidering the wisdom of

Sporkin's advice, would destroy the only copy. Investigators, however, later discovered a surviving draft.

Reagan met with his foreign policy team on December 7, and discussed the ongoing arms sales to Iran. Both Weinberger and Shultz expressed their total opposition to the policy, but Casey offered his support. Reagan said, "Well, the American people will never forgive me if I fail to get these hostages out over this legal question," as Shultz later paraphrased the president's words.[44] In early 1986, the secretaries of defense and state restated their objections in another NSC meeting led by the president. Casey and Meese continued to back the policy.[45] On January 17, Reagan signed a new finding that authorized the CIA to sell arms to Iran directly, cutting out the Israeli intermediaries.[46] That day, Reagan wrote in his diary, "I agreed to sell TOWs to Iran."[47] The following day, Weinberger's top military aide, General Colin Powell, telephoned the army's vice chief of staff to issue a secret order that four thousand TOWs, destined for Iran, be transferred to the CIA.[48] On February 1, Poindexter confided to McFarlane, now a private citizen, that although Weinberger and Shultz still disapproved of the policy, they "are cooperating." "Most importantly," he wrote, "President and VP are solid in taking the position that we have to try."[49]

McFarlane, although he no long held a government position, kept his hand in the operation. At one point he stroked North's ego, congratulating the younger man for his work. "Well done—if the world only knew how many times you have kept a semblance of integrity and gumption to US policy, they would make you Secretary of State," he wrote. "But they can't know and would complain if they did—such is the state of democracy in the late 20th century."[50] On May 25, McFarlane led a delegation including North, Secord, and Amiram Nir—a close advisor to Israeli Prime Minister Peres—on a secret mission to Tehran. They brought some Hawk spare parts requested by the Iranians as a goodwill gesture. Iranian businessman Manucher Ghorbanifar, a notorious liar (he had been the source of the dubious claim in 1981 that Qaddafi had sent assassination teams to America; see chapter 4), had proposed this amazing trip, predicting that a wholesale release of U.S. captives might follow. But McFarlane was frustrated during his three days in Tehran. The Iranians kept him waiting, sent low-level government representatives to meet him, and insisted on getting yet more weapons before any hostages would go free. Poindexter had warned against such demands, telling North beforehand, "None of this half shipment before any are released crap. It is either all or nothing." McFarlane, who had discussed the trip with Reagan before leaving, returned home to report the mission's failure personally to the president.[51]

Amid all these secret dealings with Iran, the public's attention was suddenly riveted to the opposite end of the Middle East, as renewed conflict with Libya gave Reagan the opportunity to strike at a clear target as part of the "war on terror," just as it had in 1981. In April 1986, a nightclub frequented by U.S. servicemen in West Berlin was bombed; one army soldier was killed and fifty people wounded. U.S. intelligence sources found evidence of involvement by the Libyan government. President Reagan ordered a fleet of some 200 planes to carry out airstrikes on April 15 against targets in Tripoli and Benghazi, Libya's two largest cities, including Moammar Qaddafi's residence. Qaddafi was not killed, but thirty-seven others were, including Qaddafi's daughter. Two days later, the corpses of three Beirut captives—one American and two Britons, all employees of the American University of Beirut—appeared outside the city. Qaddafi bided his time, and two years later, in 1988, Libyan operatives would plant a bomb that detonated on Pan American Airlines Flight 103 in the air over Scotland, killing all 270 people on board—two-thirds of them Americans.[52] Despite all contrary evidence, however, in 1986, many Americans remained optimistic that muscular responses to terrorism would be effective. The Gallup Poll showed 71 percent of Americans supporting the U.S. airstrikes in Libya, and in their aftermath Reagan's political standing in the realm of foreign policy was probably strengthened at home.[53]

On June 8 and June 10, 1986, the *Miami Herald* and the Associated Press ran prominent stories detailing North's involvement in Contra-aid operations after the passage of the second Boland Amendment. However, this news did not curb the momentum that the administration's aboveground public relations effort on behalf of the Contras had acquired. Reagan had never given up on the Contras, and his efforts appeared to be paying off. This "public diplomacy" program extended to outlandish claims, including charges that the Sandinistas were committing genocide against the indigenous Miskitu people, that they were antisemitic, and that they supplied sympathetic journalists, both straight and gay, with prostitutes during visits to Nicaragua.[54] In March, Reagan made an Oval Office speech in which he issued the questionable accusation "that top

Nicaraguan government officials are deeply involved in drug trafficking."[55] On June 25, the House voted, 221–209, in favor of about $100 million in new aid for the Contras, which the Senate had already approved.

If many of these charges were hard to credit, worried Democrats on Capitol Hill still hastened to denounce the Sandinistas, whose leader, Daniel Ortega, had just made an ill-timed trip to Moscow. Liberal intellectuals opposed to Reagan's policy nonetheless began to distance themselves from the Sandinistas. As the Indian writer Salman Rushdie put it, "One didn't have to like people to believe in their right not to be squashed by the United States; but it helped, it certainly helped."[56] The drug allegations, turning on their head the intermittent reports of Contra involvement in drug-trafficking, had some traction. One reporter for *Time* magazine, dismayed that his editors quashed his reports on the Contra-drug connection, claimed, "*Time* is institutionally behind the Contras. If this story was about the Sandinistas and drugs you'd have no trouble getting it in the magazine."[57] Representative Tom Foley, Democrat of Washington, stated during floor debate that even though he opposed Contra aid, "I agree with the characterizations that have been made by the president" about the Sandinistas.[58] With foes of Contra aid declaring that the Nicaraguan regime was not monstrous but merely beastly, Reagan won the day. Still, with reports circulating of unauthorized NSC actions, the House Intelligence Committee heard testimony from North in the summer of 1986. North lied with abandon. Afterward, Poindexter sent North a message: "Well done."[59]

In early October 1986, North and other U.S. officials met with an Iranian delegation in Frankfurt, West Germany, as part of a so-called "second channel" to Iran that excluded the Israelis. North brought a Bible inscribed by President Reagan, which the leader of Iran's parliament later would brandish in public to taunt the U.S. leader.[60] Eager to complete a new arms deal and get his hands on fresh cash for the Contras, North agreed that the United States would sell Iran fifteen hundred TOWs and that Iran, in exchange, would guarantee only a single American captive's release.[61] He also encouraged the Iranians to believe that he would try to gain the release of the al-Dawa prisoners. Later that month, he told the Iranians he had "already met with the Kuwaiti Foreign Minister secretly in my spare time between blowing up Nicaragua."[62]

North had to leave the deliberations early to return home and conduct damage control on another front. On October 5, Sandinista soldiers shot down a plane owned by the Enterprise, capturing one crew member, Eugene Hasenfus. (Word first came to Washington when Felix Rodriguez called Vice President Bush's staff to convey the bad news.[63]) Hasenfus soon appeared on television screens and the front pages of newspapers around the world. He told what he knew of the Enterprise's Contra supply operations, including his understanding that the Enterprise was working at the CIA's behest. The plane was owned by Southern Air Transport, once a CIA-owned airline. Like many of the former CIA personnel involved in the Enterprise, Southern Air's "independent" status seemed a bit of a legal fiction. The business card of Robert Owen, North's courier for cash to the Contras, was found in one dead crew member's wallet.[64] On October 8, Reagan disavowed any link to Hasenfus and his associates. "There was no government connection with that plane at all," the president told reporters.[65]

Less than a month later, on November 3, the Lebanese magazine *Al-Shiraa* told the story of Robert McFarlane's secret trip to Tehran, touching off a worldwide sensation. Reagan responded that the story had "no foundation," adding, "We will never pay off terrorists because that only encourages more of it."[66] On November 2, David Jacobsen had been freed in Lebanon. Five days later, Reagan presented a traumatized Jacobsen, who had been tortured by his captors, to reporters. The journalists shouted questions to Reagan about the arms-for-hostages allegations, to no avail. Reagan responded that the remaining hostages would be endangered by press inquiries into the matter. At the end of his appearance, Jacobsen turned to the reporters and shouted emotionally, "In the name of God would you please be responsible and back off."[67]

With the Iran story breaking open, Reagan led a crucial meeting in the White House on November 10. Reagan, Bush, Shultz, Weinberger, Casey, Poindexter, Regan (now the chief of staff), and Meese were present. This was damage control at the highest levels. For unstated reasons, Weinberger departed from his usual habit of writing in his diary after such meetings, instead dictating a "Memorandum for Record." Most of the first two lines of text in the declassified copy of this memorandum were blacked out, or "redacted," ostensibly on national-security grounds. The first visible sentence reads, "The President said we did not do any trading with the enemy for our hostages."[68] Likewise, Regan's notes on the meeting related that Reagan told his men, "We have not dealt directly w[ith] terrorists, no bargaining, no ransom."[69] According to Weinberger, Reagan went on to say that the purpose of the arms sales to Iran was to pave the way for "better leverage with the new government" that would follow Ruhollah Khomeini's eventual death, and that for this strategic purpose "we felt it necessary to give them some small defensive weapons." Despite these presidential disclaimers, a discussion ensued among the meeting's participants about the success or failure of the arms sales in winning the release of American captives.[70] The falsehood that the United States had approved only the sale of "some small defensive weapons" would be exposed quickly, although Reagan would try to stick to that fabrication. The denial that the arms were sold in exchange for the release of hostages would become a point of yet greater stubbornness on his part. During this meeting, Poindexter told an assortment of bold lies, including that Reagan had not approved Israel's shipment of TOWs to Iran.[71] With Poindexter's assistance, the president had established the administration's cover story.

Now events began to move fast. On the evening of November 13, Reagan addressed the nation from the Oval Office, his choice of setting indicating he understood that the Iran arms sales formed a graver matter politically than the simultaneously breaking Contra-aid affair. Reagan hewed to his story, saying that Iran had received only a "small amount of defensive weapons and spare parts." Most important, he stated, "We did not—repeat—did not trade weapons or anything else for hostages nor will we." As Shultz drily wrote later, "The story he recounted was not believed." Shultz, outraged that the Iran initiative seemed still to be moving forward despite public exposure, resolved to air his objections in the open. The secretary of state was asked, during a television appearance on November 16, if he could speak for the administration regarding policy toward Iran. Shultz answered simply, "No."[72] Three days later, Reagan held a press conference—a risky move, given that he had always stumbled over questions of fact in this setting, and the press was sure to be more aggressive with him than usual. The president braved the fourth estate only because he was perceived as hiding out, the public was confused about who was in charge of U.S. policy and what it was, and Reagan's support was falling. The press conference did not help the president. He stated three times that Israel had played no role in the arms sales to Iran. But Israel's role already had become publicly known; Reagan had not ordered his men to keep it secret. He was lying impulsively, feeling this part of the story was either unsavory or embarrassing to an ally. Shortly after the press conference ended, the White House released a statement that "there was a third country involved in our secret project with Iran," contradicting the president.[73]

On November 20, Casey and Poindexter testified before the intelligence committees. Both of them lied repeatedly, but their lies were on some points inconsistent, raising additional suspicions. In the House committee hearing, Dave McCurdy asked Casey, "Who managed the operation, Mr. Casey?" Casey answered, "I think we were all in it. It was a team." McCurdy came back, "Who headed the team? Who called the shots? Was it Poindexter or Casey?" Casey replied bluntly, "I think it was the President."[74]

The next day, a Friday, in a meeting with Poindexter and the president, Meese proposed that he, the attorney general, conduct an informal inquiry to ascertain the basic facts. Reagan assented. Someone quickly informed North of this decision, and North embarked on a weekend "shredding party," destroying a thick pile of incriminating documents.[75] Despite North's efforts, Meese's assistants during the weekend discovered one memorandum, written in early April 1986, in which North described his allocation of $12 million in proceeds from the Iranian arms sales to his other major project, Contra aid.[76] This document became famous as the "diversion memo."

Meese's inquiry was irregular in many respects. He took no notes during his weekend conversations with key officials, and made no use of professional investigators in the Justice Department. He later said he had been acting not as the attorney general but rather as Ronald Reagan's "personal counsel." As ever, Meese showed disdain bordering on contempt for any conflict of interest between his public duties and his private commitments. On Monday morning, November 24, Meese met with Reagan. Later that day, they met again in an NSPG meeting. There, Meese reported on his investigation. He did not mention the diversion. He stated that "[the] President [was] *not* informed" about the November 1985 delivery of Hawk missiles to Iran. Poindexter asserted that

McFarlane had directed the operation "all alone." Meese concluded the meeting by asking if "anyone know[s] anything else that hasn't been revealed." Although virtually all of them—including Bush, Shultz, Weinberger, and Regan—knew a good deal that contradicted what Meese had said, none spoke up.[77]

On November 25, Meese and Reagan held a press conference at which Meese disclosed the diversion, publicly tying the arms-for-hostages scandal to the shadow Contra-aid operation. Here, Meese repeated the claim that Reagan had not known of the November 1985 arms delivery. Reagan announced that he had fired North from the NSC and that Poindexter had resigned.[78] The next day, Reagan appointed the Tower Commission, noted earlier, to investigate the affair impartially and report its findings.

Yet, despite a deafening political uproar, the Iran initiative was not finished. On December 13, CIA and State Department officials met again with Iranian representatives in Frankfurt. Only afterward did Shultz persuade the president to end these contacts. Shultz expressed frustration that U.S. government officials continued to negotiate with people who demanded the release of the al-Dawa prisoners.[79]

In January 1987, the Tower Commission interviewed Reagan, and a problem with the administration's story emerged. Reagan stated that he had approved the first shipment of TOWs in August 1985. He referred to testimony that McFarlane recently had given to the Senate Foreign Relations Committee about the scandal, in which McFarlane recounted this episode similarly. But Donald Regan had told the Commission that Reagan had not approved that shipment. Regan, not the president, was sticking to the line set forth by Poindexter at the November 10 meeting. Regan was embarrassed. He and White House counsel Peter Wallison then coached the president heavily before a second scheduled interview with the Tower Commission. Regan and Wallison wished to muddy the waters of presidential memory. In February, the Board asked Reagan about this matter again. "Peter," Reagan said, "where is that piece of paper you had that you gave me this morning?" When he found the briefing document that Wallison had prepared for him, Reagan read aloud, "If the question comes up at the Tower board meeting, you might want to say that you were surprised." This was a note Wallison had written on the document. All present were shaken.[80] Perhaps Reagan, feeling besieged, was retreating into mental confusion; perhaps he was passively registering his unhappiness at being pressured into changing his story. In either case, he had sabotaged the effort to deny his responsibility.

On March 4, 1987, Reagan finally admitted the obvious. In another speech televised from the Oval Office, he said, "A few months ago, I told the American people I did not trade arms for hostages. My heart and my best intentions still tell me that is true, but the facts and evidence tell me it is not." He followed this strange construction with a fanciful narrative of declension, saying, "What began as a strategic opening to Iran deteriorated . . . into trading arms for hostages." Strenuous efforts by the First Lady and political advisers, who feared the worst politically, had moved the president to make this partial, grudging confession. He said little about the illegal Contra-aid operation; he and his advisors were evidently more worried about "Iran" than about "Contra." Opinion surveys showed that a large majority of Americans thought Reagan was not being honest. The truth was that he had always intended to trade arms for hostages, as the relevant presidential findings made explicit. In the end, this policy was a failure, even on its own terms. In eight weapons shipments in 1985 and 1986, Iran received a total of 2,004 TOW missiles and a small number of Hawks. Seemingly in return, three American hostages were released; but at least three more were taken, leading to no net gain in hostages freed.[81]

Just as Shultz had warned in 1984, Reagan had committed impeachable offenses. Soon after Meese had revealed the diversion of funds from the Iranian arms sales to the Contras, Republican senator Warren Rudman telephoned former senator Paul Laxalt, who was close to Reagan, and said, "I've got an old prosecutor's instincts. I think I can tell when something is really bad. And, Paul, this is not only bad. This is going to be a disaster." To Rudman it looked "a lot like Watergate."[82] Reagan had subverted the nation's constitutional balance of powers by running a secret foreign policy—secret from Congress and, sometimes, secret from the key national-security agencies. Reagan had had a simple reason for authorizing a new, improper realm of foreign policy run from the NSC: the policy he planned to pursue was, in substance, an illegal policy. He had ordered entire initiatives that flagrantly violated the second Boland Amendment's defunding of the U.S. war against Nicaragua, as well as the Arms Export Control Act, many times over. To implement these policies, Reagan had to break additional laws which, starting with the National

Security Act of 1947, stated that the president must inform a small number of members of Congress of covert actions abroad.

But the Tower Commission's report—produced in short order before the end of February 1987—shifted discussion in Washington away from a Watergate-style focus on presidential wrongdoing, advancing instead the alternative interpretation of the scandal: that the president had been asleep at the wheel, undone by rogue subordinates. To many who were unfamiliar with the story's details, it seemed implausible that the president or others close to the summit of power would have empowered a marine lieutenant colonel to run the illegal foreign policy that had been uncovered. Republican senator William Cohen of Maine, later in 1987, reflected the impact of the Tower Commission's conclusions. Cohen remarked that it would be a "waste of time" for anyone to attempt to elicit further clarification from Reagan's memory. He said that "with Ronald Reagan, no one is there. The sad fact is we don't have a president."[83] Such derision proved, ironically, to be a lifeline thrown to the president. Reagan's pride was hurt by all the talk of his appointees running wild, at the emerging portrait of a doddering president. But this insulting image, which echoed longstanding liberal ridicule of Reagan as a supposedly dim, aged, and inept chief executive, protected Reagan from the possible legal consequences of his actions. Reagan wanted to have things both ways—denying he had done wrong while asserting he was in command. Even as he refused to acknowledge the truth about the Iran-Contra affair, he bridled at suggestions that he had not been in charge of his own foreign policy. In a moment of frustration in May 1987, Reagan said, of the effort to circumvent the Boland Amendment, "It was my idea to begin with."[84]

Eleven

The Crisis

On January 28, 1986, as millions watched on television, the space shuttle *Challenger* exploded soon after liftoff, killing all seven crew members. President Reagan canceled his State of the Union address and, instead, gave a speech soon afterward from the Oval Office eulogizing the dead astronauts in lyrical fashion, quoting the poet John Magee Jr. in saying that the crew had "'slipped the surly bonds of Earth' to 'touch the face of God.'"[1] Reagan's words comforted a shocked nation. This was Reagan near the acme of his reign as America's ceremonial head of state, a height he reached even as his grip on government policy faltered. Later that year, in July, Reagan presided over a gala rededication of the Statue of Liberty, his favorite symbol of national pride, after extensive renovations that the nation's schoolchildren had funded with their contributions. On Independence Day, the president appeared, against the backdrop of the famous statue, as a matching sculpture of patriotism, showcased on television screens beneath a huge fireworks display over New York harbor. The actress Liza Minnelli effused, "It's what America's about, for God's sake. Our royalty is show business. We don't get kings and queens."[2]

Yet, soon after the summer of 1986, the symbolic king tumbled far and fast, amid scandal and growing public discontent with conservative rule. In November, the Democrats took control of the U.S. Senate, while maintaining a firm grip on the House. "The Reagan revolution is over," Tip O'Neill crowed.[3] When the young conservative David Brock arrived in the capital in the fall of 1986 to work at the *Washington Times*, he saw that "the conservative era ushered in by Ronald Reagan's election was fading fast."[4] A few days before Christmas, Lou Cannon, Washington's foremost expert on Ronald Reagan, wrote, "All the glitter is gone now, all the magic lost."[5] Away from Washington, on Wall Street, the sense of an impending end to the go-go years of the 1980s was palpable. "*Quick, just give me my money while there is still some left*," wrote Michael Lewis, who worked for Salomon Brothers at the time. "That was the general sentiment in the air at the end of 1986."[6] A television special, *Reagan's Way*, set to celebrate the president's seventy-sixth birthday in February 1987, was canceled due to a lack of advertisers, all "because of the Iranian thing," remarked the show's intended distributor.[7] But it was not just "the Iranian thing."

A manifold crisis enveloped the "Reagan revolution" from late 1986 through 1988—not just a crisis of conservative governance but a crisis of legitimacy for conservatism as a philosophy and movement. Conservative cadres, from lawyers to clergymen to publicists, had presented themselves as a new ruling elite, equipped not only with ideas for reinvigorating the United States but also with a moral compass that would command authority and forge social unity. The pillars of Reaganism included conservative Christianity and reverence of wealth, the latter often taking the form of cheerleading for financiers. Each of these pillars suffered major blows and showed signs of cracking during the crisis that commenced in late 1986. Less than two weeks after early November's one-two punch of the Iranian arms-sales revelations and the election returns, Ivan Boesky, the high-flying Wall Street arbitrageur, pled guilty to extensive insider trading, and it was revealed that he had cooperated extensively with prosecutors, implicating other figures in American finance.[8] A meltdown of the nation's savings-and-loans would, like the Wall Street scandals, show that the conservative program of loosening the bonds of regulation and social convention over the economy's financial sector had led to corruption and havoc. Conservative evangelists, for their part, were brought low by tawdry sex and corruption scandals. Just as damaging to the politicized version of conservative Christianity was the outcry over the government's failure to respond to the exploding AIDS crisis. The Reagan administration's slowness to address HIV/AIDS in any serious way seemed rooted in a religious condemnation of homosexuality. Surgeon General C. Everett Koop's forceful response to this challenge gave conservatives a chance to regain moral standing, yet Koop's abandonment by fellow conservatives wasted that chance. By the late 1980s, the authority of conservatism, in both the realms of economics and simple morality, was hobbled.

Running throughout this period, like a polluted stream that could not be stopped, was the Iran-Contra scandal, which further impaired the Reagan administration's capacity to govern. The televised hearings of an Iran-Contra congressional investigating committee in the spring and summer of 1987 made for captivating political theater, as Oliver North and others got their chance to tell their story in public and made the most of it. But despite North's transformation into a folk hero of military patriotism, the scandal would not go away, and Reagan could not fully recover. Reagan escaped impeachment, but at great cost to his pride—and his power. To save his job, he had to accept a new myth in place of an old one: the legend of Reagan's incompetence replaced the dented belief in his special political prowess.

The November 1986 elections put Republicans back on their heels. Twelve Republican U.S. senators brought to Washington on Reagan's coattails in 1980 had gone up for reelection, and six of them were turned out after a single term. Conservatives Jeremiah Denton of Alabama and Paula Hawkins of Florida lost to seasoned opponents, Denton to U.S. Representative Richard Shelby, the sort of shrewd moderate white Democrat who remained competitive in Southern elections throughout the 1980s, Hawkins to a popular liberal governor, Bob Graham. Democrats made a net gain of eight senators, enough to secure a firm majority of 55–45. As 1987 approached, a new Democratic leadership team in the House also prepared to challenge the president forcefully. Jim Wright of Fort Worth would replace O'Neill as House Speaker. A preacher during his teenage years, Wright was immediately identifiable by his arching, bushy eyebrows and a tight smile betraying a taut, aggressive manner. He was feared by David Stockman as a "snake oil vendor," and both Wright's populist streak and his communication skills came to the fore as he reached his ambition's summit.[9] Soon after becoming Speaker, Wright engineered passage of a new clean water bill by a vote of 306–8. Reagan vetoed it, and Congress overrode his veto. Wright moved on to steer a highway spending bill, aid to the homeless, and a bill punishing unfair trade practices through the House, all against Reagan's wishes. After Reagan held a press conference in October 1987, in which he made a series of false statements, Wright went over the transcript carefully. The president said he was frustrated that he had sent a budget to Congress, which had "simply put it on the shelf and refused even to consider it." In fact, his budget had received votes in both chambers, garnering a total of forty-five supporters. Wright told his Democratic colleagues, "I'm trying to get the public to understand this son of a bitch is a liar."[10]

Wright was a formidable parliamentary foe, but his ability to marshal forces against Reagan was enhanced in 1987 because the bedrock governing philosophy of Reaganism—that the pursuit of economic self-interest was the key to national restoration and that government should unshackle the private sector—was in trouble. The savings-and-loan (or thrift) industry had been on the rocks in the early 1980s, obligated to keep to conservative, low-earning investments and increasingly unable to compete for retail customers with banks that were offering high-interest rate checking accounts. The political system's response was to remove various restrictions from the thrifts. Soon they were playing recklessly in the bond and real estate markets. Individuals, previously faced with legal limits on how big an ownership stake they could hold in thrifts, now could take control, and some fancied themselves grandees of development and finance. The most notorious would be Charles Keating, who ran Lincoln Savings and Loan, based in Irvine, California, and eventually took his thrift's depositors down the bankruptcy hole with him, in the process sullying the reputations of five U.S. senators who, at Keating's request, met as a group with Edwin Gray, chief regulator of the thrifts, in 1987 and told him to back off from Lincoln.[11] The "rental" of the Congress through contributions from thrift operators was blatant. The major thrift deregulation bill, the Garn-St Germain Act of 1982, was mainly the work of U.S. Representative Fernand St Germain, Democrat of Rhode Island, chair of the House Banking Committee. St Germain, a man of humble origins, lived far better than his congressional salary warranted. People who could be affected by legislation before the Banking Committee cut him into lucrative business deals. This kind of thing was nothing new on Capitol Hill; it was what the writer George Washington Plunkitt had called "honest graft," as it broke no law. But rarely did it have such costly results.[12] Wright would eventually cause himself trouble with his own advocacy on behalf of Texas thrifts, but until his own downfall (see chapter 13), the thrift crisis strengthened his hand as Speaker by renewing a conviction, in Congress and among the public, of the need for government regulation.

Nothing seemed to help the savings-and-loans. In March 1985, Ohio's governor, Richard Celeste, declared a bank holiday in his state, reminiscent of actions taken in the 1930s to stem bank failures, after a big Cincinnati thrift went bust.[13] Official Washington watched events nervously. By the start of 1987, the Federal Savings and Loan Insurance Corporation, which guaranteed depositors payment up to $100,000 from the U.S. government when thrifts went bankrupt, was insolvent.[14] The magic of a free market in finance was no magic at all for these institutions, which had, for decades, played a big role in financing home construction and mortgages for a growing middle class. The nation's taxpayers eventually would pay almost $124 billion—more than the tax revenues that Reagan had raised with TEFRA in 1982—to clean up messes created by savings-and-loan officers who treated the thrifts' assets like casino chips, and who in many cases simply looted the thrifts to support lavish personal expenditures.[15] Much to their credit, under Presidents Reagan and George H. W. Bush, Justice Department personnel would prosecute 1,100 individual thrift officers, securing over 800 convictions, many of which led to prison terms.[16] But the deeper responsibility lay with the politicians of both parties who, prodded either by avarice or by ideology, urged deregulation as a cure-all.

The theme of corruption played ever louder. During Reagan's first term as president, the idea of cashing in on connections had encountered little resistance. Now, even as economic expansion continued, such behavior received public censure. Michael Deaver—like St Germain, a man of modest background—grew to crave wealth as he served the Reagans and observed the luxury of their social set. Wine-tasting outings in the mid-Atlantic region were favored recreations of his during his White House service. Like Baker, he left the White House at the start of Reagan's second term, but unlike the wealthy Baker he departed government service entirely, to begin a lobbying business in Washington (which he called a "consulting" business in an ill-fated effort to skirt restrictions on lobbying by past White House officials). In 1987, Deaver was indicted for perjuring himself in his testimony before a grand jury.[17] He was later convicted and administered a suspended prison sentence. Lyn Nofziger, formerly the head of the Office of Political Affairs for Reagan (meaning that he ran the White House's patronage shop), ran into similar trouble. He lobbied improperly for Wedtech, a military contractor in the Bronx that Meese also championed, leading to a new probe into the attorney general's dealings. Ultimately, two U.S. Representatives from New York, Mario Biaggi and Robert Garcia, as well as Stanley Friedman, the Bronx borough president, were convicted and imprisoned for bribery and extortion in the Wedtech scandal.[18]

Attorney General Meese finally escaped his troubles only by announcing he would resign in July 1988, before James McKay, the second independent counsel to investigate him, was to release a large report on Wedtech and Meese's failures to pay his taxes, as well as other matters. Meese declared himself "completely vindicated," which was untrue. McKay determined that Meese was guilty of breaking the law, but did not recommend indictment, perhaps thinking that the best solution to the problem had already been found.[19] In March 1988, a scene played out in the White House that seemed to symbolize the exhaustion of Reaganite energies at the twilight of the Reagan presidency. Arthur Burns, the number-two appointee at the Justice Department, and William Weld, head of the department's criminal division, met privately with President Reagan. Burns and Weld intended to resign in protest over Meese's leadership but wished first to explain directly to the president how profoundly Meese was damaging the government. As Weld explained that, if it were up to him, Meese would be prosecuted, Reagan fell asleep.[20] The president let Meese decide his own fate, and Meese, at last, had had enough.

The corruption scandals that overtook official life in the second half of the 1980s were bipartisan, but they called into question the basic creed only of one party, the Republicans. Biaggi, Garcia, and Friedman were Democrats. Four of the "Keating Five" were Democrats, as was St Germain. With the Democrats still ruling the U.S. House, and assuming control of the Senate in 1987, they collected large sums from business interests. When Representative Tony Coelho of California ran the fundraising effort for the Democrats in the lower chamber, he made the strongest pitch yet to corporations: the smart money would go to the people in charge on the Hill; there was no reason to steer contributions to Republicans just because they seemed more avidly pro-business. Timothy Wirth, an ambitious House Democrat from Colorado, introduced a bill in 1985 that would ban the practice known as "greenmail," in which a speculator bought up a company's stock, threatened a hostile takeover, and agreed to relent in exchange for a fat buyout. The practice was destructive; it was simply ransom paid by companies with valuable assets. The investment banking firm of Drexel Burnham Lambert, with prominent greenmailers on its client list, started giving money to Democrats, including almost $24,000 to Wirth's successful effort to move up to the Senate (which marked the end of his antigreenmail effort). Drexel's political action committee contributions jumped from $20,000 in 1984 to $177,000 in the next election cycle. The biggest recipient of Drexel money, however, was Senator Alfonse D'Amato of New York, a Republican. Known as "Senator Pothole" to his constituents for his attention to local matters, he was called "Senator Shakedown" in Washington.[21]

New York City, like Washington, proved a nest of corruption, and it was here that the fervent Reaganite belief in the merit of corporate and financial America's biggest winners—the idea that Boesky and others deserved their massive wealth—was set to explode. The instrument of Nemesis, the mythic embodiment of punishment for hubris, would be the U.S. attorney for the southern district of New York, Rudolph Giuliani. Giuliani compiled a dazzling record of indictments and convictions during his tenure, which began when he left the third-ranking position in Reagan's Justice Department to take what was, technically, a demotion. But Giuliani wanted to be at the world's media center, which he also knew to be a major nexus of graft and crime—the writer James Traub called New York in the 1980s "the sort of gorgeously foul swamp that prosecutors live for"—awaiting its Savonarola.[22] Admirers saw in Giuliani a zealous moralist who displaced his youthful priestly ambition onto powerful lawbreakers. Detractors saw a nakedly ambitious showman who maximized publicity with high-handed tactics and questionable legal methods. Giuliani won wide praise for taking on and beating organized-crime "family" heads and criminal officeholders. Then he turned his sights on Wall Street insiders, who were violating basic SEC rules by using privileged information to make millions in the stock market.

The first crack came with the indictment of Dennis Levine, an M&A specialist at Drexel and the organizer of a network of insider traders with secret bank accounts where they stored their illicit returns. He pled guilty to felony crimes in June 1986. Levine could be dismissed as a rogue trader, not a big fish. But Boesky, fresh from his triumph at Berkeley (see chapter 7), could not be. Investigators had uncovered his wrongdoing first, but had kept their discovery secret; he had led them to Levine and agreed to record their conversations. In December 1986, only six months after his "Greed is all right" speech, Boesky made his guilty plea. Now one of the great new names of unfettered capitalism had been ruined, his success suddenly seen as the result of rigging the game, not outplaying competitors. Boesky had extensive dealings with Michael Milken, the dominant force in the junk bond market, which soon would unravel under new scrutiny. In 1986, Giuliani's staff raided Drexel's New York offices and found recordings of telephone conversations dating back two years. "You're a sleaze bag," said one trader to another, after they had arranged a ruse to hide insider trading. "Welcome to the world of being a sleaze."[23] This term, "sleaze"—from the earlier adjective sleazy, which originally described cheap and slippery fabrics, but which had become a metaphor for moral shabbiness—had come into use to refer to corrupt or dirty tactics and to those who used them.

A panic rose among financial professionals as 1987 unfolded. Subpoenas and investigations spread from one financial firm to another, including Drexel, Salomon Brothers, Shearson Lehman Brothers, and Kidder Peabody. In February, Giuliani garnered worldwide attention when Martin Wigton, a Kidder vice president, was arrested dramatically in his workplace; as far away as Australia, a newspaper exulted over "Wall Street Yuppies in Handcuffs and Tears."[24] On top of the insider-trading inquiries came a burst of arrests of Wall Street employees on charges of selling cocaine, often in exchange for private financial information or client lists.[25]

Talk of congressional action against leveraged buyouts suddenly erupted. Quickly, in October, investors fled from stocks whose price had jumped on takeover rumors. The Dow Jones Industrial Average, which had reached an all-time high of over 2,700 during the summer, dropped 250 points in three trading days. The following Monday, October 19, was the worst day of all, when anxiety that had built up over the weekend found release. The market fell 508 points, a record in percentage terms for a single day, worse than any in 1929. Milken heroically stanched the bleeding, getting his stable of buyers to mop up failing stocks and bond issues. But many smaller investors lost out in crowd selling and had no reserves with which to regain their positions and ride out the wave.

As always happened, when a bull run came to its inevitable end, many were rudely disillusioned of the idea that finance was a nonstop money machine.[26]

The cultural transformation of Wall Street raiders and traders from heroes to villains was complete by the end of 1987, capped by the premier in December of Oliver Stone's film *Wall Street*. Filled with stereotypes and clichés, the movie nevertheless etched a vivid portrait of greed and abuse of position. In its most famous scene, obviously playing off Boesky's speech at Berkeley, the lead character, the reptilian Gordon Gekko, gives a speech to a shareholder meeting as he orchestrates a hostile takeover. Gekko explains that the company's management has gotten fat and lazy, feathering its own nest and failing to maximize profits. He continues, "The point is, ladies and gentleman, that greed—for lack of a better word—is good."

Greed is right.
Greed works.
Greed clarifies, cuts through, and captures the essence of the evolu-
    tionary spirit.

Pretentiously, Gekko evokes a social Darwinist ethics, with avarice the key to rejuvenation for both individual corporations and "that other malfunctioning corporation called the USA," as he concludes on a political note. But Gekko is shown to be ethically hollow even on his own terms. His advantage in the markets comes not from superior talent or even the ruthless pursuit of efficiency but from cheating. As he says to his young protégé in a more honest moment, "The public's out there throwing darts at a board, sport. I don't throw darts at a board—I bet on sure things." Pilfering privileged information and violating the law are among the true keys to his supremacy. And while he tells the shareholders, "I am not the destroyer of companies. I am the liberator of them!" this turns out to be a lie, as his takeover targets, far from becoming newly competitive, are consumed in asset sell-offs.[27] On December 20, Ivan Boesky was sentenced to three years in federal prison. Milken's turn would not come until 1990, but a long watch on his fate had already commenced.

If Wall Street insiders, savings-and-loan swindlers, and crooked politicians came to personify sleaze in the 1980s, their counterparts in the conservative movement that started collapsing in 1986 embodied another slang expression of the era: glitz. Stemming from the German word for glitter, glitz was a tastelessly flashy display, meant to convey wealth and excitement but barely diverting attention from a basic shallowness. Show business and expensive discos were glitzy. But so, perhaps oddly, were some of the Christian evangelists who presumably supplied the moral ballast for a conservative movement that bowed to the shrine of wealth. Many of the leading activists among evangelical Christians, like Jerry Falwell, comported themselves soberly. But other preachers, such as Paul and Jan Crouch and Jim and Tammy Faye Bakker, were more ostentatious. To homes across America, through Christian television networks, they beamed a vision of Christian luxury, complete with chandeliered mansions and landed estates, accented with extensive wardrobes of suits and dresses meant to denote the lives of country squires and ladies. The Bakkers' show was called *The PTL Club*; PTL stood for both Praise the Lord and People That Love. Trained in the Pentecostal Assemblies of God church, the Bakkers preached an ecumenical gospel of wealth and ease. God would provide for those who came to Him. They were more universal in their message of love than some; Tammy Faye Bakker stood out in the late 1980s for her embrace of gay AIDS sufferers and her tearful criticism of Christians who shunned those stricken with the plague. The Bakkers ended their broadcasts by saying, "God loves you, He really, really, does."

But Jim Bakker defrauded his contributors and siphoned millions from his businesses for himself and his wife, and their tacky style made them easy fodder for their critics. The journalist Frances Fitz-Gerald wrote, "They personified the most characteristic excesses of the nineteen-eighties—the greed, the love of glitz, and the shamelessness.... the Bakkers' version of the prosperity gospel could be seen as the cargo cult of junk-bond capitalism."[28] By 1987, the press, particularly the *Charlotte Observer*, and federal investigators were catching up with to Jim Bakker's games. A palatial apartment the Bakkers kept featured gold-plated bathroom fixtures. A private jet was chartered solely to fly their wardrobe from one lavish home to another. Tammy Faye joyously announced on air that she had bought Jim two giraffes for his birthday. Jim Bakker's financial chicanery got him convicted and sentenced to forty-five years in prison in 1989.

But this scandal alone did not make him an object lesson in moral hypocrisy. Rather, what brought Bakker true infamy was the bombshell news, which broke in March 1987 following his sudden resignation as head of PTL, that he had paid $265,000 in PTL funds to a former church secretary, Jessica Hahn, to prevent her from telling the world that Bakker and another pastor had coerced her into having sex with them in a Florida hotel in 1980. Bakker admitted having had a sexual "encounter" with Hahn.[29] Christian conservatives rushed to stay abreast of the vehement public anger now directed at the Bakkers. In disgrace, Bakker agreed to allow Falwell to step in temporarily as PTL chairman.

Falwell had broader concerns than the stability of PTL. He was worried that the Bakkers were damaging the image of television preachers and of Protestant evangelicals in general. Evangelical Protestants, since 1980, had felt themselves newly empowered, and this perception—even if it exaggerated the sway of preachers like Falwell—was widespread. Falwell had had a starring role in the 1984 Republican National Convention in Dallas, offering the main benediction from the podium, appearing to give his blessing to one political party. Falwell quickly took control of PTL and pushed the Bakkers and their allies out for good. He charged Jim Bakker with a long history of "homosexual problems"—in addition to his alleged heterosexual predation against Hahn—as well as financial dishonesty. Amid a public duel between the preachers, conducted largely on television, Falwell said, "What Jim Bakker needs to do, he needs to come clean about Jessica Hahn and repent. That little girl was injured for life by that terrible travesty in Florida. He has to come forward and say, 'Yes I did it,' and ask God's forgiveness."[30] For television preachers, viewership and contributions were down across the board.[31]

In early 1988, Jimmy Swaggart, an Assemblies of God television evangelist like the Bakkers, worsened the crisis. Swaggart had attacked the Bakkers over doctrine and spread the rumors about Jim Bakker's sexual past. Swaggart's active support for right-wing militias and death squads around the world made him a more overtly political figure than the Bakkers. But he, too, was undone, it seemed, by sexual misbehavior. He admitted the truth of accusations that he had had sex with prostitutes, appearing on his television show and, his face contorted, crying to the cameras, "I have sinned against You, my Lord, and I would ask that Your precious blood would wash and cleanse every stain until it is in the seas of

God's forgiveness." This display quickly became a touchstone of popular culture, endlessly parodied and mentioned. A reputation for sleaziness was spreading, indiscriminately, among television preachers. "When the Godly Make Us Vomit," read one headline about Swaggart.[32] In the decentralized world of American Protestantism, Swaggart was an independent operator, a true entrepreneur—and neither Falwell nor anyone else could control him.

Almost exactly in step with the implosion of evangelical celebrity preachers, a different ethical drama played out that also showed movement conservatism coming unglued in public. This was the havoc that the long-incubating HIV/AIDS crisis finally wreaked in the body politic. This disorder, triggered in part by activism from an unlikely source, Surgeon General Koop, and in part by new forms of agitation by advocates for gay rights and the interests of people with AIDS, made the ostrich-like stance of the Reagan administration an object of wide criticism. Koop was a fundamentalist Presbyterian immediately identifiable by the gold-trimmed uniform he wore—reviving a long-abandoned custom of surgeons general, who headed the U.S. Public Health Service—and by his long gray beard, recalling the biblical prophets as depicted in 1950s Hollywood epics. He boasted long involvement in antiabortion and biblical prophecy enterprises when Reagan nominated him in 1981, and his confirmation was delayed by liberals who mocked him as "Dr. Kook." But in 1985, after Rock Hudson died, the president made a private speech saying he planned to ask the surgeon general for a report on AIDS, and Koop took this signal and ran with it. In the fall of 1986, Koop presented a finished report as a kind of fait accompli to the White House's Domestic Policy Council, and gained approval to publish a brochure about HIV, which he did in October.[33]

Koop's materials dispelled prevalent myths about HIV, emphasizing that the virus could not be contracted through casual physical contact. Koop recommended sexual monogamy and avoiding risky behaviors, which he clearly identified as needle-sharing, anal sex, and promiscuity. But the incendiary points were these: Koop prescribed condom use and wrote, "Education about AIDS should start in early elementary school and at home," adding, "The threat of AIDS can provide an opportunity for parents to instill in their children their own moral and ethical standards."[34]

The White House, somehow, did not see the reaction coming. Almost all of this information was beyond what most American newspapers considered polite discussion in 1986. To many conservative Christians, the report was revolting and suggested Koop had lost his moral bearings. Koop insisted that he must separate his personal moral beliefs from his public-health recommendations. He added, "My position on AIDS is a very strong pro-life position. I am trying to save lives."[35] Yet he impressed many as one who had changed in the face of a human disaster. Liberals hailed this turnabout, while conservatives saw a turncoat. One employee in the federal government who had worked with Koop said that in the past, "He would make remarks about gays, ugly stuff—'homo this' and 'homo that.'" Within a year of his report's release, he seemed transformed, speaking often of the humanity of AIDS sufferers and turning his preachments against those who spurned or blamed the victims of the disease.[36]

Conservatives rallied to quarantine Koop within the Reagan administration and the Republican Party. Phyllis Schlafly deplored his "fronting for the homosexuals," and the antiabortion March for Life took back an award. Three Republican presidential candidates pulled out of a long-scheduled dinner meant to honor Koop. Secretary of Education William Bennett, a burly political brawler who had become a spokesman for conservative morals in the administration, and White House aide Gary Bauer—the types Koop later described as "political appointees who placed conservative ideology above saving lives"—railed against Koop's lax morals and led the charge in the executive branch for a presidential endorsement of a new conservative solution for the health crisis: mandatory universal testing for HIV (now that a test existed).[37] Koop, with other public-health professionals, saw this response as a recipe for discrimination and paranoia, and feared it would drive high-risk Americans away from medical care for fear of being labeled plague carriers. They called for legal protections against bias toward those with HIV. In 1986, the California legislature twice passed such antidiscrimination measures; twice the governor, Republican George Deukmejian, vetoed them.[38]

Finally, it seemed, Reagan could keep his silence no longer; he would have to choose sides in the conservative civil war over HIV, in order to end the political carnage. At the end of May 1987, he addressed the Third International Conference on AIDS, which took place in Washington. But the speech did not calm the waters. Reagan made headlines by uttering the word AIDS—only the second time he had done so publicly. But he repudiated Koop's departures from conservative wisdom. The president simply emphasized the need for moral education and the attractiveness of abstinence advocacy; the mantra of "Just Say No" could be extended from drugs to sex. Reagan would support neither sex education nor condom use. He also endorsed a limited program of testing. Some of the assembled researchers and activists booed him.[39] The president announced he would appoint an AIDS commission to compose policy prescriptions.

With Reagan hoping that a smile and conservative bromides would let him ride out the storm over AIDS, the wave of heightened public consciousness washed over him, leaving him behind. Gay-rights advocates and AIDS activists pressed ahead with interventions both temperate and unruly. At least two hundred thousand Americans traveled to the capital on October 12, 1987, to join a March on Washington for Lesbian and Gay Rights. The existential crisis of gay men had spurred a new mass-based initiative aimed at securing civil and human rights for all gay Americans—women and men—who had resolved not to keep their identities secret. Just before the march, two thousand same-sex couples, whose relationships enjoyed no legal recognition, gathered to exchange symbolic vows of commitment, underscoring the gay rights movement's gravitation toward a demand for recognition as Americans whose sexuality, in civic terms, was incidental.[40] On the National Mall, a new form of commemoration for AIDS victims came to national attention: the AIDS Quilt, organized by the NAMES Project, the inspiration of San Franciscan Cleve Jones. Those who had lost a loved one to AIDS could fashion a cloth rectangle to memorialize the dead, in whatever manner they wished. In the years to come, the Quilt would become massive, comprising forty-four thousand panels by 2002, and would be displayed all over the country.[41] Like the Vietnam Veterans Memorial, dedicated in Washington in 1982— which simply listed the names of the dead on somber black granite slabs, and invited visitors to place their own interpretation of the war's meaning on the site—the AIDS Quilt gripped the imagination of a grieving country. Even in 1987, when only 1,920 panels existed, it took three hours to lay them on the ground. Quilting epitomized American homespun culture, and its evocation was meant to appeal to Americans who had never been moved by calls for gay rights or AIDS awareness. Jones remarked (exaggerating for effect), "Every family has a quilt; it makes them think of their grandmothers. That's what we need: We need all these American grandmothers to want us to live, to be willing to say that our lives are worth defending."[42]

It was not all quilts and grandmothers, however. A lot of AIDS activists and gay-rights advocates were very angry—at all levels of government and at religious conservatives. ACT UP, which stood for AIDS Coalition to Unleash Power, led the way in venting that anger. Larry Kramer, the original angry AIDS activist and the main source of the concept for ACT UP, had penned a stream of vituperative, often profane articles about the inadequacy of America's responses to the HIV/AIDS crisis since the early 1980s. Kramer, estranged from AIDS advocacy groups that lobbied government officials, had had a huge success on the New York stage in 1985 with his play *The Normal Heart*, a barely fictionalized account of his journey through the political warfare over AIDS.[43] But his outrage was undimmed. He wanted people to become so obstreperous that their demands—for greater research funding and for readier access to experimental drugs—could not be ignored. ACT UP was a group for people who wanted to disrupt business as usual, which they did: at the New York Stock Exchange, at FDA headquarters, and, most controversially, in 1989, at a mass in New York's St. Patrick's Cathedral, led by Roman Catholic Archbishop John Cardinal O'Connor, an unrelenting foe of homosexuality, abortion, and condoms.[44] Some blamed ACT UP for alienating the straight public. But ACT UP confronted the general public with the desperation of the AIDS crisis, and the message that AIDS sufferers and their comrades were furious with those in power, like no one else had. Borrowing symbolism first deployed by gay West German radicals in the 1970s, they made their emblem the pink triangle that gay men had been forced to wear under Nazi rule—inverted from the downward-pointing direction of the original, and accompanied by the unforgettable script "Silence = Death."[45] ACT UP succeeded in its quest to make AIDS impossible to ignore. Its members were perfectly willing to sacrifice their popularity if, in the process, they could extract more forceful action on the crisis from the government and could reach the hearts of Americans with their message of urgency.

Even as Reagan was booed by scientists in May 1987—a potent signal of his lost standing—Congress had begun to stage a very public inquiry into the original scandal of the 1986–1988 period, the Iran-Contra affair. The hearings of a special Senate–House investigating committee, shown on television for hours daily from May through July, were the real broadcast spectacle of 1987. Over 70 percent of Americans watched Oliver North's testimony in July, which was broadcast live, in the daytime, by all major networks, recalling the drama of the Watergate hearings.[46]

North ended up an unexpected winner in the media drama of Iran-Contra, partly because of flawed tactics and strategy by Democratic leaders. The twenty-six committee members, seated behind two banks of raised tables, looked down on witnesses like a Roman tribunal, creating sympathy for those undergoing questioning. In fact, while the star witnesses were, in theory, vulnerable to indictment by the independent counsel, Lawrence Walsh, the committee, in return for testimony by North and others, gave them partial legal immunity, over Walsh's protests. North's truculent lawyer, Brendan Sullivan, drove a hard bargain, specifying the exact times, terms, and duration of North's testimony. He was able to do so because the committee set itself a ten-month limit to produce a final report in order to avoid the appearance of politicizing the 1988 election. The clock was ticking, and Sullivan's dilatory tactics were rewarded. While the GOP leaders in the Senate and House selected members for the committee who uniformly supported Reagan's Central America policy, the Democrats, concerned to appear evenhanded, picked both opponents and supporters of the Contras, and excluded leading critics of Reagan's policy. Of the eleven senators on the committee, only three opposed Contra aid. Of the fifteen House members, all six Republicans supported Contra aid, as did three of the nine Democrats, creating a pro-Contra majority of nine to six.[47] Public opinion, by contrast, continued to oppose Contra aid by a wide margin.[48]

Committee Democrats seemed of two minds about how to approach the president's involvement in his own policies toward Nicaragua and Iran. They wanted to saddle Reagan with ultimate responsibility. But they also spotlighted the shocking and absurd escapades that North and his confederates had organized in carrying out Reagan's policies. This took the spotlight off Reagan and bolstered the narrative of zealous subordinates run amok. Democrats also decided from the start not to take up the question of impeachment. In part they calculated that Reagan, despite his sagging poll numbers, retained a reservoir of goodwill among the public, and that the expenditure of political capital needed to pursue impeachment would prove more costly than the gain. On the path toward impeachment lay uncertainty and risk. They also knew they had a Republican president on the ropes. Reagan had fired Donald Regan as his chief of staff in January 1987, hoping this would satisfy critics and bring order to his administration. This sacrifice did not call off the hounds, but Regan's replacement with former Republican senate majority leader Howard Baker did. Baker quickly smoothed relations with Congress.[49] To many Washington insiders his ascension marked the real passing of the crisis; the hearings would be a show for the public. As things stood, Democrats were empowered legislatively. Jim Wright recalled later in explanation, "We were getting everything we wanted here in the House."[50]

North, the star witness, took his turn before the cameras in the second week of July, and threatened with his unbending defense of his actions to upend the hearings. At the NSC, North had worn business suits. For his testimony he donned his marine uniform, resplendent with ribbons won for bravery during his service in Vietnam, topped with a fresh military-style haircut. North sat erect and stared straight at his inquisitors, yielding them no moral authority even as he admitted conducting illegal operations, lying to Congress to cover them up, and then destroying uncounted incriminating public documents. He maintained that, at every step, he felt certain he was executing President Reagan's wishes, an acknowledgement that seemed to jeopardize Reagan legally. Yet North also stated that Reagan never specifically ordered him personally to commit a criminal act, thus giving Reagan a degree of legal cover. North's main defense of his unlawful behavior was simple and sweeping: "By their very nature, covert operations or special activities are a lie. There is great deceit, deception practiced in the conduct of covert operations. They are at essence a lie."[51] But, of course, those to whom executive-branch officials conducting covert operations are supposed to lie do not include the Congress. And North had run operations expressly forbidden by U.S. law. When Senator Daniel Inouye (Democrat of Hawai'i), the committee's chair, a one-armed World War II veteran whose military exploits matched North's, began to lecture North about the famous "Nuremberg principle" that men in uniform had a legal duty to disobey illegal orders, Sullivan interrupted Inouye and shouted him down.[52]

"Those of us who sat on the two-tiered dais could not fully appreciate the magnetism that North generated," Senators George Mitchell and

William Cohen (Democrat and Republican of Maine), both committee members, recalled afterward. "From a distance, North looked attractive in his Marine uniform and rows of medals, but thin and not particularly imposing. It was not until we slipped into the anteroom to drink coffee and watch the proceedings on the television sets there that we saw the dramatic transformation. His telegenic face filled the entire screen. His clear gray eyes (perpetually moist) reflected sadness, anger, sympathy. His voice was alternately soft and forceful, and it cracked at just the right emotional moment."[53] North made charged, often irrelevant declarations of his fealty to the president, his personal commitment to the Contras (whom he called the "Nicaraguan democratic resistance"), his willingness to go *mano a mano* with Palestinian terrorist Abu Nidal, and his fear for his daughter's safety from the hands of vengeful evildoers angry over North's effectiveness at thwarting their plans. He intended, he said, to tell the committee "the good, the bad, and the ugly." North's penchant for Hollywood clichés prompted comparisons with Reagan's own stagecraft, and led many commentators to see in North a charismatic figure. They declared "Olliemania" a true enthusiasm. Senator Orrin Hatch of Utah, a conservative Republican, had said before North's appearance that he found evidence that North had skimmed Enterprise funds for his personal use "sad" and "sleazy."[54] But after North's debut, committee Republicans turned about-face and became the colonel's fulsome admirers. Sullivan, meanwhile, whispered advice in North's ear before North replied to questions and stacked piles of pro-North telegrams on the witness table during North's testimony.

To some, North became a hero. Arthur Liman, the lead lawyer for Senate Democrats on the committee, on returning to the hearing room after a lunch break on North's last day of testimony saw, to his dismay, that Senate policemen were lined up to have their photographs taken with a smiling North.[55] For a time it appeared that North's prestige might even extend to the Contras themselves. Those committee Democrats who opposed Contra aid seemed tentative; the pro-Contra pleadings by North and other witnesses went largely unrebutted. Representative David Bonior, a passionate opponent of Contra aid (and not a member of the committee), said in frustration, "I've been getting calls about the hearings from activists all over the country saying, 'What the hell is going on?' The idea was, if we stuck to process questions and constitutional questions, they were so important it would be easy to carry the day for us. We didn't want to debate the policy itself. I'm not sure that was right. The House Republicans are all arguing the policy."[56] However, North's popularity was easily exaggerated. One entrepreneur who produced thousands of "Ollie North" action figures had to eat most of his outlay, selling only a paltry few. By August, Olliemania, an expression of the traditional American attraction to military heroes—an attraction that had temporarily weakened during the 1970s—had subsided, and an opinion poll showed that almost two-thirds of the public considered North's actions "more wrong than right."[57]

When Poindexter, former national security adviser and navy rear admiral, a nuclear physicist with a low profile and a cold, uninviting manner, testified before the committee in mid-July, he sealed off any remaining avenue of approach to the president regarding the infamous "diversion" of funds from the Iranian arms sales to the Contras. Reagan's safety on this one issue, by no means the most important one, gave his defenders an opening to assert that there was no "smoking gun" that could incriminate the president in any important way. Poindexter maintained that he had "made a very deliberate decision" not to discuss the diversion with Reagan and not to pass on a memorandum from North describing it, "so that I could insulate him from the decision and provide some future deniability for the President if it ever leaked out."[58] Poindexter's audacity seemed to taunt and frustrate the committee. He may well have been lying about whether he had told Reagan of the diversion; he was, after all, openly admitting that his purpose always had been to falsify history and conceal presidential misconduct. There was no way to prove whether he was being truthful. Yet he harmed his credibility when he answered 184 different questions during his testimony with "I don't recall" or some variation of that reply.[59] This made him the champion of forgetfulness in the whole affair, but this was a measure only of degree. Other witnesses, both during the hearings and in later legal proceedings, also were afflicted with memory loss.

After the dust of the committee hearings settled, it was clear that North and Poindexter, as well as Richard Secord, North's main contractor for delivering arms to the Contras and the Iranians, were scapegoats whose culpability drew fire away from the president. During the hearings they were careful, as noted earlier, in saying they could not confirm Reagan's specific knowledge of their wrongdoing, aware that if they alienated Reagan's supporters on the committee they risked retribution from Republicans determined to protect the president. But later they sang a different tune, complaining—in their own interest, to be sure, but still significantly—that they had taken the fall for the president. After Secord pled guilty to a single felony count in exchange for a suspended sentence in 1990, he stated angrily, "I think former President Reagan has been hiding out. I think it's cowardly. I believed earlier and I still believe that he was well aware of the general outlines of the so-called Iran-Contra affair." North published a memoir, *Under Fire*, in which he portrayed Reagan and George Bush as fully aware of the illegal Contra supply operation and the Iranian arms sales and argued that Reagan also knew of the diversion. "I am . . . convinced," North wrote. *"President Reagan knew everything."* The White House had claimed that when Reagan telephoned North to fire him, the president asked North to give "the entire truth" to investigators. North's recollection was different. The president had said, "Ollie, you have to understand, I just didn't know," North wrote. North took this to be a cover story that Reagan was asking him to support.[60]

By summer's end, congressional leaders, looking a bit like television producers who had lost control of their own show and knowing that the drama had passed its climax, girded for other battles. The looming fight was to be over Reagan's nomination, announced in July, of Robert Bork, a well-known conservative judge, to replace the retiring Supreme Court justice Lewis Powell Jr. Senator Edward Kennedy made a harsh speech against Bork, signaling the administration that it faced a struggle. Kennedy declared:

> Robert Bork's America is a land in which women would be forced into back-alley abortions, blacks would sit at segregated lunch counters, rogue police could break down citizens' doors in midnight raids, schoolchildren could not be taught about evolution, writers and artists could be censored at the whim of government, and the doors of the Federal courts would be shut on the fingers of millions of citizens for whom the judiciary is—and is often the only—protector of the individual rights that are the heart of our democracy.[61]

Bork, like many conservatives, derided the liberal Warren Court of the 1954–1969 years for supposedly inventing rights not found in the Constitution. He also had denigrated the *Roe v. Wade* decision of 1973, although he was coy concerning whether he would vote to overturn it. Kennedy's implication that Bork would not have supported the unanimous 1954 *Brown v. Board of Education* decision, which outlawed racial segregation in public schooling, was the most savage blow against Bork's reputation. If Kennedy's statement was taken to mean that Bork would consider undoing the *Brown* decision, this was absurd. But beyond individual cases, Kennedy was arguing that judges tended to be relatively sympathetic or unsympathetic to the weak, and that Bork was one who would afflict the afflicted and comfort the comfortable in general. Bork insisted that he followed the "original intent" of the Constitution's drafters, not present-day emotional tides and not the sympathy for the powerful of which Kennedy accused him. This "originalist" position echoed a series of speeches Meese had made as attorney general.[62]

Reagan fought and lost the Bork fight, and this result was another signal of how far both the president and the conservative movement had weakened compared to their earlier powers. Reagan may have thought that nominating Bork would revive conservative spirits, but instead it galvanized liberals, who mounted an impressive organizing effort that emboldened Senate Democrats. Bork's efforts to save himself only helped sink his nomination. He appeared arrogant when testifying before the Senate Judiciary Committee, lecturing questioners whose expertise in the law he disdained. More viscerally, Bork made a poor impression. Republicans and Democrats alike had seen in the Iran-Contra hearings that, in the theater of politics, appearances mattered. To many, Oliver North had appeared a brave patriot, a leading man straight from central casting. In contrast, Bork, who, with his jutting red beard, now turning gray, affected a Mephistophelean look, proved to have little allure on camera. His glowering face and his dyspeptic, haughty manner won no one over. After the committee's negative recommendation, the Senate rejected Bork, 42–58, by a bigger margin than any other judicial nominee in U.S. history.[63]

When Reagan sought television airtime for a speech defending Bork, the networks refused him. "Even had his speech been broadcast," opined the liberal journalist Haynes Johnson, "there is no reason to believe it would have made the slightest difference. The public seems to have tuned Reagan out, just as the Congress increasingly treats him as irrelevant."[64] Reagan's second choice to replace Powell, Douglas Ginsburg, withdrew his name in embarrassment following revelations that he had smoked marijuana while a professor at Harvard Law School. For an administration that deemed marijuana a "gateway drug" leading to harder stuff, this was a problem. On his third try, Reagan turned to the mild-mannered Anthony Kennedy, whom the Senate approved by a vote of 97–0. Yet the Bork struggle would be what everyone remembered from the fall of 1987. Conservatives invented a new verb, "borking," to refer to character assassination.[65] Liberals had no regrets, thinking Bork a genuine extremist and a partisan. In a final demonstration of Reagan's loss of political control, in March 1988, Congress voted to override Reagan's veto of the Civil Rights Restoration Act. Congress had passed the law with strong bipartisan support in order to reverse a Supreme Court ruling that had narrowed the application of federal civil rights laws to institutions that accepted U.S. government funding. No president had vetoed a civil rights law since Andrew Johnson during the Reconstruction era. Reagan had run his last election campaign, and he seemingly threw appearances to the wind. He said the law would "unjustifiably extend the power of the federal government over the decisions and affairs of private organizations"—the same reasoning that underlay Reagan's opposition, in principle, to federal civil rights laws going back to the 1960s. Others in his party saw danger in this hostility to hard-fought compromise legislation on civil rights; they did not wish to antagonize women and senior citizens, in addition to African Americans and other nonwhite Americans, all of whom would be protected by the law. Seventy-three senators and 292 representatives voted to negate Reagan's action.[66]

Aggressively conservative jurists, flamboyant conservative preachers, self-righteous Wall Street "masters of the universe" and lesser acolytes of unregulated finance, and champions of military confrontation in the Third World—all of them were in retreat by late 1987, along with the crusading conservative president to whom each group had looked as their liege. News reports of corrupt and improper dealings among political and social elites had come to seem normal, and continued throughout 1988. Now, many observers easily referred to the sleaze, the glitz, and the sanctimony of would-be conservative leaders of all kinds. The widely expressed passions for unrestrained capitalism and "traditional values" so characteristic of the early 1980s seemed outworn; now, each cause was on the defensive. By 1988, a widespread public yearning to turn the page on Reaganite conservatism was palpable. Whether the public was willing to embrace any alternative on offer was, however, another matter, a question that only further political competition would answer.

Twelve

Strength Through Peace

Increasingly hamstrung by political turmoil in the United States starting in 1986, and disabled most of all in domestic policy, Ronald Reagan salvaged his presidency in dramatic fashion, through peacemaking abroad. Even as the Iran-Contra scandal engulfed some areas of his foreign policy, he made history by pressing forward, in a way few could have foreseen in 1980, toward peaceful relations with the Soviet Union. Together with Mikhail Gorbachev, who took the helm in the Soviet Union in 1985, Reagan effectively ended the Cold War. The USSR under Gorbachev negotiated an exit from the arms race, leaving America an unmatched power in the world. After Reagan left office, President George H. W. Bush would continue amicable relations with Moscow and would solidify America's supreme international position. Reagan had promised Americans "peace through strength," pledging that a military buildup would make the Soviets more tractable. Decades after the presidencies of Reagan and Bush, many continued to see, in the end of the Cold War, a vindication of this U.S. strategy. But the irony of Reagan's Cold War triumph is that he gained his historic achievement by renouncing some of his own long-standing positions and agreeing to return to diplomacy and détente. By consenting to the idea of strategic parity between the superpowers—an idea Reagan always had resisted previously—he gained strategic primacy for America. The formula for success was strength through peace, more than peace through strength.

After Yuri Andropov died in February 1984—little more than a year after becoming the top leader in Moscow—and was replaced by the in-

firm Konstantin Chernenko, a joke made the rounds in Moscow: Margaret Thatcher, who had gone to Andropov's funeral, telephoned Ronald
Reagan, who had not attended, to say, "You should have come. They did
it very well. I'm definitely coming back next year."[1] Chernenko died on
March 10, 1985, his tenure even briefer than Andropov's. The next day,
the Soviet press announced both his death and Mikhail Gorbachev's
ascension to the post of general secretary of the Communist Party of
the Soviet Union (CPSU). Aged fifty-four, Gorbachev represented "the
generation of wartime children" of the 1940s.[2] He had risen swiftly in
the hopeful, reformist milieu of post-Stalin Soviet Communism. When
he reached the pinnacle of power in 1985, some saw in him an "almost
complete preoccupation . . . with domestic matters."[3] He wanted to focus
his energies on the urgent need for economic reform in his country. The
Cold War appeared as a costly diversion. Soviet military spending, after
remaining flat in the early 1980s, had started to rise, in a belated response
to Reagan's buildup.[4] In 1986, Gorbachev would say he had to "do everything . . . to weaken the grip of expenses on defense." He sometimes expressed confidence that his country could maintain strategic parity with
the Americans. But at least once he stated to the Politburo, "Our goal is
to prevent the next round of the arms race," for fear the USSR "will be
pulled into an arms race that is beyond our capabilities . . . we are at the
limits of our capabilities."[5]

Gorbachev needed a breakthrough in superpower relations. When
meeting George Bush at Chernenko's funeral, Gorbachev said, "The
USSR has never intended to fight the United States. . . . There has [sic]
never been such madmen in the Soviet leadership, and there are none
now." Bush invited Gorbachev to meet with Reagan.[6] Gorbachev quickly
issued dramatic proposals, beginning in April 1985, when he announced
a six-month moratorium on further deployment of intermediate-range
nuclear missiles, and then proposed to the United States a joint moratorium on nuclear weapons testing. Reagan turned down this proposition,
but Gorbachev pushed ahead with a unilateral test ban.[7]

When Gorbachev took over, Shultz and his counterpart, Andrei Gromyko (soon to be replaced by Eduard Shevardnadze, a political leader
from Soviet Georgia with no experience in foreign policy), were trying
to restart arms-control talks. Shultz had encouraged Reagan's presentation of SDI as a path to a nuclear arms–free world. He engineered a writ

of U.S. intentions that he took to his January 1985 sessions with Gromyko stating, "During the next 10 years, the U.S. objective is a radical reduction in the power of existing and planned offensive nuclear arms." This statement affirmed, "A world free of nuclear arms is an ultimate objective to which we, the Soviet Union, and all other nations can agree." Gromyko, frustrated by the American commitment to SDI, retorted, "Why do it at all? Why not just eliminate nuclear missiles themselves?" The two men agreed to resume arms-control negotiations, on ice since late 1983. Two days after his second inauguration, Reagan repeated what had become a familiar refrain, saying in a statement released to the press, "I have no more important goal than reducing and, ultimately, eliminating nuclear weapons."[8] The two governments resolved that Reagan and Gorbachev would meet face to face in Geneva to discuss arms control.

The Geneva summit was set for November 1985, and in September, Shevardnadze came to Washington to deliver a broad Soviet proposal. Gorbachev advocated 50 percent reductions in overall strategic offensive nuclear weapons—meaning nuclear weapons that each country could deliver directly to the other's territory—by both governments, down to six thousand nuclear "charges" apiece. He also proposed a halt to all work on "space-strike weapons," Soviet parlance for SDI. The United States countered with more specific proposals designed to cut most deeply into ICBMs, the area of greatest Soviet strength, and refused out of hand to freeze SDI. Shultz found Shevardnadze's message "clever and . . . weighted heavily against us." Its proposed cuts would affect U.S. missiles based in European NATO allies and aimed at the Soviet Union, but not Soviet missiles aimed at Western Europe. It also encompassed bombers, an area of U.S. advantage, which the Americans wished to keep off the bargaining table.[9] At this impasse, the Geneva summit produced no tangible gains. Behind the scenes, Gorbachev and Reagan did not warm to each other. Gorbachev told Reagan, "Make no mistake, we can match you, whatever you do."[10]

Despite the distance between them, the two leaders signed off on a "Joint Statement" at the summit's end that, conceptually, was significant. It affirmed that their governments "agreed that a nuclear war cannot be won and must never be fought," and asserted that each side "will not seek to achieve military superiority."[11] The first of these ideas had become a staple of Reagan's speeches. But the second was inconsistent with his long record of statements identifying strategic superiority as his central military goal. The new line echoed a statement that Margaret Thatcher, seeking to ease tensions in Europe, had extracted from Reagan in late 1984. Its repetition suggested that the American president might really be prepared to renounce his long-held aim. An insistence on making strategic parity the basis of arms reductions was the longtime Soviet position. Georgi Arbatov, an America specialist in the USSR, had expressed this view in 1982, asserting that "if history showed something convincing it was the fact that it was precisely parity . . . which insured more stable conditions and opened the opportunity for successful talks on disarmament."[12] By 1985, Reagan was embracing this logic, in word if not yet in deed. Perhaps anticipating attacks from Reagan's right, Robert McFarlane, in early December, gave a speech asserting that Reagan was not changing course. He declared, "There are new opportunities before us now not because the President is changing his approach but precisely because he *isn't* changing it."[13]

Gorbachev pressed forward aggressively. In January 1986, he proposed to the United States a three-stage process of eliminating all nuclear weapons and all ballistic missiles by the year 2000. Many top advisers to Reagan, including Nitze, reportedly viewed Gorbachev's announcement as a public-relations stunt.[14] Shultz, while criticizing some elements in the proposal, acknowledged that it was "a blockbuster," and advised Reagan that the president would be unwise to dismiss it. According to Shultz, Reagan responded by asking, "Why wait until the end of the century for a world without nuclear weapons?"[15] Reagan's diary entry for that day was less positive. "At the very least it is a h—l of a propaganda move," he wrote. "We'd be hard put to explain how we could turn it down."[16]

In late February and early March of 1986, Gorbachev displayed his command of the Soviet political system and trumpeted key concepts of his "new thinking" at the twenty-seventh CPSU Congress. The interdependence of nations was his main theme.[17] Gorbachev's ideas were influenced by his encounters with Western European social democrats, such as Swedish Prime Minister Olof Palme, who led a commission in the 1980s that promoted the concept of a Europe-wide "common security," and Prime Minister Felipe González of Spain.[18] The race for supremacy between the superpowers was an outworn concept, Gorbachev told the delegates. "In our time," he declared, "genuine equal security is guaranteed not by the highest possible, but by the lowest possible level of the strategic balance, from which it is essential to exclude entirely nuclear and other types of weapons of mass destruction."[19] Even matching the United States in all important military technologies was unnecessary; instead, "reasonable sufficiency" in the nation's defenses ought to be the goal.[20] Gorbachev expressed confidence that he would secure American cooperation, and suggested that he would make the United States offers it could not refuse. "Will the ruling elites of the capitalist world" embrace the new thinking? he asked rhetorically. He could not say. But "we cannot take no for an answer to the question: Will mankind survive or not?"[21] What he said of this philosophical question he might have said of his specific proposals: he was not planning to take no for an answer.[22]

But American mistrust of the Soviets lingered. In 1985, the U.S. government had disclosed a series of grievous security breaches, including CIA, FBI, and military personnel spying for the USSR, usually for cash. American officials feared the U.S. embassy in Moscow was hopelessly "bugged." At the same time, the USSR uncovered U.S. intelligence operatives in the Soviet Union, some of them fingered by Americans on the Soviet payroll. Each government expelled some of the other's diplomatic personnel.[23] A new tempest broke when the Soviets arrested Nicholas Daniloff, an American journalist who had been compromised by his CIA contacts, on charges of espionage. In March, in an act that Shultz labeled "cold-blooded murder," an East German soldier shot U.S. Army Major Arthur Nicholson outside Berlin, as Nicholson, an intelligence operative, was photographing a Soviet military facility. Nicholson then bled to death waiting for medical help.[24] World affairs augured poorly for a superpower thaw. In 1986, after the United States bombed Libya (see chapter 10), Gorbachev told the Politburo, "We just cannot work with this gang."[25] Another U.S. intervention, close to Soviet borders, was far more threatening. The United States was expanding its military aid to the Afghan mujahideen, appropriating $250 million in 1985, more than double the level of 1984, to help them fight the Soviets. U.S. congressmen of both parties were eager to advertise their support for the nationalist uprising against the occupying Red Army; this was an emotionally satisfying reversal of America's Vietnam experience. Gorbachev, for his part, at the 1986 CPSU Congress signaled his impatience with a war he called a "bleeding wound."[26]

President Reagan, in an action long urged by Weinberger and Assistant Secretary of Defense Richard Perle, stated, in May 1986, that the United States would breach the arms limits described in the unratified SALT II agreement, exceeding those ceilings by year's end. The United States and the USSR had complied voluntarily with these guidelines since 1979. This agreement had been useful from the American viewpoint, as SALT II restrained the deployment of further multiple-warhead ICBMs by the Soviets. But the United States charged the Soviets with violations of other treaty provisions. Kenneth Adelman, the chief arms control official in the U.S. government, said that "in essence, we're not bound by SALT II any more."[27] NATO allies, gathered in Canada for a meeting immediately afterward, were outraged. Joe Clark, the Canadian External Affairs Minister in the Progressive Conservative government of Brian Mulroney, a supporter of Reagan's, called the U.S. announcement "profoundly disturbing."[28] Reagan retracted his commitment to break through the limits during 1986, but continued to say that the United States might exceed them in the future. Reagan underlined the ambiguity of his stance toward the USSR when he stated at a June press conference, "We're not seeking to achieve superiority over them, but we're certainly not going to let them go on increasing their superiority over us." He was reasserting his newfound embrace of strategic parity as a goal while reviving his old campaign theme that the Soviets held the lead in the arms race.[29]

But this was a hypothetical discussion of future actions, and Gorbachev had more urgent concerns. On April 26, 1986, the graphite core of one of the nuclear reactors at the power plant in Chernobyl, in the Ukraine, had exploded and caught fire. The Soviet leadership at first responded with its time-honored method of denial, but Swedish authorities soon reported the dangerous radioactive particles borne on the winds out of the East. Belatedly, the Ukrainian government evacuated the area. Emergency workers and volunteers, many of them doomed, made heroic efforts to smother the fire and stop the deadly emissions. After waiting almost three weeks, Moscow revealed the essential facts of the story. Gorbachev and his top aides were shaken. The destruction around Chernobyl seemed almost apocalyptic. In a television address on May 14, Gorbachev asserted that "the accident at Chernobyl showed again what an abyss will open if nuclear war befalls mankind. . . . For inherent in the nuclear arsenals stockpiled are thousands of disasters far more horrible than the

Chernobyl one."[30] Later, he implored Soviet officials to consider that "if the peaceful atom is attended by such risk, what does that say about the nuclear weapon!"[31]

Against this background of devastation, Gorbachev brushed aside American debates over SALT II. In a June report to the CPSU Central Committee, he said that the USSR had to take the initiative "to clear the road to a reduction of nuclear arms."[32] In September, Shevardnadze came to Washington and, almost in passing, suggested that Reagan and Gorbachev arrange "a quick one-on-one meeting, let us say in Iceland or in London, maybe just for one day," to lay plans for a full-fledged summit later on. Reagan said yes; "I opt for Iceland," he added.[33] The meeting was set for October. Daniloff was freed through an exchange for a Soviet spy held in America. Both sides, it turned out, could distinguish major prospects from minor distractions. Still, as he left for Reykjavik, Reagan said he was "curious about what brought about this flat-out invitation to meet right now."[34]

The October 1986 talks in Iceland turned out to be ones of high drama, during which Gorbachev and Reagan broached the idea of completely eliminating nuclear weapons. But the two leaders, after skating to the edge of a nonnuclear world, pulled back amid acrimony over SDI. Emerging into public view at summit's end with no agreement secured, both men wore grim and angry expressions, and many observers thought the meetings a failure. Ultimately, however, the talks provided unexpected inspiration to those who pined for a farewell to nuclear arms. Most important, Reykjavik became the gateway to the Cold War's end.

Facilities for the two countries' delegations were spare, and the Americans did not expect intensive discussions. But Reagan and Shultz brought Paul Nitze, whom Shultz had taken on as his personal adviser regarding arms control. Nitze, a fit and energetic seventy-nine, was a link to the Cold War's early years. Despite his regrettable tendency to indulge in personal attacks against his political opponents, Nitze was renowned as a negotiator for his comfort with technical detail. Nitze had worked for arms control in the past. As recently as 1982, as the U.S. negotiator in the intermediate-range nuclear forces (INF) talks in Geneva, he almost secured a compromise with his Soviet counterpart using informal means, in what was known as the "walk in the woods" episode.[35] Yet, as the author of NSC 68 and the intellectual leader of the Committee on the Present

Danger (see chapter 2), Nitze was anyone's match for anti-Soviet rhetoric, and his stature among arms-control skeptics was such that he could provide political cover if attractive disarmament agreements seemed on offer. At Reykjavik, the Soviets called him *starik*, "the old man," a term of respect. There, Nitze would pursue an ardent effort to forge a comprehensive Strategic Arms Reduction Treaty (START) with Soviet Marshal Sergei Akhromeyev.[36]

At Reykjavik, Gorbachev immediately proposed 50 percent cuts in strategic arms generally, including heavy ICBMs. He moved further toward the U.S. position on INF, the "zero option" that Reagan had advanced in 1981. And he reduced the proposed period of guaranteed compliance with the ABM Treaty to ten years from earlier, lengthier demands, while stating he would consider work on SDI compatible with the treaty so long as it stayed in the "laboratory." Both men talked of their ultimate goal of eliminating all nuclear weapons, but each resisted the other's idea about how to reach that goal. Reagan presented SDI as the path to disarmament, while for Gorbachev it was the great impediment. Gorbachev focused on filling in the details of his January proposal to eliminate nuclear weapons in phases by the year 2000, a course of negotiation that Reagan evaded. Their teams nonetheless worked through the night, achieving remarkable progress on INF and START, mainly through Soviet capitulations. Yet SDI was blocking everything, and only the two nations' leaders could clear the obstacle. On October 12, the second and last day of planned meetings, Reagan, to Gorbachev's disgust, wanted to shake hands on INF and START while not addressing SDI. "No, let's go home," Gorbachev told his aides. "We've accomplished nothing."[37] He wanted a comprehensive "package"; only with American concessions on SDI could Gorbachev sell Soviet concessions on INF and START to his own doubters in Moscow. But the two sides merely broke for lunch and agreed to return for another session, beyond the summit's scheduled end-time. Reagan still proposed that the two sides agree to everything except the future of the ABM Treaty. That question could be put off until a "real" summit meeting planned for Washington in 1987. "But without that there's no package," Gorbachev replied. The U.S. team had been polishing an idea of its own: eliminating all ballistic missiles within ten years, rather than all strategic nuclear arms and delivery systems. This idea, consistent with long-standing U.S. positions, targeted the ICBMs on which the Soviets banked heavily. Reagan brought this proposal to Gorbachev. It omitted the term "laboratory" in discussing SDI testing, as Gorbachev noted immediately.

Here the bargaining reached dizzying heights of ambition, despite the imbalance in the new U.S. proposal. Gorbachev seemed baffled by the shift from cutting strategic arms to cutting ballistic missiles. Reagan "said he had received the message . . . that the Soviets were mainly interested in ballistic missiles." "Gorbachev said no, they had in mind strategic offensive weapons." Ballistic missiles covered only land- and sea-based nuclear weapons, not the bombers and cruise missiles where the United States had a big edge. After the leaders circled around this difference at length, Reagan finally "asked whether Gorbachev was saying that beginning in the first five-year period and then going on in the second we would be reducing all nuclear weapons—cruise missiles, battlefield weapons, sub-launched and the like. It would be fine with him [Reagan] if we eliminated all nuclear weapons." Reagan had abandoned his team's negotiating position of fixing on the elimination of ballistic missiles alone. "Gorbachev said we can do that. We can eliminate them." Shultz jumped in to add, "Let's do it."[38]

But SDI still loomed. Gorbachev had to have some limits on it to placate those in his own government who feared he was tearing down Soviet defenses. Gorbachev "could not do without the word 'laboratory.'" Reagan replied that "from the beginning of the [ABM] Treaty there had been this difference" in interpretation. "There was a sort of liberal interpretation"—one that supposedly allowed testing of ABM components outside of laboratories—"and also one that confined this strictly to laboratories. This was a legitimate difference. But we had gone a long way, and what the hell difference did it make." Reagan "was three steps away from becoming a great President," Gorbachev told Reagan. Yet, Gorbachev complained, "The American side has essentially not made any concessions, not a single major step to meet us halfway. It's hard to do business on that basis."[39] Reagan said "he had promised the American people he would not give up SDI." He "could not give in." "Is that your final position?" demanded Gorbachev. "If so, we can end our meeting at this point." "Yes it is," said Reagan.[40] Gorbachev said that if he came home empty-handed on this point, "he would be called a dummy (*durak*) and not a leader."[41] As the negotiations fell apart, both leaders expressed recriminations. "Even though our meeting is ending this way, I have a clear conscience before my people and before you," said Gorbachev. "I have done everything I could." Reagan responded, "It's too bad we have to part this way. We were so close to an agreement. I think you didn't want to achieve an agreement anyway. I'm very sorry."[42] Nothing was achieved in Reykjavik—or so it appeared.

The two leaders walked into the darkness outside, the summit over. Gorbachev met with assembled reporters. "I looked at the audience and this is what I decided: That I have to talk constructive, be constructive," he said later. He spoke in detail of the tantalizing discussions in Iceland, which, he implied, need not go back to square one. Some Soviet officials, despite their vexation over Reagan's stubbornness concerning SDI, came away feeling more sympathetic toward him than before. One of them, Aleksander Yakovlev, said, "In Reykjavik I first saw his human hesitation about what decision to make, and it seemed to me he wasn't acting. . . . On the one hand . . . he was interested in the idea of universal nuclear disarmament, on the other hand sticking to the idea of such a funny toy as SDI."[43] Reagan had exerted himself; his frustration showed. As his car drove away from the meeting site, he muttered to himself, "Laboratory, laboratory, laboratory."[44] He came home to face severe criticism from his right flank over even the proposal to eliminate ballistic missiles, let alone to scrap all nuclear weapons. Richard Nixon opined, "No summit since Yalta has threatened Western interests so much as the two days at Reykjavik."[45] The NATO allies, who had requested the intermediate-range weapons and then had withstood strong domestic protest to receive them, had not been consulted before Reagan pledged the missiles' removal.

As the summit ended, Nitze punctuated the drama by voicing to Shultz one of the great open secrets of the Cold War. The idea of eliminating nuclear weapons may have been rather new to Reagan, but the Soviets had cherished that goal for a long time. "The Kremlin sees a nonnuclear world as removing the one really fatal threat to them," Nitze said. "So it is attractive to them. After all, no one is going to attack them conventionally."[46] Gorbachev placed his own coda on the summit as he parted with Iceland's prime minister, Steingrimur Hermannsson, at the airport. According to Hermannsson's later account, Gorbachev assured him that "there will be more coming out of this meeting than anyone realizes." He predicted, "This is the beginning of the end of the Cold War."[47]

Returning home to the United States only weeks before midterm elections—just as the public revelations of, first, the covert Contra-aid program, and then, the sale of arms to Iran hit the news and engulfed official Washington—Reagan took to the campaign trail and defended his decision to choose SDI over historic arms-reduction agreements. "We can either bet on American technology to keep us safe," said the president in South Dakota, "or on Soviet promises. And each has its own track record. I'll bet on American technology any time."[48] Reagan was more cautious in private. In December, after disappointing election returns gave control of the Senate to the Democrats, Weinberger approached Reagan with a proposal to fund a rocket that could launch at least some pieces of an envisioned missile-defense system into space. Reagan congratulated Weinberger on this progress, but then stopped his secretary of defense cold by asking how this idea could be reconciled with the verbal commitment Reagan had made in Reykjavik, where he had said he did not wish to bring SDI out of the laboratory for ten years.[49]

Meanwhile, SDI was in trouble on Capitol Hill. In technical terms, few in Washington had taken it seriously. Instead, it had found favor as a boondoggle to military contractors. Now, however, senators respected for their knowledge of defense matters were offended by Reagan's aggressive push to reinterpret the ABM Treaty to allow testing of SDI components. Sam Nunn, a conservative Georgia Democrat who chaired the Senate Armed Services Committee and frequently voted for Reagan's proposals, led a tough resistance to this revision, making a series of lengthy speeches on the Senate floor on the matter. In 1987, Nunn called this a "constitutional confrontation of profound dimensions."[50] Reviewing the testimony given during Senate hearings prior to the treaty's 1972 ratification, he was certain that, in the understanding of the senators who voted in favor, the treaty disallowed development and testing of anti–ballistic missile equipment using yet-undiscovered techniques. But this was just the opening that SDI proponents thought they needed, and claimed they saw. In November, Nunn's committee released a report terming the effort to rewrite the treaty "the most flagrant abuse of the Constitution's treaty power in 200 years of American history."[51] A reduction in funding for the program soon followed.[52]

As support for SDI was faltering in America, Gorbachev decided to simply step around it, rather than continue trying to remove it from his path. The Russian nuclear physicist Andrei Sakharov, known as the father of the Soviet thermonuclear bomb but more recently a political dissident, personally lobbied Gorbachev to disregard SDI as a scientific impossibility and no strategic threat. He encouraged Gorbachev to stand up to Soviet defense hawks who reflexively feared an American first-strike technology. By ignoring SDI, Gorbachev could untie the "package" he had wanted and come to terms with Reagan in discrete areas individually. In February 1987, Gorbachev and Shevardnadze gave up all remaining objections to the "zero option" on INF. The Soviets agreed to remove intermediate-range nuclear missiles from both Europe and Asia, and dropped their demands for the elimination of British and French missiles. They no longer demanded limits on SDI as the price.[53] In Shultz's view, "The Soviets were picking up on our ideas and playing them back to us as though they had just invented them."[54] Reagan and Gorbachev would sign the Treaty on Intermediate-Range Nuclear Forces in Washington in late 1987. Shultz traveled to Moscow to take care of details in April, even as a majority of seventy U.S. senators, because of continuing spy revelations, supported a resolution disapproving of his visit. He found himself confronted by a frustrated Gorbachev. "You think we are weak," Gorbachev complained. "You pocket our concessions. So what have you brought?"[55] Shultz had brought nothing.

In terms of rhetoric as well as negotiating substance, Reagan continued to play tough with the Soviets. In June 1987, Reagan, perhaps seeking to deflect conservative criticism of his alleged coziness with Gorbachev, issued his most famous challenge to communism, speaking at the Brandenburg Gate in Berlin and echoing John Kennedy's words delivered in the same city in 1963. Reagan's voice rose as he said, "General Secretary Gorbachev, if you seek peace, if you seek prosperity for the Soviet Union and Eastern Europe, if you seek liberalization: Come here to this gate! Mr. Gorbachev, open this gate! Mr. Gorbachev, tear down this wall!"[56] This challenge represented something of a reversion to Reagan's first-term posture.

But nothing could weaken Gorbachev's desire to escape the arms race. He came to Washington in December to sign the INF Treaty. It required the Soviets to dismantle more than four times as many nuclear weapons as it did the Americans.[57] Some American hawks continued to lament disarmament. Kissinger wrote, "I could not shake a melancholy feeling as

I watched the leaders of the country whose nuclear guarantee had protected free peoples for forty years embrace Gorbachev's evocation of a
nuclear-free world—a goal put forward, if with less panache, by every
Soviet leader since Stalin."[58] But such doomsayers were few. Gorbachev
enjoyed approval ratings with the American public edging past 70 percent, numbers that any president would envy.[59] Americans' relief that
the nightmarish specter of nuclear war—so palpable in 1983—was lifting bordered on euphoria. The conservative evangelist Billy Graham said
that Gorbachev described a "beautiful picture of the world in which we
are all brothers."[60] Reagan took the opportunity to tell Gorbachev that
the United States was proceeding with SDI. "We are going forward with
the research and development necessary to see if this is a workable concept, and if it is, we are going to deploy it." Gorbachev replied, with a hint
of amusement, "Who am I to tell you what to do? I think you're wasting
money. I don't think it will work. But if that's what you want to do, go
ahead."[61]

The INF Treaty seemed unimpressive to some arms-reduction advocates, as it only eliminated less than one-twentieth of the world's nuclear
weapons. But it was very important. This was the first time the superpowers ever had agreed to destroy a category of nuclear weapons. Some
Europeans feared the strategic consequences, but many others had clamored for the denuclearization of Europe. If the INF Treaty did not reach
this goal, it went partway toward it. The treaty included unprecedented
and intrusive mutual inspection provisions, ones that laid the ground-
work for future accords. The Soviets had suddenly embraced with the
zeal of converts the very proposals for arms-reduction verification that
the United States traditionally had advanced, confident that the Soviets
would resist them. One U.S. diplomat noted, "The Soviet verification
package was essentially the same as ours. But they played the hand in a
way that let us choke on our own vomit."[62]

Prospects for a START treaty—a wide-ranging agreement that would
cut levels of strategic nuclear weaponry—were cloudy. The Senate ratified the INF Treaty in a lopsided vote of 93–5, but conservative Republicans were unhappy, and "the naysayers' real pint of blood was taken from
the efforts to conclude a START Treaty," in Shultz's view.[63] Reagan and
Shultz saw little hope for another big deal. In March 1988, Shevardnadze
returned to Washington for discussions with both the president and the

secretary of state about withdrawing conventional arms from Europe. Reagan and Gorbachev had agreed that they would meet yet again, this time in Moscow, and Shevardnadze hoped that the leaders would have a major new agreement to sign there. But that would not happen. After leaving the U.S. capital, clearly frustrated, Shevardnadze told a group of journalists, "Let me say, in all honesty, we were amazed at the response of our American partners. They have shown, to put it very mildly, no great enthusiasm to discuss the issue."[64]

Reagan's Moscow visit, at the end of May 1988, was like a victory lap for the American president. He and Gorbachev walked like old friends, arms around one another's waists. A reporter asked Reagan if he still thought the Soviet Union was an evil empire. "That was another time, another era," said Reagan.[65] For him, the Cold War was over. Visiting his former enemy, "Reagan had no major negotiating objectives."[66] The climax of his visit was his lecture to students at Moscow State University, standing before a huge bust of Lenin. Reagan spoke glowingly of microprocessors and the computer revolution, arguing that free enterprise was leading to a better, more integrated world. "The explorers of the modern era are the entrepreneurs, men with vision," he said. He welcomed "a growing friendship and closeness between our two peoples," but he gave no quarter to socialist values. Economic and political freedoms were of a piece, he explained. He warned Gorbachev against backsliding in his program of greater openness. Using a favorite rhetorical device, he illustrated his point with a movie reference. "It's like that scene in the cowboy movie *Butch Cassidy and the Sundance Kid*, which some here in Moscow recently had a chance to see," he said, naming a 1969 film set in America's Old West. "The posse is closing in on the two outlaws, Butch and Sundance, who find themselves trapped on the edge of a cliff." The point of the anecdote was that for Russia, as for the Wild West protagonists in the movie, there was no going backward, despite the dangers that lay ahead. "And, by the way, both Butch and Sundance made it," Reagan remarked. (This was true of the particular scene he described. He did not mention that the two lovable rogues charge into certain death against overwhelming odds at the film's finish.)[67]

During their private meetings, Gorbachev handed Reagan a proposed joint statement. It affirmed "peaceful coexistence as a universal principle of international affairs." It committed both leaders to "noninterference in internal affairs" of other states and to "freedom of sociopolitical choice," a phrase Gorbachev often used, which suggested he planned to lift the yoke of Soviet power off the necks of Eastern European nations. Reagan said this seemed all right. But when he showed it to his advisers, they were aghast. "Peaceful coexistence" was a phrase obnoxious to all conservatives who had loathed détente. Moreover, Gorbachev may have meant the statement to restrain U.S. efforts to undermine the Nicaraguan government. America would accept no such conditions. The president reported back to Gorbachev that the proposed statement was no good. "You had no objection to this" when you first saw the draft, Gorbachev retorted.[68] Tired of Reagan's lectures on human rights, Gorbachev, who believed there were at most three hundred political prisoners in the USSR, argued that America was not unblemished itself. "Recently," he said, "the Soviets had become much more self-critical, but the U.S. had not."[69] However, Reagan would grant no gestures of political equivalence between the two nations.

Despite this disappointment, Gorbachev no longer would wait for the United States to join him in disarmament measures. In December 1988, he made an historic address to the UN General Assembly, four years after Reagan had made his own pivotal speech there. The Soviet leader reiterated his concept of national "freedom of choice" regarding social systems, and announced that his government planned to remove a half-million military personnel from Europe in the next two years, including six tank divisions then in central Europe.[70] These cuts in conventional arms erased the basic justification for the containment strategy of America and NATO throughout the Cold War: the threat of a land invasion of Western Europe by the Red Army. Gorbachev argued that "all of us, and primarily the stronger of us, must exercise self-restraint and totally rule out an outward-oriented use of force." Rejecting potential criticism that such ideas were "too romantic," he avowed, "I am convinced that we are not floating above reality."[71]

In the remainder of the decade, the changes from Moscow and Eastern Europe came rapidly. Some were tangible and far-reaching, others rhetorical yet profound. Starting in mid-1989, the Warsaw Pact nations, beginning with Poland, broke free of Soviet control, and Gorbachev, far from trying to stop them, seemed to urge the process on (see chapter 14). The Red Army departed Afghanistan, leaving Moscow's client state to fight

off the mujahideen, which the United States continued to arm. Shevardnadze, in October 1989, told the Supreme Soviet that the 1979 invasion
of Afghanistan had "violated norms of behavior, and gone against common human interests"—a far cry from anything any U.S. president ever
said about the Vietnam War.[72] In early 1990, he agreed to conventional-
arms terms set forth by James Baker, who had become secretary of state
under President Bush. The Soviets would remove 370,000 troops from
central Europe, the United States only 60,000.[73] The Treaty on Conventional Forces in Europe was signed later that year. Further Soviet concessions paved the way for a START agreement (signed in 1991). In February
1990, Gorbachev, facing quickening opposition from conservative forces
in the CPSU, succeeded in getting Article 6 of the USSR's Constitution,
which assigned the party the "leading role" in Soviet society, stricken.
The CPSU officially changed its goal from "communism" to "democratic
socialism."[74] This substitution expressed Gorbachev's deepest hopes, of
returning Russian socialism to the fold of European social democracy.[75]

Gorbachev's bravado was something of a façade, concealing deep institutional rot within his regime and economic disarray in his society.
The Soviets had staged their own military buildup for a time, early in the
1980s, but they abandoned that course after Gorbachev took power. Reagan did not bankrupt them.[76] However, the Soviet *nomenklatura*'s customary belief that they held the keys to the future faltered in the 1980s,
and perhaps the new anti-Soviet offensive that Reagan spearheaded contributed to this loss of heart. Richard Pipes claimed that "Reagan's ideological offensive and his military buildup rattled the Russians, robbing
them of the confidence, acquired in the 1960s and 1970s, that they had
the United States on the ropes."[77] What is certain is that Reagan's very
tough negotiating stance ensured that almost all the concessions on the
path to a new détente came from the Soviet side.

But the key moment in the transformation in the U.S.–Soviet relationship came when Reagan relinquished his longtime belief that one country or the other had to enjoy military predominance and that the United
States must assert its supremacy. Gorbachev had secured from Reagan
a deepened commitment to the idea of strategic parity, and the Soviet
leader had pursued disarmament based on the concepts of military "sufficiency" and "common security." All these ideas were closely tied to détente. Reagan, an enemy of détente in its earlier form, proved willing to

embrace such ideas when they appeared as the threshold to peace with continued U.S. strength, and not, as he had feared in the 1970s, as a ruse cloaking Soviet aggression. He grasped that Gorbachev was undertaking a phased surrender, opting out of the arms race. Reagan, unlike some conservatives, recognized the shape of victory. Once the insistence on strategic inequality vanished, the way was open for arms reductions negotiated from a shared understanding of strategic equality, mutual interests, and the needs of the world—a return to détente. Ironically, Reagan's abandonment of his hawk's commitment to U.S. primacy was exactly what, in the end, created unquestionable American supremacy. The Cold War had shaped America and the world for over forty years. Reagan had vowed to revitalize America's side in the conflict, to keep the Communists from winning. Now it was all over: no more Politburo, no more refuseniks, no more Captive Nations Week. Not only maps of the physical world, but psychological maps of the political world, would have to be redrawn. The long conflict ended, to the world's relief, without a bang. America had won—by default and through negotiations, not through armed conflict. Now there would be only one superpower.

Thirteen

The Election of Willie Horton

As 1988 unfolded and America's attention turned to the competition to succeed Ronald Reagan, despite widespread elation over the dramatic easing of Cold War fears, a palpable sense of exhaustion with Reaganism—a premonition of unpaid bills coming due, in more than only a literal sense—hovered over the political scene. In this way, it seemed that Reagan and the conservatism he had championed would be on the ballot once again, and that the electorate might well bring in a negative verdict. Yet Reagan's vice president, George H. W. Bush, would prevail in 1988, winning the White House with a campaign that succeeded in smothering a brewing backlash against Reaganite economics. Bush effectively took Reagan off the ballot, and began to alter American conservatism by amplifying concerns which, while they had been components of Reaganite governance up to 1988, had received less attention than questions of economics and foreign policy. Bush focused on local controversies that were freighted with symbolic significance and that served to discredit the Democratic nominee, Governor Michael Dukakis of Massachusetts. Bush's campaign set the stage for what would become known, in the 1990s, as the "culture wars," a political era dominated by polarizing controversies relating to race, sex, crime, and patriotism. In this way, Bush lifted the most divisive and emotionally volatile elements of Reaganism out of the realm of undercurrents and secondary themes, and fashioned them into the central thrust of a retooled conservatism.

Numerous ambitious men slugged it out to win both parties' presidential nominations in a year with no incumbent on the ballot. Among the

Republicans, the main competition was between Bush and Senator Robert Dole of Kansas. Neither was a favorite of movement conservatives. Bush, lean and tall, seemed to epitomize the fabled "eastern establishment," historically an object of mistrust within the grassroots right. He had relocated from Connecticut to Texas as an adult, but maintained a beloved, large family estate on the Maine coast. Bush never shed his image as a preppie gone southwest, although he continued trying during the 1988 campaign, particularly by broadcasting his affection for fried pork rinds. Bush had always been a successful sportsman, but far from displaying the physical ease and self-control that some athletes do, he often appeared overexcited when under pressure, making herky-jerky movements with his long limbs, his voice rising to a whiny pitch. However, the vice president was well liked by most who knew him personally. He had cemented his standing as a faithful party man with his unwavering, usually silent, support for Reagan ever since Reagan had made Bush his running mate in 1980. While Reagan now endorsed Bush for president, he did so with little fanfare, as if Reagan were a father who felt his son needed to prove his own mettle. Bush was dogged by questions about his involvement in Iran-Contra—he said, less than honestly, that he had been "out of the loop"—and about his independence and his toughness. Bush could be petulant. He and his family were incensed by a *Time* magazine cover that raised what it labeled "The Wimp Factor" as a problem for Bush. Dole, an able legislator with an arm crippled by a war injury and a bitter sense of humor, won in Iowa, where Bush had prevailed in 1980. But Bush came back to win in New Hampshire. Marion "Pat" Robertson, a successful television evangelist and, like Bush, the son of a U.S. senator, made a strong showing in the caucus states of Iowa and Michigan, where campaigns relied on highly motivated supporters to do more than cast a ballot, but his appeal soon faded. As the contests moved to the South, Bush's devotion to Reagan proved more boon than bane with Republican voters, and the vice president began to cruise toward the GOP nomination.

In a less tidy Democratic field, Dukakis emerged gradually as a palatable, if unexciting, leader. To those outside Washington, Gary Hart, the 1984 runner-up to Mondale, had seemed assured of the Democratic nomination. However, revelations of the married Hart's philandering, rumored in Washington to be extensive, came to light and swiftly crushed his candidacy in late 1987.[1] With Hart gone, seven Democrats remained in the running, each with limited appeal, mocked by some as the "seven dwarves."[2] Representative Richard Gephardt of Missouri, playing to blue-collar voters angry over industrial imports from countries that protected their own home markets, came in first in the Iowa caucuses, but proved unable to build on this success. Dukakis won the New Hampshire primary soon afterward, but his status as a near–favorite son diminished the importance of his victory.

Jesse Jackson, who had toured the country's industrial heartland in recent years, marching with labor unions protesting plant shutdowns and wage cuts, ran again in 1988, and he became a bigger factor than he had been in 1984, now a true contender for the nomination. Jackson proved to have a cross-racial populist appeal among the Democratic faithful in 1988. However, just as important in bolstering Jackson's odds this time around was the fact that no one else could compete with him for African American voters the way that Mondale had in 1984. Dukakis boasted of the "Massachusetts miracle," an economic boom fueled by high-technology companies and military contractors, while Jackson denounced the "economic violence" of deindustrialization and mingy relief policies. In a set of primaries in March, dubbed "Super Tuesday" and designed to give more weight to conservative Southern white voters in the party, Dukakis and Jackson, frustrating those plans, finished in a virtual tie for the most delegates gained. Then Jackson shocked the nation's political elites by winning the Michigan caucuses. Soon, white voters coalesced around Dukakis, giving him an edge in the contest. Jackson complained that even Dukakis's staffers sympathized with Jackson's fury against Reaganism, but believed that only a more cautious politician like Dukakis could win in November. They "were pulling for me; working for him and hoping I would keep raising the right issues," Jackson said. "They wanted me to be the tugboat and provide the energy and wanted him to be the ship to carry them across."[3]

Dukakis and Bush seemed destined to wage a contest marked by an absence of charisma. Next to Bush, Dukakis's short stature was so notable that the Democrat's campaign insisted he have a platform to stand on, behind his podium, during their debates. Dukakis, a graduate of Harvard Law School and the son of a Greek immigrant who had made good as a physician, simply appeared too "ethnic" for some. He had heavy, dark eyebrows and a prominent nose. He was ridiculed when, at one point during the campaign, he donned a combat helmet and drove a small tank around to demonstrate his comfort with armaments. But Dukakis's temperament, cool verging on frigid, detracted from his appeal more than did his appearance.

Personalities aside, policy issues in 1988 seemed to be cutting in the Democrats' favor, in contrast to 1980 and 1984. On the home front, in some ways Reaganism appeared the victim of its own successes. Conservatives had addressed the major concerns, inflation and taxes, that had powered them forward in 1978–1980. Bush pledged never to raise taxes as president, which shored up his Republican support. But the broader public did not chafe under taxation, or inflation, the way it had eight years earlier. Regarding other pressing domestic issues, Reaganism's failings, not its successes, put Bush at a disadvantage. On the challenges of fiscal policy, neglected infrastructure, and social crises including HIV/AIDS, homelessness, and farm foreclosures, Reaganism simply had no answers to offer. On the international scene, the threat that Communist states posed to U.S. security, which had been the basis of the Republican foreign policy appeal throughout the Cold War, no longer seemed real to most Americans. Here, Reagan's successful peacemaking with Gorbachev, whether a triumph of Reaganite doctrine or a deviation from it, removed another old card from Bush's hand. Although Bush could boast of the incumbent administration's achievements in superpower relations, this triumph was far less potent than the traditional GOP pledge to protect Americans from fearsome enemies. As the summer nominating conventions approached, Dukakis looked to be in a strong position if he ran hard on domestic policy and offered a plausible recipe for progress on the nation's unmet needs.

Bush and his campaign manager, Lee Atwater, would decide how to address this unfavorable political environment. Their decision would rivet the nation's attention, wrest command of the campaign from Dukakis, and buy time for conservatives to regroup and fight another day on new political terrain. The Bush campaign conducted standard "opposition research" on Dukakis's record in Massachusetts, probing for vulnerabilities. Atwater's team found two state-level imbroglios that Atwater realized were political dynamite.

One of them concerned Governor Dukakis's veto of a bill that the Massachusetts legislature had passed, in 1976, requiring public-school teachers to lead their students in a daily avowal of the Pledge of Allegiance. Dukakis believed the Pledge bill, if it became law, would be ruled unconstitutional by U.S. courts, because of precedents that protected the rights of members of religious minorities to refuse to make oaths of any kind; thus, he saw the bill as pointless grandstanding. But many Americans surely would have little patience with such legal reasoning and would feel, as members of the Massachusetts legislature had calculated their own constituents would, that resisting this measure reflected insufficient patriotism.

But it was the second of the Bay State controversies that became the burning core of Bush's campaign. It centered on a man named "Willie" Horton. In 1986, while serving a life sentence with no possibility of parole after a conviction for murder, Horton fled from a weekend prison furlough in Massachusetts and brutalized a Maryland couple, twice raping Angela Miller and torturing her fiancé, Clifford Barnes, over the course of a night. When Dukakis became governor in 1975, he inherited the furlough program, intended to promote good behavior by inmates who longed for a taste of freedom. First-degree murderers like Horton were not eligible. But the state Supreme Judicial Court ruled that they could not be excluded from the program. The legislature, in 1976, sent Dukakis a bill defying the Court ruling and forbidding furloughs for such inmates. Dukakis vetoed the bill, seeing it—like the Pledge of Allegiance bill—as sure to be struck down in court. But after intense coverage of the Horton case in the local news media, Dukakis reluctantly signed a bill in April 1988—just as he was emerging as his party's likely presidential candidate—removing only murderers sentenced to life without the possibility of parole from the program.

On May 26, the Bush campaign's brain trust, comprised of Atwater, media advisor Roger Ailes, pollster Robert Teeter, chief fundraiser Nicholas Brady, and Craig Fuller, Bush's chief of staff, visited a nondescript building in Paramus, New Jersey. Fifteen white voters, mainly middle-income and Catholic, gathered before a two-way mirror. They had voted for Reagan in 1984, but now said they planned to support Dukakis. A moderator leading the group quickly realized, however, that the participants knew little about Dukakis. The moderator then asked what they would think if they knew Dukakis had vetoed a bill requiring a recitation of the Pledge of Allegiance in Massachusetts classrooms. What if he had granted a furlough to a murderer who committed rape while free? With this information in hand, the focus group turned on Dukakis. "Basically, their mouths fell open," said an executive at the research firm that conducted the focus group.[4] The Bush campaign leadership knew they had found what they needed.

Atwater traveled to Bush's Maine home to share the attack strategy against Dukakis with his candidate. Bush, seeing opinion polls showing him well behind, by all reports calmly endorsed Atwater's plan. Horton's crimes and the Pledge veto would be their main issues. These could discredit Dukakis and take the campaign's focus away from the more familiar national policy agenda that seemed tilted against Bush. The vice president, far from showing squeamishness about running for the White House on a tale of rape, assault, and murder, would display what many found a surprising lustiness in leading the charge against Dukakis.

Under the unofficial rules of American politics, Bush had no obligation to refrain from using these matters against Dukakis. Crime was a major issue of public concern in the 1980s—even if the federal government's role in fighting crime remained relatively minor—and the Horton story, as well as the Pledge-bill veto, were familiar flashpoints in Massachusetts. Nonetheless, the way Bush and Atwater used these issues—obsessively focused on the emotionally explosive details of the Horton case, and determined to make Dukakis appear alien and personally repellent, a man friendly to rapists—made their campaign a master class in demagoguery. "The only question is whether we depict Willie Horton with a knife in his hand or without it," Roger Ailes, chief of media for the Bush campaign, told *Time* magazine, almost jauntily.[5] Bush captained his campaign, and it became his legacy in American politics. Virtually no one outside the Bush team's leadership could imagine that a gruesome crime story could form the essential basis for a presidential campaign. Yet it did. Bush and Atwater painted Dukakis as unpatriotic—and as Willie Horton's patron. "What is it about the American flag that upsets this man so much?"[6] Bush cried out at one campaign appearance. Floyd Brown, a political operative working for a group that produced a crude television advertisement attacking Dukakis, told reporters, "When we're through, people are going to think that Willie Horton is Michael Dukakis's nephew."[7] The Maryland GOP disseminated a flyer pairing photographs of Horton and Dukakis with the text, "Is This Your Pro-Family Team for 1988?"[8] As the campaign wore on, Bush himself began to recount Horton's horrible acts in "vivid detail," wrote one reporter.[9] Republicans also spread baseless rumors about Dukakis's mental health and his wife's political past. No one had seen national politics go this far into the gutter, no one had experienced such an atmosphere of reckless abandon at high levels of responsibility, since the heyday of Joseph McCarthy in the early 1950s.

The specter of racial fear was palpable in the campaign. Everyone knew that the Horton story was especially potent because Horton was a black man who had raped a white woman. One Bush campaign official said privately of the Horton story, "It's a wonderful mix of liberalism and a big black rapist."[10] Atwater told a gathering of Republicans in Atlanta, "There is a story about a fellow named Willie Horton who for all I know may end up to be Dukakis's running mate. . . . On Monday I saw in the driveway of [Dukakis's] house: Jesse Jackson. So anyway, maybe he'll put this Willie Horton guy on the ticket after all is said and done."[11] Aside from the sheer outrageousness of Atwater "joking" that Dukakis might make Horton his vice-presidential pick, the only reason to mention Jackson and Horton in the same breath was that both were black men. The frequent use of Horton's photograph in Republican campaign materials ensured that no one would be uncertain about Horton's race. In September, a pro-Bush political action committee fielded a low-budget television advertisement about Horton's crimes; the campaign stated it was uninvolved. But the journalist Elizabeth Drew noted, "People in the Bush campaign knew all there is to know about the various ways in which an 'independent' group can be made helpful to a Presidential campaign. Before it even ran, one Bush campaign official read me the text of the 'independent' group's ad featuring Clifford Barnes."[12] The campaign's spokesman would pin Horton's police "mug shot" over his desk.[13]

Bush portrayed Dukakis as a liberal snob out of touch with ordinary Americans' concerns. This thread tied together the soft-on-rapists charge and the claim that Dukakis was a deficient patriot. Dukakis's perverse loyalties, Bush said, were part of the Democrat's liberalism, "born in Harvard Yard's boutique."[14] Bush, himself the scion of a wealthy, powerful blue-blood family, counteracted the potential unpopularity of his elite background by arguing that he was a man of the people in his heart, and that Dukakis was, in contrast, animated only by the rights of criminals and dissenters. Bush ridiculed Dukakis's membership in the ACLU. "I am not a card-carrying member of the ACLU," Bush told a crowd. "I am for the people."[15] Bush also regularly criticized Dukakis for the pollution of Boston Harbor, a problem that Dukakis had taken some steps to improve. This issue helped blunt Dukakis's effort to tie Bush to the Reagan administration's record of lax environmental regulation.[16]

As the Democratic convention started, Jackson, reacting peevishly to the news that Senator Lloyd Bentsen of Texas, a conservative choice and a skilled politician, would be the Democrats' vice-presidential nominee, threatened to upstage Dukakis. Jackson addressed a simultaneous meeting of the NAACP, finishing an intense speech by saying, "I may not be on the ticket but I'm qualified!"—rebuffing a criticism he had faced throughout his presidential campaigns. Jackson then repeated, along with the crowd, "Qualified! Qualified! Qualified!" Meetings were arranged hastily, and Bentsen, who got on better with Jackson than did Dukakis, helped calm the waters. Convention speakers shifted the focus to Bush, ridiculing him as a creature of privilege. Keynote speaker Ann Richards, the Texas state treasurer, made headlines by mocking the vice president's verbal awkwardness, saying, "Poor George, he can't help it—he was born with a silver foot in his mouth." Jim Hightower, another Texas liberal, called Bush "a man who was born on third base and thinks he hit a triple." Edward Kennedy roused the crowd with a taunting refrain of "Where was George?" as he delivered a speech lambasting Bush's claim that he had been uninvolved in the Iran-Contra affair.[17] Senator John Kerry of Massachusetts called the Reagan years a time of "moral darkness" in America.[18]

Dukakis's acceptance speech made a positive impression—a testament to the public's receptivity to the Democratic appeal in 1988, since the nominee's speech took a questionable strategic approach to the contest. Dukakis spoke forcefully at the podium (which was decorated, rather oddly, in salmon, cream, and lavender instead of bold red, white, and blue) about the need for a bright future and his record of economic achievement. In his signature line, he declared that "this election isn't about ideology. It's about competence."[19] With the incumbent president's capacities widely questioned, this was no idle concern. Yet it was strange that Dukakis basically eschewed a focus on the political issues that had dominated news headlines for some months and years. He and other Democrats criticized the Republican record on HIV/AIDS, the farm crisis, financial deregulation, deindustrialization, and corruption in government, but Dukakis attributed these failures to ineptness, not to a governing dogma of hostility to government itself. Technique, not substance, was the ground on which he laid claim to the mantle of leadership. This was a sincere expression of his managerial passions. As the commentator Sidney Blumenthal observed, Dukakis was part of the Watergate generation of Democrats who had entered high office in the mid-1970s, embodying "a curious regression to a pre–New Deal liberalism, a Yankee reformism whose energy was drawn from moral outrage at corruption and whose god was efficiency."[20] Dukakis's belief that he could win the presidency by running a larger version of a gubernatorial campaign, where nonideological problem-solving was often rated at a premium, would prove his downfall.

Even in Dukakis's moment of triumph in Atlanta, indications surfaced that the Republican campaign against him would be an onslaught far more personal and fearsome than anything he anticipated. Right-wing elements began spreading the story that Dukakis had received psychiatric treatment during two episodes of depression, one after his brother was struck and killed by a car and the other following Dukakis's loss of his governorship in 1978. The Bush campaign urged the story along.[21] Dukakis felt compelled to produce his personal physician to assure the press corps that the candidate never had been treated for depression. But the open talk of his mental health made an impact. One top Dukakis operative said, "We dropped eight points in a week."[22] Seeking to shift the conversation onto the outgoing Reagan administration's record, Dukakis criticized the corruption scandals surrounding Meese and other federal officials. "The fish rots from the head down," he said, hanging responsibility on the president. Reagan struck back, hard and low. Days later, he told a group of reporters, when asked about Dukakis, "I'm not going to pick on an invalid." Reagan, before this moment, always had been more sinned against than sinner where accusations of incompetence were concerned. He soon expressed regret for his remark, but his retraction received little attention.[23]

As the Republican convention in New Orleans neared, Bush, his personal insecurities outweighing other considerations, risked his election by choosing as his running mate Senator J. Danforth ("Dan") Quayle of Indiana, the most callow and unintelligent candidate for vice president in modern history. Quayle was the dull issue of a provincial dynasty. His family owned the most conservative newspapers in a conservative state. Bush, perfectly subservient to Reagan, chose the one potential running mate on whom he could count for a similar servility. Quayle quickly damaged himself, admitting in television interviews that "phone calls were made" on his behalf when he had sought, successfully, to gain entry into the National Guard during the Vietnam War as a way of avoiding combat. It also appeared that Indiana University's law school had admitted him despite his poor college grades, using a program designed to benefit disadvantaged students.[24] He fumbled his way through an interview with an eleven-year-old girl from a children's newspaper. She asked Quayle about abortion rights, and he responded by telling her that he would oppose allowing her to obtain an abortion even if her father impregnated her (which was a more severe position than Bush's). Quayle then told the girl that he would approve "a D and C," or a dilation and curettage, in such a case. Quayle called this "a perfectly normal procedure that I would not put into the category of abortion," although it was, in fact, a common form of abortion.[25] But despite clamorous criticism of Quayle as a weak, even disastrous, choice, Bush stuck by Quayle, resisting calls to dump him from the ticket and keeping him away from the press as much as possible.

Bush maintained a glaring spotlight on Dukakis. Now emphasizing the Pledge-bill veto, Bush visited flag factories in Ohio and New Jersey on the campaign trail and concluded his speech accepting his party's presidential nomination, in New Orleans, by leading the assembly in the Pledge. "Should public school teachers be required to lead our children in the pledge of allegiance?" Bush asked. "My opponent says no—but I say yes." He went on, "Should society be allowed to impose the death penalty on those who commit crimes of extraordinary cruelty and violence? My opponent says no—but I say yes." Finally Bush declared, effectively bringing Willie Horton on-stage with him at the pinnacle of his political career, "I'm the one who believes it is a scandal to give a weekend furlough to a hardened first-degree killer who hasn't even served enough time to be eligible for parole."[26]

The Republican convention intensified the GOP effort to dispute Dukakis's patriotism. The harshest attacks on Dukakis in New Orleans came from the convention's keynote speaker, Governor Thomas Kean of New Jersey, previously known for his moderation and civility. Kean (with a touch of homophobia) ridiculed the Democrats' "pastel patriotism," and went on, "The liberal Democrats are trying to hide more than the colors in our flag—they are trying to hide their true colors." Kean charged, "They want to weaken America. But they won't admit it."[27] Bush, in addition to his flag-factory visits, stood before a bank of flags whenever he could on the campaign trail. The standards "surround him on the stump like flowers at a mafia funeral," a reporter wrote mordantly. Appearing before the Veterans of Foreign Wars to defend Quayle's service record, Bush said defiantly that Quayle "did not go to Canada, he did not burn his draft card and he damn sure didn't burn the American flag." Days later, Senator Steve Symms of Idaho alleged, falsely, that photographs existed showing that Kitty Dukakis, the governor's wife, had been just such a flag-burner.[28]

In his convention speech, Bush also sought to present himself in a softer light, avowing his commitment to voluntarism as a means of creating a decent society. He invoked the metaphor of "a thousand points of light" to describe the moral illumination provided by those performing charitable works. This was a traditional conservative theme; neighborly benevolence, not government entitlement, should provide for the needy. Yet, at the end of Reagan's presidency, even this conservative vision positioned Bush as relatively sensitive to the realities of social distress. It was aimed at moderate voters concerned over the social costs of Reaganism. "I want a kinder, gentler nation," said Bush, implicitly criticizing Reagan's legacy. At the same time, Bush sought to motivate his party's conservative base to turn out strongly for him in November by reiterating his no-tax pledge. He said he knew that, once he became president, "The Congress will push me to raise taxes, and I'll say no, and they'll push, and I'll say no, and they'll push again, and I'll say to them, 'Read my lips: No new taxes!'"[29]

Bush and Dukakis debated twice. While Bush failed to charm the public in these encounters, Dukakis emerged from them badly scathed. At first, it did not appear that this would be the result. In their first meeting, Dukakis aggressively criticized the Reagan record and tied Bush to it, placing the vice president on the defensive. When Bush said, "I hope people don't think that I'm questioning his patriotism," Dukakis retorted, "Of course, the vice president's questioning my patriotism. I don't think there's any question about that. And I resent it. I resent it."[30] But at the second debate, Dukakis departed from this assertive tone. One of the journalists moderating the debate, Bernard Shaw, opened the event by asking Dukakis, "Governor, if Kitty Dukakis were raped and murdered, would you favor an irrevocable death penalty for the killer?" In reply to this astounding question, Dukakis said, with a calm that faintly suggested weariness over such antics, "No, I don't, Bernard. And I think you know I've opposed the death penalty during all my life. I don't see any evidence that it's a deterrent." Viewers were amazed at Dukakis's failure to show anger—either at the hypothetical assailant against his wife or at a reporter seeking to sensationalize a serious occasion. At the first debate, Bush had said plaintively, after stumbling over his own practiced lines, "Wouldn't it be nice to be perfect? . . . Wouldn't it be nice to be the ice man so you never make a mistake?"[31] This waspish lament was unattractive, resembling a child's angry response to an argument he cannot meet. Nonetheless, in light of the bizarre exchange between Dukakis and Shaw, Bush had stuck a damaging label—"the ice man"—on Dukakis, who seemed a bloodless legalist, rational to a fault.

As Bush pulled away in the opinion polls, Dukakis finally threw caution to the winds, but in a strange manner. On the campaign trail in California, he had planned to rebut Bush's charge that Dukakis's liberalism was dangerous and nearly un-American. "The L-crowd doesn't like it," crowed Bush, when he called Dukakis a liberal. Dukakis was supposed to say he was simply a Roosevelt-Truman-Kennedy Democrat. Instead, he announced, to his staff's dismay, "Yes, I'm a liberal," then subsequently struggled to explain what he thought this meant. With two weeks remaining, Dukakis suddenly embraced the rhetoric of economic populism that he had previously resisted. "George Bush is on their side, I'm on your side!" he said. Dukakis hardly needed to say who "they" were; they were the wealthy. "I'm on your side" became his constant refrain in the contest's last days, when Dukakis wore himself out with a punishing schedule of campaigning.[32] This theme roused the Democratic faithful. One of them, the labor lawyer Thomas Geoghegan, called this the ritualized "last ten days" of presidential campaigning in this era. "Every four years," he wrote,

the same thing happens . . . : The Democratic candidate stumbles, falls further and further behind, and then, in the last ten days. . . . he goes around like an old-time Democrat. He marches with the unions. . . . When the next presidential campaign begins, no one will have the slightest memory of the last ten days, until everything collapses again, and the next last ten days come around, and we all have to go back into Detroit, Pittsburgh, and Akron, the fleshpots of the old New Deal, and slum around for working-class votes.[33]

By the fall, the Pledge issue appeared to be losing effectiveness, and Bush's campaign renewed its emphasis on the Horton case. Now, another pro-Bush group sponsored a speaking tour featuring Clifford Barnes and the sister of the man Horton was convicted of murdering in 1974.[34] Barnes, in a television advertisement, said, "Mike Dukakis and Willie Horton changed our lives forever. . . . We are worried people don't know enough about Mike Dukakis." The original "independent" advertisement about Horton stopped airing after two weeks, in early October, but at that time the Bush campaign itself started broadcasting its own best-known television advertisement, known as "Revolving Door." Shot in black-and-white, it showed men walking in and out of a prison; the narration and captions suggested, inaccurately, that hundreds of *murderers* had been furloughed in the Massachusetts program and that "many" had escaped and remained at large. Most of the actors playing the prisoners were white. Yet it stood as testimony to the powerful racial current in the Horton controversy that many viewers, primed by the extensive previous discussion of the Horton case, mistakenly recalled most of the men in the advertisement as black.[35] On Labor Day 1988, Bush, campaigning in California, declared, "No more furloughs for people to rape, pillage, and plunder in the United States!"[36]

In late October, independent researchers conducted a set of focus groups designed to learn what information voters had taken from campaign advertisements and coverage. Of the ninety-three participants, eighty-eight noted that Horton was black, eighty-one that Angela Miller was white. One woman, a waitress in Dallas, asked to summarize what she knew of the case, stated:

Willy [sic] Horton is a killer—black—supposed to be gassed or electrocuted when Dukakis was governor. . . . But he vetoed all death penalties. . . . [Horton] broke into a home, a married home—in a small town—Maryland—and then tied up the husband. . . . He stayed there for a whole afternoon. . . . He kept raping the wife. . . . He was black and the wife was white. Even when she begged him because she might be pregnant. Her husband went crazy. He couldn't do anything because Horton had shot him and stabbed him. . . . He still can't forgive himself. That's why he is against Dukakis.[37]

The scenario of a black man raping and terrorizing a white woman and man in their own home was so upsetting to white Americans that some embroidered the awful story with additional details drawn from some deep cultural store of imagined horrors. The Bush campaign had sliced through the media clutter and reached the "low-information voter," a storied, elusive prey for campaign professionals.

Bush, with his relentless message that liberals posed a danger to Americans, preserved the Reagan coalition at the presidential level. Bush swept the South and the Mountain West; Reagan himself, in the end, campaigned energetically in California, helping secure that state for Bush, too. The popular vote count gave Bush a solid victory margin of almost eight points, 53.4 percent to 45.7 percent for Dukakis, yielding an Electoral College victory of 426–111. Rural areas and older voters were weaker for Bush than for Reagan in 1984, but Bush performed well in many suburbs and won convincingly among political independents and voters below age thirty. Men preferred Bush by twelve points, and Bush nosed past Dukakis among women, due to white women favoring him strongly.[38] The congressional elections, meanwhile, kept the Democrats' majorities in both the House and Senate almost exactly as they had been. Bush had no coattails at all. He had won no mandate to do anything except pledge allegiance to the flag and not free imprisoned murderers.

"The Presidential campaign of 1988 did something new to our Presidential elections," Elizabeth Drew, who had been studiously nonpartisan during the campaign, worried when it was over. "A degradation occurred which we may have to live with for a long time."[39] The Bush campaign provided a road-map for Republicans facing inauspicious political environments, showing that furious attacks on the decency and patriotism of Democrats could carry the day. Democrats would remember the 1988 Republican campaign bitterly as merely an updated version of old Southern race-baiting campaigns. Atwater defended himself, in part, by denying that he harbored any racist intent. Many a Democrat scoffed at these protestations with a reference to Atwater's training in South Carolina politics. The evidence suggests that Atwater was, indeed, no racist. However, this line of defense hardly put Atwater, Roger Ailes, or Bush in a flattering light. It only revealed their campaign as a monument to political cynicism. The Democrats, for their part, had missed a large opportunity. Atwater, in a postelection analysis, said he had feared the Democrats would stick to their convention theme of lambasting Bush as a wealthy highbrow. He told *Time* that if he had run the Dukakis campaign he would have depicted Bush and the GOP as "a bunch of rich, old snobs," complete with footage of Bush playing tennis, accompanied by narration saying, "No wonder he wants to cut capital gains taxes on the wealthy." This might be divisive, said Atwater, but, in his view, "It would work."[40]

The highly personal attack on one's political rival was emerging as the primary method of Republicans with their backs against the wall in the late 1980s, as events in Congress confirmed. In the U.S. House, a seemingly permanent Democratic majority had left Republicans with scant role in governance. Many House Republicans, led by Representative Newt Gingrich of Georgia, responded by making condemnations of the House leadership almost their full-time job. Gingrich had organized a large number of younger House Republicans into the Conservative Opportunity Society (COS). Starting in 1983, its members had begun making numerous one-minute speeches, as well as longer "special order" speeches, usually late at night, on the House floor. The cable television service C-SPAN had begun broadcasting House business, with the camera staying trained on the speaker; COS members made grievous charges against House Democrats in their speeches, knowing that viewers would not see the empty House chamber to which they declaimed. Robert Michel, the House Republican leader, blanched at the Georgia upstart's tactics and feared a challenge from him.[41]

Gingrich, in turn, feared Jim Wright once the Texan took over the speakership, and devoted himself to rallying opposition to what he called Wright's corruption. "If Wright consolidates his power, he will be a very, very formidable man," Gingrich said. "We have to take him on early to prevent that." Gingrich knew of no corrupt practices by Wright, and some of the journalists whom Gingrich hectored to raise the alarm against Wright were unimpressed. But Gingrich persisted. He said of Wright,

"He's from Texas. He's been in politics over thirty years. An aggressive investigator with subpoena powers might find something."[42] Eventually, reporters started looking into Wright's personal finances, and found evidence of business deals in which Wright had been made a partner, clearly because of his public position. In late 1987, Gingrich planned to file ethics charges against Wright and prepared a dossier for the committee. Perhaps the most damaging evidence against the Speaker was an arrangement in which he received unusually high royalty rates from sales of a book of his writings and speeches, published by a company owned by a man who did contract work for Wright's campaigns. It appeared that Wright's campaign funds thus were laundered through this company to end up enriching Wright personally. Wright also had applied pressure against savings-and-loan regulators on behalf of Texas thrift operators.

As the inquiry dragged on, in March 1989, the Senate rejected President Bush's nomination of former senator John Tower of Texas to be secretary of defense, by a vote of 47 to 53. A prominent conservative, Paul Weyrich, initiated the activism against Tower by airing his concerns about Tower's excessive drinking and womanizing—well known in Washington. Senator Sam Nunn stated that the secretary of defense "must be a person suited by personal conduct, discretion, and judgment to serve second only to the President in the chain of command for military operations; to set the highest leadership example for the men and women in uniform," concluding, "Tower cannot meet these standards." In an acrimonious atmosphere, one observer, Chris Matthews, who had served as an aide to Tip O'Neill, said, "The Democrats got Robert Bork. The Republicans got Michael Dukakis. The Democrats got John Tower. The Republicans will get . . . Jim Wright."[43] It was a bit fanciful to link all these career flameouts as a sequence of tit-for-tat partisanship; each had distinct causes. Nonetheless, this perception made headway.

Wright found himself with few backers in the end. Although he had succeeded in steering the ship of government policy in his brief time as Speaker, he had driven his party's members hard—harder than O'Neill had—demanding loyalty in vote after vote. His position weakened in mid-May when Pamela Small revealed that, in 1973, she had been savagely attacked and almost killed by a young man named John Mack, who then had become a reclamation project of Wright, rising from a menial post to become the Speaker's top aide.[44] By the end of May, his support having crumbled, Wright resolved to resign both his speakership and his House seat. He was quickly replaced by his deputy, Representative Tom Foley of Washington, a cerebral type whose career was untouched by any trace of scandal. Foley's ascension had been guaranteed only days earlier, when Tony Coelho, the third-ranking House Democrat, who had risen fast through his prodigious fundraising for Democratic House candidates, had announced his own resignation following revelations he had improperly received financial largesse from Drexel Burnham Lambert. Drexel's controversial star broker, Michael Milken, was close to Coehlo.[45]

But the political warfare continued. Sensational rumors concerning Foley's relations with male teenagers suddenly raced through Washington. The talk was groundless, and its origin was obscure. Gingrich's staff pushed the story along, but it may have started with Democrats supportive of Wright, in the hope that fears of a Foley speakership would shore up Wright's support.[46] Soon the Republican National Committee, now run by Lee Atwater, issued a press release titled "TOM FOLEY: OUT OF THE LIBERAL CLOSET." This document compared Foley's voting record to that of the liberal Representative Barney Frank of Massachusetts, one of two openly gay members of Congress. Mark Goodin, Atwater's deputy, wrote a cover note for the release, stating that Foley was, in reality, a liberal, even if "many in the Democratic Party and the media will be portraying him as the 'darling' of the moderates." Seeking to put an end to the matter, Frank contacted Michel and reportedly threatened to "out" some secretly gay Republican senators. Goodin had to resign his position, but Bush intervened to spare Atwater. When reporters asked Bush about the press release, the president said, unconvincingly in light of the campaign he had run the previous year, "Disgusting. It's against everything that I have tried to stand for in political life."[47]

As president, Bush displayed two different tendencies, each of which showed the evolution of American conservatism after Ronald Reagan's departure from the scene. On the one hand, in some respects, primarily in fiscal policy, Bush wished to govern more responsibly than Reagan had. On the other hand, Bush continued to pursue some of his incendiary campaign themes. Bush's drive to address the federal government's deficits alienated him from conservative Republicans. Bush's culture war politics, by contrast, energized conservatives, who wished to press matters that seemed politically promising and that had been neglected under Reagan in favor of economic and foreign policy.

The budget situation could not be put off. Despite agreements reached under Reagan, the final Gramm-Rudman budget targets (see chapter 9) remained unmet, and the severe spending cuts required by the law threatened to take effect. Bush also was worried that, with no serious action on the deficits, jittery bond markets might bring on a recession. After dawdling for some time, Bush, in the summer of 1990, authorized negotiations with congressional Democrats. The need for tax increases, as well as spending reductions, as part of a compact to which the Democratic leaders of the Congress would assent was obvious. Privately, Bush appeared nonplussed at congressional Republicans who had taken his no-new-taxes pledge seriously. "You don't understand," he said in one meeting. "I'm here to govern."[48] Reagan had corralled Republican votes for a series of tax increases following his signature tax cuts of 1981. But Bush lacked Reagan's authority with conservatives, had never cut taxes as Reagan had, and, unlike Reagan, had made an airtight vow never to increase taxes. A majority of Republicans in the House, roused by Gingrich, repudiated the budget the White House had negotiated. After this abandonment, Bush agreed to a further compromise with the Democrats, accepting that a budget could pass only with overwhelmingly Democratic support. On the day after the 1990 elections, in which Republicans suffered a net loss of eight House seats and one Senate seat, Bush signed the budget deal. It included $140 billion in new taxes over five years, some of which would come from raising the marginal income-tax rate for top earners from 28 percent to 31.5 percent, and over $350 billion in reduced spending over the same five years.[49] A recession had already begun, in mid-1990.

On other issues, Bush remained the culture warrior of 1988. He vetoed a bill that would have allowed public funding of abortions to end pregnancies resulting from rape or incest. He defended the rule that forbade any family-planning facility that received federal funds from discussing abortion with female clients.[50] In 1990, he nominated David Souter to be a justice on the Supreme Court, one who ultimately would vote to uphold abortion rights. But Souter, a moderate, replaced a formidable liberal leader, Justice William Brennan, so his appointment still shifted the Court's weight to the right. Bush also vetoed a civil rights bill intended to reverse the effects of a 1989 ruling on employment discrimination, calling it a quota measure.[51] (In contrast, he happily signed the Americans with Disabilities Act; he would gain little politically by not doing so.[52])

In September 1989, Bush called for a huge drug-war bill. "Drugs are sapping our strength as a nation," he warned in a speech from the Oval Office. He brandished a bag of crack that, he said, police had confiscated from a drug-peddler right across the street from the White House itself, in Lafayette Park. "Let there be no mistake: This stuff is poison," said the president. This was a set-up job: the dealer was enticed to the park so that Bush could portray the danger as lapping at the very door of power. Bush proposed "more prisons, more jails, more courts, more prosecutors"—urging "an almost $1.5 billion increase" in federal funds for such measures, and $2 billion over five years for interdiction and military aid to prevent drug importation from the South. He also endorsed smaller amounts, $321 million and $250 million, respectively, for expanded drug treatment and drug education efforts. This fight was truly to be like a war, said the president. "Victory—victory over drugs—is our cause, a just cause."[53] Senator Joseph Biden of Delaware gave a speech in response for the Democrats: "Not tough enough," he said.[54] The parties continued their bidding war over prison construction, police militarization, and long mandatory sentences for drug-related convictions.

Most strikingly, Bush maintained his determination to make an issue of honor for the nation's flag. He backed a proposed amendment to the U.S. Constitution that would ban flag "desecration." In October 1988, in the heat of the presidential campaign in which the treatment of the star-spangled banner had been a flashpoint, the U.S. Supreme Court had announced that it would review the case of a Texas man convicted for his involvement in the public burning of a U.S. flag in 1984. Gregory Lee Johnson had been found guilty of violating a state law prohibiting the "desecration of a venerated object," but the Texas Court of Appeals had declared the conviction had violated Johnson's freedom of expression. On June 21, 1989, the U.S. Supreme Court upheld that decision, ruling, 5–4, in *Texas v. Johnson*, that the U.S. Constitution's First Amendment gave license to destroy the nation's flag. Justice Anthony Kennedy joined the majority but wrote an anguished concurring opinion that concluded, "The hard fact is that sometimes we must make decisions we do not like."[55]

An embarrassing interval ensued in which members of the Congress competed with one another by offering ever more hysterical calls for the need to protect the flag against an alleged rising tide of physical assaults. One journalist reflected afterward, "I've worked on the Hill a long, long time . . . and I don't think I've ever seen a time when people were so scared. . . . The Democrats were determined that the Republicans were not going to outflag them this time."[56] The House of Representatives passed a resolution renaming Independence Day "Take Pride in the Flag Day"; one Democrat, Representative Andrew Jacobs of Indiana, worried aloud that to "designate only 1 day a year makes you wonder about the 364, in a way, does it not?"[57] Yet Congress lacked the majorities needed to pass a constitutional amendment in the face of the *Johnson* ruling. Democrats, looking for political cover, rallied instead behind a Flag Protection Act, a simple law, passed overwhelmingly and signed by President Bush, which the high court then, unsurprisingly, overturned in June 1990.

The culture wars beckoned, and would not be stilled for some time. Conflicts over economic inequality and social distress that had seemed ready to burst the fabric of American politics in 1988 had had their destructive energies drained and redirected toward arguments over who would keep drugs and rapists away from America's children and women and who could salute the flag most fervently. In the shadow of the 1988 campaign, cynical posturing and triviality dominated national politics. Conservatives, however, despite their newfound methods of political success, were torn between die-hard antitax commitments and establishmentarian concerns over government debt. A recession was underway, and the Cold War was ending. As Reaganism's heyday faded, and conservatives struggled to hold their coalition together between election contests, the largest questions of domestic and foreign policy found no response in the new formula for political power.

Fourteen

The Free World

As the Cold War drew to a close, Washington worked its will abroad, no longer fearing a negative response from any foe. The new power of the United States resulted from the raw facts of military and economic might. At the same time, waves of peace and democracy were advancing in parts of the world that had known strife and oppression for many years. Few had foreseen either of these developments at the decade's start, when Ronald Reagan had marshaled American forces for what turned out to be the closing episodes in the Cold War. Reagan had vowed his support for anticommunist "freedom fighters" around the world. The commentator Charles Krauthammer dubbed this a "Reagan Doctrine," recalling older Republican cries for a "rollback" of Communist power.[1] But Reagan supported freedom and democracy only against left-wing states; hence, these were halfway commitments at best. While rock-steady in his opposition to dictatorship in Eastern Europe, Reagan was only intermittently a friend to the cause of freedom elsewhere. When America arrived at the pinnacle of its power, during the presidency of George H. W. Bush, the United States responded with marked ambivalence to the ascendancy of freedom. Thus, it squandered the opportunity it enjoyed, with the demise of Soviet power, to consolidate its authority for a post–Cold War world. Power was one thing; authority was another.

The triumph of democracy abroad most widely heralded in the United States in the mid-1980s occurred in the Philippines. Ferdinand Marcos, long the violent and corrupt U.S. client ruler there, fled to sanctuary in Hawai'i in February 1986, in the face of massive protests that observers called "people power." Marcos was displaced by Corazon Aquino, widow of Marcos's rival Benigno Aquino, who had been assassinated in full view of television cameras in Manila in 1983. Stanley Karnow, a longtime Asia reporter with a gimlet eye, wrote, "Marcos was not overthrown . . . because Filipinos clamored for the return of democracy. He crumbled under the sheer weight of his venality, which bankrupted the country, alienating the Manila business community and the Catholic hierarchy, his most enthusiastic supporters at the beginning. They crystallized around Cory Aquino, who represented the old oligarchy that Marcos had dispossessed."[2] Marcos agreed to a presidential election in 1986, which he probably thought he could rig.

Powerful Americans were abandoning Marcos politically, but Reagan staunchly supported his friend. A brewing insurgency led by the Communist New People's Army (NPA) alarmed U.S. leaders. To Reagan, this rising threat meant sticking with Marcos no matter what. The *New York Times* editor A. M. Rosenthal, visiting the White House, poisoned Reagan's receptive mind against Aquino, calling her an "empty-headed housewife . . . a dazed, vacant woman."[3] Others in Reagan's government saw in Aquino, educated in the United States and quite conservative, an upgrade from Marcos. These included Admiral William Crowe, head of the U.S. Pacific Command; Michael Armacost, first as U.S. ambassador in Manila and then as a key aide to Shultz in Washington; Paul Wolfowitz, the assistant secretary of state for East Asian and Pacific affairs, glad of a chance to show that his professed commitment to spreading democracy was serious; and Richard Armitage, an undersecretary of defense with long experience in East Asia.[4] They led a back-channel effort to foster rebellion against Marcos within the Filipino armed forces and business class.

Republican senator Richard Lugar of Indiana and Democratic congressman Jack Murtha traveled to Manila to observe the 1986 elections, and afterward briefed Reagan on Marcos's brazen electoral fraud. Reagan disregarded Lugar and Murtha, stating that he saw "the possibility of fraud, although it could have been that all of that was occurring on both sides." Stephen Bosworth, the desperate U.S. ambassador in Manila, counseled Aquino to ignore Reagan's remarks. "That wasn't the full U.S. position you heard," he said.[5] Events on the ground outstripped Reagan's stubbornness. The Filipino army suffered large defections and huge crowds protected the rebels. Marcos's troops declined to shoot to keep him in office. Reagan, unhappily, accepted Marcos's departure. With the president sulking, Shultz invited Aquino to Washington, where she addressed Congress and received a rapturous welcome. A raucous democracy returned to the Philippines; but challenging the rotten social structure and culture of corruption that had festered under Marcos was not part of Aquino's mission. In 1987, Aquino declared "total war" on the Communists; President Bush ordered U.S. forces to help put down a rightist coup attempt against her in 1989.[6]

The Filipino events were part of a contagion of protest for democracy in East Asia. In the Republic of Korea, home to a massive U.S. military presence, no network of powerful Americans urged rebellion. Here, there was no leftist insurgency; instead, university students and labor activists led a protest movement against a repressive regime that had reneged on promises of reform. The International Olympic Committee had awarded the 1988 Summer Games to Seoul, and democracy activists escalated their militancy, knowing the government would want to restore order before the world's athletes, leaders, and tourists converged on their capital city. The U.S. State Department urged compromise, fearing chaos. After massive demonstrations in June 1987, the U.S.-backed president, Chun Doo Hwan, agreed to a December election to choose his successor. Unionization and strikes among industrial workers spread across the country as reform forces showed their political muscle. But the opposition was divided. Its two chief leaders, Kim Dae Jung, sometimes called "the Nelson Mandela of Asia," and Kim Young Sam, both resolved to run against Roh Tae Woo, the regime's candidate. The conservative Roh won with a plurality of 36.6 percent, as "the two Kims" split the reform vote. Thus, partial democratization did not threaten the U.S. military presence, and panic did not erupt in Washington.[7]

The reform tide reached the Communist Chinese state as well, and the United States responded timidly to a bloody PRC crackdown against protesters in 1989, reflecting the widening economic flows between the two nations—cheap Chinese goods to America and U.S. investment to China. When Reagan, long a stalwart supporter of Taiwan, had visited the PRC in 1984, he had been sufficiently impressed with the emergence of capitalism there that he had come home and spoken of "so-called Communist China."[8] His hostility to Beijing became a thing of the past. Bush had been the de facto U.S. ambassador in Beijing in the 1970s and served as Reagan's emissary to the rulers there as early as the 1980 presidential campaign. In 1989, a visit from Gorbachev to Beijing helped spark an inchoate but unsettling uprising by students and workers against China's elite. The protesters gained wide support from citizens angry at Communist Party insiders feathering their own nests. On April 15, students began gathering in the tens of thousands in Tiananmen Square, the enormous public space in the capital, overseen by a huge poster image of Mao Zedong's face. As the weeks passed, workers and city residents joined the students, swelling the crowd to several hundred thousand, almost a city within a city. On the night of June 4, the People's Liberation Army moved on the square and perpetrated a massacre, quite possibly killing thousands. Reacting to the violence, President Bush suspended arms sales to the PRC. But he sent Brent Scowcroft, his national security adviser, on a secret mission to Beijing later that month, reassuring China's leaders that their diplomatic ties with America remained intact at a time when the PRC was an object of global antipathy. News of Scowcroft's visit, complete with a toast he made to his hosts, leaked out, and critics were unsparing. Bush, they said, coddled the "butchers of Beijing."[9]

In Latin America, the democratic trend first took hold in South America, where the elimination of any possibility of socialism—of "another Cuba"—had been secured through years of rightist dictatorship. These sometimes vicious regimes had been firmly, sometimes warmly, supported by the U.S. government. But to many in Washington, a restoration of democracy now seemed safe far to the south, and in the mid-1980s, Reagan's State Department began to balance its hemispheric stance by endorsing democratization in South America. First the Argentine junta, weakened by the Falklands debacle, fell in 1983, and an elected president took office. The United States was more closely tied to Augusto Pinochet's Chilean dictatorship. Yet Elliott Abrams, assistant secretary of state for inter-American affairs, said in 1985, "We support a transition to democracy" in Chile. The United States voted aye on five of nine UN resolutions criticizing Pinochet's human rights record between 1986 and 1988.[10] Unwisely, Pinochet agreed to hold a plebiscite in 1988 on the continuation of his rule. A vigorous, creative democracy coalition, with aid from the United States, channeled through the government-funded National Endowment for Democracy (NED), pulled off an upset, dealing Pinochet a 55 percent negative vote.[11] Patricio Aylwin, a Christian Democrat, was elected president one year later, although Pinochet and the military retained partial power and immunity from prosecution for their crimes.

The U.S. hand lay heavier on Central America, and there the Reagan administration, even as it preached democracy, tried in vain to stop an outbreak of peace. A critical event was the election of Oscar Arias as president of Costa Rica in 1986. Arias refused to allow the United States to continue using his country as a staging ground for the war against Nicaragua. Abrams, a hardliner on this matter, had crudely remarked to a colleague, "We'll have to squeeze his balls." Richard Secord, adding a racist touch, told Oliver North, "Boy needs to be straightened out by heavy weights." After a browbeating from Abrams, Arias said defiantly, "Friendship should not mean being servile. A friend who does everything you want is not a friend, but a slave."[12] Arias, against U.S. wishes, helped bring the Sandinistas and Contra leaders together for negotiations, and engineered agreement among the leaders of five Central American nations on the terms of a peace deal. After Jim Wright became House Speaker, the Reagan administration, in an unusual diplomatic move, brought Wright into the talks, hoping to smooth the path for new Contra aid by coopting him. But when the Sandinistas, led by Daniel Ortega, signaled agreement to most demands made of them, Reagan tried to scotch the deal and turned on Wright, depicting the Speaker as a Communist dupe. "We started with the Wright-Reagan plan," said the president. "Now we've got the Wright-Ortega plan." Wright fought back, terming the attacks on him redbaiting. "I'm not afraid of the bastard," he said, meaning President Reagan.[13] Wright persisted in his diplomacy, dealing personally with both sides in the conflict, challenging the executive branch's monopoly on foreign relations and infuriating Republicans.

With negotiations promising peace, Reagan was unable to keep the Contra war going. In 1988, Congress turned down Reagan's last serious bid for Contra aid. The Sandinistas and the Contras signed a peace agreement the next year. Attention turned to the Nicaraguan elections, scheduled for 1990. The Sandinistas had made enemies domestically, on the basis of class and region, although they had mobilized wide support among the poor with education and healthcare initiatives. However, Washington was not content to let the internal dynamics of Nicaraguan politics decide the regime's fate. What the United States had done for the opposition in Chile, it could do for the opposition in Nicaragua. The NED, the CIA, and the Republican Party spent lavishly to support Ortega's challenger for the presidency, Violeta Chamorro, the editor of the main opposition newspaper in Managua, *La Prensa*, which long had received U.S. government largesse. Chamorro won by almost fourteen percentage points.[14]

Regarding El Salvador, Washington's counterinsurgency fever did not break until Bush became president. In November 1989, amid a new rebel offensive, the Salvadoran army high command ordered the murder of a distinguished group of dissident Jesuit scholars in their homes on the campus of the *Universidad Centroamericana* in San Salvador. The new U.S. House Speaker, Thomas Foley, sensed the rising disgust in his caucus over the seemingly endless butchery committed by a government the United States was supposed to be reforming. Democrats' fear of appearing soft on communism in Central America was dissipating as the Cold War wound down. They also seemed less afraid of Bush than they had been of Reagan. Representative Joseph Moakley, Democrat of Massachusetts, led a congressional investigation in El Salvador, and his damning report helped sway his colleagues to support halving aid to the regime. "Enough is enough," he said.[15] As in Nicaragua, political life in El Salvador would achieve a semblance of normalcy as the 1990s unfolded. The basic issues of social justice raised in the civil war went largely unaddressed, but the terror abated.

The emotional debates over U.S. interference in Central American affairs during the 1980s had wracked the political scene, poisoning U.S. civic life even as the peoples of Nicaragua, El Salvador, and Guatemala experienced massive suffering and trauma. Inside the United States, unnamed parties perpetrated a wave of burglaries and assaults against those who protested Washington's policy in Central America. The FBI targeted groups like the Committee in Solidarity with the People of El Salvador, compiling lists of activists, harassing them, and recruiting right-wing university students to spy on them.[16] Many responded to these infringements on their liberty with bravado or insouciance, but this effort at political repression remains an ugly episode, and soon became an embarrassment to be forgotten. To the south, however, the era's events were unforgettable. One Honduran businessman noted of his own country's experience, "It is as though a hurricane passed through."[17]

When Bush took the helm in 1989, the hurricane moved to Panama. In 1988, the Department of Justice had indicted Panama's ruler, Manuel Noriega, on drug-trafficking charges. Noriega had made Panama a haven for drug merchants and money launderers. But he was also a highly paid U.S. informant.[18] Now, the war on drugs in the United States created political pressure to make a show of high-profile law enforcement. The Senate voted, 83–10, to register outrage over rumors that the DOJ would quash the indictment in return for Noriega's quiet exit from power. "You tell me how I and people like me can go to . . . children and their parents today and tell them to say 'no' to drugs when we've got an Administration in Washington that can't say no to Noriega," said Democratic presidential candidate Dukakis. Shultz, indeed, had dispatched an emissary, Michael Kozak, to negotiate a deal with Noriega. When Kozak returned to Washington for a key meeting, Shultz warned him, "You will be attacked by the vice president. . . . He will do everything he can to derail you." Politically, Bush could not afford to do otherwise. Reagan, who liked the idea of a deal to avert a confrontation, encountered fierce arguments from Meese and others. "All the law enforcement people I know strongly oppose this," Meese said. Reagan shot back, "You've just lowered my respect for people in the law enforcement field."[19] The issue went unresolved. After becoming president, Bush decided to make a new antidrug push, both domestically and internationally, and Noriega, now not merely a liability, became an opportunity for a display of steel.

Noriega stole a presidential election in 1989, keeping the real winner, Guillermo Endara, from taking office. Such things had happened many times in Latin America, with little reaction from the United States. One year earlier, the ruling party in Mexico had stolen the presidential election from a social-democratic challenger, Cuauhtémoc Cárdenas, claiming that the computers tallying the vote had failed and later announcing that the apparent margin of victory for Cárdenas had vanished mysteriously. Advisers to Cárdenas were murdered. The United States barely acknowledged these events.[20] But now Bush, declaring himself democracy's champion and pointing to incidents of violence and harassment against a handful of U.S. military personnel in Panama, determined to oust Noriega through a full-scale invasion. On December 20, Operation Just Cause commenced. (Some U.S. officers called it "Operation Just Because."[21]) Pliant U.S. media outlets amplified U.S. Army claims that large piles of cocaine had been found in Noriega's residence; they turned out to be tamales.[22] The Organization of American States and the UN General Assembly damned the invasion as unlawful. Panamanian defense forces were easily overwhelmed. Noriega was brought to Miami for trial, and Endara took office. Little changed in Panama, but Bush was now a warrior president.

If the U.S. stance toward peace and democracy was a mixed one regarding Latin America in the late 1980s, it seemed almost schizoid in southern Africa. South Africa for years had pursued wars against leftist forces in neighboring Mozambique, Namibia, and Angola, with support from Washington. However, the U.S. State Department, under Shultz, yearned for a regional policy that was more strategically rational and internationally defensible. Mozambique became the chink in the armor of Reagan's backing for Pretoria. Shultz brought the Mozambican president, Samora Machel, to the White House to meet Reagan in 1985, and the two leaders found they got on well. Washington, persuaded that Machel had kept the USSR at arm's length, began to aid Mozambique, switching sides in the conflict there. Some American rightists provided private funds to the RENAMO rebels in Mozambique, and others, organized in a group called Free the Eagle, lobbied the White House to join them, calling this a vital Cold War battle. But the State Department released a damning report in 1988 on RENAMO.[23] Assistant Secretary of State Chester Crocker called them "an African Khmer Rouge" and another official accused them of perpetrating "one of the most cruel holocausts . . . since World War II."[24] With this breach opened between America and South Africa, and with Gorbachev pressing Reagan to negotiate an end to superpower support for the region's wars, late in 1988, the United States and the USSR agreed they would get out of Angola, as did the Cubans and South Africans. Reagan still sympathized with Pretoria, but now he confined himself to supporting conservative forces within South Africa regarding that country's own internal dynamics. Bush, upon becoming president, seemed free of Reagan's personal attachment to the old regime.

The South African regime—watching its pillar of outside support weakening, and besieged within its country's borders by a courageous democracy movement, based primarily in trade unions and churches—began reconciling itself to the prospect of democracy and an end to apartheid. A new president, F. W. de Klerk, secretly negotiated with Nelson Mandela, still a prisoner, and then announced that Mandela and other rebel leaders would go free—an event that occurred in February 1990, to a global celebration. President Bush reached out to Mandela, who later noted that Bush "included me on his short list of world leaders whom he briefed on important issues."[25] The longtime conservative argument that only quiet, friendly counsels of moderation would bring positive change to South Africa stood discredited. Namibia gained its independence in 1990. However, peace did not come to Angola. As historian Odd Arne Westad notes, "The only outside power that reserved the right to continued intervention in the region was the United States, which doubled its aid to Jonas Savimbi's UNITA . . . in 1990," seemingly determined to show that it would still fund a war against Communists somewhere.[26]

In contrast to his treatment of apartheid South Africa, Reagan ruled out "constructive engagement" with Communist regimes—although he eventually engaged diplomatically with the Soviets. Bush, campaigning for the presidency in June 1988, came close to siding with those who feared Reagan had gone soft on the USSR. "The Cold War is not over," said the vice president. Two days after Bush's inauguration, Scowcroft agreed, "I think the Cold War is not over."[27] In the following years, Bush and his team skillfully made certain that Gorbachev's defeat on key strategic issues would be complete and unmitigated. Bush managed to appear supportive of Gorbachev, while in substance giving him no quarter. In the end, Bush helped undermine Gorbachev's political position in the Soviet Union itself, and the USSR started to come apart sooner than most Americans had expected.

Bush privately was warm toward Gorbachev. When the two men met alone briefly in December 1987 in Washington, Bush supposedly told Gorbachev that Reagan's coterie was a bunch of "marginal intellectual thugs."[28] Bush recalled that, using a Chinese phrase, he told Gorbachev to disregard the "empty cannons of rhetoric" that would issue from the Republican camp during the 1988 election campaign.[29] Bush did not wish to alienate Gorbachev; in fact, he appeared worried that the Soviet satellites were moving out of Moscow's orbit too fast. The Polish ruler Wojciech Jaruzelski, who had outlawed Solidarity in 1981, was on the verge of losing power to the group he had banned. He had agreed to limited parliamentary elections, and in June 1989, Solidarity's candidates won 260 of the 261 seats it was allowed to contest. Bush considered Jaruzelski a "real class act." After meeting with Hungarian reformers in spring 1989, Bush remarked, "These really aren't the right guys to be running this place. At least not yet." Bush seemed willing to consider Henry Kissinger's proposal that the United States refrain from interfering in Eastern Europe in exchange for a Soviet pledge not to use violent repression there. That idea appeared to die when James Baker, the new secretary of state, revealed it to public view. However, it got a new lease on life in December 1989, when Bush and Gorbachev met for their first formal summit, a shipboard affair on choppy seas near the island nation of Malta, and discussed such a tacit agreement.[30] Appearances were deceiving. Despite Bush's concern for stability, he gave Gorbachev no help with the key nations where crises brought down the Soviet empire.

Americans at large were most attuned, regarding Eastern Europe, to rapidly developing changes in Poland and Czechoslovakia. The Kremlin and its enemies had always seen Poland as vitally important, the path of either communism's westward spread or an eastward invasion of Russia. But by 1989, Gorbachev seemed glad to be rid of the Polish problem, having given up the age-old Russian fear of a land attack. His supporters in the CPSU had concluded, too, that "the roots of socialism have penetrated too deeply" for democratization to wipe out socialism in Eastern Europe.[31] In August, he telephoned Jaruzelski and indicated no objection to the Polish ruler's invitation to Tadeusz Mazowiecki, a Solidarity leader, to form a new government.[32] Gorbachev optimistically (and wrongly) expected Poland to remain part of the Warsaw Pact. Indirect Soviet control of Poland ended without a pitched confrontation between dissenters and the state.

If the transition to postcommunism was peaceful in Poland, it was positively festive in Czechoslovakia. In late 1989, a group of free-spirited rebels, led by the playwright Václav Havel and others, simply took over in Prague when the Communist government resigned in the face of massive people power. The Czech events became known as the Velvet Revolution, denoting both the triumph of nonviolence and Havel's affection for the Velvet Underground, Lou Reed's New York rock-and-roll band—figurative bohemia intersecting with the real place.[33] Havel was elected president and got a hero's welcome when he traveled to Washington to address Congress in February 1990. Dispensing existentialist philosophy, Havel reflected that he had taken from life "one great certainty: Consciousness precedes Being, and not the other way around, as the Marxists claim." The line sparked enormous applause in the House chamber, indicating appreciation for Havel's rebuke to Marxism, rather than wide appreciation among his audience for the writings of Jean-Paul Sartre, which Havel paraphrased closely.[34]

Yet while American eyes were fixed in amazement on Warsaw and Prague, President Bush was concerned with events in Bonn and Berlin, the capitals, respectively, of West Germany (the Federal Republic of Germany, or FRG) and East Germany (the German Democratic Republic, or GDR). The fate of Germany, potentially the most powerful nation in Europe, had been the issue that, more than any other, had caused and shaped the Cold War in the 1940s; the resolution of Germany's fate in the late 1980s would define the Cold War's final disposition of power in Europe. With Gorbachev's support in Moscow eroding, and his government's finances collapsing, the Soviet leader had his hand out for German charity. Helmut Kohl was willing, up to a point, to give it, essentially purchasing Gorbachev's acquiescence in the FRG's absorption of the GDR. Bush, wanting what Kohl wanted—and seeing how much Kohl wanted it—let Kohl do the heavy lifting to achieve America's strategic objective in the heart of Europe: a united Germany, inside NATO.[35]

Gorbachev's position in the GDR was untenable. He did not have the funds to maintain the Soviet military presence there, and, without that presence, Gorbachev would lose his leverage over the GDR leadership. Kohl and Bush got progressively tougher with him. As Mary Elise Sarotte notes, "In the West, while Bonn and Washington publicly expressed sympathy for Gorbachev's reformist goals in 1989–90, they privately sensed that they did not really need to accommodate him."[36] Gorbachev evidently had ruled out using force within Europe. His critics lamented that he "had no guts for blood."[37] He ordered Soviet troops stationed in the GDR to stay in their barracks if Erich Honecker, the East German ruler, attempted to repress popular unrest. In June 1989, Bush, traveling in Europe, spoke in Mainz, applauding the relaxation of border controls by Hungary and urging, "Let Berlin be next! Let Berlin be next!"[38] In September, Hungary opened its borders, allowing vacationing East Germans to escape to Austria. Honecker's own security chief, soon to depose him, refused to use violence against mass demonstrations in Leipzig. In October, Gorbachev, in Helsinki, reiterated his position that each country could choose its own political system. The USSR, he conceded, had "no . . . moral or political right" to intervene in Eastern Europe. His aide Gennadi Gerasimov remarked jovially to reporters that the Brezhnev Doctrine had been displaced by the "Frank Sinatra Doctrine," referring to the Sinatra song "My Way." "Hungary and Poland are doing it their way," he said.[39]

Little remained to prevent the East German regime's collapse. On November 9, panicky GDR authorities opened the gate in the Wall on Bornholmer Street, and almost seventy thousand people streamed out of East Berlin overnight. About three million East Germans exercised their new tourist opportunities in the Federal Republic over the following three days.[40] The GDR authorities could not get the stopper back in the bottle. Ironically, dissidents who had suffered under the East German regime tried, in their way, as hard as anyone to preserve some version of socialism, seeking to stave off de facto annexation by the West. They were swept aside by an East German populace eager to share in the affluence of the FRG.

With Germany unified, the United States would achieve one of its two German goals. The other was to make a united Germany a NATO member. Years later, Gorbachev claimed that he had extracted a series of verbal promises from Germany and America to the effect that NATO's borders would not move east. But he failed to get any written assurances, and Bush and Kohl soon felt comfortable rejecting his ideas.[41] Bush remarked privately of Gorbachev's demands, "To hell with that! We prevailed, they didn't. We can't let the Soviets clutch victory from the jaws of defeat."[42] In October 1990, the Federal Republic incorporated the Democratic Republic, and Germany was a NATO member. Bush, to secure victory, had only needed to remain impassive in the face of Gorbachev's entreaties for a better deal. Bush had lamented aloud during the 1988 campaign that he was no "ice man," but in conducting international relations his own sangfroid served him well. Still, he was doing the obvious. It is hard to imagine any U.S. president interfering in European political dynamics in order to produce a different outcome, when the future seemed to be falling into America's lap.

A greater test came within the borders of the USSR, whose collapse Bush did not foresee. Here Bush simply stayed out of the way. The downfall of Communist power in Eastern Europe exerted a negative feedback effect on the Soviet Union. Gorbachev was losing support on both his left and right flanks. Liberals found him half-hearted; the pride of true-believer Communists and Russian nationalists was deeply wounded by the loss of the empire. Only in trying to hold the Union together would Gorbachev use violence to repress nationalist uprisings. In January 1990, Soviet troops killed at least 120 in Baku, the capital of Azerbaijan and a major oil port. Bush expressed sympathy for Gorbachev, explaining to *Newsweek* magazine that this was "a situation where the Soviet Union is trying to put down ethnic conflict, internal conflict," and that "a lot of pontificating from leaders in other countries" would do nothing to help matters.[43] But the three Baltic nations, Lithuania, Latvia, and Estonia, succeeded in opening a gap in the walls of the Soviet Union itself. In August 1989, marking the symbolically weighty fiftieth anniversary of the Nazi-Soviet pact that had consigned their nations to Soviet annexation, two million Balts formed a human chain stretching from the Estonian capital of Tallinn, through Riga, to Vilnius, the Lithuanian capital and the leading source of Baltic resistance.[44] In Vilnius, people power forced the government to agree to free parliamentary elections in March 1990, leading to a nationalist majority. The Lithuanians promptly declared the 1940 Soviet takeover of their country illegal—always the U.S. position—and then declared independence from Moscow. Latvia soon followed suit. There would be no confrontation between the people and the state, as the two were united in revolt against Soviet power. Bush cautioned his NSC that a public show of support for the Lithuanians would lead to another disaster like the Soviet repression of the Hungarian uprising in 1956, an uprising the United States had encouraged.[45] Kohl, eager to keep a pliant Gorbachev in power, called the Lithuanian prime minister and asked her to cease agitating for her country's independence.[46]

Gorbachev's strong disinclination to use violence inside Europe was fatal for the USSR. For, while Gorbachev might well lose Lithuania if he ordered violence, he clearly would lose it if he refrained from violence.[47] In June 1990, Lithuania withdrew its declaration of independence, but this only bought Moscow some extra time. Bush watched and did nothing, despite harsh criticism within Congress. He reminded Gorbachev, "I have conducted myself in ways not to complicate your life. That's why I have not jumped up and down on the Berlin Wall."[48] But Gorbachev, to stave off utter defeat, needed more than good taste from his American counterpart, as Bush no doubt could see. Bush played his hand deftly during the final collapse of America's Cold War enemy. He made a good show of commiseration with Gorbachev, thus leaving U.S. fingerprints invisible on the political and social wreckage that many Russians, despite their newfound freedoms, saw mounting all around them.

For most of the Cold War, the U.S. military had referred to the industrial heartland of its European NATO allies as the "Central Region," the place where World War III was expected to break out. But in the 1980s, the United States dubbed the Persian Gulf the new central region. In 1983, President Reagan formed a new U.S. military command centered in the Gulf; it was called, revealingly, Central Command.[49] Before this time, the U.S. military's capacity to respond swiftly to events in the Middle East had been unimpressive, as the events in Lebanon in 1982 and 1983 showed. Lebanon, Israel, and Libya figured large in American news reports in the 1980s. But the deepest U.S. involvements in Western Asia during this era lay in the Gulf and in Afghanistan.

The leading advocates of support to the Afghan mujahideen, Zbigniew Brzezinski, Carter's national security adviser, and William Casey, Reagan's DCI, linked Afghanistan to the Gulf, asserting implausibly that the Soviets hoped to send their forces in Afghanistan slicing through hundreds of miles of Pakistani or Iranian territory to the Gulf's mouth. The Red Army had its hands full propping up its unpopular client regime in Kabul. The main motive for U.S. aid to that regime's domestic enemies, which Carter had initiated, was to pin the Red Army down and bleed its finances and morale.[50] When Reagan became president, he and the Saudis quickly agreed that the two governments would fund the mujahideen equally, with the Saudi money channeled through Washington; in fiscal year 1985, this combined aid shot up to $500 billion, with the American half of that sum equaling all previous U.S. assistance.[51] With few U.S. assets close to the action, the money was disbursed by the Pakistani government of dictator Zia ul-Haq, who had seized power in 1977. Islamabad was determined to push Soviet influence out of Afghanistan, and Washington would propitiate Zia. Shultz emphasized to Reagan in 1982, "We must remember that without Zia's support, the Afghan resistance, key to making the Soviets pay a heavy price for their Afghan adventure, is effectively dead."[52] In March 1985, Reagan changed the U.S. aim, from "making the Soviets pay a heavy price" to the ouster of Soviet forces, and he signed off on a host of newly aggressive tactics, which included providing tactical intelligence and equipment to the rebels.[53] Before 1986, the U.S. and Saudi money purchased arms on the world market. Starting then, the CIA directly supplied U.S. weapons to the rebels, including Stinger shoulder-launched missiles for use against Soviet helicopters.[54]

The Americans, eager to inflict a defeat on the Soviets, did not blanch at the strange bedfellows they took on in the mujahideen. The rebels were less Afghan nationalists than a mix of Pashtun tribalists and foreign volunteers, the two constituencies joined by a passionate, politically charged version of Islam. They were inspired with a lethal hatred for Communists and a vision of a puritan Sunni Islamic republic rising across the Khyber Pass. The mujahideen were violent and extreme enough that, for the purposes of U.S. policy, their sanguinary outlook was best left a bit cloudy to the eyes of the American public. But government insiders were aware of the tools they employed to torment the Soviets. One defense analyst later observed, "In Afghanistan, we made a deliberate choice. . . . what we [had] to do is to throw the worst crazies against them that we can find, and there was a lot of collateral damage. We knew exactly who these people were, and what their organizations were like. . . . Then, we allowed them to get rid of, just kill all the moderate leaders."[55] Osama bin Laden, a Saudi fundamentalist who made a name for himself by funneling money and volunteers from Arab countries to the mujahideen in the 1980s, opened a recruitment office with his confederates in Tucson, a city with a large Arab American population, in 1986.[56]

In Moscow, Gorbachev was anxious to leave Afghanistan, but also concerned to prevent a hostile government, which might spread Islamic revolution, from taking power on his country's southern border. Gorbachev urged his Afghan puppet, Babrak Karmal—who only held power because Soviet forces had murdered his main rival—to pursue a moderate course domestically. "Forget about socialism, and share real power with . . . the warlords," Gorbachev advised brusquely. "Restore the status of Islam."[57] In November 1986, having replaced Karmal with Muhammad Najibullah, a brutal but skilled subordinate, Gorbachev told the Politburo he planned to withdraw the Red Army within two years. "We have set a clear goal:

Help speed up the process so we have a friendly neutral country, and get out of there."[58] In April 1988, the USSR, the United States, Afghanistan, and Pakistan signed a set of accords providing for the departure of foreign forces and noninterference in Afghan affairs. But Zia told Reagan he would continue aiding the mujahideen. "We'll just lie about it. That's what we've been doing for eight years."[59] Pakistani and U.S. aid continued on one side, Soviet aid on the other. Bush, after becoming president, "paid hardly any attention to Afghanistan," according to journalist Steve Coll. "CIA officers who met the president reported that he seemed barely aware that the war there was continuing."[60]

Bush was focused, instead, on the Persian Gulf. The Gulf's egress through the Strait of Hormuz, which ran between Iran to the north and Oman to the south, became the scene of an undeclared, many-sided "tanker war" in the late 1980s. Iraq's invasion of Iran in 1980, subsequently backed by Kuwait and Saudi Arabia, had become a horrible mire, with a half-million killed over eight years with no gain for either party.[61] The United States sided with Iraq (while secretly selling weapons to Iran as well), providing Saddam Hussein with intelligence and materiel, despite his extensive use of chemical weapons. In 1987, Kuwait asked for protection against Iranian attacks on its oil tankers, and the Reagan administration resolved to "reflag" Kuwaiti tankers as American, protected by U.S. Navy ships. In May, an Iraqi jet hit the USS *Stark* with two missiles, killing thirty-seven sailors. Iraq pleaded human error. Washington, far from punishing Iraq, used the incident to turn up the heat on Iran, which it blamed for the whole situation. President Reagan insisted, "The villain in the piece is Iran."[62] In July, the U.S. House voted to disapprove the reflagging policy, and the Senate was stopped from doing the same only by a Republican filibuster. In April 1988, an Iranian mine damaged a U.S. ship. The U.S. Navy responded powerfully, destroying Iranian oil platforms and sea craft.[63]

Then, on July 3, 1988, in waterways crowded with the navies of over ten nations, the USS *Vincennes* shot down a low-flying Iran Air civilian jet, IR655, on its scheduled flight path in the daytime, apparently mistaking it for an Iranian fighter jet. The *Vincennes* was in Iran's territorial waters, although the U.S. Navy claimed otherwise. All 290 passengers were killed. President Reagan, who had execrated the Soviet Union when its officers shot down KAL007 in 1983, expressed only perfunctory regret.

The brother of the downed plane's pilot wrote in anguish to the *Vincennes*'s captain that "the U.S. government . . . showed neither remorse nor compassion for the loss of innocent lives." The sailors of the *Vincennes* received combat action ribbons when they returned home to a warm welcome.[64]

The Iran–Iraq War finally ended in 1988, leaving Iraq bitter. Saddam felt his country had shouldered the burden for the Kuwaitis and Saudis, and he accused Kuwait of behaving ungratefully. Iraq also long had coveted Kuwaiti oil fields, viewing the border between the two countries as a vestige of British imperialism. In July 1990, Saddam vented his frustration to the U.S. ambassador in Baghdad, April Glaspie. Glaspie demanded of Saddam, "What are your intentions?" as she recounted to her superiors afterward. She got no clear reply. Nonetheless, Glaspie told Saddam, regarding "the border question," that the United States "took no position on these Arab affairs." She did not seem alarmed.[65]

On August 2, Iraqi forces invaded Kuwait, quickly advancing to the capital, Kuwait City. This move was a major disruption in a region designated strategically vital by the United States, potentially a threat to the certain flow of oil on favorable terms to the industrialized world. As Glaspie later explained, "I didn't think—and nobody else did—that the Iraqis were going to take all of Kuwait."[66] President Bush called the invasion a threat to a lawful world, and began comparing Saddam to Adolf Hitler. "This will not stand. This will not stand, this aggression against Kuwait," he declared.[67] Saddam's criminal history suddenly became news, his "vast and cruel" police state now a fit subject for outrage.[68] Bush succeeded in securing a UN Security Council resolution demanding Iraqi withdrawal. Iraq, a staunch defender of the Palestinian cause, tried to link diplomatic progress on the Israel–Palestine conflict to any negotiated withdrawal of its troops from Kuwait. The United States opposed such immediate linkage, demanding that Iraq simply vacate Kuwait. But, to Israel's consternation, Bush and Baker promised Arab governments that an international conference on the Palestine question would follow a favorable resolution of the Kuwait problem. This assurance made it easier for Arab countries to join a mobilization aimed at forcing the Iraqis back across the Kuwaiti border, and many did so.

By October, Bush had dispatched two hundred thousand U.S. troops to Saudi Arabia, purportedly to deter an Iraqi advance into that country, before Congress had made itself heard. The next month, he doubled that number. The U.S. commander, General H. Norman Schwarzkopf, rebuked reporters who questioned America's motives. The Iraqi invasion was "an international rape of the first order," he told them. "We all 'tsk-tsk' when some old lady is raped in New York and twenty-four people know about it and do nothing . . . it's not just a question of oil. There's not a single serviceman out there who thinks that—not any I've met."[69] Even if Schwarzkopf had not met such servicemen, they existed. One marine later recalled, "We joke[d] about having transferred from the Marine Corps to the Oil Corps."[70] Gorbachev, beset by troubles at home, supported Bush, telling Baker, "What's really important is that we stick together."[71] The Saudi ambassador to the United States, Prince Bandar, swatted away warnings of a morass, saying that when war came, it would be "over in a matter of hours. Do you know what happens to tanks in the desert? They are absolutely unprotected targets for the air force, in which we"—by which he meant the United States primarily—"have an overwhelming superiority."[72] As 1990 ended, the U.S. Senate prepared to debate whether to authorize war against Iraq, but many doubted a negative outcome would deter Bush.

At the end of the 1980s, America's reach was global, and it had no rivals. The Reaganite goal in foreign affairs—to make the United States supremely powerful around the world—had been accomplished. Reagan's military buildup had not created America's preeminence—the fall of Soviet power did that—but the buildup put America in position to capitalize, at least militarily, on its now unchecked powers. Whether American power was matched by a global desire for U.S. leadership was a question seldom asked by Americans. The U.S. ascendancy coincided with dramatic breakthroughs toward peace and democracy all around the globe. But only in Eastern Europe was the march of freedom publicly and unambiguously urged forward by the United States, and only there were the two big shifts in power relations—between the United States and the rest of the world, and within nations in many regions—definitely linked.

Neoconservative thinkers who had lamented the decline of confrontation in U.S.–Soviet relations took heart from the prospect of a new assertion of U.S. primacy. One of them, Francis Fukuyama, argued that "history" had ended with the U.S. victory in the Cold War. In his view, the United States was the whole world's future; no alternative social models would emerge.[73] Krauthammer declared the world newly "uni-polar," dominated by a lone superpower.[74] Anxieties over America's de-cline, reflected in the success of Yale University historian Paul Kennedy's 1987 work, *The Rise and Fall of Great Powers*, which intimated U.S. power was in danger of collapsing through "imperial overstretch," suddenly faded.[75] The outstanding new reality in the world was Washington's lack of military inhibition. Bush seemed eager to use his swollen powers. The dawning epoch of U.S. preeminence looked to be an age of steel and fire, not one of peace and idealism; an era of generals and diplomats, not one of people power. Some worried, despite assurances like those of Prince Bandar, about the military outcome of a looming war in the desert. But when war came, in early 1991, American power would sweep those con-cerns aside. The fighting would not last long. It would clip Saddam's wings, ending his martial adventurism outside Iraq's borders, while leav-ing him in power in his country. Bush's vision for the Middle East would stand confirmed as one of stability, not transformation.

But, in late 1990, this outcome lay in the future. As senators debated in Washington, the brute facts of American strength seemed to carry an awesome momentum. The very presence of a huge U.S. force in Saudi Arabia became an argument for war. The soldiers could not wait in these conditions forever, it was said. One American serviceman described it: "After . . . six weeks of deployment, the desert is in us, one particle at a time. . . . Sand has invaded my body: ears and eyes and nose and mouth, ass crack and piss hole. The desert is everywhere."[76] The expedition was costly; the weather would turn, making action difficult. As the last month of the last year of the decade ran out, the world waited for the clash, and for the new order it might bring.

Fifteen

Top of the Heap

A new America took shape in the 1980s, and it included plenty of winners. Others could, at least, imagine themselves winners. Playing the lottery became a legal, and sometimes obsessive, pastime for low-income Americans in the 1980s, as state governments starved for funds ran games of chance to finance their operations. In Illinois, lottery revenues were $98 million in 1980 and rose over fifteenfold, to $1.5 billion, in the next ten years.[1] The dream of storybook riches shone ever brighter. Increasingly, Americans dreamed of finding themselves at the "top of the heap," to quote a song popularized when Frank Sinatra released it in 1980.[2] The society in which immense riches were real and formed the substance of widespread aspiration was the America that Reaganite conservatives celebrated and did their best to create.

The big winners, in truth, were those already on top. Conservatives helped fashion a winner-take-more society in the 1980s, moving the United States in the direction of economic laissez-faire. This was the crucial decade within a longer history of wealth concentration.[3] The economic history of the United States from the end of World War II until the early twenty-first century divides into two parts. Between 1946 and 1976, in an era of income equalization, the average income of the top 1 percent of income earners rose by less than 10 percent, while that of the bottom 90 percent increased by about 75 percent. Between 1976 and 2007, the situation was dramatically different: the average income of the top 1 percent virtually *tripled*, while that of the bottom 90 percent increased only about 15 percent.[4]

It was in the 1980s that the shape of the second of these long periods became unavoidably clear. The growth phase of the 1980s did not bring pervasive affluence. Reaganite tax policies also eased the public burden on the wealthy, but brought little or no relief to less affluent Americans. These changes in taxation meant that the tax system did less to ameliorate growing inequality in the 1980s than it would have if the government had left federal rates alone. Taking total federal taxes into account, the 20 percent of U.S. households with the lowest incomes saw, on average, *no* economic benefit between 1980 and 1990. The next 40 percent saw paltry gains, on average in the middling single digits. Yet the top 1 percent averaged a hefty increase of 72.8 percent in income.[5] The gains within "the one percent," as a later generation would call them, were even more skewed toward the very top, as one could see by examining those gains closely. As a result of these highly uneven income gains, the total income share taken by the top 1 percent, which had grown by 10 percent during the 1970s, increased by almost 50 percent in the 1980s. The income share of the top one-hundredth of 1 percent had risen by an impressive 30 percent in the 1970s, but it spiked in the 1980s, climbing by more than 75 percent.[6]

Working-class America treaded water over the course of the 1980s. Real hourly and weekly wages for young blue-collar men flatlined. The government refused to raise the federal minimum wage after 1981—from $3.35 per hour—for an unprecedented nine years. In 1990, Congress and President Bush agreed to raise it to $3.80, but if the 1981 rate had merely kept pace with inflation it would have been over $4.50.[7] Only the steadily increasing participation of women in paid labor and a lengthening of the average work week kept the incomes of working-class families, particularly younger ones, afloat. In 1990, for one-quarter of full-time workers, "full-time" meant at least forty-nine hours per week on the job, and for almost one-eighth of workers it meant *sixty* hours or longer.[8]

Even working more hours was not enough to compensate for the growing imbalance in the new economy. Working- and middle-class incomes were not adequate to purchase enough goods and services to sustain economic growth. Debt had to fill the gap. This, and not pervasive moral failings among the American people, explains the growing private indebtedness that took off in the 1980s. In the estimation of one scholar of finance, the ratio of household debt to gross domestic product (GDP) "turned a corner and broke through 50%" in the 1980s, "hitting 60% in 1988."[9] Public debt might fall or rise with policy shifts after 1990, but private debt would continue to ascend ever higher until the edifice came crashing down—in what economists delicately termed "deleveraging"—after the financial crisis of 2007–2008. But even then, the imbalance between supply and demand in the economy, which stemmed from worsening economic inequality, would ensure the perpetuation of massive debt. This indebtedness was a structural component of the new American economy hailed by Reaganites.

As already noted, Reagan's tax policies reinforced the trend toward inequality. Democratic senator George Mitchell, the Senate's majority leader at the end of the 1980s, commented that increases in the Social Security tax rate during the decade, in tandem with Reagan's income-tax cuts, meant that "there has been a shift of about $80 billion in annual revenue collections from the progressive income tax to the regressive payroll tax."[10] The payroll tax was regressive because, unlike the income tax that it partly replaced, it took no account of one's ability to pay, levying the same rate on all workers—and effectively taxed the rich at a lower rate, because income above a certain threshold was exempt. (That upper limit benefited approximately the 6 percent highest-earning Americans.)[11]

The stated goal of these changes was to foster investment and enhance economic growth. But the great leap forward predicted by supply-side advocates did not materialize. Economic growth in the 1980s was almost indistinguishable from what it had been in the 1970s. The economy grew by 36.7 percent in the 1970s and by 37.6 percent in the 1980s.[12] National savings, which, according to supply-side doctrine, should have risen after the tax cuts, fell sharply instead, from a yearly average of 8.9 percent of GDP in the 1970s to one of 3.7 percent during the 1981–1988 years.[13]

By the standard of another conservative goal—shrinking the size of the federal government—the conservative scoresheet for the 1980s was a weak one. The tax burden of government on the economy did not decline in the decade of Reaganism. Federal government tax collections were 19 percent of GDP in 1980 and 18 percent in 1990, while federal expenditures were higher and virtually identical in both years. Taxation at all levels of American government was 29 percent of GDP in both 1980 and 1990.[14] Society's overall tax obligation had simply shifted down the income scale. President Reagan's fiscal policies—large tax cuts not off-set by reduced spending—roughly tripled America's public debt in dollar terms. The federal government's debt amounted to 26.2 percent of GDP at the end of 1980, but this figure jumped to 42.8 percent by the end of 1990.[15] It was left to Bush and others to grapple with Reaganism's fiscal legacy.

Other economic policies of the 1980s besides changes in the tax code also helped usher in the newly unequal society. The Federal Reserve and the Treasury Department pursued tight-money and high-dollar policies until, respectively, 1983 and 1985, devastating America's manufacturing sector, eliminating tens of thousands of unionized jobs and killing off firms where pay had been relatively egalitarian. "Two-thirds of the man-ufacturing jobs lost in the 1981–1982 recession were never regained," ac-cording to economic historian John Sloan.[16] The union membership rate of private-sector American workers, which had declined from 24.2 per-cent to 20.1 percent between 1973 and 1980, dropped faster in the 1980s, falling to 11.9 percent by 1990.[17]

What replaced manufacturing in the new economy were financial firms, insurance companies, and real estate enterprise, often called the FIRE sector of the economy. The debt markets became enormous, var-ied, and highly profitable. With U.S. Treasury securities and (after 1985) U.S. properties attractive investments, foreign cash engorged U.S. ac-count books to finance ballooning public and private debt. Between 1982 and 1989, foreign holdings of U.S. government debt doubled, and direct foreign investment in the United States more than tripled.[18] Many Americans were alarmed by headlines about a real estate division of the Mitsubishi Group buying Rockefeller Center in 1989; by the late 1980s, it was estimated that foreign ownership of downtown commercial prop-erty was 20 percent in Manhattan and almost half in Los Angeles.[19] War-ren Buffett, famous as an investor and one of the country's richest men, said, "We are much like a wealthy family that annually sells acreage so that it can sustain a lifestyle unwarranted by its current output. Until the plantation is gone, it's all pleasure and no pain."[20] New kinds of bonds proliferated, not only junk bonds but also collateralized mortgage obliga-tions, which were first devised in 1983.[21] The FIRE sector had accounted for about 22 percent of America's corporate profits in 1980, and produced about 28 percent in 1990—the year it surpassed the national profit share of manufacturing, which was heading downward. As with income trends, these developments would continue after the 1980s.[22]

Finance was Reaganism's true heartland. The ethos of finance and related enterprises was rather gleefully Darwinian: those at the top should take what they could, and they could take a lot. No impediments stood in their way; the FIRE sector's unionization rate was just 3.1 percent in 1990.[23] The economists Thomas Piketty and Emmanuel Saez conclude that the new great fortunes of the era derived less from investment income than from massive salaries and bonuses.[24] They document a pattern of increasing concentration of income at the top for the whole period from the late 1960s onward, but the trend first became truly striking during the 1980s. Chief executive officers (CEOs) of big corporations saw their pay rocket upward starting in the 1980s. Figures from large firms show the ratio of CEO pay to that of the average American worker had risen in the 1970s, from about 28 to around 40 in 1980. Between 1980 and 1990, this curve bent more sharply, with the ratio reaching about 75. (It would rise astronomically in the following years, attaining a shocking 299 in the late 1990s.)[25] However, it was in the FIRE sector, more than any other, that huge compensation packages for executives—a key source of rising income inequality—became the new cultural norm. In the era of deindustrialization and financialization, firms in the most dynamic economic sector were directing the lion's share of their profit streams to those at the top.

If the giants of finance were the top of the heap in the 1980s, their king, as they called him, was Michael Milken. In 1990, Milken finally had his date with destiny in the person of Rudolph Giuliani. They looked almost like cousins, both of them intensely focused, pale-skinned, each sporting an unconvincing black hairpiece. Milken and his associates had engaged in insider trading and secretly spread around their security holdings in order to evade public disclosure requirements. They displayed, according to journalist Connie Bruck, a "willingness to treat the law as if it were a stultifying system of rules and regulations meant for the world's less able."[26] Drexel ousted Milken in late 1988, hoping to save the firm. But this was like cutting off both its arms. Milken's operation alone had made Drexel the most profitable investment bank in the country by 1986. Drexel was bankrupt before Milken finally agreed, in 1990, to plead guilty to six criminal charges. He had to pay $600 million and was sentenced to serve ten years. He eventually served two. Milken's personal disgrace was real, but there would be no turning back from the new landscape of American finance that he had done much to shape.

Milken had stood at the nexus of far-reaching changes in American capitalism. He had shown that there were huge, previously untapped sources of investment wealth in America, and had used them to make merchant princes out of obscure executives. In the process, he transformed American business by pumping up debt levels, forcing the dismantling of inefficient and poorly managed conglomerates, and upsetting the familiar gentility of corporate culture. Drexel's signal takeover was its assault on Revlon, a renowned cosmetics company. Milken anointed Ronald Perelman, by all accounts an unpleasant man with a Napoleon complex, as the principal in the takeover. This upstart symbolized, in Bruck's judgment, "a class war," with "the Drexel arrivistes" playing the outsiders—although many Americans might have had difficulty seeing any "class" divide between warring upper-class factions.[27] In October 1989, the stock market took a new dive, as companies financed with junk bonds started to default.[28] Amid the wreckage, many experts saw stronger, pared-down companies emerge. Economists generally viewed the takeover wave of the 1980s as a way to undo a previous generation's ill-conceived mergers, and they doubted that the takeovers were a major source of job losses, despite popular perceptions.[29] Indeed, a major corporation like General Electric, never a takeover target, eliminated one hundred thousand jobs in the decade's first half under its chief, Jack Welch.[30] Milken, Boesky, and their confederates became lightning rods for public anger over the perception that the new economy was a game rigged for insiders. Welch, meanwhile, was hailed as a management genius.

Far less controversy attended the rise of wealthy business heroes in areas other than finance, and nowhere was this clearer than in the information technology (IT) sector, which made the United States again a world leader in new industries. By 1990, Bill Gates, a Harvard dropout who started Microsoft, was IT's most prominent face. For those intoxicated by the new world of IT, Microsoft epitomized a new meritocracy, a corporate America that left behind the hierarchy and rigidity associated with companies like IBM—the company that, ironically, launched Microsoft. In the early 1980s, Gates, who was twenty-five but looked like a teenager, nabbed the contract to supply an operating system for the personal computer (PC) that IBM had in the works. Between 1985 and 1989, IBM lost half its world market share of PCs, going from one-half to a quarter.[31] But Microsoft was well on its way to near-monopoly status in software, as it made a fortune from IBM "clones" running its system.

Gates pictured a world in which the computer was a household appliance as well as a standard tool at desks in businesses everywhere, replacing the typewriter. Business purchase of microcomputers increased almost tenfold between 1981 and 1985, rising from 344,000 to 3,290,000. This was only the start.[32] Gates combined a broad and deep grasp of IT with coolheaded negotiating skills (his father was a prominent Seattle lawyer) and a vision of commercial supremacy that brooked no obstacle. Detractors carped that he was uncreative, making Milken-like millions by copying others' inventions. "He lets things get out in the market and be tried first before he moves into them," observed one colleague.[33] In 1990, Gates unveiled Microsoft's third effort to imitate the Apple Macintosh computer's graphical user interface system of manipulating a handheld device (a mouse) to point and click on screen "icons," rather than entering text-based commands. With Windows 3.0, as the product was called, Microsoft finally got a passable competitor to market. Windows would expand its province, becoming the dominant operating system on PCs. Microsoft, with no debt and huge cash reserves, showed a capacity to overcome repeated product failures and to persist in capturing the software world one step at a time by flooding the marketplace with decent, if not great, programs. Its triumph in operating systems would give it leverage it would use to destroy early leaders in spreadsheet and word-processing programs. A new economy may have been emerging in 1990, but corporate giants who dominated through power and position—an old phenomenon in American business—were far from an extinct breed.

IT was what most Americans meant when they began to talk about the "new economy," but the "old economy" continued to loom large in the picture of American employment and profit, and nowhere was this truer than in retail sales. Yet the old was becoming new; in the 1980s, retail witnessed huge changes, largely wrought by an Arkansan whose provincial image concealed transformative innovation powered by leading-edge technology. The man was Sam Walton, founder of Wal-Mart, a billionaire usually seen wearing a baseball cap, standard attire for older men throughout America's South and Midwest. Wal-Mart was the country's fourth–biggest earning discount retail chain in 1981, and it moved up from there, selling everything from gum and pajamas to car batteries and cat food. Like Mao Zedong's Communists sweeping out of remote rural base areas in the 1930s, Walton's forces gathered strength in the deep interior fastness of the Ozarks, refining their methods, then stormed into America's small-town and far suburban landscape, threatening the cities with encirclement. Wal-Mart's doorway greeters, blue smocks, stark store interiors, and morning employee group cheer—an imitation of a ritual Walton had observed in a Korean shoe factory—became famous in the 1980s.[34] Walton built "the world's largest private, integrated satellite communication network" to track sales minutely and refine his management of inventory.[35] To facilitate this computerization of sales data, he required that everything sold in Wal-Mart have a Universal Product Code, or barcode, on it, and the barcode soon became ubiquitous in American life.

Walton broke both town and country merchants by underpricing them. He had an eye for wasted effort and expense. To avoid problems with efficient provisioning of his small-town stores, he first built his distribution centers in promising areas, and then built his stores in orbit around them. He nickeled and dimed his employees, keeping as many as possible below full-time hours to deny them benefits. He continually transferred his managers without mercy and fired 10 to 15 percent of them yearly no matter how well the company did. Fiercely anti-union, Walton flew to the scene in 1982 as warehouse workers in one locality prepared to vote on whether to organize. "He told us that if the union got in, the warehouse would be closed," said one witness, even though to have done so for that reason would have been illegal.[36] Walton could withstand a fine from the NLRB; he would not tolerate a union. It became part of middle America's folklore that a Wal-Mart store on a nearby highway meant ruin for independent shopkeepers. "Wal-Mart just cannibalized Main Street," said one financial analyst.[37] "People come in and say we're robbing them," a small-town Oklahoma pharmacist lamented in 1987. Drugs were cheaper at Wal-Mart.[38] With half the country's households working more hours merely to maintain their income levels, consumers had become highly price-sensitive.

Wal-Mart brought the planet's goods to the American shopper, becoming the portal to a world of globalized production, shipment, and sales. Along with manufacturers like IBM and Nike, a new leader in athletic shoes, Wal-Mart exploited the sharp drop in transoceanic shipping costs wrought in the 1970s by the advent of cargo "containerization."[39] Wal-Mart established offices in Hong Kong and Taiwan in the early 1980s. By 1989, it had ninety full-time employees working in East Asia (which Walton, with an old-time touch, called the Orient). A tidal wave of cheap products from Asia, dealing death blows to various sickly U.S. industries—particularly textiles and clothing—was borne in on the hurricane named Wal-Mart. In the first half of the 1980s, more than 250 clothing factories closed in the United States.[40] In the globalized economy of "disintegrated production," insecure workers and low prices were two sides of the same coin.[41]

If Walton brought the world to American consumers in a newly globalized economy, U.S. companies had products and images to show the world as well. In some cases, American "manufacturers" were really contractors and headquarters for contingent suppliers elsewhere, but the image and brand of the finished product were all-American. The epitome of this new "flexible" manufacturing corporation was Nike. It was headquartered in Oregon, but its own employees merely designed products there; Nike had its shoes made by contractors in various Asian workshops, and sold them to Americans and Europeans at a huge markup. The face of Nike—and, in a way, the face of America in the dawning era of globalization—was not its CEO, Phil Knight, but its greatest product endorser, the basketball star Michael Jordan. In an era of changing racial attitudes and identities, two African American men, Jordan and Bill Cosby, were reputed to be the two celebrities most highly regarded by their countrymen.[42] By 1990, Jordan was likely the most famous living American. Stanley Crouch underlined the sweep of cultural change with his choice of words when he wrote that "in 1960, if white girls in the suburbs had had posters of a Negro that dark on the wall, there would have been hell to pay."[43]

The mounting reverence toward Jordan was a celebration of individual prowess and fearsome competitive drive, displayed by Jordan in a game where teamwork, ironically, was the key to victory. (Only in 1991 would Jordan win the first of his six professional championships.) Individual sports, like tennis, golf, or running, lacked the mass popularity needed for the kind of global celebrity that Jordan assumed. Basketball was well established in Europe, and as the 1990s began, Nike saw big new fields of potential customers in Third World countries like China, where the sport was taking root. Jordan seemed tailor-made as the pitchman for the U.S. export sector: a handsome man who was the most spectacular player ever in a game with an expanding, worldwide following second only to football (i.e., soccer), in a burgeoning age of globalized visual communications; an archetype of individual aspiration and excellence for a youthful world bursting with desire for achievement and betterment; a black man from the First World who thereby embodied racial complexity and blunted charges of U.S. cultural imperialism. In 1989 and 1990, Jordan encountered public-relations difficulties with reports that black male teenagers in America's cities were literally killing and dying for "Air Jordans," the coveted shoes stolen off murder victims' feet.[44] Jordan's image survived this shock, however, with Jordan keeping silent. "Just do it" was the slogan Nike used starting in 1986—one that would endure through many campaigns, eventually involving a legion of star endorsers from many sports. The spirit of the 1980s lived on triumphant in the phrase, full of the message that life was a struggle won by single-minded warriors, and that to compete and to win was a cause more glorious than any other.

The new economy was alternately gendered male and female. As of 1990, in the world of advertising, faux warrior heroes were almost exclusively men. The IT sector suffered from a nerdy version of machismo. In the world of high finance, profane men who swaggered and bullied were often worshipped and imitated. Yet in the lower economic reaches of the expanding service sector, workers were heavily female. The non-FIRE service sector was relatively labor-intensive and featured thin profit margins, and its share of the nation's jobs, which included retail clerking, tending bar, teaching school, cutting hair, lawyering, and cleaning hotel rooms, grew in the 1980s from about 24 percent to 30 percent.[45] In an era of factory shutdowns, long-term layoffs, and job-shifting across national borders by manufacturers, men increasingly held service jobs. But women long had been concentrated in this economic sector, and expanded their reach into new service occupations during the 1980s. Between 1980 and 1990, the percentage of American women working full-time for pay increased from 51.5 percent to 57.5 percent; the ratio of their average yearly pay to that of American men improved from 0.60 to 0.72.[46] The percentages of women among architects, lawyers, college professors, insurance adjustors, and bartenders increased. But progress toward equality, while noticeable, was very gradual, and contrary trends toward inequality cut against these gains. By 1995, about one fifth of the nation's families were led by single women, and of these, about 70 percent had incomes of $25,000 or less.[47]

If American women were slowly making headway in their quest for economic parity with men as the 1980s ended, many women remained concerned, not only over economic and social conditions, but also over the continuing controversy surrounding abortion. Reagan's installation of conservative federal judges guaranteed that abortion would remain a contested issue. In early July 1989, the U.S. Supreme Court ruled, 5–4, in *Webster v. Reproductive Health Services*, to reverse lower-court rulings and uphold the constitutionality of several restrictions that the state of Missouri had placed on abortion, such as forbidding public employees or public hospitals to perform abortions regardless of whether public funds paid for the procedure.[48] "What I heard is they upheld *Roe v. Wade*," one woman told a reporter after the decision. But another, a young mother of two, said, "This is awful, I'm totally depressed."[49] *Webster* went far enough to lead some abortion-rights activists to fear *Roe* was effectively a dead letter.[50]

Democrats, aware that most women were pro-choice, capitalized on the ruling. One Democrat who did so was Ann Richards, antagonist of George H. W. Bush in 1988, who, in a marquee political contest in 1990, became the second woman and the first modern liberal elected governor of Texas.[51] Richards had risen through the political ranks like many women. She had begun as a homemaker who did endless campaign scut work and learned more about how to identify and turn out supporters for candidates than almost anyone. Richards eventually was recruited to run state legislative campaigns and then became a candidate. She was serving as state treasurer when the call came asking this obscure figure with a sharp tongue and snow-white hair to give the keynote address to the Democrats' 1988 convention in Atlanta. The Ferraro gambit in 1984 had flopped, but the Democrats would keep trying to exploit the potential they saw for gains among women voters. In 1990, Richards survived a brutal Democratic primary in which her main opponent was the state's attorney general, Jim Mattox. Mattox made highly personal attacks on Richards, a recovering alcoholic, demanding that she say whether she had used illegal drugs, peddling allegations off the record to journalists concerning Richards's drug use and sexuality, and publicly accusing her of past cocaine use.[52] Richards became her party's nominee mainly because Mattox, who had compiled a strong record as state attorney general, made himself repellent.

The appeal to women saved Richards, who rose from the political dead in the closing weeks of her fall 1990 campaign against the Republican nominee, the highly conservative Clayton Williams, a self-styled cowboy multimillionaire. One-fourth of Republican women crossed over to give Richards a narrow victory.[53] "Claytie" became infamous during the GOP primary race when he remarked that bad weather is "like rape. If it's inevitable, you might as well lie back and enjoy it," and reminisced about being "serviced" in bordellos near the Mexican border in his youth.[54] Yet he went on to win the primary easily and was far ahead in polls against Richards until Labor Day. At a public forum in the campaign's closing days, Williams revived the issue of sexism when he refused to shake Richards's hand. Suddenly, he was attacked for his churlishness. Bob Bullock, a conservative Democrat running for lieutenant governor, shouted at a campaign rally, "You men, now you listen to me! In Texas a man shakes a woman's hand! I'm here to tell you Clayton Williams is no man!"[55]

"This race really drove white men and women in opposite directions," remarked one analyst.[56] Richards's victory signaled the growing political divergence of the sexes. Ironically, as male-dominated manufacturing jobs disappeared, and the slow convergence of men's and women's work experiences advanced inexorably, women and men were drifting apart politically. Scholars concluded that men judged the state of the nation's economy based on their own fortunes and prospects, while women reached verdicts based on their perceptions of the country's economy as a whole. This divergence led the two groups—at least among white Americans—toward different judgments on conservatism.[57] Such findings confounded certain gender stereotypes, as they showed men relying more on the authority of personal experience, with women preferring a more analytical perspective—even as they confirmed others by showing men to be more individualistic and women more concerned with communal well-being. The gender gap, as of 1990, was not enormous, and did not jeopardize Republican fortunes in general. The GOP advantage with men was often more powerful than its liabilities with women. Female Democrats were not storming the halls of power en masse; there was no nationwide tide of liberal sentiment to carry them. Richards needed some luck, in the form of obnoxious opponents, to win her 1990 race; the same year, Dianne Feinstein of San Francisco lost her bid to become governor of California, defeated by Republican U.S. senator Pete Wilson of San Diego. However, the discrepancy between American men's and women's partisan preferences would continue to grow.

Issues of gender were newly salient in American politics as the 1980s ended. Any coherent stance toward these matters was beyond the imagination of Ronald Reagan, the man who had created the new gender gap in American politics. Some of the civic concerns that had fueled the rise of both Reagan and Reaganism, like fear of communism and worries about inflation, had receded dramatically, even as other matters increased in urgency. American conservatives adjusted to a new political environment; but in doing so, in some ways, they left Reagan's own political style and appeal behind them.

The relationship of post-1990 conservatives to Reaganism was an ambivalent one. Some elements of the Reaganite formula lived on in the conservative movement and the Republican Party. Fiercely unapologetic patriotism and a belief in U.S. military preponderance remained fundamental tenets for most conservatives. So did faith in unrestrained business as a source of social good, and the cherished ideal of hardy individualism, free from entanglements with the state. But the conservatism of Bush and his supporters departed from Reagan's in other respects. Fiscally, it was more responsible; politically, it was coarser. The balance of sentiment on the American right, as of 1990, was tipping away from the embrace of hedonism that had marked the 1980s, and toward cultural traditionalism. In terms of foreign policy, Americans looked back to Reagan for little guidance as a new age of resource wars in the Persian Gulf vicinity dawned. Later in the 1990s, foreign policy neoconservatives would call for "a neo-Reaganite foreign policy of military supremacy and moral confidence." These were undeniably Reaganite values. But Americans would find it hard to say, after the Cold War's conclusion, exactly what foreign policies those values should dictate.[58]

Just as aspects of Reaganism lived on, so did Reagan's personal legend. At his presidency's end, Reagan shucked off the worst effects of scandal and emerged an honored figure. His farewell address in 1989 was graceful, yet self-satisfied. At one and the same time, he downplayed his own role as an individual in creating change and boasted of a nation made "more prosperous, more secure, and happier" because of his leadership. "All in all, not bad," he said, in grading his accomplishments in office; "not bad at all."[59] The Reagans moved back to their ranch in the hills near Santa Barbara, but the former president ventured out in the ensuing years to make highly paid appearances before business groups. Some found this unbecoming; previously, among ex-presidents, only Gerald Ford had cashed in on his status in this way. (Americans would become accustomed to this habit over time, as retired presidents of both parties would follow suit.) In November 1990, Reagan's memoir, *An American Life*, was published. It exuded his characteristic combination of self-effacement and complacency.[60] Even before Reagan drifted into senescence in the mid-1990s—a victim of Alzheimer's disease—he became a symbol of the 1980s, a totem of the conservative narrative of recent American history: the man who saved the country from self-doubt and liberal failure. Conservatives emphatically identified Reagan with their creed and their movement—the way liberals long had identified their own cause with Franklin Roosevelt—and for decades would proclaim themselves Reagan's heirs, even as they swore they would never do things that Reagan had done, such as raise taxes or approve an amnesty for undocumented immigrants. Understanding Reaganism is more important than knowing Reagan. But there is no interpreting the 1980s without arriving at a judgment on Reagan, who, it seems likely, will always be closely tied to our memories of that era.

He was a great success in many ways. He was an ideologue who recognized political realities and bowed to them when necessary, taking his gains where he could. He defied those who had said, during the 1970s, that the presidency had become an impotent office, the president the chief in name only of a system beyond anyone's control. Where Reagan led, many followed. Neither the childlike analytical capacities that Reagan sometimes displayed nor the peculiarly passive stance he took toward much of his own government's operations negates that achievement in leadership. He did restore national confidence and the traditional American belief in the beneficence of U.S. power. At great expense, he left the United States in a position to dominate the world through force of arms, its military loaded for bear.

The historian David T. Courtwright observes, mischievously but accurately, "Reagan was to money what [Hugh] Hefner was to sex: an iconic cheerleader for a profound moral change in an age when celebrities created as well as reflected values."[61] Reagan led a movement that wrenched political debate in America away from concern over poverty and unemployment, which remained problems in the 1980s and at times grew markedly worse. One of Reaganism's basic components was the idea that Americans should get what they could, when they could. Surely this attitude bore some connection to the impressive corruption that marked Reagan's presidential administration. In the George H. W. Bush years, even as the previous regime's misdeeds continued to make news, the realization that the new president's own son, Neil, had been recruited as an officer at a thrift that had gone belly-up, costing the taxpayers millions of dollars, threatened to mark the entire Republican Party as unethical and greedy.[62] Corruption in government was nothing new, and it certainly was not the exclusive property of one party (as discussed in chapter 11, the savings-and-loan crisis resulted from a sterling example of bipartisan collaboration). But it was snowballing, seemingly out of control, in the late 1980s, and it was not hard to trace the problem back to a creed that celebrated individual enrichment—one rightly identified with Reagan.

Neither the public corruption of the 1980s nor the failure of conservatives to reduce the scale of government restored luster to the idea of big-government liberalism. To the contrary, Reaganism, both in theory and in reality, reinforced the cloud of suspicion that had gathered over government in America during the 1960s and 1970s. It was Reagan's legacy to render axiomatic, for broadened swaths of the American public, the evils of taxation and the unsavory character of regulation. The vision of the free economy and the weak state, only partially fulfilled, was renewed as a social ideal—except for sectors of the population deemed overloaded with criminal elements. For them, the prescriptions administered were narrowed legal rights, tougher police methods, more prisons, and dramatically expanded incarceration. For most Americans, the state should be weak; for the dangerous classes, the state would be exceptionally strong. This was big-government conservatism.

Regarding questions of culture, Reaganism was Janus-faced—now traditionalist, now libertarian. The Reaganite achievement in cultural terms, therefore, could not satisfy the entire movement. Reagan himself had promised a return to what he termed traditional moral values. By this measure, his accomplishment was slender. In 1990, his country was less traditional, and not more moral, than it had been in 1980. But Reagan himself embodied the divided mind of conservatism on cultural matters. His admiration of unfettered wealth was the instinct that echoed and amplified throughout American culture during the 1980s. The cultural mood of the 1970s, with its nod toward the virtues of simple living and its cultivated homespun populism, gave way to an emphasis on glitz and glamour. Some Americans were repulsed by the sybaritic aspect of 1980s culture. In the late 1980s, the unfitness of the contemporary rich for social leadership became a widely heard theme, fodder for satire in fictions like *The Bonfire of the Vanities* and for outrage in nonfiction works like *The Politics of Rich and Poor*, an analysis by the conservative strategist Kevin Phillips published in 1990. Yet the high status of wealth would survive this time of testing, to receive fresh boosts in the 1990s and beyond— from many Democrats as well as Republicans.[63]

The United States was, and remained, a fiercely proud and immensely powerful country, but from the 1970s onward, many Americans feared an inevitable decline both in their nation's position in the world and in the possibilities of upward mobility within American society. Addressing the first of these concerns, Reagan embraced both pride and power with an unreserved strength and clarity that made him a patriotic icon, one with resonance beyond the limits of party. Addressing the second, he stirred Americans by retrieving deeply familiar rhetoric of boundless aspiration and personal ambition. This was the two-pronged meaning of his invocation of Paine's assurance, "We have it in our power to begin the world over again." Reagan's success in linking political conservatism to the cause of national revitalization through military strength, on one side, and to the idea of individual self-betterment, on the other, explains why conservatives and Republicans, a quarter-century after his presidency ended, continued to treat Reagan as their political touchstone. This success also explains why many others remained somewhat awestruck by Reagan as a political figure, even if they disagreed strongly with the political stands he took. Nothing wins like winning.

To Reagan's most devoted conservative admirers, he was the hero who tamed American politics and Soviet power. In 2001, Peggy Noonan, who had been Reagan's most talented speechwriter, rebuked Reagan's critics: "They called him stupid. They called him warlike. They called him unsophisticated, lazy, a mere actor, a cornball blowhard who believes in a mythic America that never existed." She herself, she recalled, had once agreed with some of these criticisms, at least to a degree. But now, she wrote, "We were wrong."[64] Three years before Reagan's death in 2004, his greatness seemed unquestionable to Noonan. Many other conservative writers agreed, and book-length encomiums to Reagan became a lucrative branch of American publishing starting in the early 2000s. As Noonan noted, virtually all Republican presidential aspirants in 2000 (as afterward) claimed to be Reagan's political reincarnation.

But for all of Reagan's achievements, he was not, despite his admirers' seemingly limitless praise, a great man. He scorned far greater men, like King and Mandela, who knew real danger as they led their peoples' struggles against lethal tyrannies. Reagan lacked the capacity to recognize the moral stature of such figures, and in this he surely embodied the spirit of Reaganism as a movement. This was not solely a matter of race. Reagan and his followers were deeply suspicious of movements of, by, and for the underprivileged.

Reagan was not a stupid man, but he sometimes took refuge in stupid lies. He was little troubled by the mass killings committed during his presidency by the Central American regimes that he armed and defended to the hilt. Reagan aggressively advanced grisly counterinsurgency policies in order to prevent socialists from taking power in small countries of no strategic importance to the United States. Reaganite efforts to justify this violent course of action in human terms now appear terribly weak, even detached from reality. In *An American Life*, Reagan explained his views concerning the conflict in El Salvador. "Yes, it is true there were extreme right-wing outlaw elements in that country, including members of the government security forces, who were guilty of flagrant and grave human-rights abuses," he wrote. "But the brutal pro-Marxist rebels who were slaughtering innocent peasants, burning and pillaging their crops, destroying electrical power lines, and blowing up dams in their campaign to wrest control of the country were infinitely more barbaric."[65] Yet three years later, the Commission on the Truth for El Salvador compiled accounts of twenty-two thousand atrocities committed in that country between 1980 and 1991, and revealed, in its thorough and impartial report, that testimony by Salvadorans attributed almost 85 percent of this violence to the regime and its death squads, and only about 5 percent to the insurgents.[66]

The grieving families, the mounds of corpses: these meant nothing to Reagan and his cadres, and were for nothing. The ordeal of the peoples of El Salvador and Guatemala—and that of Nicaragua, where Reagan stubbornly waged indirect war against the Sandinistas—played no role in ending the Cold War, a marvelous development that transpired when Reagan, in his singular change of heart, turned his back on his whole political history and embraced superpower diplomacy and the concepts of détente. The peoples to the south were left to bury their dead. In the United States, Americans were freed of the fear with which they had lived for decades, the fear of a terrible nuclear war.

As Reagan walked into his figurative sunset, his people knew that they inhabited a colossus bestride the world. Their national life was now one of power and debt, of opulence and struggle, of realities both born of conservatism and beyond conservatives' imagining. Despite conservatism's limitations, in the 1990s and into the twenty-first century, Reaganism would remain part of the political air Americans breathed. The tangible achievement of Reaganism was sometimes distorted or obscured by the simple antigovernment rhetoric of conservatives. Not a destruction of government, but a shift in the balance of the state's burdens, financial and punitive, was that achievement's substance. Yet perhaps Reaganism's deeper accomplishment was intangible, a triumph of ideas. In the realm of political legitimacy, Reagan and his followers damaged the cause of government action on behalf of the less fortunate, and added lasting ballast to the presumption in favor of leaving inequality intact. In sum, they reordered the relationships that define government's essence: whom it taxes, whom it enriches, whom it seeks to protect, and on whom it uses force. Few leaders or movements in their country's history had secured more.

Notes

Introduction

1. "U.S. Elections: How Groups Voted in 1984," Roper Center Public Opinion Archives, accessed June 10, 2009, http://www.ropercenter.uconn.edu/elections/how _groups_voted/voted_84.html.

2. Thomas Paine, *Common Sense* (1776), in Thomas Paine, *Collected Writings* (New York: Library of America, 1995), 52; "Ronald Reagan's Announcement for Presidential Candidacy," November 13, 1979, http://www.reagan.utexas.edu/archives/reference/ 11.13.79.html; Ronald Reagan, "Address Accepting the Presidential Nomination at the Republican National Convention in Detroit," July 17, 1980. Gerhard Peters and John T. Woolley, *The American Presidency Project*, http://www.presidency.ucsb.edu/ws/index .php?pid=25970.

3. See Mark Lilla, "A Tale of Two Reactions," *New York Review of Books*, May 14, 1998, reprinted in *Left Hooks, Right Crosses: A Decade of Political Writing*, ed. Christopher Hitchens and Christopher Caldwell (New York: Thunder's Mouth Press/Nation Books, 2002), 257–69 and Daniel T. Rodgers, *Age of Fracture* (Cambridge, MA: Belknap Press of Harvard University Press, 2011), 270. James Livingston and David T. Courtwright argue that American culture simply became more liberal in the late twentieth century. But the truth is that cultural developments provoked division and ambivalence among both liberals and conservatives. James Livingston, *The World Turned Inside Out: American Thought and Culture at the End of the Twentieth Century* (Lanham, MD: Rowman and Littlefield, 2010); David T. Courtwright, *No Right Turn: Conservative Politics in a Liberal America* (Cambridge, MA: Harvard University Press, 2010).

4. For a recent effort to weigh the matter judiciously, see John Prados, *How the Cold War Ended: Debating and Doing History* (Washington, DC: Potomac Books, 2010).

5. Meg Jacobs and Julian E. Zelizer, *Conservatives in Power: The Reagan Years, 1981– 1989: A Brief History with Documents* (Boston, MA: Bedford/St. Martin's, 2011), 28–32, makes this argument persuasively. For greater elaboration, see the comparative study by Paul Pierson, *Dismantling the Welfare State? Reagan, Thatcher, and the Politics of Retrenchment* (Cambridge: Cambridge University Press, 1994).

6. Michael Stewart Foley, *Front Porch Politics: The Forgotten Heyday of American Activism in the 1970s and 1980s* (New York: Hill and Wang, 2013). Also see Bradford Martin, *The Other Eighties: A Secret History of America in the Age of Reagan* (New York: Hill and Wang, 2011).

7. The American National Election Studies (ANES) Guide to Public Opinion and Electoral Behavior, based at the University of Michigan, shows that self-identified conservatives of all degrees ("slightly" to "extremely") totaled 26 percent in both 1980 and 1990. The total figures for liberals in those years were, respectively, 17 and 16 percent. The percentage of respondents saying that the federal government was too powerful fell from 49 in 1980 to 33 in 1988. On some issues dividing liberals from conservatives, the U.S. population clearly became more liberal during the 1980s, for example on the question of gender equality. See the tables, accessed February 1, 2011, collected at http://www.electionstudies.org/nesguide/gd-index.htm#2. Larry M. Bartels, *Unequal Democracy: The Political Economy of the New Gilded Age* (Princeton, NJ: Russell Sage Foundation and Princeton University Press, 2008), 79.

8. On intellectual trends, see Rodgers, *Age of Fracture*; for a summation of the common wisdom among political observers, see the work of two British journalists, Adrian Wooldridge and John Micklethwait, *The Right Nation: Conservative Power in America* (New York: Penguin, 2004).

9. Paine, *Common Sense*, in Paine, *Collected Writings*, 6.

10. Works claiming Paine for the left include Eric Foner, *Tom Paine and Revolutionary America*, updated edition (New York: Oxford University Press, 2004) and Harvey J. Kaye, *Tom Paine and the Promise of America* (New York: Hill and Wang, 2006).

11. "Key Facts at a Glance: Incarceration Rate, 1980–1990," U.S. Bureau of Justice Statistics, http://bjs.ojp.usdoj.gov/content/glance/tables/incrttab.cfm. Those imprisoned were very disproportionately black. For a harsh account, see Michelle Alexander, *The New Jim Crow: Mass Incarceration in the Age of Colorblindness* (New York: New Press, 2010). Also see David Garland, *The Culture of Control: Crime and Social Order in Contemporary Society* (Chicago: University of Chicago Press, 2001).

12. Sean Wilentz, *The Age of Reagan: A History, 1974–2008* (New York: Harper, 2008), 135; Richard Hofstadter, *The American Political Tradition, and the Men Who Made It* (1948; repr., New York: Vintage, 1989), 333. Reagan was born one year before Wilson was elected president. Wilson was the unmarried name of Nelle, Ronald Reagan's mother. Reagan and Wilson were namesakes only in the sense that they shared a name.

13. Haynes Johnson, *Sleepwalking through History: America in the Reagan Years* (New York: Norton, 1991), 176–84. On housing, see Roger Biles, *The Fate of Cities: Urban America and the Federal Government, 1945–2000* (Lawrence: University Press of Kansas, 2011), 279–84. On the Defense Department scandal (now all but forgotten), see Andy Pasztor, *When the Pentagon Was for Sale: Inside America's Biggest Defense Scandal* (New York: Scribner, 1995).

14. Jeff Chang, *Can't Stop Won't Stop: A History of the Hip-Hop Generation* (New York: Picador, 2005), 319.

15. Stephen Tuck, *We Ain't What We Ought to Be: The Black Freedom Struggle from Emancipation to Obama* (Cambridge, MA: Belknap Press of Harvard University Press, 2010), 380.

16. Anne Edwards, *Early Reagan* (New York: William Morrow, 1987), 203, 205.

17. Michael and Ron Jr. each underwent this induction into the tragic life at age four-teen. Edmund Morris, *Dutch: A Memoir of Ronald Reagan* (New York: Modern Library, 1999), 216. Reagan caused puzzlement in later years when he repeatedly claimed that he had been among the troops that liberated the camps and shot the footage. Reagan had spent World War II in Los Angeles, making army training films—but saying he was an eyewitness made for a more dramatic story.

18. Lou Cannon, *President Reagan: The Role of a Lifetime* (New York: PublicAffairs, 2000), 462.

19. Ibid., 456–57.

20. Jeffrey M. Jones, Frank Newport, and Lydia Saad, "Ronald Reagan from the People's Perspective: A Gallup Poll Review," accessed May 14, 2009, http://www.gallup.com/poll/11887/Ronald-Reagan-From-Peoples-Perspective-Gallup-Poll-Review.aspx.

21. Martin Kasindorf, "The Teflon Is Gone: Reagan's Transition to Private Life Has Been Tainted by Accusations That He Is Cashing in on His Old Job," *Newsday*, March 13, 1990.

22. John Kerry, U.S. Senator of Massachusetts, made the first comment in a speech to the Democratic National Convention in July 1988; Bill Clinton, who unseated Bush in 1992, made the second in October 1991. Walter V. Robinson, "Dukakis Sweeps to the Nomination; Jackson's Forces Make It Unanimous," *Boston Globe*, July 21, 1988; Spencer Rich, "Clinton Vows to 'Honor Middle-Class Values,'" *Washington Post*, October 24, 1991.

23. This was U.S. Representative Henry Hyde of Illinois. William Neikirk, "Amid Much Rhetoric, Reagan Airport Is Approved," *Chicago Tribune*, February 5, 1998.

24. Jones, Newport, and Saad, "Ronald Reagan."

1. The Time Is Now

1. *The Killers*, directed by Don Siegel (1964; Irvington, NY: Criterion, 2003), DVD.

2. Lou Cannon, *Governor Reagan: His Rise to Power* (New York: PublicAffairs, 2003), chapter 8, gives a careful account of Reagan's changing politics during his Hollywood days.

3. GE employed Reagan as a spokesman from 1954 to 1962. Thomas W. Evans, *The Education of Ronald Reagan: The General Electric Years and the Untold Story of His Conversion to Conservatism* (New York: Columbia University Press, 2006).

4. Ronald Reagan, "A Time for Choosing," reproduced in Evans, *Education of Ronald Reagan*, 239, 249.

5. Lisa McGirr, *Suburban Warriors: The Origins of the New American Right* (Princeton, NJ: Princeton University Press, 2002), a study of Orange County, California, is the best study of the JBS and the new right in its heyday. For an older view, see Daniel Bell, ed., *The Radical Right: The New American Right Expanded and Updated* (Garden City, NY: Doubleday, 1964).

6. *Washington Post*, July 15, 1964, quoted in Jeremy D. Mayer, *Running on Race: Racial Politics in Presidential Campaigns, 1960–2000* (New York: Random House, 2002), 56.

7. Taylor Branch, *Pillar of Fire: America in the King Years, 1963–65* (New York: Simon and Schuster, 1999), 403–4.

8. Of thirty-three Senate Republicans, twenty-seven voted aye and six voted nay.

9. Matthew Dallek, *The Right Moment: Ronald Reagan's First Victory and the Decisive Turning Point in American Politics* (New York: Oxford University Press, 2004), 193.

10. Footage of this scene is featured in the documentary film *Berkeley in the Sixties*, directed by Mark Kitchell (1990; First Run Features, 2002), DVD.

11. Todd Gitlin, *The Sixties: Years of Hope, Days of Rage* (New York: Bantam, 1993), 357–58; Cannon, *Governor Reagan*, 191–92, 275; Lou Cannon, *President Reagan: The Role of a Lifetime* (New York: PublicAffairs, 2000), 630.

12. Adam Clymer, *Drawing the Line at the Big Ditch: The Panama Canal Treaties and the Rise of the Right* (Lawrence: University Press of Kansas, 2008), 23, 39; Andrew E. Busch, *Reagan's Victory: The Presidential Election of 1980 and the Rise of the Right* (Lawrence: University Press of Kansas, 2005), 47; Julian E. Zelizer, "Conservatives, Carter, and the Politics of National Security," in *Rightward Bound: Making America Conservative in the 1970s*, ed. Bruce J. Schulman and Julian E. Zelizer (Cambridge, MA: Harvard University Press, 2008), 273–75.

13. Donald T. Critchlow, *Phyllis Schlafly and Grassroots Conservatism: A Woman's Crusade* (Princeton, NJ: Princeton University Press, 2005).

14. Some claimed that Reagan's professional jealousy of his first wife, the Hollywood star Jane Wyman, broke up their marriage, but not all agree. For differing accounts, see Edmund Morris, *Dutch: A Memoir of Ronald Reagan* (New York: Modern Library, 1999), 220, and Anne Edwards, *Early Reagan* (New York: William Morrow, 1987), 320–21, 331, 355. Nancy Reagan encountered persistent criticism as a supposedly controlling and domineering spouse, but her husband was happy in their relationship.

15. Mayer, *Running on Race*, 135.

16. Meg Jacobs, "The Conservative Struggle and the Energy Crisis," in *Rightward Bound*, 197–98. OPEC nations were angry over U.S. support for Israel in a Middle East war of that year. But they also reacted against the falling value of the U.S. dollar, the denomination in which they counted their oil revenues. William Greider, *Secrets of the Temple: How the Federal Reserve Runs the Country* (New York: Simon and Schuster, 1987), 337–40.

17. The average rise in worker productivity was 2.8 percent per year between 1945 and 1973. Dean Baker, *The United States Since 1980* (Cambridge: Cambridge University Press, 2007), 45.

18. Ibid., 46.

19. Austin Ranney, "The Carter Administration," in *The American Elections of 1980*, ed. Austin Ranney (Washington, DC: American Enterprise Institute for Public Policy Research, 1981), 28–29; Larry M. Bartels, *Unequal Democracy: The Political Economy of the New Gilded Age* (Princeton, NJ: Princeton University Press and Russell Sage Foundation, 2008), 46.

20. Burton I. Kaufman, *The Presidency of James Earl Carter, Jr.* (Lawrence: University Press of Kansas, 1993), 114.

21. Peter N. Carroll, *It Seemed Like Nothing Happened: America in the 1970s* (New Brunswick, NJ: Rutgers University Press, 1990), 132. This quotation was from 1974, but expresses a pervasive concern of the era.

22. See W. Carl Biven, *Jimmy Carter's Economy: Policy in an Age of Limits* (Chapel Hill: University of North Carolina Press, 2002), 4–5, 192–93.

23. Carter needed to trim some $15 billion from his budget to meet his target of a $30 billion deficit, but he had told NATO member countries they each should increase military spending by 3 percent over the inflation rate per year in the near future. The cuts would have to occur elsewhere. Kaufman, *Presidency of James Earl Carter*, 115; Zelizer, "Conservatives, Carter, and the Politics of National Security," 277.

24. Edward Berkowitz, *Something Happened: A Political and Cultural Overview of the Seventies* (New York: Columbia University Press, 2006), 125.

25. Biven, *Jimmy Carter's Economy*, 240–46.

26. Kaufman, *Presidency of James Earl Carter*, 169; Biven, *Jimmy Carter's Economy*, 243.

27. Soon after the crisis began, Ruhollah Khomeini ordered thirteen hostages, either female or African American, released, leaving fifty-two imprisoned. Jimmy Carter, *Keeping Faith: Memoirs of a President* (New York: Bantam, 1982), 465.

28. David Farber, *Taken Hostage: The Iran Hostage Crisis and America's First Encounter with Radical Islam* (Princeton, NJ: Princeton University Press, 2005), 152.

29. Ranney, "Carter Administration," 34.

30. In July 1980, Carter signed Presidential Directive (PD) 59, initiating this military buildup. This action indicated a move away from reliance on the deterrent effect of Mutual Assured Destruction (MAD), the idea that nuclear war between the superpowers was unthinkable because both understood that if either of them launched a first strike, the other would be utterly devastated by a counterstrike. George C. Herring, *From Colony to Superpower: U.S. Foreign Relations Since 1776* (New York: Oxford University Press, 2008), 853–56.

31. William Safire, "The Four I's," *New York Times*, March 27, 1980; Kaufman, *Presidency of James Earl Carter*, 136.

32. Kaufman, *Presidency of James Earl Carter*, 171. Busch, *Reagan's Victory*, 75–78, gives good coverage of the Carter-Kennedy battle, and Timothy Stanley, *Kennedy vs. Carter: The 1980 Battle for the Democratic Party's Soul* (Lawrence: University Press of Kansas, 2010) covers it completely.

33. Jimmy Carter, "Energy and National Goals" (July 15, 1979), reproduced in Daniel Horowitz, *Jimmy Carter and the Energy Crisis of the 1970s: The "Crisis of Confidence" Speech of July 15, 1979: A Brief History with Documents* (Boston: Bedford/St. Martin's, 2005), 113.

34. Isaac William Martin, *The Permanent Tax Revolt: How the Property Tax Transformed American Politics* (Stanford, CA: Stanford University Press, 2008); Robert Kuttner, *Revolt of the Haves: Tax Rebellions and Hard Times* (New York: Simon and Schuster, 1980); Bruce J. Schulman, *The Seventies: The Great Shift in American Culture, Society, and Politics* (New York: The Free Press, 2001), chapter 8. According to Busch, in November 1978, sixteen states saw ballot measures limiting or cutting taxes, and these passed in twelve states. Busch, *Reagan's Victory*, 24–25.

35. See Monica Prasad, "The Popular Origins of Neoliberalism in the Reagan Tax Cut of 1981," *Journal of Policy History* 24, no. 3 (2012): 353–59.

36. Kaufman, *Presidency of James Earl Carter*, 115; Busch, *Reagan's Victory*, 25.

37. "Our Country" (January 9, 1978), in *Reagan's Path to Victory: The Shaping of Ronald Reagan's Vision: Collected Writings*, ed. Kiron K. Skinner, Annelise Anderson, and Martin Anderson (New York: Free Press, 2004), 253.

38. Elizabeth Drew, *Portrait of an Election: The 1980 Presidential Campaign* (New York: Simon and Schuster, 1981), 120.

39. Ibid., 110.

40. Ibid., 190.

41. Ronald Reagan, "Address Accepting the Presidential Nomination at the Republican National Convention in Detroit" (July 17, 1980) in *The American Presidency Project*, ed. Gerhard Peters and John T. Woolley, http://www.presidency.ucsb.edu/ws/index .php?pid=25970. Unless noted otherwise, subsequent references to presidential statements and nomination convention speeches are to this same online archive. Franklin D. Roosevelt, "Acceptance Speech for the Renomination for the Presidency, Philadelphia, Pa." (June 27, 1936), http://www.presidency.ucsb.edu/ws/index.php?pid=15314. Reagan's speech quoted extensively from passages in Roosevelt's 1932 acceptance speech that stressed the need for restraint in government spending.

42. Reagan, "Address Accepting the Presidential Nomination."

43. Richard Wirthlin, "Memorandum I: Some Initial Strategic and Tactical Considerations for the 1980 Presidential Campaign, drafted March 28, 1980," reproduced in Drew, *Portrait of an Election*, 353, 357.

44. Albert R. Hunt, "The Campaign and the Issues," in *The American Elections of 1980*, 165.

45. Adam Clymer, "Labor Day Symbols Vital to 3 Seeking Presidency," *New York Times*, September 1, 1980.

46. Douglas E. Kneeland, "Reagan Campaigns at Mississippi Fair," *New York Times*, August 4, 1980; Joseph Crespino, *In Search of Another Country: Mississippi and the Conservative Counterrevolution* (Princeton, NJ: Princeton University Press, 2007), 1.

47. Hunt, "Campaign and the Issues," 155; Mayer, *Running on Race*, 170.

48. Crespino, *In Search of Another Country*, 256.

49. Mayer, *Running on Race*, 164–65. Mayer uses this same description in telling a story about Reagan in 1968, and notes "the faint trace of a disturbing pattern." Ibid., 165n.

50. Garry Wills, *Reagan's America: Innocents at Home* (Garden City, NY: Doubleday, 1987), chapter 2.

51. Howell Raines, "Reagan Backs Evangelicals in Their Political Activities," *New York Times*, August 23, 1980; Sara Diamond, *Not by Politics Alone: The Enduring Influence of the Christian Right* (New York: The Guilford Press, 1998), 68.

52. Transcript of "Liberty Park/Hope Campaign 80," *The Living Room Candidate: Presidential Campaign Commercials 1952–1988* (created by the Museum of the Moving Image), accessed May 26, 2009, http://www.livingroomcandidate.org/commercials/ 1980.

53. These results were in the Gallup Poll. Frank Newport, "History Shows Presidential Job Approval Ratings Can Plummet Rapidly," Gallup News Service, February 11, 1998, accessed June 8, 2009, http://www.gallup.com/poll/4258/history-shows -presidential-job-approval-ratings-can-plummet-rapidly.aspx.

54. In 1980 Carter proposed a 4.5 percent increase in the nation's military budget for each of the next five years. Zelizer, "Conservatives, Carter, and the Politics of National Security," 282.

55. Drew, *Portrait of an Election*, 266.

56. Ibid., 322.

57. Gary Sick, *October Surprise: America's Hostages in Iran and the Election of Ronald Reagan* (New York: Crown, 1991). Written by a reputable former Carter NSC official, *October Surprise* was the main source of the accusation, implicating Reagan's campaign manager, Casey, in particular; some versions charged that George H. W. Bush also met with Iranians to "fix" the hostage release. After this book's publication, both the U.S. Senate and House deputed inquiries into the matter; both reached exculpatory conclusions, although the Senate committee less emphatically. See Joe Stork, "October Reprise: A Critical Review of the 'October Surprise' Scenario and Its Critics," *Middle East Journal* 47, no. 3 (Summer 1993): 509–17. Iran announced the hostages were headed for freedom only minutes after Carter left office.

58. Another contretemps stirred Washington in 1983, when journalist Laurence Barrett revealed that the Reagan campaign, in advance of the debate, had acquired Carter's briefing papers (others alleged that Reagan's campaign also obtained additional Carter campaign materials). Laurence I. Barrett, *Gambling with History: Ronald Reagan in the White House* (Garden City, NY: Doubleday, 1983), 383; Craig Unger, *House of Bush, House of Saud: The Hidden Relationship between the World's Two Most Powerful Dynasties* (London: Gibson Square Books, 2004), 309–10n60. Such skullduggery, while improper, played no discernible role in the campaign's outcome.

59. Busch, *Reagan's Victory*, 116, 119.

60. Hunt, "Campaign and the Issues," 170.

61. Walter Dean Burnham, "Into the 1980s with Ronald Reagan," in Walter Dean Burnham, *The Current Crisis in American Politics* (New York: Oxford University Press, 1982), 301–7. John Anderson, a liberal Republican House member who ran as an independent, garnered 6.6 percent of the national vote and may have pushed a few states to Reagan.

62. Ibid., 288–89.

63. Carter won 45 percent of the Jewish vote, and Anderson got 14 percent. "The History of the Jewish Vote," May 27, 2009, RiskingHemlock, accessed May 28, 2009, http://riskinghemlock.blogspot.com/2009/05/history-of-jewish-vote.html. Elizabeth Holmes, "Democratic Hold on Jewish Vote Could Slip," *Wall Street Journal*, May 15, 2008.

64. Busch, *Reagan's Victory*, 153–54; Austin Ranney, "Carter Administration," 1–2; "Appendix F: Congressional by State and Region, 1980," in *The American Elections of 1980*, 370–75.

65. Thomas E. Mann and Norman J. Ornstein, "The Republican Surge in Congress," in *American Elections of 1980*, 299.

66. Drew, *Portrait of an Election*, 341.

67. These were the results of *New York Times*/CBS News Poll. Adam Clymer, "Displeasure with Carter Turned Many to Reagan," *New York Times*, November 9, 1980.

68. William Schneider, "The November 4 Vote for President: What Did It Mean?" in *The American Elections of 1980*, 247–48.

69. See Prasad, "Popular Origins of Neoliberalism," 353–54 on this point.

70. See the issue analysis in Schneider, "November 4 Vote," 227–40.

71. Drew, *Portrait of an Election*, 345.

72. Bob Schieffer and Gary Paul Gates, *The Acting President: Ronald Reagan and the Supporting Players Who Helped Him Create the Illusion That Held America Spellbound* (New York: Dutton, 1989), 16.

2. The Agenda

1. It was Stockman himself who dubbed the paper "alarmist." David A. Stockman, *The Triumph of Politics: Why the Reagan Revolution Failed* (New York: Harper and Row, 1986), 71.

2. Laurence I. Barrett, *Gambling with History: Ronald Reagan in the White House* (Garden City, NY: Doubleday, 1983), 62. These quotations are from an interview Barrett, a reporter for *Time* magazine, conducted with Reagan on July 24, 1982.

3. Lou Cannon, *President Reagan: The Role of a Lifetime* (New York: PublicAffairs, 2000), 68, 69.

4. Ayn Rand, *Atlas Shrugged* (1957; repr., New York: Plume, 1999). On Rand, see Jennifer Burns, *Goddess of the Market: Ayn Rand and the American Right* (New York: Oxford University Press, 2009).

5. John W. Sloan, *The Reagan Effect: Economics and Presidential Leadership* (Lawrence: University Press of Kansas, 1999), 118. The words are Sloan's, not Regan's.

6. Ibid., 118.

7. Dean Baker, *The United States Since 1980* (Cambridge: Cambridge University Press, 2007), 66–67.

8. Paul Krugman, *Peddling Prosperity: Economic Sense and Nonsense in the Age of Diminished Expectations* (New York: Norton, 1994), chapter 3. Krugman calls the supply-siders "cranks." He wrote this well before he became known as a liberal public-affairs commentator; in *Peddling Prosperity*, Krugman punctures economic nostrums current among both Republicans and Democrats in the 1980s and early 1990s.

9. Mark Blyth, *Great Transformations: Economic Ideas and Institutional Change in the Twentieth Century* (Cambridge: Cambridge University Press, 2002), 165.

10. Paul Craig Roberts, *The Supply-Side Revolution: An Insider's Account of Policymaking in Washington* (Cambridge, MA: Harvard University Press, 1985), 27.

11. For a recent review of international data, see Mathias Trabandt and Harald Uhlig, "How Far Are We from the Slippery Slope? The Laffer Curve Revisited," *NBER Working Paper 15343* (Cambridge, MA: National Bureau of Economic Research, September 2009).

12. Sloan, *Reagan Effect*, 117.

13. Alan Greenspan, *The Age of Turbulence: Adventures in a New World* (New York: Penguin, 2007), 92. Reagan had tapped an Economic Policy Board during the transition period to advise him; it included eminent conservative economists, including Milton Friedman and Arthur Burns as well as Greenspan. Elizabeth Drew, *Portrait of a Campaign: The 1980 Presidential Election* (New York: Simon and Schuster, 1981), 274–75.

14. Roberts, *Supply-Side Revolution*, 23.

15. Robert Shogan, "Bush Ends His Waiting Game, Attacks Reagan," *Los Angeles Times*, April 14, 1980.

16. See Robert M. Collins, *More: The Politics of Economic Growth in Postwar America* (New York: Oxford University Press, 2002), chapter 6.

17. Bruce J. Schulman, "Slouching toward the Supply Side: Jimmy Carter and the New American Political Economy," in *The Carter Presidency: Policy Choices in the Post–New Deal Era*, ed. Gary M. Fink and Hugh Davis Graham (Lawrence: University Press of Kansas, 1998), 66. The italics appeared in the original text of the speech, by Stuart Eizenstat.

18. Roberts, *Supply-Side Revolution*, 63.

19. Michael Lind, *Up From Conservatism: Why the Right Is Wrong for America* (New York: Free Press, 1997), 132.

20. See John Prados, *The Soviet Estimate: U.S. Intelligence Analysis and Russian Military Strength* (New York: The Dial Press, 1982), 248–57 and Anne Hessing Cahn, *Killing Détente: The Right Attacks the CIA* (University Park: Pennsylvania State University Press, 1998), chapters 7–9. Richard Pipes, *Vixi: Memoirs of a Non-Belonger* (New Haven, CT: Yale University Press, 2003), 132–43, defends Team B's work.

21. Prados, *Soviet Estimate* offers a balanced view of the CIA's work and Cahn, *Killing Détente* defends the Agency's estimates vigorously.

22. Melvyn P. Leffler, *For the Soul of Mankind: The United States, the Soviet Union, and the Cold War* (New York: Hill and Wang, 2007), 315.

23. Julian E. Zelizer, "Conservatives, Carter, and the Politics of National Security," in *Rightward Bound: Making America Conservative in the 1970s*, ed. Julian E. Zelizer and Bruce J. Schulman (Cambridge, MA: Harvard University Press, 2008), 269.

24. Norman Podhoretz, *The Present Danger* (New York: Simon and Schuster, 1980).

25. Garry Wills, *Reagan's America: Innocents at Home* (Garden City, NY: Doubleday, 1987), 338.

26. Ronald Reagan, "Inaugural Address," January 20, 1981. Gerhard Peters and John T. Woolley, *The American Presidency Project*, http://www.presidency.ucsb.edu/ws/index.php?pid=43130. Unless noted otherwise, subsequent references to presidential statements and nominating convention speeches come from this online archive.

27. George C. Herring, *From Colony to Superpower: U.S. Foreign Relations Since 1776* (New York: Oxford University Press, 2008), 818–19.

28. Leffler, *For the Soul of Mankind*, 255.

29. Ronald Reagan, "The President's News Conference," January 29, 1981, http://www.presidency.ucsb.edu/ws/index.php?pid=44101.

30. Reagan, "Inaugural Address."

31. Walter LaFeber, *America, Russia, and the Cold War, 1945–1984*, 5th. ed. (New York: Knopf, 1985), 303.

32. These increases continued a curve of rising military spending in the late 1970s. Those post–Vietnam War increases had begun with a modest rise of 3.5 percent in 1974 and ended with increases of 11.3 percent in 1979 and 15.2 percent in 1980. The first two years of the Reagan administration would represent the high-water mark for these increases in percentage terms. In comparison, during a similar peacetime period

of national urgency over the arms race with the Soviet Union in the early 1960s, U.S. military spending increased by 3.1 percent in 1961, 5.5 percent in 1962, and 2 percent in 1963. These figures represent total budget outlays for "National Defense" as found in Table 3.1—Outlays by Superfunction and Function: 1940–2016 in *Budget of the U.S. Government, Fiscal Year 2012: Historical Tables* (Washington, DC: Government Printing Office, 2010), 47–55.

33. The Reagan campaign had some $400,000 remaining in its coffers, which it put to this purpose, along with $1,100,000 that resulted from two different dedicated fund-raising efforts aimed at readying the new administration to take power. Bob Schieffer and Gary Paul Gates, *The Acting President: Ronald Reagan and the Supporting Players Who Helped Him Create the Illusion That Held America Spellbound* (New York: Dutton, 1989), 18.

34. G. Calvin Mackenzie, quoted in Barrett, *Gambling with History*, 72.

35. Andrew Gamble, *The Free Economy and the Strong State: The Politics of Thatcherism* (Durham, NC: Duke University Press, 1988).

36. Reagan, "Inaugural Address."

37. Desmond S. King and Rogers M. Smith, *Still a House Divided: Race and Politics in Obama's America* (Princeton, NJ: Princeton University Press, 2011), 123.

38. On the facts of the *Griggs* case, see Robert C. Smith, *Racism in the Post–Civil Rights Era: Now You See It, Now You Don't* (Albany: State University of New York Press, 1995), 58–59.

39. See Hugh Davis Graham, "Civil Rights Policy," in *The Reagan Presidency: Pragmatic Conservatism and Its Legacies*, ed. W. Elliot Brownlee and Hugh Davis Graham (Lawrence: University Press of Kansas, 2003), 283–92.

40. Ibid., 123, 160; D. Lee Bawden and John L. Palmer, "Social Policy: Challenging the Welfare State," in *The Reagan Record: An Assessment of America's Changing Domestic Priorities*, ed. John L. Palmer and Isabel V. Sawhill (Cambridge, MA: Ballinger, 1984), 205, 206.

41. Barrett, *Gambling with History*, 419.

42. Wiliam Kleinknecht, *The Man Who Sold the World: Ronald Reagan and the Betrayal of Main Street America* (New York: Nation Books, 2009), 62–63.

43. William A. Niskanen, *Reaganomics: An Insider's Account of the Politics and the People* (New York: Oxford University Press, 1988), 21.

44. Paul R. Portney, "Natural Resources and the Environment: More Controversy Than Change," in *Reagan Record*, 148.

45. Philip Shabecoff, "Rita Lavelle Gets 6-Month Term and Is Fined $10,000 for Perjury," *New York Times*, January 10, 1984, A1.

46. Kleinknecht, *Man Who Sold the World*, 108, 109.

47. Ronald Reagan, "Executive Order 12291—Federal Regulation," February 17, 1981, http://www.presidency.ucsb.edu/ws/index.php?pid=43424.

48. Barrett, *Gambling with History*, 16.

49. Kleinknecht, *Man Who Sold the World*, 215.

50. Reagan, "Inaugural Address."

3. Victory on Capitol Hill

1. Haynes Johnson, *Sleepwalking Through History: America in the Reagan Years* (New York: Anchor, 1991), 19.

2. William Kleinknecht, *The Man Who Sold the World: Ronald Reagan and the Betrayal of Main Street America* (New York: Nation Books, 2009), 57.

3. Sidney Blumenthal, "Reaganism and the Neo-Kitsch Esthetic," in *The Reagan Legacy*, ed. Sidney Blumenthal and Thomas Byrne Edsall (New York: Pantheon, 1988), 252, 253.

4. Lewis H. Lapham, "The Precarious Eden," *Harper's*, March 1981, reprinted in *Reagan as President: Contemporary Views of the Man, His Politics, and His Policies*, ed. Paul Boyer (Chicago: Ivan R. Dee, 1990), 39.

5. Laurence I. Barrett, *Gambling with History: Ronald Reagan in the White House* (Garden City, NY: Doubleday, 1983), 470.

6. "For Mrs. Reagan, Gifts Mean High Fashion at No Cost," *New York Times*, January 16, 1982; Steven V. Roberts, "First Lady Expresses 'Regrets' on Wardrobe," *New York Times*, October 17, 1988; Robert D. Hershey Jr., "Gifts and Loans to Nancy Reagan Stir I.R.S. Interest in High Fashion," *New York Times*, December 6, 1989.

7. Leslie Bennetts, "With a New First Lady, a New Style," *New York Times*, January 25, 1981.

8. Karl Gerard Brandt, *Ronald Reagan and the House Democrats: Gridlock, Partisanship, and the Fiscal Crisis* (Columbia: University of Missouri Press, 2009), 9–10.

9. John W. Sloan, *The Reagan Effect: Economics and Presidential Leadership* (Lawrence: University Press of Kansas, 1999), 124.

10. Bob Schieffer and Gary Paul Gates, *The Acting President: Ronald Reagan and the Supporting Players Who Helped Him Create the Illusion That Held America Spellbound* (New York: Dutton, 1989), 24.

11. Sloan, *Reagan Effect*, 124.

12. Ibid., 122.

13. Lou Cannon, *President Reagan: The Role of a Lifetime* (New York: PublicAffairs, 2000), 91.

14. Sloan, *Reagan Effect*, 124.

15. Cannon, *President Reagan*, 78.

16. See Katharine Graham, *Personal History* (New York: Knopf, 1997).

17. Schieffer and Gates, *Acting President*, 6.

18. Cannon, *President Reagan*, 50.

19. William Niskanen, *Reaganomics: An Insider's Account of the Policies and the People* (New York: Oxford University Press, 1988), 301.

20. A photocopy of this memorandum is reproduced in Schieffer and Gates, *Acting President*, 83.

21. Baker, as chief of staff, had a corps of loyal subordinates who could alert him to any unscheduled meeting between Meese and Reagan. Ibid., 85.

22. For example, Alexander Haig, *Caveat: Reagan, Realism, and Foreign Policy* (New York: Macmillan, 1984), 83. Haig had served President Richard Nixon as chief of staff.

23. Niskanen, *Reaganomics*, 301.

24. This remark came from Robert Carleson, head of the Cabinet Council on Human Resources. Cannon, *President Reagan*, 152.

25. Mark Hertsgaard, *On Bended Knee: The Press and the Reagan Presidency* (New York: Farrar, Straus and Giroux, 1988), 34–37. Larry Speakes became press secretary after James Brady, who first held the job, was incapacitated after being shot by John Hinckley Jr.

26. Sloan, *Reagan Effect*, 134–35.

27. David A. Stockman, *The Triumph of Politics: Why the Reagan Revolution Failed* (New York: Harper and Row, 1986), 92.

28. William Greider, "The Education of David Stockman," *Atlantic Monthly* 248 (December 1981), 51.

29. Barrett, *Gambling with History*, 178.

30. Stockman, *Triumph of Politics*, 108–9.

31. Barrett, *Gambling with History*, 178; Stockman, *Triumph of Politics*, 291.

32. Cannon, *President Reagan*, 216–17; Stockman, *Triumph of Politics*, 97–98.

33. Greider, "Education of David Stockman," 32.

34. Ibid., 39; Stockman, *Triumph of Politics*, 124.

35. Brandt, *Ronald Reagan and the House Democrats*, 17.

36. Barrett, *Gambling with History*, 168.

37. See the account in Del Quentin Wilber, *Rawhide Down: The Near Assassination of Ronald Reagan* (New York: Henry Holt, 2011), chapter 6. A helpful drawing of the scene is provided in ibid., 76.

38. Lou Cannon, *Reagan* (New York: G. P. Putnam's Sons, 1982), 403.

39. Herbert L. Abrams, *"The President Has Been Shot": Confusion, Disability, and the 25th Amendment* (New York: Norton, 1992), 57.

40. Barrett, *Gambling with History*, 111.

41. Cannon, *President Reagan*, 404; Wilber, *Rawhide Down*, 147. The surgeon who made this remark, Joseph Giordano, was a liberal Democrat.

42. Wilber, *Rawhide Down*, 215.

43. Brandt, *Ronald Reagan and the House Democrats*, 36.

44. Barrett, *Gambling with History*, 154.

45. Brandt, *Ronald Reagan and the House Democrats*, 37, 43.

46. Barrett, *Gambling with History*, 163.

47. Greider, "Education of David Stockman," 35.

48. Ibid., 30.

49. Brandt, *Ronald Reagan and the House Democrats*, 48–49; Barrett, *Gambling with History*, 161 (quoting Breaux); Kurt Andersen, Gary Lee, and Peter Staler, "Clinch River: A Breeder for Baker," *Time*, August 3, 1981.

50. Gregory B. Bills, "The Budget: A Failure of Discipline," in *The Reagan Record: An Assessment of America's Changing Domestic Priorities*, ed. John L. Palmer and Isabel V. Sawhill (Cambridge, MA: Ballinger, 1984), 113.

51. D. Lee Bawden and John L. Palmer, "Social Policy: Challenging the Welfare State," in *The Reagan Record*, 192. As part of its push to restrict poor relief to those truly unable to work, the administration reduced welfare benefits from the Aid to Families with Dependent Children program (AFDC) in proportion to the income that families on welfare earned through work.

52. Alan Greenspan, *The Age of Turbulence: Adventures in a New World* (New York: Penguin, 2007), 87.

53. Stockman, *Triumph of Politics*, 87, 223.

54. Reagan also agreed to give up the idea that the first year's tax cuts would apply retroactively to January 1, 1981; instead they applied starting on October 1. The original proposal for a 30 percent reduction in marginal rates would have amounted to an effective 27 percent rate shrinkage, as W. Elliot Brownlee and C. Eugene Steuerle explain: "The tax cut program would apply each 10 percent cut to a successively lower rate of taxation.... More precisely, the net tax cut percentage, pt, was: $pt=1-[(1-.1)x(1-.1)x(1-.1)]$." Brownlee and Steuerle, "Taxation," in *The Reagan Presidency: Pragmatic Conservatism and Its Legacies*, ed. W. Elliot Brownlee and Hugh Davis Graham (Lawrence: University Press of Kansas, 2003), 175n5. The same math applied to the eventual 5:10:10 rate reductions.

55. Barrett, *Gambling with History*, 144–45.

56. Greider, "Education of David Stockman," 46.

57. ERTA also "indexed" tax brackets to inflation, to address the "bracket creep" problem, and allowed bigger deductions for contributions to Individual Retirement Accounts, the contents of which would not be taxed until the accrued wealth in the accounts was withdrawn.

58. Greider, "Education of David Stockman," 51.

59. Stockman, *Triumph of Politics*, 407.

60. Sloan, *Reagan Effect*, 145.

61. Stockman, *Triumph of Politics*, 310, 311–12.

62. Ibid., 319.

63. Mark Blyth, *Great Transformations: Economic Ideas and Institutional Change in the Twentieth Century* (Cambridge: Cambridge University Press, 2002), 178n106; Perry D. Quick, "Business: Reagan's Industrial Policy," in *The Reagan Record*, 297, 298, 300 (Table 9.3); Bills, "The Budget," 119.

64. "Effects of the 1981 Tax Act on the Distribution of Income and Taxes Paid," 22 (figures calculated from those in Table II.7), http://www.cbo.gov/ftpdocs/61xx/doc6173/doc20a-Entire.pdf. The CBO used its definition of Expanded Adjusted Gross Income (EAGI) per tax return to derive its numbers, in 1983 dollars.

65. Greider, "Education of David Stockman," 47.

4. An Aggressive Foreign Policy

1. Alexander Cockburn, "The Network" (March 4, 1981), in Alexander Cockburn, *Corruptions of Empire: Life Studies and the Reagan Era* (London: Verso, 1987), 263.

2. Laurence I. Barrett, *Gambling with History: Ronald Reagan in the White House* (Garden City, NY: Doubleday, 1983), 305.

3. Richard Pipes, *Vixi: Memoirs of a Non-Belonger* (New Haven, CT: Yale University Press, 2003), 194.

4. Barrett, *Gambling with History*, 294.

5. Jeremi Suri, "Explaining the End of the Cold War: A New Historical Consensus?" *Journal of Cold War Studies* 4, no. 4 (Fall 2002): 71.

6. Ronald Reagan, "Address to Members of the British Parliament," June 8, 1982. Gerhard Peters and John T. Woolley, *The American Presidency Project*, http://www.presidency.ucsb.edu/ws/index.php?pid=42614.

7. David E. Hoffman, *The Dead Hand: The Untold Story of the Cold War Arms Race and Its Dangerous Legacy* (New York: Doubleday, 2009), 44.

8. Barry R. Posen and Stephen Van Evera, "Defense Policy and the Reagan Administration: Departure from Containment," *International Security* 8, no. 1 (Summer 1983): 29–30.

9. Barrett, *Gambling with History*, 306.

10. Lou Cannon, *President Reagan: The Role of a Lifetime* (New York: PublicAffairs, 2000), 133–39, gives a scathing account of the MX affair.

11. Bernard T. Feld, "The Hands Move Closer to Midnight," *Bulletin of the Atomic Scientists*, January 1, 1980, cited in Pipes, *Vixi*, 190.

12. J. Peter Scoblic, *U.S. vs. Them: How a Half Century of Conservatism Has Undermined America's Security* (New York: Viking, 2008), 126–27, 130.

13. Richard Halloran, "Pentagon Draws Up First Strategy for Fighting a Long Nuclear War," *New York Times*, May 30, 1982.

14. Lawrence S. Wittner, *Toward Nuclear Abolition: A History of the World Nuclear Disarmament Movement, 1971 to the Present* (Stanford, CA: Stanford University Press, 2003), 177, 184, 197, 257–58, 264–65.

15. "The Wider Ripples of the Allen Affair," *Economist*, December 5, 1981.

16. Barrett, *Gambling with History*, 241.

17. Richard Reeves, *President Reagan: The Triumph of Imagination* (New York: Simon and Schuster, 2005), 30.

18. Pipes, *Vixi*, 166.

19. Haig gave the impression that he believed, erroneously, that the secretary of state followed the vice president directly in the presidential line of succession; Haig later wrote that he was familiar with the correct line of succession from his service as White House chief of staff in Nixon's last months as president. Alexander M. Haig Jr., *Caveat: Realism, Reagan, and Foreign Policy* (New York: Macmillan, 1984), 156–57, 164.

20. For details, see Tracy Dahlby, "Allen Seen in Tokyo as Key Link to U.S.," *Washington Post*, December 6, 1981.

21. "Terrorism: Dubious Evidence," *Economist*, May 9, 1981.

22. Bob Woodward, *Veil: The Wars of the CIA, 1981–1987* (New York: Pocket Books, 1988), 125–28.

23. Claire Sterling, "Who *Were* Those 'Student' Terrorists?" *Washington Post*, January 23, 1981; Claire Sterling, "Terrorism: Tracing the International Network," *New York Times Magazine*, March 1, 1981.

24. Blaine Harden, "Terrorism: Are the Reasons for It as Simple as Ronald Reagan, Alexander Haig and Claire Sterling Would Have Us Believe?" *Washington Post Magazine*, March 15, 1981.

25. Henry Allen, "The Politics of Fear: Claire Sterling and 'The Terror Network,'" *Washington Post*, April 11, 1981.

26. See Arnaud de Borchgrave and Robert Moss, *The Spike* (New York: Crown, 1980).

27. Emily Yoffe, "De Borchgrave: A Cold Warrior's Battle with a World He Sees Full of Dupes, Deception and Disinformation," *Washington Post Magazine*, July 8, 1984.

28. William M. LeoGrande, *Our Own Backyard: The United States in Central America, 1977–1992* (Chapel Hill: University of North Carolina Press, 1998), 449.

29. Barrett, *Gambling with History*, 200.

30. Jeane J. Kirkpatrick, "Dictatorships and Double Standards," *Commentary* 68, no. 5 (November 1979): 34–45.

31. Sara Diamond, *Spiritual Warfare: The Politics of the Christian Right* (Boston: South End Press, 1989), 17.

32. LeoGrande, *Our Own Backyard*, 252.

33. Diamond, *Spiritual Warfare*, 34.

34. Douglas Little, "To the Shores of Tripoli: America, Qaddafi, and Libyan Revolution, 1969–89," *International History Review* 35, no. 1 (January 2013): 84–85.

35. Barrett, *Gambling with History*, 212.

36. Ibid., 216; Woodward, *Veil*, 194–201.

37. "Palestine" (March 27, 1979), in *Reagan, In His Own Hand: The Writings of Ronald Reagan that Reveal His Revolutionary Vision for America*, ed. Kiron K. Skinner, Annelise Anderson, and Martin Anderson (New York: Free Press, 2001), 215.

38. Barrett, *Gambling with History*, 275, 445. AWACS stood for Airborne Warning and Control System.

39. Avi Shlaim, *The Iron Wall: Israel and the Arab World* (New York: Norton, 2001), 404.

40. Cannon, *President Reagan*, 350. This phone exchange was related by Geoffrey Kemp, an NSC staff member. George Shultz wrote that Reagan told him on August 12 that "another Holocaust was taking place." George P. Shultz, *Turmoil and Triumph: My Years as Secretary of State* (New York: Scribner's, 1993), 70.

41. Christian Smith, *Resisting Reagan: The U.S. Central America Peace Movement* (Chicago: University of Chicago Press, 1996), 9.

42. Cecilia Menjívar and Néstor Rodríguez, "State Terror in the U.S.–Latin American Interstate Regime," in *When States Kill: Latin America, the U.S., and Technologies of Terror*, ed. Cecilia Menjívar and Néstor Rodríguez (Austin: University of Texas Press, 2005), 15 (italics in original).

43. Smith, *Resisting Reagan*, 34.

44. Philip Geyelin, "Exiles in Training," *Washington Post*, April 7, 1981. This article discussed the efforts of David Bonior, a Democratic U.S. representative from Michigan, to call attention to the impropriety of such activities occurring on U.S. soil. Bonior did not charge the U.S. government with funding the operation.

45. Christopher Dickey, *With the Contras: A Reporter in the Wilds of Nicaragua* (New York: Simon and Schuster, 1985), 104.

46. Bob Levin and others, "Storm Over El Salvador," *Newsweek*, March 16, 1981.

47. LeoGrande, *Our Own Backyard*, 80, 81.

48. This was a member of the Maximiliano Hernandez Brigade. Levin and others, "Storm Over El Salvador."

49. LeoGrande, *Our Own Backyard*, 63.

50. Joan Didion, *Salvador* (London: Chatto & Windus/The Hogarth Press, 1983), 92.

51. "Film Preserves Haig's Words on Murders" (letter from William P. Ford, dated April 1, 1991), *New York Times*, April 12, 1993.

52. Edward Walsh, "Kin of Slain Nuns Denounce Haig for 'Smear Campaign,'" *Washington Post*, March 20, 1981.

53. Judith Miller, "House Panel, 8–7, Votes $5 Million in Extra Military Aid to El Salvador," *New York Times*, March 25, 1981.

54. Smith, *Resisting Reagan*, 35; Greg Grandin, *Empire's Workshop: Latin America, the United States, and the Rise of the New Imperialism* (New York: Holt, 2006), 71.

55. Mark Danner, *The Massacre at El Mozote: A Parable of the Cold War* (New York: Vintage, 1993).

56. Smith, *Resisting Reagan*, 153.

57. LeoGrande, *Our Own Backyard*, 179, 180. In 1996, peace accords were signed ending the civil conflict in Guatemala. These accords mandated the establishment of a Commission for Historical Clarification, whose report concluded that the Guatemalan state committed acts of genocide against the Mayan people, who constituted a majority of the Guatemalan population, specifically between 1981 and 1983. The report, *Guatemala: Memory of Silence*, published in 1999, is available at the website of Yale University's Genocide Studies Program, accessed January 20, 2011, http://shr.aaas.org/guatemala/ceh/report/english/toc.html.

58. This issue had arisen in 1981, in awkward but finally successful Senate confirmation hearings after Reagan had nominated Clark to be deputy secretary of state. Judith Miller, "State Dept. Nominee Is Challenged," *New York Times*, February 3, 1981. The NSC job did not require Senate confirmation.

59. Dickey, *With the Contras*, 146.

60. At least five hundred were killed at Kwangju, and perhaps more than two thousand—roughly on the order of the Tiananmen massacre of 1989. Bruce Cumings, *Korea's Place in the Sun: A Modern History*, updated ed. (New York: Norton, 2005), 382–83. Also see Henry Scott-Stokes and Lee Jai Eui, eds., *The Kwangju Uprising: Eyewitness Press Accounts of Korea's Tiananmen* (Armonk, NY: M. E. Sharpe, 2000). The United States, which effectively had command of the ROK's military, did not intervene.

61. Stanley Karnow, *In Our Image: America's Empire in the Philippines* (New York: Ballantine, 1989), 401. Carter had granted Marcos $500 million in military and "military-related" aid for the five-year period between 1979 and 1984. In 1983, Reagan pledged $900 million for the succeeding five years. Walden Bello, *U.S. Sponsored Low-Intensity Conflict in the Philippines* (Food First Development Report No. 2) (San Francisco: Institute for Food and Development Policy, 1987), 63.

5. The Purge

1. John W. Sloan, *The Reagan Effect: Economics and Presidential Leadership* (Lawrence: University Press of Kansas, 1999), 233.

2. William Greider, *Secrets of the Temple: How the Federal Reserve Runs the Country* (New York: Touchstone, 1989), 587.

3. See Judith Stein, *Pivotal Decade: How the United States Traded Factories for Finance in the Seventies* (New Haven, CT: Yale University Press, 2010) for a critique of the Democrats' failure on this score.

4. D. Lee Bawden and John L. Palmer, "Social Policy: Challenging the Welfare State," in *The Reagan Record: An Assessment of America's Changing Domestic Priorities*, ed. John L. Palmer and Isabel V. Sawhill (Cambridge, MA: Ballinger, 1984), 190. On the low proportion of the unemployed receiving UI in the 1980s, also see Bennett Harrison and Barry Bluestone, *The Great U-Turn: Corporate Restructuring and the Polarizing of America* (New York: Basic Books, 1988), 93; Greider, *Secrets of the Temple*, 454.

5. Bawden and Palmer, "Social Policy: Challenging the Welfare State," 197–98. These figures measured poverty as defined by total cash income, including government benefits.

6. Joseph A. McCartin, *Collision Course: Ronald Reagan, the Air Traffic Controllers, and the Strike That Changed America* (New York: Oxford University Press, 2011), 291, 294.

7. Ronald Reagan, "Remarks on Signing the Economic Recovery Tax Act of 1981 and the Omnibus Budget Reconciliation Act of 1981, and a Question-and-Answer Session With Reporters," August 13, 1981. Gerhard Peters and John T. Woolley, *The American Presidency Project*, http://www.presidency.ucsb.edu/ws.index.php?pid=44161. Unless otherwise noted, subsequent references to presidential statements and nominating convention speeches are to this same online archive.

8. McCartin, *Collision Course*, 318, 334.

9. Jefferson Cowie, *Stayin' Alive: The 1970s and the Last Days of the Working Class* (New York: The New Press, 2010), 363.

10. Ibid., 293, 302.

11. Lou Cannon, *President Reagan: The Role of a Lifetime* (New York: PublicAffairs, 2000), 437.

12. McCartin, *Collision Course*, 348, 351. On the Phelps Dodge strike, see Barbara Kingsolver, *Holding the Line: Women in the Great Arizona Mine Strike of 1983* (Ithaca, NY: ILR Press, 1996); on the Hormel strike, see Peter Rachleff, *Hard-Pressed in the Heartland: The Hormel Strike and the Future of the Labor Movement* (Boston: South End Press, 1999).

13. "Beige Book: National Summary, November 10, 1981"; this and all Beige Books available at http://www.minneapolisfed.org/bb/reports/1981/81–11-su.cfm. The official name for this report was the "Summary of Commentary on Current Economic Conditions by Federal Reserve District." Known as Red Books until 1983, they first were released to the public in that year, and at that time the report's informal name was changed to the Beige Book. Archives of pre-1983 summaries generally refer to them as Beige Books.

14. "Beige Book: National Summary, March 23, 1982," http://www.minneapolisfed.org/bb/reports/1982/82–03-su.cfm.

15. These were the *Milwaukee Spring v. United Auto Workers of America* case and the *Otis Elevator* case. Harrison and Bluestone, *The Great U-Turn*, 101; Mark Blyth, *Great Transformations: Economic Ideas and Institutional Change in the Twentieth Century* (Cambridge: Cambridge University Press, 2002), 182–83. The NLRB's members served terms of fixed length; a new president could replace them only gradually.

16. Greider, *Secrets of the Temple*, 419.

17. Sloan, *Reagan Effect*, 227.

18. Paul Craig Roberts, *The Supply-Side Revolution: An Insider's Account of Policymaking in Washington* (Cambridge, MA: Harvard University Press, 1984), 225.

19. Greider, *Secrets of the Temple*, 381–82; Richard Reeves, *President Reagan: The Triumph of Imagination* (New York: Simon and Schuster, 2005), 24–25.

20. Paul Krugman, *Peddling Prosperity: Economic Sense and Nonsense in an Age of Diminished Expectations* (New York: Norton, 1994), 173.

21. This measure of the money supply was known as M-1. Greider, *Secrets of the Temple*, Appendix B, 724.

22. Greider, *Secrets of the Temple*, 375.

23. "Current Recession Began in July," National Bureau of Economic Research Press Release, January 6, 1982.

24. Greider, *Secrets of the Temple*, Appendix B, 724–25; "Recovery Began in November," National Bureau of Economic Research Press Release, July 8, 1983.

25. "Beige Book: National Summary, September 30, 1981," http://www.minneapolisfed.org/bb/reports/1981/81-09-su.cfm; "Beige Book: National Summary, November 10, 1981"; "Beige Book: National Summary, December 16, 1981," http://www.minneapolisfed.org/bb/reports/1981/81-12-su.cfm; "Beige Book: National Summary, January 27, 1982," http://www.minneapolisfed.org/bb/reports/1982/82-01-su.cfm; "Beige Book: National Summary, March 23, 1982."

26. Reagan's first budget was for fiscal year 1982, which began in October 1981. By September, the meaning of changes in myriad social programs had become specific.

27. "Still Cutting School Lunch Corners," *New York Times*, November 2, 1981; Ward Sinclair, "School Lunches Flunk GAO Nutrition Test," *Washington Post*, September 15, 1981; Jane E. Brody, "School Food: New Intent," *New York Times*, September 14, 1981.

28. Russell Baker, "Observer: Gipper, Scrooge and Santa," *New York Times*, September 12, 1981.

29. Mary Thornton and Martin Schram, "U.S. Holds the Ketchup in Schools," *Washington Post*, September 26, 1981. One change in the federal school lunch regulations would have allowed nonmeat items such as tofu, nuts, and seeds to count toward protein allotments. Another would have made one ounce of meat a serving size. Democrats in 1981 could not resist making fun of tofu along with the parsimonious proposed serving sizes.

30. Eric Pianin and others, "250,000 March to Protest Reagan's Policies," *Washington Post*, September 20, 1981.

31. Richard Cohen, "Remote," *Washington Post*, September 15, 1981.

32. Steven R. Weisman, "Reagan Abandons Proposal to Pare School Nutrition," *New York Times*, September 25, 1981.

33. "Still Cutting School Lunch Corners," *New York Times*, November 2, 1981; Robert Pear, "President Gets Revised Proposals for Standards on School Lunches," *New York Times*, November 18, 1981.

34. Seth S. King, "U.S. Jobless Rate Rose in February to 8.8 percent from 8.5 percent," *New York Times*, March 6, 1982.

35. Steven R. Weisman, "Reagan Quoted as Assailing TV Coverage of the Recession," *New York Times*, March 18, 1982; Cannon, *President Reagan*, 227.

36. Adam Clymer, "Reagan Evoking Rising Concern, New Poll Shows," *New York Times*, March 19, 1982; Hedrick Smith, "Blue-Collar Workers' Support for Reagan Declines," *New York Times*, March 8, 1982.

37. Clymer, "Reagan Evoking Rising Concern."

38. U.S. Representative Patricia Schroeder, Democrat of Colorado, was credited with applying this term to Reagan. Cannon, *President Reagan*, 182n.

39. Howell Raines, "A Rare Presidential Journey into Public View," *New York Times*, March 18, 1982.

40. Steven R. Weisman, "White House Assails CBS news, but a Bid for Reply Is Rejected," *New York Times*, April 23, 1982.

41. Mark Crispin Miller, "*Virtù, Inc.*," *New Republic*, April 7, 1982, reprinted in *Reagan as President: Contemporary Views of the Man, His Politics, and His Policies*, ed. Paul Boyer (Chicago: Ivan R. Dee, 1990), 79.

42. Greider, *Secrets of the Temple*, 455.

43. Gareth Davies, "The Welfare State," in *The Reagan Presidency: Pragmatic Conservatism and Its Legacies*, ed. W. Elliot Brownlee and Hugh Davis Graham (Lawrence: University Press of Kansas, 2003), 216.

44. Davies, "Welfare State," 215, 219.

45. Albert R. Hunt, "National Politics and the 1982 Campaign," in *The American Elections of 1982*, ed. Thomas E. Mann and Norman J. Ornstein (Washington, DC: American Enterprise Institute for Public Policy Research, 1983), 13.

46. Bill Peterson, "Abortion, School Prayer Issues Shuffle the Cards in the Senate," *Washington Post*, September 28, 1982. The Hyde Amendment, named for U.S. Representative Henry Hyde, already barred the use of Medicaid funds for abortions. Helms's measure would have used federal funds as leverage to further limit the availability of abortion—for example, by barring medical schools receiving such monies from training medical students in abortion techniques. The Helms bill also would have placed Congress on record as stating that the *Roe v. Wade* decision of 1973 had been wrongly decided.

47. Helen Dewar, "GOP's 'Old Center' Holds, Despite New Right Senators," *Washington Post*, August 23, 1982; Bill Peterson, "New-Right Knight Dulls His Senate Sword," *Washington Post*, September 21, 1982.

48. Steven R. Weisman, "Reagan Neutral on Bid to Curb Court on Prayer," *New York Times*, September 9, 1982.

49. Bill Peterson and Herbert H. Denton, "President Backs Foes of Abortion; Reagan Attempting to Regain Support of Conservatives," *Washington Post*, September 9, 1982.

50. John F. Bibby, "State House Elections at Midterm," in *The American Elections of 1982*, 111, 121.

51. Thomas E. Mann and Norman J. Ornstein, "Sending a Message: Voters and Congress in 1982," in *American Elections of 1982*, 148–49.

52. Hunt, "National Politics and the 1982 Campaign," 30.

53. Larry Sabato, "Parties, PACs, and Independent Groups," in *American Elections of 1982*, 85.

54. Mann and Ornstein summarized the model developed by Edward R. Tufte and refined by Gary C. Jacobson and Samuel Kernell, which was based on election results between 1946 and 1978. Tufte's model predicted a loss of between forty-five and fifty-nine House seats for the Republicans in 1982. Yet Jacobson and Kernell anticipated the shift would be smaller. Mann and Ornstein, "Sending a Message," 139–40; Sabato, "Parties, PACs, and Independent Groups," 80–81.

55. Mann and Ornstein, "Sending a Message," 140.

56. See Mark A. Smith, "Economic Insecurity, Party Reputations, and the Republican Ascendance," in *The Transformation of American Politics: Activist Government and the Rise of Conservatism*, ed. Paul Pierson and Theda Skocpol (Princeton, NJ: Princeton University Press, 2007), 135–59. The Republicans had begun to regain some of their lost advantage on economic issues even during 1982. See Figure 6.1, 143.

57. "Reagan Steadies Position in Poll," *New York Times*, May 16, 1982; Adam Clymer, "Poll Finds Support Off for G.O.P. and Its Policy but Not for Reagan," *New York Times*, May 28, 1982; "Reagan Steady in Gallup Poll," *New York Times*, July 8, 1982.

58. Greider, *Secrets of the Temple*, 413.

59. Marilyn Moon and Isabel V. Sawhill, "Family Incomes: Gainers and Losers," in *Reagan Record*, 334.

60. Greider, *Secrets of the Temple*, 563–64.

61. "Beige Book: National Summary, March 23, 1983," http://www.minneapolisfed.org/bb/reports/1983/83–03-su.cfm; "Beige Book: National Summary, December 6, 1983," http://www.minneapolisfed.org/bb/reports/1983/83–12-su.cfm; "Beige Book: National Summary, March 13, 1984," http://www.minneapolisfed.org/bb/reports/1984/84–03-su.cfm.

62. Eric Alterman, *It Ain't No Sin to Be Glad You're Alive: The Promise of Bruce Springsteen* (Boston: Little, Brown, 1999), 25–26; Bruce Springsteen, *Nebraska* (1982), Columbia B0000025T6, CD, 1990.

63. See Cowie, *Stayin' Alive*, chapters 6–8 for the broader sweep of this process.

6. 1983: The World at the Brink

1. George P. Shultz, *Turmoil and Triumph: My Years as Secretary of State* (New York: Scribner's, 1993), 310.

2. William M. LeoGrande, *Our Own Backyard: The United States in Central America, 1977–1992* (Chapel Hill: University of North Carolina Press, 1998), 202.

3. Ronald Reagan, "Address Before a Joint Session of the Congress on Central America," April 27, 1983. Gerhard Peters and John T. Woolley, *The American Presidency Project*, http://www.presidency.ucsb.edu/ws/index.php?pid=41245. Unless otherwise noted, subsequent references to presidential statements and nominating convention speeches are to this same online archive.

4. "Transcript of Democrat's Response to Reagan Speech on Central America," *New York Times*, April 28, 1983.

5. Joan Didion, *Salvador* (London: Chatto & Windus/The Hogarth Press, 1983), 19.

6. LeoGrande, *Our Own Backyard*, 215.

7. Shultz, *Turmoil and Triumph*, 3.

8. Garry Wills, *Reagan's America: Innocents at Home* (Garden City, NY: Doubleday, 1986), 350.

9. On November 28, 1984, Weinberger delivered a speech at the National Press Club in Washington, in which he described the exacting criteria, in his view, for the use of U.S. force abroad. Brad Knickerbocker, "Weinberger Spells Out Conditions for Deployment of US Troops," *Christian Science Monitor*, November 30, 1984; Richard Halloran, "Shultz and Weinberger: Disputing Use of Force," *New York Times*, November 30, 1984; "The Weinberger Doctrine," *Washington Post*, November 30, 1984, was a favorable editorial.

10. Shultz, *Turmoil and Triumph*, 303.

11. Ibid., 306.

12. LeoGrande, *Our Own Backyard*, 314–17.

13. Shultz, *Turmoil and Triumph*, 312–13.

14. Ibid., 228.

15. LeoGrande, *Our Own Backyard*, 234.

16. Ibid., 228–30; quote on 230.

17. Bob Woodward, *Veil: The Secret Wars of the CIA, 1981–1987* (New York: Pocket Books, 1988), 315.

18. Ronald Reagan, "Remarks at the Annual Convention of the National Association of Evangelicals in Orlando, Florida," March 8, 1983, http://www.presidency.ucsb.edu/ws/index.php?pid=41023&st=&st1=.

19. Alexander Solzhenitsyn had used the term in 1975, and the head of French intelligence had used it in conversation with Reagan in 1980. Edmund Morris, *Dutch: A Memoir of Ronald Reagan* (New York: Modern Library, 1999), 472.

20. Ronald Reagan, "Address to the Nation on Defense and National Security," March 23, 1983, http://www.presidency.ucsb.edu/ws/index.php?pid=41093.

21. Phyllis Schlafly and Chester Ward, *Strike from Space: A Megadeath Mystery* (Alton, IL: Pere Marquette Press, 1965).

22. See Frances FitzGerald, *Way Out There in the Blue: Reagan, Star Wars and the End of the Cold War* (New York: Simon and Schuster, 2000), 96.

23. Ibid., 373–76, 402–3, on the early, disappointing technical evaluations of SDI research and development in 1985, 1986, and 1987. Further tests occurred in the 1990s, when funding for missile-defense research continued, albeit not under the rubric of SDI. Defense contractors Boeing and TRW were accused of faking the results of tests. Theodore Postol, a nuclear engineer and professor at the Massachusetts Institute of Technology, became the most dogged critic of missile-defense advocates. For one account, see Charles P. Pierce, "Going Postol," *Boston Globe Magazine*, October 23, 2005.

24. J. Peter Scoblic, *U.S. vs. Them: How a Half Century of Conservatism Has Undermined America's Security* (New York: Viking, 2008).

25. FitzGerald, *Way Out There*, 28.

26. Ibid., 27.

27. "Peace" (August 18, 1980), in *Reagan, in His Own Hand: the Writings of Ronald Reagan that Reveal His Revolutionary Vision for America*, ed. Kiron K. Skinner, Annelise Anderson and Martin Anderson (New York: Free Press, 2001), 481–82.

28. Morris, *Dutch*, 474, 478.

29. Hugo Young, *One of Us: A Biography of Margaret Thatcher*, final ed. (London: Macmillan London, 1991), 398.

30. Wills, *Reagan's America*, 359–60.

31. FitzGerald, *Way Out There*, 258–64.

32. "Bishops Condemn Nuclear Race," *Miami Herald,* May 4, 1983; "Anti-Nuclear Support Expected by Bishops," *Miami Herald*, May 5, 1983.

33. David Maraniss, "House Passes Nuclear Freeze Resolution; Opponents Win on Arms Amendment," *Washington Post*, May 5, 1983. The issue cut across party lines; forty-three Democrats joined 106 Republicans in opposition.

34. "242 Christians Arrested in Arms Protest," *Miami Herald*, May 24, 1983.

35. Shultz, *Turmoil and Triumph*, 359–60; an image of Reagan's handwritten letter is on 359.

36. Some have argued that Reagan for many years, even decades, before this had desired nuclear abolition, but the evidence shows otherwise. See Doug Rossinow, "The Legend of Reagan the Peacemaker," *Raritan* 32, no. 3 (Winter 2013): 56–76.

37. David Crist, *The Twilight War: The Secret History of America's Thirty-Year Conflict with Iran* (New York: Penguin, 2012), 115.

38. Murray Sayle, "Closing the File on Flight 007," *New Yorker*, December 13, 1993, 90–102.

39. Benjamin B. Fischer, *A Cold War Conundrum: The 1983 Soviet War Scare* (CIA Center for the Study of Intelligence, 1997), accessed February 23, 2010, https://www.cia.gov/library/center-for-the-study-of-intelligence/csi-publications/books-and-monographs/a-cold-war-conundrum/source.htm. Also see Nathan Bennett Jones, "Operation RYAN, Able Archer 83, and Miscalculation: The War Scare of 1983" (paper delivered at the International Graduate Student Conference on the Cold War, University of California at Santa Barbara, Santa Barbara, CA, April 14–16, 2008), available at http://www.wilsoncenter.org/topics/docs/08%2004%2001%20Nathan%20Jones%20Operation%20RYAN%20Able%20Archer%2083%20and%20Miscalculation%20IGSCCW.pdf

40. RYAN was the English transliteration of the Russian *Raketno-Yadernoe Napadenie*, which means "Nuclear Missile Attack." David E. Hoffman, *The Dead Hand: The Untold Story of the Cold War Arms Race and Its Dangerous Legacy* (New York: Doubleday, 2009), 36.

41. Shultz, *Turmoil and Triumph*, 362.

42. Ronald Reagan, "Address to the Nation on the Soviet Attack on a Korean Civilian Airliner," September 5, 1983, http://www.presidency.ucsb.edu/ws/index.php?pid=41788.

43. Hoffman, *Dead Hand*, 6–11.

44. Ronald Reagan, *An American Life: The Autobiography* (New York: Simon and Schuster, 1990), 448; Shultz, *Turmoil and Triumph*, 320.

45. Jane Mayer and Doyle McManus, *Landslide: The Unmaking of the President, 1984–1988* (Boston: Houghton Mifflin, 1988), 59.

46. Cannon, *President Reagan*, 391.

47. The OECS was led by Prime Minister Eugenia Charles of Dominica. The United States was funding a road project in Dominica, and the CIA reportedly had provided funds to Charles's political party. Woodward, *Veil*, 325.

48. Shultz, *Turmoil and Triumph*, 332.

49. Ronald Reagan, "Address to the Nation on Events in Lebanon and Grenada," October 27, 1983, http://www.presidency.ucsb.edu/ws/index.php?pid=40696.

50. Woodward, *Veil*, 331.

51. Hoffman, *Dead Hand*, 87–88, 91–92, 94–95, 98–100; John Prados, *How the Cold War Ended: Debating and Doing History* (Washington, DC: Potomac Books, 2011), 56–57. Gordievsky's account was published in Christopher Andrew and Oleg Gordievsky, *Comrade Kryuchkov's Instructions: Top Secret Files on KGB Foreign Operations, 1975–1985* (Stanford, CA: Stanford University Press, 1991). Some claim that Gordievsky met with Reagan in the White House to discuss the matter. Prados, *How the Cold War Ended*, 57.

52. Shultz, *Turmoil and Triumph*, 372.

53. Ronald Reagan, *The Reagan Diaries*, ed. Douglas Brinkley (New York: Harper-Collins, 2007), 199.

54. Ibid., 189.

55. Shultz, *Turmoil and Triumph*, 376.

56. In preparing to broadcast his weekly radio address on National Public Radio on August 11, 1984, Reagan said, "My fellow Americans, I'm pleased to tell you today that I've signed legislation that will outlaw Russia forever. We begin bombing in five minutes." Accessed January 18, 2011; a sound recording of Reagan's joke is available at http://upload.wikimedia.org/wikipedia/commons/0/01/ReaganBeginsBombing Russia.org.

57. *Reagan Diaries*, 186 (entry for October 10, 1983).

58. Nena, *99 Luftballons* (1983), Sbme Special Mkts. B0012GMUWM, CD, 2008.

59. *WarGames*, directed by John Badham (1983; Santa Monica, CA: MGM Home Entertainment, 2008), DVD; Cannon, *President Reagan*, 38.

60. Ronald Reagan, "Address to the Nation and Other Countries on United States–Soviet Relations," January 16, 1984, http://www.presidency.ucsb.edu/ws/?pid=39806. See Beth A. Fischer, *The Reagan Reversal: Foreign Policy and the End of the Cold War* (Columbia: University of Missouri Press, 1997) for a detailed discussion of this speech as a turning point in U.S. policy toward the Soviet Union.

61. John Newhouse, *War and Peace in the Nuclear Age* (New York: Knopf, 1989), 370.

62. Raymond Garthoff, *The Great Transition: American-Soviet Relations and the End of the Cold War* (Washington, DC: Brookings Institution, 1994), 170.

63. Ibid., 161.

7. The High Eighties

1. *Chariots of Fire*, directed by Hugh Hudson (1981; Burbank, CA: Warner Home Video, 2005), DVD.

2. *The Great Gatsby*, directed by Jack Clayton (1974; Hollywood, CA: Paramount Home Video, 2003), DVD; "Here Comes the Preppie Look," *Time*, April 28, 1980; Stephen Koepp, "Selling a Dream of Elegance and the Good Life," *Time*, September 1, 1986.

3. Lisa Birnbach, ed., *The Official Preppy Handbook* (New York: Workman, 1980). The term's spelling varied.

4. Paul Fussell, *Class* (New York: Ballantine, 1984), 52, 60.

5. Internet Movie Database, http://www.imdb.com/title/tt0086750/.

6. *Arthur*, directed by Steve Gordon (1981; Burbank, CA: Warner Home Video, 1997), DVD; Internet Movie Database, http://www.imdb.com/year/1981/.

7. See Anthony Haden-Guest, *The Last Party: Studio 54, Disco, and the Culture of the Night* (New York: William Morrow, 1997) and Alice Echols, *Hot Stuff: Disco and the Remaking of American Culture* (New York: Norton, 2010).

8. Marie Brenner, "Jerry Rubin's Last-Chance Salon," *New York*, June 8, 1981.

9. Sidney Blumenthal, "Reaganism and the Neokitsch Aesthetic," in *The Reagan Legacy*, ed. Sidney Blumenthal and Thomas Byrne Edsall (New York: Pantheon Books, 1988), 266.

10. Jan Greenberg and Sandra Jordan, *Andy Warhol: Prince of Pop* (New York: Delacorte Press, 2004), 121.

11. Robert Hughes, "The Rise of Andy Warhol," review of *Andy Warhol: Das Grafische Werk, 1962–1980*, by Hermann Wünsche, and *Andy Warhol: A Print Retrospective*, *New York Review of Books*, February 18, 1982. Warhol died in 1987.

12. Dominic Streatfeild, *Cocaine: An Unauthorized Biography* (New York: Thomas Dunne Books, 2001), 238, 239.

13. Murray Chass, "Hernandez of the Mets Tells Jury of His Experiences with Cocaine," *New York Times*, September 7, 1985; Jeff Pearlman, *The Bad Guys Won! A Season of Brawling, Boozing, Bimbo-chasing, and Championship Baseball with Straw, Doc, Mookie, Nails, The Kid, and the Rest of the 1986 Mets, the Rowdiest Team Ever to Put on a New York Uniform—and Maybe the Best* (New York: Harper, 2004).

14. *Fast Times at Ridgemont High*, directed by Amy Heckerling (1982; Universal City, CA: Universal Studios, 2007), DVD.

15. *Scarface*, directed by Brian De Palma (1983; Universal City, CA: Universal Studios, 1998), DVD.

16. On Nixon's efforts, see Michael Massing, *The Fix* (New York: Simon and Schuster, 1998).

17. See the report from the U.S. General Accounting Office, "Youth Illicit Drug Prevention: DARE Long-Term Evaluations and Federal Efforts to Identify Effective Programs" (January 15, 2003), http://www.gao.gov/new.items/d03172r.pdf.

18. Streatfeild, *Cocaine*, 293.

19. See Henry H. Brownstein, *The Rise and Fall of a Violent Crime Wave: Crack Cocaine and the Social Construction of a Crime Problem* (Guilderland, NY: Harrow and Heston, 1996), 37–40.

20. John Corry, "CBS on 'Crack Street,'" *New York Times*, September 4, 1986.

21. Christopher Jencks, *The Homeless* (Cambridge, MA: Harvard University Press, 1994), 43. These cities excluded the largest of all, New York City. In the borough of Manhattan, the figure was higher, at 65 percent.

22. Craig Reinarman and Harry G. Levine, eds., *Crack in America: Demon Drugs and Social Justice* (Berkeley: University of California Press, 1997) is a compendium of doubters from the left.

23. See David Rudovsky, "The Impact of the War on Drugs on Procedural Fairness and Racial Equality," *University of Chicago Legal Forum* (1994): 237–74; Randall Kennedy, *Race, Crime, and the Law* (New York: Vintage, 1998), chapter 10; and David F. Musto, *The American Disease: Origins of Narcotic Control*, 3rd ed. (New York: Oxford University Press, 1999), 273–80.

24. Tom Wolfe, *The Bonfire of the Vanities* (New York: Farrar, Straus & Giroux, 1987).

25. Michael Lewis, *Liar's Poker: Rising through the Wreckage on Wall Street* (New York: Norton, 1989).

26. James B. Stewart, *Den of Thieves* (New York: Simon and Schuster Paperbacks, 1992), 261; Bethany Moreton, *To Serve God and Wal-Mart: The Making of Christian Free Enterprise* (Cambridge, MA: Harvard University Press, 2009), 250. On Rand (an atheist), see Jennifer Burns, *Goddess of the Market: Ayn Rand and the American Right* (New York: Oxford University Press, 2009).

27. Stewart, *Den of Thieves*, 97.

28. Gerald F. Davis and Suzanne K. Stout, "Organization Theory and the Market for Corporate Control: A Dynamic Analysis of the Characteristics of Large Takeover Targets, 1980–1990," *Administrative Science Quarterly* 37, no. 4 (December 1992): 605.

29. The issue was December 31, 1984.

30. Joan Didion, *Political Fictions* (New York: Vintage, 2001), 95.

31. John Casey, "At Dartmouth: The Clash of '89," *New York Times Magazine*, February 26, 1989; Didion, *Political Fictions*, 95–96.

32. George F. Gilder, *Sexual Suicide* (New York: Quadrangle, 1973); George Gilder, *Wealth and Poverty* (New York: Bantam, 1981). On popular efforts to resolve this tension, see Linda Kintz, *Between Jesus and the Market: The Emotions that Matter in Right-Wing America* (Durham, NC: Duke University Press, 1997).

33. David Brock, *Blinded by the Right: The Conscience of an Ex-Conservative* (New York: Crown Publishers, 2002); Marvin Liebman, *Coming Out Conservative: An Autobiography* (San Francisco: Chronicle, 1992); Susan B. Trento, *The Power House: Robert Keith Gray and the Selling of Access and Influence in Washington* (New York: St. Martin's Press, 1992).

34. Allan Bloom, *The Closing of the American Mind: How Higher Education Has Failed Democracy and Impoverished the Souls of Today's Students* (New York: Simon and Schuster, 1987); Saul Bellow, *Ravelstein* (New York: Viking, 2000). Despite the subtitle of Bloom's book, democracy was not a real concern of his. He was a proud elitist.

35. Bellow, *Ravelstein*. See D. T. Max, "With Friends Like Saul Bellow," *New York Times Magazine*, April 16, 2000. Donald Lazere, "'The Closing of the American Mind,' 20 Years Later," *Inside Higher Ed*, September 18, 2007, http://www.insidehighered.com/layout/set/print/views/2007/09/18/lazere.

36. Edwin Diamond, "Sexual Hysteria: The New New Journalism," *New York*, June 22, 1987.

37. Randy Shilts, *And the Band Played On: People, Politics, and the AIDS Epidemic* (New York: St. Martin's Press, 1987), 311.

38. Edmund Morris, *Dutch: A Memoir of Ronald Reagan* (New York: Modern Library, 1999), 458.

39. Jonathan Engel, *The Epidemic: A Global History of AIDS* (New York: Smithsonian Books/HarperCollins, 2006), 71.

40. Shilts, *Band Played On*, 407.

41. Engel, *Epidemic*, 7.

42. The yearly figures, as reported by the U.S. Centers for Disease Control (CDC) in its Year-End HIV/AIDS Surveillance reports, are available at http://www.cdc.gov/hiv/topics/surveillance/resources/reports/past.htm#surveillance. These initial numbers were invariably revised upward as time passed. By 2000, updated figures showed that over 440,000 Americans had died from AIDS. Engel, *Epidemic*, 291.

43. Engel, *Epidemic*, 11.

44. For a valuable guide to the sexual politics of HIV at this time, see Jennifer Brier, *Infectious Ideas: U.S. Political Responses to the AIDS Crisis* (Chapel Hill: University of North Carolina Press, 2009).

45. Engel, *Epidemic*, 45.

46. Ibid., 18.

47. Shilts, *Band Played On*, 377; Engel, *Epidemic*, 16.

48. Shilts, *Band Played On*, 311. The chief of public health in the city reported to the board of supervisors, not to the mayor.

49. For a sympathetic account, see Richard Socarides, "Ed Koch and the Politics of the Closet," *New Yorker Online*, February 2, 2013, http://www.newyorker.com/online/blogs/newsdesk/2013/02/the-private-life-of-ed-koch.html; for a somewhat more critical one, see Mary Elizabeth Williams, "Ed Koch's Enduring, Uneasy Gay Legacy," *Salon*, February 1, 2013, http://www.salon.com/2013/02/01/ed_kochs_enduring_uneasy_gay_legacy/.

50. Shilts, *Band Played On*, 285–86.

51. Ibid., 544.

52. Ibid., 576.

53. 478 U.S. 186 *Bowers v. Hardwick* (No. 85–140), June 30, 1986, available at http://www.law.cornell.edu/supremecourt/text/478/186; "High Court Rules Laws on Sodomy Outweigh Privacy," *Washington Post*, July 1, 1986. The policeman had entered Hardwick's home on an unrelated matter.

54. "Family in AIDS Case Quits Florida Town after House Burns," *New York Times*, August 30, 1987; Stephen Buckley, "Slow Change of Heart," *St. Petersburg Times*, September 2, 2001.

55. Frederic Jameson, "Postmodernism and Consumer Society" (1985), quoted in Catherine Constable, "Postmodernism and Film," in *The Cambridge Companion to Postmodernism*, ed. Steven Connor (Cambridge: Cambridge University Press, 2004), 48.

56. Don DeLillo, *White Noise: Text and Criticism*, ed. Mark Osteen (New York: Penguin, 1998), 310.

57. This conundrum was made explicit in Jean-François Lyotard, *The Postmodern Condition: A Report on Knowledge* (Manchester: Manchester University Press, 1984), a work published in France in 1979.

58. *Liquid Sky*, directed by Slava Tsukerman (1983; n.l.: WINTERtainment, 2003), DVD.

59. This was Ken Tucker, quoted in Theo Cateforis, *Are We Not New Wave? Modern Pop at the Turn of the 1980s* (Ann Arbor: University of Michigan Press, 2011), 211.

60. Madonna, *Madonna* (1983), Warner Bros. B00005J6T1, CD, 2006; Cateforis, *Are We Not New Wave?*, 106.

61. Madonna, *Like a Virgin* (1984), Warner Bros. B00005J6SZ, CD, 2001; *Gentlemen Prefer Blondes*, directed by Howard Hawks (1953; Beverly Hills, CA: Twentieth-Century Fox Home Entertainment, 2006), DVD.

62. Madonna, *Like a Prayer* (1989), Sire B000002LGQ, CD, 1990.

63. Prince, *1999* (1982), Warner Bros. B000002KY8, CD, 1990; Prince, *Music from the Motion Picture "Purple Rain"* (1984), Warner Bros. B000002L68, CD, 1990; Prince, *Lovesexy* (1988), Warner Bros. B000002LE6, CD, 1990.

64. Michael Jackson, *Thriller* (1982), Sony B00005QGAZ, CD, 2001; Michael Jackson, *Bad* (1987), Sony B00000269M, CD, 1990.

65. "The 25 Best-Selling Albums of All-Time," *Entertainment Weekly*, May 3, 1996, http://www.ew.com/ew/article/0,,292340,00.html.

8. Days of Fear

1. Philip Jenkins, *Decade of Nightmares: The End of the Sixties and the Making of Eighties America* (New York: Oxford University Press, 2006), 137, 237.

2. Craig Werner, *A Change Is Gonna Come: Music, Race and the Soul of America* (New York: Plume, 1999), 245.

3. Alice Walker, "Each One, Pull One," in Alice Walker, *Horses Make a Landscape Look More Beautiful* (San Diego, CA: Harcourt Brace Jovanovich, 1984), 51.

4. Andrew Hacker, *Two Nations: Black and White, Separate, Hostile, Unequal* (New York: Charles Scribner's Sons, 1992), 201.

5. Table 4, "Proportion of Black and White Populations Living in the Suburbs of the Fifteen Largest Metropolitan Areas in 1990, 1970–1990," in Stephen Thernstrom and Abigail Thernstrom, *America in Black and White: One Nation, Indivisible* (New York: Simon and Schuster, 1997), 213.

6. Ibid., 198–99.

7. Table 1, "Black Elected Officials, 1960–1995," in Thernstrom and Thernstrom, *America in Black and White*, 289.

8. Trey Ellis, "The New Black Aesthetic," *Callaloo* 38 (Winter 1989): 234, 237.

9. Sut Jhally and Justin Lewis, *Enlightened Racism: The Cosby Show, Audiences, and the Myth of the American Dream* (Boulder, CO: Westview Press, 1992), 95.

10. Thomas J. Sugrue, *Sweet Land of Liberty: The Forgotten Struggle for Civil Rights in the North* (New York: Random House, 2008), 510–13; Bart Landry, *The New Black Middle Class* (Berkeley: University of California Press, 1987).

11. Robert J. Norrell, *The House I Live In: Race in the American Century* (New York: Oxford University Press, 2006), 309; John Bound and Richard B. Freeman, "What Went Wrong? The Erosion of Relative Earnings and Employment Among Young Black Men in the 1980s," *Quarterly Journal of Economics* 107, no. 1 (February 1992): 201–32.

12. I derived these figures from the numbers in Table Ae1–28, "Households, by race and sex of householder and household type: 1850–1990," in *Historical Statistics of the United States*, Millennial Edition On Line, ed. Susan B. Carter et al. (Cambridge: Cambridge University Press, 2006).

13. Quoted in Werner, *Change Is Gonna Come*, 291.

14. Alex Kotlowitz, *There Are No Children Here: The Story of Two Boys Growing Up in the Other America* (New York: Anchor, 1992), 25.

15. Ibid., 22, 239–41.

16. Oscar Lewis, *Five Families: Mexican Case Studies in the Culture of Poverty* (New York: Basic Books, 1959) and Michael Harrington, *The Other America: Poverty in the United States* (New York: Macmillan, 1962) were landmarks of left-wing analysis that advanced the idea of a culture of poverty. *The Negro Family: A Case for National Action*, a government report released by U.S. assistant secretary of labor Daniel Patrick Moynihan in 1965, made similar points from a liberal point of view, stressing the expected efficacy of public spending to create new job opportunities for those long mired in poverty. Edward C. Banfield, *The Unheavenly City: The Nature and Future of Our Urban Crisis* (Boston: Little, Brown, 1968) advanced the conservative argument that some people

were simply impervious to assistance. Banfield's perspective was the one that received fresh support in the 1980s, even, in qualified form, from the social democrat William Julius Wilson, who concluded that "ghetto pathologies," although ultimately rooted in economic exclusion, played a role in keeping the underclass poor. William Julius Wilson, *The Truly Disadvantaged: The Inner City, the Underclass, and Public Policy* (Chicago: University of Chicago Press, 1990).

17. See Table 2, "Poverty Status, by Family Relationship, Race, and Hispanic Origin," in the Historical Poverty Tables, U.S. Census Bureau, http://www.census.gov/hhes/www/poverty/data/historical/people.html.

18. Hacker, *Two Nations*, 103.

19. The articles were then published as a book. Ken Auletta, *The Underclass* (New York: Random House, 1982).

20. Charles Murray, *Losing Ground: American Social Policy, 1950–1980* (New York: Basic Books, 1984).

21. "Poverty Status, by Family Relationship, Race, and Hispanic Origin"; Christopher Jencks, *Rethinking Social Policy: Race, Poverty, and the Underclass* (Cambridge, MA: Harvard University Press, 1992), 149.

22. Ibid., 193; Table 5.14 on 193.

23. Ibid., 195–96. Murray's antiwelfare argument and the culture of poverty thesis pointed toward similar policy conclusions, but Murray did not think the poor had distinctive values.

24. Tera Hunter, "'It's a Man's Man's Man's World': Specters of the Old Re-Newed in Afro-American Culture and Criticism," *Callaloo* 38 (Winter 1989): 248; Hacker, *Two Nations*, 115. "She Watch Channel Zero?!" was on *It Takes a Nation of Millions to Hold Us Back* (1988), Sony B00000EHNW, CD, 1990; "Sophisticated Bitch" was on Public Enemy, *Yo! Bum Rush the Show* (1987), Def Jam B00000024JZ, CD, 1990.

25. Christopher Jencks, *The Homeless* (Cambridge, MA: Harvard University Press, 1994), chapter 3.

26. Michael Stewart Foley, *Front Porch Politics: The Forgotten Heyday of American Activism in the 1970s and 1980s* (New York: Hill and Wang, 2013), 268.

27. Jencks, *The Homeless*, 37–40, 94–98. The administration stopped this purge during 1983, and the numbers of Americans receiving Social Security disability then rose, even though homelessness appeared to continue expanding. Jencks's explanation for this parallel rise is "that many other traditional sources of support for the mentally ill were drying up during the 1980s, making more people eligible for federal benefits." Ibid., 38.

28. Ibid., 16.

29. Jonathan Kozol, *Rachel and Her Children: Homeless Families in America* (New York: Crown, 1988).

30. Foley, *Front Porch Politics*, 274–75.

31. "Fasting Wins Concessions on Shelter for Homeless," *New York Times*, November 5, 1984; Robert Pear, "Homeless in Capital Resisting Move," *New York Times*, November 16, 1985; "Homeless Shelter Operator Begins New Fast in Capital," *New York Times*, February 14, 1986; "Around the Nation; U.S. Shelter Funds Bring End to Hunger Strike," *New York Times*, June 5, 1986; David S. Hilzenrath, "Advocates for Homeless Be-

gin Fast to Pressure Metro," *Washington Post*, November 10, 1987; Karlyn Barker, "Refurbished D.C. Shelter for Homeless Opens," *Washington Post*, February 20, 1987; Michael Abramowitz, "Snyder, CCNV Tear Down Fences at 4 Metro Stops," *Washington Post*, December 26, 1988.

32. Catherine McNicol Stock, *Rural Radicals: Righteous Rage in the American Grain* (Ithaca, NY: Cornell University Press, 1996), 157.

33. See the splendid account in Foley, *Front Porch Politics*, chapter 8. Also see Neil E. Harl, *The Farm Debt Crisis of the 1980s* (Ames: Iowa State University Press, 1990), and Mary Summers, "From the Heartland to Seattle: The Family Farm Movement of the 1980s and the Legacy of Agrarian State Building," in *The Countryside in the Age of the Modern State: Political Histories of Rural America*, ed. Catherine McNicol Stock and Robert D. Johnston (Ithaca, NY: Cornell University Press, 2001), 304–25.

34. *Country*, directed by Richard Pearce (1984; Walt Disney Video, 2003), DVD; *The River*, directed by Mark Rydell (1984; University City, CA: Universal Studios, 1999), DVD; Ronald Reagan, entry dated October 5, 1984, in *The Reagan Diaries*, ed. Douglas Brinkley (New York: HarperCollins, 2007), 271.

35. Kahl barricaded himself with a weapons cache and the marshals threw in a grenade, blowing him to bits. James Corcoran, *Bitter Harvest: Gordon Kahl and the Posse Comitatus: Murder in the Heartland* (New York: Viking, 1990); Stock, *Rural Radicals*, 171.

36. Jenkins, *Decade of Nightmares*, 169–70; Patricia A. Turner, *I Heard It Through the Grapevine: Rumor in African-American Culture* (Berkeley: University of California Press, 1993), 123–27, 144–51; James Baldwin, *The Evidence of Things Not Seen* (New York: Henry Holt, 1985).

37. Michelle Smith and Lawrence Pazder, *Michelle Remembers: The True Story of a Year-Long Contest Between Innocence and Evil* (New York: Congdon and Lattès, 1980); Jenkins, *Decade of Nightmares*, 171, 256, 264, 272. Also see Barry Glassner, *The Culture of Fear: Why Americans Are Afraid of the Wrong Things* (New York: Basic Books, 1999), chapter 3. The major blow against the Satanic abuse allegations came from Dorothy Rabinowitz, who won a Pulitzer Prize largely on the basis of a string of *Wall Street Journal* editorials she wrote questioning a set of prosecutions in Massachusetts, subsequently compiled in book form. Dorothy Rabinowitz, *No Crueler Tyrannies: Accusation, False Witness, and Other Terrors of Our Times* (New York: Free Press, 2003).

38. David Garland, *The Culture of Crime: Crime and Social Order in Contemporary Society* (Chicago, IL: University of Chicago Press, 2001), 106. For data, see Figure 1 "Index of offenses known to police per 100,000 population United States, 1950–1998," in ibid., 208.

39. Hacker, *Two Nations*, 182–83. These percentages represent instances of these crimes in which the perpetrator's race was identified.

40. Randall Kennedy, *Race, Crime, and the Law* (New York: Vintage, 1998), 20; Thernstrom and Thernstrom, *America in Black and White*, 266. The corresponding death rate for white males in the same age group also increased sharply, by 50 percent—yet this was but one-sixth the size of the increase for black youths.

41. See Michael W. Flamm, *Law and Order: Street Crime, Civil Unrest, and the Crisis of Liberalism in the 1960s* (New York: Columbia University Press, 2007).

42. Hacker, *Two Nations*, 183.

43. Thernstrom and Thernstrom, *America in Black and White*, 250. The Thernstroms cite a study from 1995 that found a 32 percent "in the system" rate for black men in 1995—4.5 times the rate for young white men and 2.5 times the rate for young Latinos.

44. Bound and Freeman, "What Went Wrong?" 226–27.

45. See Diane M. Pinderhughes, *Race and Ethnicity in Chicago Politics* (Urbana: University of Illinois Press, 1987), and Gary Rivlin, *Fire on the Prairie: Chicago's Harold Washington and the Politics of Race* (New York: Henry Holt, 1992).

46. In 1980, New York City's non-Hispanic white population was 52 percent of the whole, and 43 percent in 1990. Joshua B. Freeman, *Working-Class New York: Life and Labor since World War II* (New York: The Free Press, 2000), 303.

47. John Hull Mollenkopf, *A Phoenix Rises in the Ashes: The Rise and Fall of the Koch Coalition in New York City Politics* (Princeton, NJ: Princeton University Press, 1992), 110–13.

48. Melinda Beck with Ronald Henkoff, "The McDuffie Case," *Newsweek*, June 2, 1980.

49. Herbert Denton, "Riot without Rhetoric," *Washington Post*, July 30, 1980.

50. George Lardner Jr. and Margot Hornblower, "Miami: Brutality Was Not Expected," *Washington Post*, May 25, 1980.

51. For this argument, see Ronald Walters, "White Racial Nationalism in the United States," *Without Prejudice* 1, no. 1 (Fall 1987), available at http://www.eaford.org/publications/2/White%20Racial%20Nationalism%20in%20the%20United%20States.pdf, specifically concerning the first half of the 1980s.

52. Freeman, *Working-Class New York*, 283.

53. Isabel Wilkerson, "Jury Acquits All Transit Officers in 1983 Death of Michael Stewart," *New York Times*, November 25, 1985.

54. "Graffiti Limbo" was on Michelle Shocked, *Short Sharp Shocked* (1988), Mighty Sound B0000CBLA8, CD, 2003.

55. Jeff Gammage, "The Murder That Galvanized Asian American Activism," *Philadelphia Inquirer*, March 5, 2010; Lynette Clemetson, "A Slaying in 1982 Maintains Its Grip on Asian-Americans," *New York Times*, June 18, 2002; William Wei, *The Asian American Movement* (Philadelphia: Temple University Press, 1993), 193–94, 252.

56. Esther B. Fein, "Angry Citizens in Many Cities Supporting Goetz," *New York Times*, January 7, 1985.

57. Murray Kempton, "What Is to Be Done with Him?" *Newsday*, June 12, 1987.

58. Stanley Crouch, "I, the Jury," in Stanley Crouch, *Notes of a Hanging Judge: Essays and Reviews, 1979–1989* (New York: Oxford University Press, 1991), 130; Adam Nossiter, "Bronx Jury Orders Goetz to Pay Man He Paralyzed $43 Million," *New York Times*, April 24, 1996.

59. Kirk Johnson, "Acquittal Won in Shooting of 4 Youths—Prison Term Possible on Weapons Charges," *New York Times*, June 17, 1986.

60. Otto Friedrich, Roger Franklin, and Raji Samghabad, "Not Guilty," *Time*, June 29, 1987.

61. Barbara Whitaker, "The New York Poll: City Supports Goetz Verdict," *Newsday*, June 28, 1987.

62. The men Goetz shot had carried screwdrivers, and many later believed these had been sharpened to points, making them suitable as deadly weapons, but this was not true. They had planned to use the screwdrivers to break open and burglarize games in

an arcade, and on their way they evidently just saw Goetz as an easy mark, a way to pick up some pocket money on their way to a bigger score.

63. Reed Albergotti et al., "Racism Comes Home: The Howard Beach Case," The Queens Spin (part of a set of retrospective articles written for the Queens Tribune), http://www.queenstribune.comanniversary2003/howardbeach.htm.

64. Ibid.

65. Joyce Purnick, "A Break with the Past: Koch and Racial Attack," New York Times, January 6, 1987.

66. Joseph P. Fried, "3 in Howard Beach Attack Are Guilty of Manslaughter," New York Times, December 22, 1987; Joseph P. Fried, "Howard Beach Defendant Given Maximum Term of 10 to 30 Years," New York Times, January 23, 1988; Joseph P. Fried, "2 Men Start Jail Terms in Howard Beach Case," New York Times, April 24, 1990.

67. This is the story reconstructed in Robert D. McFadden et al., Outrage: The Story Behind the Tawana Brawley Hoax (New York: Bantam, 1990), by six New York Times reporters. In their version, Tawana Brawley's mother, Glenda, was her daughter's collaborator, and the two did not intend to involve the authorities. Glenda was supposed to "find" Tawana on the premises of an apartment complex where the family recently had lived, but she was late and neighbors found the teenager and called the police. See chapter 31 for the journalists' narrative of Tawana Brawley's "missing days." My discussion of the Brawley case is largely drawn from Outrage, which remains the only substantive history of the case and whose contents have never been seriously challenged (in fact, Al Sharpton was an important source for the authors).

68. Robert D. McFadden, "27 Brutality Charges Now Filed in Clash," New York Times, August 9, 1988.

69. Todd S. Purdum, "Melee in Tompkins Sq. Park: Violence and Its Provocation," New York Times, August 14, 1988.

70. Sydney H. Schanberg, "A Journey through the Tangled Case of the Central Park Jogger," Village Voice, November 20–26, 2002; Rivka Gewirtz Little, "Ash-Blond Ambition," Village Voice, November 20–26, 2002; Susan Saulny, "Convictions and Charges Voided in '89 Central Park Jogger Attack," New York Times, December 20, 2002.

71. Robert D. McFadden, "Boys' Guilt Likely in Rape of Jogger, Police Panel Says," New York Times, January 28, 2003; Marc Santora, "Prosecutor Rejects Theory of Boys' Attack on Jogger," New York Times, January 31, 2003; Jim Dwyer, "One Trail, Two Conclusions," New York Times, February 2, 2003; Bob Herbert, "That Terrible Time," New York Times, December 9, 2002.

72. Do the Right Thing, directed by Spike Lee (1989; Irvington, NY: Criterion, 2001), DVD.

73. See Cheryl L. Keyes, Rap Music and Street Consciousness (Urbana: University of Illinois Press, 2004), 79–80, 99–100.

74. Straight Outta Compton (1988), Priority Records B00006JJ51, CD, 2002.

75. Eithne Quinn, Nuthin' but a "G" Thang: The Culture and Commerce of Gangsta Rap (New York: Columbia University Press, 2005), 44.

76. Jeff Chang, Can't Stop Won't Stop: A History of the Hip-Hop Generation (New York: Picador, 2005), 388.

77. See Pyong Gap Min, Caught in the Middle: Korean Merchants in America's Multiethnic Cities (Berkeley: University of California Press, 1996), and Claire Jean Kim, Bitter

Fruit: The Politics of Black-Korean Conflict in New York City (New Haven, CT: Yale University Press, 2000). Also see Roger Waldinger, *Still the Promised Land? African-Americans and New Immigrants in Postindustrial New York* (Cambridge, MA: Harvard University Press, 1996), and Min Zhou, "Revisiting Ethnic Entrepreneurship: Convergencies, Controversies, and Conceptual Advancements," *International Migration Review* 38, no. 3 (Fall 2004): 1040–74.

78. See Table 1, "Nativity of the Population and Place of Birth of the Native Population: 1850 to 2000," in Campbell Gibson and Kay Jung, *Historical Census Statistics on the Foreign-Born Population of the United States: 1850 to 2000*, U.S. Census Bureau Working Paper No. 81 (February 2006), http://www.census.gov/population/www/documentation/twps0081/twps0081.pdf, 103.

79. Table 2, "World Region of Birth of the Foreign-Born Population: 1850 to 1930 and 1960 to 2000," in ibid., 104; Joel Perlmann and Roger Waldinger, "Second Generation Decline? Children of Immigrants, Past and Present—A Reconsideration," *International Migration Review* 31, no. 4 (Winter 1997): 900.

80. Nancy Foner, *From Ellis Island to JFK: New York's Two Great Waves of Immigration* (New Haven, CT/New York: Yale University Press/Russell Sage Foundation, 2000), 10–11; Table 2, "Foreign-Born Residents of New York City, by Country of Birth," is on 11. New York's Italian immigrants were older, the legacy of an earlier wave of immigration.

81. Melani McAlister, *Epic Encounters: Culture, Media, and U.S. Interests in the Middle East since 1945*, updated ed. (Berkeley: University of California Press, 2005), 247.

82. Perlmann and Waldinger, "Second Generation Decline?," 899. For a less sanguine view, see Alejandro Portes and Min Zhou, "The New Second Generation: Segmented Assimilation and Its Variants," *Annals of the American Academy of Political and Social Sciences* 530 (November 1993): 74–96.

83. Hacker, *Two Nations*, 145.

84. Mike Davis, *City of Quartz: Excavating the Future in Los Angeles* (New York: Vintage, 1992), 104.

85. See Saskia Sassen, "America's Immigration 'Problem,'" in Saskia Sassen, *Globalization and Its Discontents: Essays on the New Mobility of People and Money* (New York: The New Press, 1998), 31–54.

86. In 1990, 885,000 people became legal residents under this provision of the law, 1,100,000 in 1991. Foner, *From Ellis Island to JFK*, 249n73. See Otis L. Graham Jr., "Failing the Test: Immigration Reform," in *The Reagan Presidency: Pragmatic Conservatism and Its Legacies*, ed. W. Elliot Brownlee and Hugh Davis Graham (Lawrence: University Press of Kansas, 2003), 259–82. Graham shared the frustration of some conservatives that Reagan did so little to restrict immigration. But there was more than one conservative position on immigration.

87. Tracy Chapman, *Tracy Chapman* (1988), Elektra/Bea B000002H5I, CD, 1990.

9. The Winner

1. Martha Derthick and Steven M. Teles, "Riding the Third Rail: Social Security Reform," in *The Reagan Presidency: Pragmatic Conservatism and Its Legacies*, ed. W. El-

liot Brownlee and Hugh Davis Graham (Lawrence: University Press of Kansas, 2003), 198–99.

2. Ibid., 202.

3. Karlyn Barker and Peter Perl, "250,000 Assemble to Mark '63 March," *Washington Post*, August 28, 1963, A1.

4. Helen Dewar, "Helms Loses, 76–12; Delay of King Bill Defeated," *Washington Post*, October 19, 1983; Don Wolfensberger, "The Martin Luther King, Jr. Holiday: The Long Struggle in Congress; An Introductory Essay" (seminar on "The Martin Luther King, Jr. Holiday: How Did It Happen?," Woodrow Wilson International Center for Scholars, January 14, 2008), 6, 7. For abundant detail, see David L. Chappell, *Waking from the Dream: The Struggle for Civil Rights in the Shadow of Martin Luther King, Jr.* (New York: Random House, 2014), chapter 4.

5. Juan Williams, "Reagan Calls Mrs. King to Explain," *Washington Post*, October 22, 1983. Chappell notes that Reagan had spoken positively about King's life and work in January 1983, on King's birthday. Chappell, *Waking from the Dream*, 114.

6. Wolfensberger, "Martin Luther King, Jr. Holiday," 8.

7. Karl Gerard Brandt, *Ronald Reagan and the House Democrats: Gridlock, Partisanship, and the Fiscal Crisis* (Columbia: University of Missouri Press, 2009), 120, 122, 130.

8. Donovan was not indicted, but investigators made clear that they saw him as not proven guilty rather than innocent. George Lardner Jr., "Prosecutor Ends Inquiry on Donovan," *Washington Post*, September 14, 1982; Joel Brinkley, "More Than a Dozen in Administration Accused of Impropriety," *New York Times*, March 28, 1984; Tom Morganthau, "'Country-Club Ethics,'" *Newsweek*, April 2, 1984, 28–29.

9. Mark Starr et al., "A Nomination in Trouble," *Newsweek*, March 26, 1984, 36–37.

10. William M. LeoGrande, *Our Own Backyard: The United States in Central America, 1977–1992* (Chapel Hill: University of North Carolina Press, 1998), 332, 334, 335, 336–37, 340.

11. Ibid., 339, 345 (emphases added).

12. Steven M. Gillon, *The Democrats' Dilemma: Walter F. Mondale and the Liberal Legacy* (New York: Columbia University Press, 1992), 317.

13. Peter N. Carroll, *It Seemed Like Nothing Happened: America in the 1970s* (New Brunswick, NJ: Rutgers University Press, 1990), 318.

14. George Lardner Jr., "ACLU Report on '82 Calls Administration an 'Implacable Foe,'" *Washington Post*, October 11, 1982.

15. Gillon, *Democrats' Dilemma*, 342.

16. Chappell, *Waking from the Dream*, chapter 5, gives an outstanding account of Jackson's political journey.

17. Tom Morganthau et al., "Jesse Wins a 'Syria Primary,'" *Newsweek*, January 16, 1984, 14–15.

18. Chappell, *Waking from the Dream*, 133–36. Controversy also dogged Jackson over allegations that he had exaggerated his physical and political proximity to Martin Luther King Jr. at the time of King's murder in 1968. Chappell's careful account absolves Jackson of these charges. Ibid., 138–43.

19. Gillon, *Democrats' Dilemma*, 352.

20. Bernard Weinraub, "Geraldine Ferraro Is Chosen by Mondale as Running Mate, First Woman on Major Ticket," *New York Times*, July 12, 1984.

21. Jane Mayer and Doyle McManus, *Landslide: The Unmaking of the President, 1984–1988* (Boston: Houghton Mifflin, 1988), 4.

22. Bruce Springsteen, *Born in the U.S.A.* (1984; Sony, B0000025UW, 1990); Jon Pareles, "Bruce Springsteen—Rock's Popular Populist," *New York Times*, August 18, 1985.

23. Mayer and McManus, *Landslide*, 14.

24. John Brady, *Bad Boy: The Life and Politics of Lee Atwater* (Reading, MA: Addison Wesley, 1997), 91, 118, 120.

25. Thomas Byrne Edsall, "The Reagan Legacy," in *The Reagan Legacy*, ed. Sidney Blumenthal and Thomas Byrne Edsall (New York: Pantheon, 1988), 29. Republicans counted 466,000 new voters in the state in these years, the Democrats, 226,000.

26. Lawrence Summers and Paul Krugman were the economists who reportedly deflated the industrial-policy balloon at an August 1983 gathering in Jackson Hole, Wyoming. Paul Krugman, *Peddling Prosperity: Economic Sense and Nonsense in the Age of Diminished Expectations* (New York: Norton, 1994), 255; Mark Blyth, *Great Transformations: Economic Ideas and Institutional Change in the Twentieth Century* (Cambridge: Cambridge University Press, 2002), 192–93.

27. Walter F. Mondale, "Address Accepting the Presidential Nomination at the Democratic National Convention in San Francisco," July 19, 1984. Gerhard Peters and John T. Woolley, *The American Presidency Project*, http://www.presidency.ucsb.edu/ws/index.php?pid=25972. Unless noted otherwise, subsequent references to presidential statements and nominating convention speeches are to this same online archive.

28. Albert R. Hunt, "The Campaign and the Issues," in *The American Elections of 1984*, ed. Austin Ranney (Durham, NC: Duke University Press, 1985), 132.

29. Hunt, "Campaign and the Issues," 140.

30. Ronald Reagan, "Remarks Accepting the Presidential Nomination at the Republican National Convention in Dallas, Texas," August 23, 1984, http://www.presidency.ucsb.edu/ws/index.php?pid=40290.

31. Ibid.

32. Tom Shales, "Battle Hymn of the Republicans," *Washington Post*, August 24, 1984.

33. Gillon, *Democrats' Dilemma*, 393.

34. William Schneider, "The November 6 Vote for President: What Did It Mean?" in *American Elections of 1984*, 203.

35. Michael J. Robinson, "Where's the Beef? Media and Media Elites in 1984," in *American Elections of 1984*, 181; Hunt, "The Campaign and the Issues," 155.

36. Gillon, *Democrats' Dilemma*, 383, 385.

37. Schneider, "The November 6 Vote for President," 203, 212.

38. Gillon, *Democrats' Dilemma*, 394.

39. Raymond E. Wolfinger, "Dealignment, Realignment, and Mandates in the 1984 Election," in *American Elections of 1984*, 291.

40. John Ehrman, *The Eighties: America in the Age of Reagan* (New Haven, CT: Yale University Press, 2005), 66.

41. Edsall, "Reagan Legacy," Table 1, 22.

42. Kent B. Germany, "Lyndon B. Johnson and Civil Rights: Introduction to the Digital Edition," *Presidential Recordings of Lyndon B. Johnson: Digital Edition*, http://presidentialrecordings.rotunda.upress.virginia.edu/essays?series=CivilRights.

43. See Thomas Byrne Edsall and Mary B. Edsall, *Chain Reaction: The Impact of Race, Rights, and Taxes on American Politics* (New York: Norton, 1991) for a detailed analysis. Larry M. Bartels, *Unequal Democracy: The Political Economy of the New Gilded Age* (Princeton, NJ: Russell Sage Foundation and Princeton University Press, 2008), 75–78, shows that the decline in the Democratic share of the white vote nationally between 1952 and 2004 was due exclusively to increasing white Southern support for Republicans. However, this does not mean that the racially charged antipathy for liberalism was not also present in the rest of the country, as the evidence assembled by the Edsalls indicates it was.

44. Edsall, "Reagan Legacy," 31.

45. Gillon, *Democrats' Dilemma*, 395.

46. Ibid., 382.

47. Mayer and McManus, *Landslide*, 18. Mayer and McManus write that it was Mondale's attacks on Reagan as "old and disengaged" that needled the president.

48. William Schneider, "The Political Legacy of the Reagan Years," in *The Reagan Legacy*, 90.

49. Barry Sussman, quoted in Nelson W. Polsby, "The Democratic Nomination and the Evolution of the Party System," in *American Elections of 1984*, 44.

50. Schneider, "November 6 Vote for President," 220.

51. Ehrman, *The Eighties*, 85.

52. Brandt, *Ronald Reagan and the House Democrats*, 137.

53. Ibid., 216. On the longer-term trend toward more partisan voting, see Julian E. Zelizer, *On Capitol Hill: The Struggle to Reform Congress and Its Consequences, 1948–2000* (Cambridge: Cambridge University Press, 2004), 235.

54. See Kenneth S. Baer, *Reinventing Democrats: The Politics of Liberalism from Reagan to Clinton* (Lawrence: University Press of Kansas, 2000).

55. Regan, pushed out of his position in late 1987 in a White House effort to contain the political damage done by the Iran-Contra affair, soon divulged his disappointment with Reagan's leadership, as well as the attention-grabbing revelation that Nancy Reagan's consultations with an astrologer determined the scheduling of many of the president's activities, in Donald T. Regan, *For the Record: From Wall Street to Washington* (San Diego, CA: Harcourt Brace Jovanovich, 1988).

56. Robert Kaiser, "Ed Meese Out of His Depth," *Washington Post*, February 3, 1985.

57. Julia Malone, "Senate Panel Questions Meese about Controversial Home Sale," *Christian Science Monitor*, January 31, 1985; Mark Starr with Ann McDaniel, "Ed Meese Faces the Senate," *Newsweek*, February 11, 1985; Leslie Maitland Werner, "Senate Approves Meese to Become Attorney General," *New York Times*, February 24, 1985; Kaiser, "Ed Meese."

58. See Darrell M. West, "Gramm-Rudman-Hollings and the Politics of Deficit Reduction," *Annals of the American Academy of Political and Social Science*, 499 (September 1988): 90–100. A Democratic senator, Ernest Hollings of South Carolina, joined Gramm and Rudman but later grew disillusioned with this policy course.

59. W. Elliot Brownlee and C. Eugene Steuerle, "Taxation," in *Reagan Presidency*, 168–73; Jeffrey H. Birnbaum and Alan S. Murray, *Showdown at Gucci Gulch: Lawmakers, Lobbyists, and the Unlikely Triumph of Tax Reform* (New York: Random House, 1987).

60. David M. O'Brien, "Federal Judgeships in Retrospect," in *Reagan Presidency*, 328 (Table 14.1), 337–40; Nancy Scherer, "Blacks on the Bench," *Political Science Quarterly* 119, no. 4 (2004): 657 (Table 1); A. Leon Higginbotham, "The Case of the Missing Black Judges," *New York Times*, July 29, 1992; Lou Cannon, *President Reagan: The Role of a Lifetime* (New York: PublicAffairs, 2000), 720–21.

61. Herman Schwartz, "O'Connor as a 'Centrist'? Not When Minorities Are Involved," *Los Angeles Times*, April 12, 1998. These forty-one cases were those decided by only one or two votes.

62. Michael Meyer with Lynda Wright, "Rehnquist's Rocky Road," *Newsweek*, August 11, 1986.

63. See Cannon, *President Reagan*, 506–20, for a detailed account.

64. Francis Njubi Nesbitt, *Race for Sanctions: African Americans against Apartheid, 1946–1994* (Bloomington: Indiana University Press, 2004); David L. Hostetter, *Movement Matters: American Antiapartheid Activism and the Rise of Multicultural Politics* (New York: Routledge, 2009).

65. Nesbitt, *Race for Sanctions*, 134–35, 140–42.

10. Arms and the Man

1. Jane Mayer and Doyle McManus, *Landslide: The Unmaking of the President, 1984–1988* (Boston: Houghton Mifflin, 1988), 78–79.

2. Minutes, NSPG Meeting on Central America, June 25, 1984, 9, reproduced as Document 21 in *The Iran-Contra Scandal: The Declassified History*, ed. Peter Kornbluh and Malcolm Byrne (New York: The New Press, 1993), 77. The NSPG was an elite committee of the NSC, with responsibility for overseeing covert operations. The committee had gone by other names in previous administrations. In 1990, Baker told Lou Cannon that he had warned against such third-party solicitations at an NSPG meeting in the summer of 1984. What meeting Baker referred to remains unclear. Lou Cannon, *President Reagan: The Role of a Lifetime* (New York: PublicAffairs, 2000), 333. Baker testified during the congressional investigations of the scandal that he had voiced doubts about the legality of these activities, but would not confirm that he had raised the issue of impeachment. However, McFarlane agreed that Baker had done so, and Shultz's assistant, Charles Hill, also testified that Shultz had related Baker's view identically at the time. Theodore Draper, *A Very Thin Line: The Iran-Contra Affairs* (New York: Hill and Wang, 1991), 76n.

3. Minutes, NSPG Meeting on Central America, June 25, 1984, 14, in *Iran-Contra Scandal*, 82.

4. Ibid., 82.

5. U.S. Government Stipulation on Quid Pro Quos with other Governments as Part of Contra Operations, April 6, 1989, reproduced as Document 23 in *Iran-Contra Scandal*, 85–97.

6. Joanne Omang, "McFarlane Aide Facilitates Policy; Marine Officer Nurtures Connections with Contras, Conservatives," *Washington Post*, August 11, 1985; Draper, *Very Thin Line*, 113.

7. North and John Poindexter, national security adviser from December 1985 to November 1987, disagreed sharply about whether they sought presidential approval for

this "diversion" of funds to the Contras; many Americans became urgently concerned about whether Reagan knew of this diversion after the affair came to light. Investigators never produced documentary evidence of such knowledge, and Reagan consistently denied approving it. North testified that he had prepared five or six memoranda for the president's eyes concerning the diversion, but that he had shredded his copies of them. Poindexter recalled no such documents, and stated that he intentionally shielded Reagan from knowledge of the diversion. *Report of the Congressional Committees Investigating the Iran-Contra Affair, with the Minority Views*, abridged ed. (New York: Random House/ Times Books, 1988), 199–200, 235–36.

8. The report of the Independent Counsel for the Iran-Contra scandal, Lawrence Walsh, persuasively explains that the 1984 Boland Amendment's proscriptions covered the NSC. Lawrence E. Walsh, Independent Counsel, *Iran-Contra: The Final Report* (New York: Times Books, 1994), 67–69. Defenders of the NSC's novel operational role argued that it was not an "intelligence" agency, and therefore was not covered by the second Boland Amendment's blanket prohibition against Contra aid by any such agency. Ironically, Attorney General Meese, in 1986, sought and received a legal memorandum from the DOJ's Office of Legal Counsel, justifying a November 1985 arms shipment to Iran (discussed below) by arguing that the NSC was, in fact, an intelligence agency. Ibid., 455–56.

9. Mayer and McManus, *Landslide*, 68; Robert Timberg, *The Nightingale's Song* (New York: Simon and Schuster, 1995), 203.

10. Timberg, *Nightingale's Song*, 207–11.

11. Mayer and McManus, *Landslide*, 69.

12. Cannon, *President Reagan*, 565.

13. Draper, *Very Thin Line*, 35–36.

14. Gregg denied that Bush and Rodriguez discussed this matter, despite what the printed agenda stated. Walsh, *Iran-Contra*, 491–93; Mayer and McManus, *Landslide*, 218; Draper, *Very Thin Line*, 352–53, 574–75.

15. Draper, *Very Thin Line*, 71–73.

16. Abrams lied about his fundraising activities during Senate testimony, leading to a conviction for perjury, which was ultimately overturned. Draper, *Very Thin Line*, 363–73. The $10 billion never reached the Contras because North's secretary, Fawn Hall, supplied an incorrect bank-account number to Abrams.

17. Ibid., 54–70. Carl Channell was the public face of this private fundraising effort.

18. Alexander Cockburn and Jeffrey St. Clair, *Whiteout: The CIA, Drugs and the Press* (London: Verso, 1998), 35. See the materials collected in "The Contras, Cocaine, and Covert Operations," National Security Archive Electronic Briefing Book No. 2, http:// www.gwu.edu/~nsarchiv/NSAEBB/NSAEBB2/nsaebb2.htm.

19. *Report of the Congressional Committees*, 295.

20. Draper, *Very Thin Line*, 33.

21. U.S. Government Stipulation on Quid Pro Quos, paragraphs 58, 62–64, in *Iran-Contra Scandal*, 91–92.

22. David Hoffman and Joanne Omang, "Reagan Attacks 'Totalitarian' Nicaragua in Push for Rebel Aid," *Washington Post*, July 19, 1984; Robert Parry and Peter Kornbluh, "Reagan's Pro-Contra Propaganda Machine," *Washington Post*, September 4, 1988.

23. William M. LeoGrande, *Our Own Backyard: The United States in Central America, 1977–1992* (Chapel Hill: University of North Carolina Press, 1998), 435.

24. Draper, *Very Thin Line*, 111–13.

25. *Report of the Congressional Committees*, 117–19. North took over a year to finish this job.

26. Robert McFarlane, draft of letter to Congressman Michael Barnes, September 12, 1985, reproduced as Document 55 in *Iran-Contra Scandal*, 202.

27. Bob Woodward, *Veil: The Secret Wars of the CIA, 1981–1987* (New York: Pocket Books, 1988), 455. According to Woodward, Casey went directly to Saudi Ambassador Bandar, outside normal CIA channels, to contract out the job. Joseph E. Persico, *Casey: From the OSS to the CIA* (New York: Viking, 1990), 429–30, questions Woodward's account. Woodward offers no documentation, presumably basing his version on confidential interviews. Persico gives no proof of any kind for his alternative account. He concedes that the Unites States was at least indirectly responsible for the bombing by funding Lebanese groups that—he conjectures—really did the job.

28. Cannon, *President Reagan*, 536, 539. According to some reports, the hijackers selected passengers with Jewish- or Israeli-sounding names as those to be kept hostage the longest. See William E. Smith, "Terror Aboard Flight 847," *Time*, June 24, 2001.

29. Four hijackers were convicted in Italian courts, but two of them later escaped from prison (one was recaptured). Italy declined to hold Mohammed Zaydan, often known as Abu Abbas, thought to be the leader of the group that carried out the hijacking, for arrest. He found refuge in Iraq, where U.S. forces captured him after invading the country in 2003. Zaydan died in U.S. military custody in 2004. David Johnston, "Leader of '85 Achille Lauro Attack Dies at Prison in Iraq," *New York Times*, March 10, 2004.

30. Mayer and McManus, *Landslide*, 101–3.

31. The president made this remark in regard to arms sales to Iran, discussed below. Reagan said that "he could answer charges of illegality" more easily than those of inaction. Diary, Caspar W. Weinberger, December 7, 1985, reproduced as Document 14 in "The Iran-Contra Affair 20 Years On," National Security Archive Electronic Briefing Book No. 210, posted November 24, 2006, from http://www.gwu.edu/~nsarchiv/NSAEBB/NSAEBB210/14-Weinberger%20Diaries%20Dec%207%20handwritten.pdf.

32. See Trita Parsi, *Treacherous Alliance: The Secret Dealings of Israel, Iran, and the U.S.* (New Haven, CT: Yale University Press, 2007), 91–92, 127–28.

33. Bob Woodward and Walter Pincus, "Israeli Sale Said Allowed by Haig in '81," *Washington Post*, November 29, 1986. The Act required that the U.S. president approve retransfer of arms from a legitimate recipient to a third country, and it required that the president inform Congress if he learned of improper retransfers. Transfer of U.S. government arms either to the Contras or to Iran was prohibited by law during the period at issue, and Reagan, of course, knew of the transfers and kept them secret from Congress. Compliance with the Act often entailed "end-user certificates" in which foreign governments stated that they would not export weapons they bought from the United States, and one part of the Iran-Contra deceptions involved the Reagan administration pressuring foreign governments to produce fraudulent certificates that would conceal the actual destination of U.S. weapons.

34. Shultz learned of Ledeen's mission after it began, and he questioned McFarlane sharply on the matter. McFarlane lied to Shultz, telling the secretary of state that Ledeen had acted on his own. Draper, *Very Thin Line*, 140–41. Trita Parsi contends that

Peres communicated directly with McFarlane to instigate the scheme. Parsi, *Treacherous Alliance*, 116–17.

35. Lou Cannon, "President Assails 'Terrorist' Nations; Unspecified Action Is Threatened," *Washington Post*, July 9, 1985. Cannon's article noted that Nicaragua was not classified by the U.S. State Department as a terrorist nation.

36. *The Tower Commission Report: The Full Text of the President's Special Review Board* (New York: Bantam/Times Books, 1987), 24–25; *Report of the Congressional Committees*, 147–48.

37. TOW was an acronym for Tube-launched, Optically tracked, Wire-guided missiles. Donald Regan confirmed McFarlane's recollection of this briefing. Cannon, *President Reagan*, 551. Exactly what was said at this meeting remains in dispute. See Edmund Morris, *Dutch: A Memoir of Ronald Reagan* (New York: Modern Library, 1999), 603–7.

38. *Report of the Congressional Committees*, 150–51; David Crist, *The Twilight War: The Secret History of America's Thirty-Year Conflict with Iran* (New York: Penguin, 2012), 180.

39. *Report of the Congressional Committees*, 151; Morris, *Dutch*, 542.

40. *Report of the Congressional Committees*, 155–56, 302. Hawk missiles were surface-to-air missiles, used mainly against aircraft. They sometimes were used against missiles, but not as effectively. After the weapon's introduction in the 1960s, the name was sometimes used as an acronym for "Homing All the Way Killer." This shipment ran into much trouble; in the end, only eighteen missiles were delivered.

41. This was in an interview with the Special Review Board (the Tower Commission). Cannon, *President Reagan*, 551; *Report of the Congressional Committees*, 158.

42. Ibid., 172.

43. Unsigned Draft Presidential Finding on "Hostage Rescue—Middle East," ca. November 26, 1985, reproduced as Document 63 in *Iran-Contra Scandal*, 231.

44. Cannon, *President Reagan*, 560; *Report of the Congressional Committees*, 175.

45. *Report of the Congressional Committees*, 179–80.

46. John Poindexter, Memorandum for the President, "Covert Action Finding Regarding Iran," with Signed Finding Attached, January 17, 1986, reproduced as Document 64 in *Iran-Contra Scandal*, 232–35.

47. Cannon, *President Reagan*, 566.

48. *Report of the Congressional Committees*, 186–87.

49. "The Iran-Contra Scandal: A Chronology of Events," in *Iran-Contra Scandal*, 397, citing Secure Equipment, February 1, 1986, 16:33; Senators William S. Cohen and George J. Mitchell, *Men of Zeal: A Candid Inside Story of the Iran-Contra Hearings* (New York: Viking, 1988), 271.

50. *Report of the Congressional Committees*, 193.

51. Ibid., 212.

52. Douglas Little, "To the Shores of Tripoli: America, Qaddafi, and the Libyan Revolution, 1969–89," *International History Review* 35, no. 1 (January 2013): 89–91.

53. "Tension over Libya: Thousands Take to the Streets," *New York Times*, April 20, 1986.

54. Parry and Kornbluh, "Reagan's Pro-Contra Propaganda Machine."

55. Cockburn and St. Clair, *Whiteout*, 317.

56. Salman Rushdie, *The Jaguar's Smile: A Nicaraguan Journey* (New York: Viking, 1987), 13.

57. The reporter was Lawrence Zuckerman. Cockburn and St. Clair, *Whiteout*, 310.

58. LeoGrande, *Our Own Backyard*, 474.

59. Woodward, *Veil*, 543.

60. Loren Jenkins, "Iranian Displays Bible Signed 'Ronald Reagan,'" *Washington Post*, January 29, 1987.

61. Albert Hakim, Memorandum of Understanding, "Translation by Albert Hakim of the Farse [*sic*] Original of the '9 Points,'" October 8, 1986, reproduced as Document 84 in *Iran-Contra Scandal*, 302–3; *Report of the Congressional Committees*, 224–26.

62. *Report of the Congressional Committees*, 228.

63. Draper, *Very Thin Line*, 352.

64. James LeMoyne, "U.S. Prisoner in Nicaragua Says C.I.A. Ran Contra Supply Flights," *New York Times*, October 10, 1986. North had arranged for Owen to be paid by the Nicaraguan Humanitarian Assistance Office, which Congress had created to channel nonlethal aid to the Contras.

65. Mayer and McManus, *Landslide*, 274.

66. Cannon, *President Reagan*, 601.

67. Ibid., 602.

68. Caspar Weinberger, Memorandum for the Record, "Meeting on November 10, 1986, with the President, Vice President, Secretary Shultz, DCI Casey, Attorney General Meese, Don Regan, Admiral Poindexter, and Al Keel, in the Oval Office," Undated, 1, reproduced as Document 86 in *Iran-Contra Scandal*, 315.

69. *Report of the Congressional Committees*, 257.

70. Weinberger, Memorandum for the Record, 3, in *Iran-Contra Scandal*, 317.

71. Cannon, *President Reagan*, 604–5.

72. George P. Shultz, *Turmoil and Triumph: My Years as Secretary of State* (New York: Scribner's, 1993), 819, 822–23.

73. *New York Times*, December 4, 1986.

74. Cannon, *President Reagan*, 615–16; Woodward, *Veil*, 570–71.

75. McFarlane testified that North used this phrase (which North denied) in a mid-day conversation on the twenty-first. Robert Earl, North's deputy, testified that North told him on that same day that he (North) had met with Meese already, but neither Meese nor North corroborated Earl's recollection. *Report of the Congressional Committees*, 267.

76. Ibid., 305–16; Walter Pincus and David Ottoway, "Up to $30 Million Transferred," *Washington Post*, November 26, 1986; Oliver North, "Release of American Hostages in Beirut," ca. April 4, 1986 (the "Diversion Memo"), reproduced as Document 88 in *Iran-Contra Scandal*, 319–23.

77. Walsh, *Iran-Contra*, 542. The first Meese quotation and the Poindexter quotation are from Weinberger's notes of the meeting; the second Meese quotation comes from Regan's notes.

78. Ronald Reagan, Transcript of News Conference, November 25, 1986, reproduced as Document 89 in *Iran-Contra Scandal*, 324–25.

79. Woodward, *Veil*, 583–84.

80. Cannon, *President Reagan*, 630–31.

81. Walsh, *Iran-Contra*, 10, 12–13, 15, 19–20, 21, 22; Morris, *Dutch*, 612. Of the eighteen Hawk missiles that the Iranians received in November 1985, they test-fired one, found

it faulty, and returned the remaining seventeen in February 1986, after taking posses-sion of a shipment of five hundred TOWs. By one common reckoning, the weapons earned Benjamin Weir, David Jacobsen, and Lawrence Jenco their freedom, but three more Americans—Frank Reed, Joseph Cicippio, and Edward Tracy—were seized in Beirut while the secret arms sales to Iran were ongoing, for a net gain of zero hostages released. Ibid., 607. However, Terry Anderson, an American journalist in Beirut, also was kidnapped in 1985 (and freed six years later).

82. Haynes Johnson, *Sleepwalking Through History: America in the Reagan Years* (New York: Anchor, 1991), 327.

83. Ibid., 636n.

84. Draper, *Very Thin Line*, 570.

11. The Crisis

1. Peter Grier, "Challenger Explosion: How President Reagan Responded," *Christian Science Monitor*—SCMonitor.com, January 28, 2011, http://www.csmonitor.com/layout/set/print/content/view/print/359636. The Magee poem was called "High Flight." Peggy Noonan wrote Reagan's speech.

2. Sidney Blumenthal, "Reaganism and the Neokitsch Aesthetic," in *The Reagan Era*, ed. Sidney Blumenthal and Thomas Byrne Edsall (New York: Pantheon, 1988), 282.

3. Peter Osterlund, "Democrats Not Planning Senate Revolt," *Christian Science Monitor*, November 6, 1986.

4. David Brock, *Blinded by the Right: The Conscience of an Ex-Conservative* (New York: Crown, 2002), 21.

5. Lou Cannon, "Why the Band Has Stopped Playing for Ronald Reagan," *Washington Post*, December 21, 1986.

6. Michael Lewis, *Liar's Poker: Rising Through the Wreckage on Wall Street* (New York: Norton, 2010), 247.

7. Blumenthal, "Reaganism and the Neokitsch Aesthetic," 283.

8. Connie Bruck, *The Predator's Ball: The Inside Story of Drexel Burnham and the Rise of the Junk Bond Raiders* (New York: Penguin, 1989), chapter 15; Eric Gelman and Bill Powell et al., "The Secret World of Ivan Boesky," *Newsweek*, December 1, 1986.

9. David Stockman, *The Triumph of Politics: Why the Reagan Revolution Failed* (New York: Harper & Row, 1986), 266.

10. John M. Barry, *The Ambition and the Power* (New York: Viking, 1989), 435, 480–81.

11. The "Keating Five" were Alan Cranston of California, Dennis DeConcini of Arizona, Donald Riegle of Michigan, John Glenn of Ohio (all Democrats), and John McCain of Arizona (a Republican). Philip Shenon, "5 Senators Struggle to Avoid Keating Inquiry Fallout," *New York Times*, November 22, 1989; Richard L. Berke, "Aftermath of the Keating Verdicts: Damage Control, Political Glee," *New York Times*, March 1, 1991.

12. Lou Cannon, *President Reagan: The Role of a Lifetime* (New York: PublicAffairs, 2000), 740–44; Brooks Jackson, *Honest Graft: Big Money and the American Political Process*, rev. ed. (Washington, DC: Farragut Publishing Company, 1990).

13. Caroline Rand Herron and Michael Wright, "Bank Holiday in Ohio," *New York Times*, March 17, 1985; Eileen Ogintz and Laurie Cohen, "Ohio Governor OKs Savings Rescue Plan," *Chicago Tribune*, March 20, 1985.

14. Monica Langley, "FSLIC Is Now Operating at a Deficit, Probably Is Billions in Red, GAO Finds," *Wall Street Journal*, February 25, 1987; Kathleen Day, "Auditors Seek FSLIC Writeoff," *Washington Post*, February 26, 1987. In 1989, the government would abolish the FSLIC and replace it with the Resolution Trust Corporation, charged with liquidating failed thrifts.

15. For a breakdown of these costs, see Table 4, "Estimated Savings and Loan Resolution Cost, 1986–1995," in Timothy Curry and Lynn Shibut, "The Cost of the Savings and Loan Crisis: Truth and Consequences," *FDIC Banking Review* 13, no. 2 (2000): 31, http://www.fdic.gov/bank/analytical/banking/2000dec/brv13n2_2.pdf. For a full discussion, see this entire article (26–35) and *History of the Eighties—Lessons for the Future*, vol. 1: *An Examination of the Banking Crises of the 1980s and Early 1990s* (FDIC Division of Research and Statistics, 1997), chapter 1, http://www.fdic.gov/bank/historical/history/3_85.pdf.

16. "Two Financial Crises Compared: The Savings and Loan Debacle and the Mortgage Mess," *New York Times*, April 13, 2011.

17. John S. DeMott, "The Bill Comes Due for Deaver," *Time*, March 30, 1987.

18. Clifford D. May, "Wedtech Scandal Gets Messier and Messier," *New York Times*, June 7, 1987; "Nofziger Loses Bid to Dismiss Indictment Under Ethics Law," *New York Times*, October 22, 1987; "A Web of Corruption," *New York Times*, August 5, 1988; "Biaggi Sentenced to an 8-Year Term in Wedtech Case," *New York Times*, November 19, 1988.

19. Ruth Marcus, "Justice Dept. Report Sharply Criticizes Meese," *Washington Post*, January 17, 1989; Eloise Salholz with Ann McDaniel and Thomas M. Defrank, "Meese's Long Goodbye," *Newsweek*, July 18, 1988; George Lardner Jr., "McKay Reports Four 'Probable' Meese Offenses," *Washington Post*, July 19, 1988; Philip Shenon, "The McKay Report: An Ambiguous Conclusion to a 14-Month Investigation," *New York Times*, July 19, 1988; James N. Baker with Richard Sandza, "Meese Plays the Martyr," *Newsweek*, August 1, 1988.

20. Christopher Drew and George de Lama, "2 Meese Aides Resign After Urging Ouster," *Chicago Tribune*, March 30, 1988; Philip Shenon, "Former Aides Assail Meese's Leadership," *New York Times*, July 27, 1988; Cannon, *President Reagan*, 718–20.

21. James B. Stewart, *Den of Thieves* (New York: Simon and Schuster Paperbacks, 1992), 256.

22. James Traub, *Too Good to Be True: The Outlandish Story of Wedtech* (New York: Doubleday, 1990), 302.

23. Stewart, *Den of Thieves*, 412.

24. James Sterngold, "With Key Executives' Arrest, Wall Street Faces Challenge," *New York Times*, February 15, 1987; David Pauly et al., "New Arrests on Wall Street," *Newsweek*, February 23, 1987; David A. Vise and Steve Coll, "Wall Street's Long Year of Turmoil," *Washington Post*, May 10, 1987; David Dale, "Wall Street Yuppies in Handcuffs and Tears," *Sydney Morning Herald*, February 21, 1987.

25. Peter Kerr, "15 Employees of Wall Street Firms Are Arrested on Cocaine Charges," *New York Times*, April 17, 1987; Pat Widder, "16 Charged in Drug Probe on Wall St.," *Chicago Tribune*, April 17, 1987.

26. Eric Gelman, "Stocks Plunge 508 Points, a Drop of 22.6%," *New York Times*, October 20, 1987. See the readings collected in part 1 of *Panic: The Story of Modern Financial Insanity*, ed. Michael Lewis (New York: Norton, 2008).

27. *Wall Street*, directed by Oliver Stone (1987; Twentieth-Century Fox, 2000), DVD.

28. Frances FitzGerald, "Jim and Tammy," *New Yorker*, April 23, 1990, 86.

29. Richard N. Ostling, "TV's Unholy Row," *Time*, April 6, 1987.

30. Russell Chandler, "Bakkers' $1.6-Million PTL Salaries Cut Off by Falwell," *Los Angeles Times*, April 29, 1987; "Falwell to Bakker: 'Come Clean about Jessica Hahn and Repent,'" Albany *Times Union*, May 27, 1987.

31. Richard N. Ostling, "Enterprising Evangelism," *Time*, August 3, 1987.

32. Art Harris, "Swaggart Steps Down for 'Sin'," *Washington Post*, February 22, 1988; Art Harris, "Jimmy Swaggart and the Snare of Sin," *Washington Post*, February 25, 1988; Des Colquhoun, "When the Godly Make Us Vomit," *Advertiser*, February 24, 1988.

33. "Journal Publishes Dr. Koop's Personal Account of the AIDS Controversy," *PR Newswire*, March 31, 2001, http://www.prnewswire.com/news-releases/journal -publishes-dr-koops-personal-account-of-the-aids-controversy-118977359.html; Dick Polman, "A Realignment on Koop AIDS Stance Pleases Early Foes, Riles Allies," *Philadelphia Inquirer*, April 12, 1987; Steven Chapple and David Talbot, "From *Burning Desires*" (1989), in *While the World Sleeps: Writing from the First Twenty Years of the Global AIDS Plague*, ed. Chris Bull (New York: Thunder's Mouth, 2003), 142–43.

34. *Surgeon General's Report on Acquired Immune Deficiency Syndrome* (Washington, DC: United States Public Health Service, 1986).

35. Polman, "Realignment on Koop."

36. Chapple and Talbot, "*Burning Desires*," 141, 152.

37. Polman, "Realignment on Koop"; Maureen Dowd, "Dr. Koop Defends His Crusade on AIDS," *New York Times*, April 6, 1987; Chapple and Talbot, "*Burning Desires*," 143–44, 146–50; "Journal Publishes Dr. Koop's."

38. Randy Shilts, *And the Band Played On: Politics, People, and the AIDS Epidemic* (New York: St. Martin's Griffin, 1987), 587–88.

39. Ibid., 595; Chapple and Talbot, "*Burning Desires*," 151.

40. Lena Williams, "200,000 March in Capital to Seek Gay Rights and Money for AIDS," *New York Times*, October 12, 1987; Linda Wheeler, "2,000 Gay Couples Exchange Vows in Ceremony of Rights," *Washington Post*, October 11, 1987. March organizers estimated the crowd at more than three hundred thousand.

41. Christopher Capozzola, "A Very American Epidemic: Memory Politics and Identity Politics in the AIDS Memorial Quilt, 1985–1993," in *The World the 60s Made: Politics and Culture in Recent America*, ed. Van Gosse and Richard Moser (Philadelphia: Temple University Press, 2003), 219.

42. Sandra G. Boodman, "A Somber Crowd Dedicates Quilt to AIDS Victims," *Washington Post*, October 12, 1987; Capozzola, "Very American Epidemic," 226.

43. Larry Kramer, *The Normal Heart and the Destiny of Me: Two Plays* (New York: Grove Press, 2000).

44. Douglas Crimp and Adam Rolston, "Stop the Church" (1990), in *While the World Sleeps*, 171–77; Douglas Crimp and Adam Rolston, "Seize Control of the FDA," in ibid., 179–82.

45. See the writings collected in Larry Kramer, *Reports from the Holocaust: The Story of an AIDS Activist* (New York: St. Martin's Press, 1994).

46. David Thelen, *Becoming Citizens in the Age of Television: How Americans Challenged the Media and Seized Political Initiative during the Iran-Contra Debate* (Chicago: University of Chicago Press, 1996), 18.

47. Senators William S. Cohen and George J. Mitchell, *Men of Zeal: A Candid Inside Story of the Iran-Contra Hearings* (New York: Viking, 1988), 18–22; Holly Sklar, *Washington's War on Nicaragua* (Boston: South End Press, 1988), 348.

48. Public support for Contra aid never polled higher than 40 percent of the public, and was usually lower. Thelen, *Becoming Citizens*, 39.

49. See Cannon, *President Reagan*, 650–58, for an account that reflects this sentiment.

50. Julian E. Zelizer, *Arsenal of Democracy: The Politics of National Security—from World War II to the War on Terrorism* (New York: Basic Books, 2010), 347.

51. Cohen and Mitchell, *Men of Zeal*, 155.

52. Thelen, *Becoming Citizens*, 43–44.

53. Cohen and Mitchell, *Men of Zeal*, 162–63.

54. Ibid., 121.

55. Haynes Johnson, *Sleepwalking through History: America in the Reagan Years* (New York: Norton, 1991), 363.

56. Barry, *Ambition and the Power*, 303.

57. Thelen, *Becoming Citizens*, 40; Lawrence E. Walsh, *Firewall: The Iran-Contra Conspiracy and Cover-up* (New York: Norton, 1997), 141.

58. Cohen and Mitchell, *Men of Zeal*, 200.

59. Ibid., 194–95.

60. Walsh, *Firewall*, 223, 303–4; Oliver L. North with William Novak, *Under Fire: An American Story* (New York: HarperCollins/Zondervan, 1991), 12, 15–17.

61. Edward M. Kennedy, "Robert Bork's America" (July 1, 1987), in *Conservatives in Power: The Reagan Years, 1981–1989: A Brief History with Documents*, ed. Meg Jacobs and Julian E. Zelizer (New York: Bedford/St. Martin's, 2011), 132–33.

62. See Bruce Ackerman, "Robert Bork's Grand Inquisition," *Yale Law Review* 99, no. 6 (April 1990): 1419–39.

63. Steven V. Roberts, "9–5 Panel Vote Against Bork Sends Nomination to Senate Amid Predictions of Defeat," *New York Times*, October 7, 1987; Arlen Specter, "Why I Voted Against Bork," *New York Times*, October 9, 1987; Edward Walsh and Ruth Marcus, "Bork Rejected for High Court," *Washington Post*, October 24, 1987.

64. Haynes Johnson, "The Ebb Tide of Influence," *Washington Post*, October 16, 1987.

65. Cannon, *President Reagan*, 723–28, sympathizes somewhat with Bork. Also see Stuart Taylor Jr., "Of Bork and Tactics," *New York Times*, October 21, 1987.

66. Norman C. Amaker, *Civil Rights and the Reagan Administration* (Washington, DC: The Urban Institute Press, 1988), 73–74; David L. Chappell, *Waking from the Dream: The Struggle for Civil Rights in the Shadow of Martin Luther King, Jr.* (New York: Random House, 2014), 145. The Supreme Court decision was *Grove City College v. Bell* (1984), which held that only the financial aid department of Grove City College in Pennsylvania, a school with a strong religious conservative philosophy, not the college itself, was liable for violations of women's equal rights, as established under Title IX of the Edu-

cation Amendments of 1972 to the Higher Education Act of 1965. (Grove City College stated it did not take federal money, but students with federal financial aid attended the college and paid it tuition.) The decision was widely perceived as establishing precedent that would apply to groups other than women who were protected by numerous federal civil rights laws. See Hugh Davis Graham, "The Storm Over Grove City College: Civil Rights Regulation, Higher Education, and the Reagan Administration," *History of Education Quarterly* 38, no. 4 (Winter 1998): 407–29. Republican and Democratic members of Congress formed wide support for the Restoration Act by agreeing to state that no action by any institution regarding abortion would trigger the law's provisions.

12. Strength Through Peace

1. Archie Brown, *The Gorbachev Factor* (Oxford: Oxford University Press, 1996), 83.

2. Gorbachev quoted in Melvyn P. Leffler, *For the Soul of Mankind: The United States, the Soviet Union, and the Cold War* (New York: Hill and Wang, 2007), 367.

3. Dusko Doder, "U.S. Concession or 'Coercive' Ploy? Deteriorating Ties, Suspicion Fueled Moscow's Quick Rebuff," *Washington Post*, June 16, 1985.

4. In November 1984, the Soviet government publicized an increase in the defense budget of "nearly 12 percent." Raymond L. Garthoff, *The Great Transition: American-Soviet Relations and the End of the Cold War* (Washington, DC: Brookings Institution, 1994), 189.

5. These statements are from 1986. Leffler, *For the Soul of Mankind*, 376.

6. Ibid., 338–39.

7. Matthew Evangelista, "Turning Points in Arms Control," in *Ending the Cold War: Interpretations, Causation, and the Study of International Relations,* ed. Richard K. Herrmann and Richard Ned Lebow (New York: Palgrave Macmillan, 2004), 84. The moratorium, extended several times, lasted nineteen months without U.S. reciprocation until Gorbachev, under pressure from his military, approved a resumption of testing.

8. George P. Shultz, *Turmoil and Triumph: My Years as Secretary of State* (New York: Scribner's, 1993), 511, 515, 522.

9. Garthoff, *Great Transition*, 229; Shultz, *Turmoil and Triumph*, 576.

10. Shultz, *Turmoil and Triumph*, 600–1.

11. Garthoff, *Great Transition*, 240.

12. Ibid., 88.

13. Ibid., 247.

14. Paul Lettow, *Ronald Reagan and His Quest to Abolish Nuclear Weapons* (New York: Random House, 2005), 191.

15. Shultz, *Turmoil and Triumph*, 699, 700.

16. Richard Rhodes, *Arsenals of Folly: The Making of the Nuclear Arms Race* (New York: Knopf, 2007), 221.

17. Garthoff, *Great Transition*, 257.

18. Brown, *Gorbachev Factor*, 116–17. The Palme Commission's official name was the Independent Commission on Disarmament and Security Issues; it issued its major report in 1982, titled *Common Security: A Blueprint for Survival.*

19. Don Oberdorfer, *From the Cold War to a New Era: The United States and the Soviet Union, 1983–1991*, updated ed. (Baltimore, MD: The Johns Hopkins University Press, 1998), 160.

20. Brown, *Gorbachev Factor*, 221.

21. Leffler, *For the Soul of Mankind*, 388.

22. Ibid., 389.

23. Garthoff, *Great Transition*, 224–25, 284–85; David E. Hoffman, *The Dead Hand: The Untold Story of the Cold War Arms Race and Its Dangerous Legacy* (New York: Doubleday, 2009), chapter 9.

24. Shultz, *Turmoil and Triumph*, 534.

25. Odd Arne Westad, *The Global Cold War: Third World Interventions and the Making of Our Times* (Cambridge: Cambridge University Press, 2007), 372.

26. Brown, *Gorbachev Factor*, 221. See Steve Coll, *Ghost Wars: The Secret History of the CIA, Afghanistan, and bin Laden, from the Soviet Invasion to September 10, 2001* (New York: Penguin, 2005), 102, 151, and chapter 14.

27. Don Oberdorfer, "U.S. Is 'No Longer Bound' by SALT II, Weinberger Says," *Washington Post*, May 29, 1986.

28. Bernard Gwertzman, "NATO Faults U.S. on Intent to Drop 1979 Arms Treaty," *New York Times*, May 30, 1986.

29. David Hoffman, "Reagan Calls SALT II Dead; U.S. to Seek a 'Better Deal,'" *Washington Post*, June 13, 1986.

30. Matthew Evangelista, *Unarmed Forces: The Transnational Movement to End the Cold War* (Ithaca, NY: Cornell University Press, 1999), 274.

31. Brown, *Gorbachev Factor*, 231. Rhodes, *Arsenals of Folly*, chapter 1, provides an engrossing account of the Chernobyl disaster.

32. Garthoff, *Great Transition*, 278.

33. Edmund Morris, *Dutch: A Memoir of Ronald Reagan* (New York: Modern Library, 1999), 591.

34. Oberdorfer, *From the Cold War*, 188.

35. See Paul H. Nitze, with Ann M. Smith and Steven L. Rearden, *From Hiroshima to Glasnost: At the Center of Decision: A Memoir* (New York: Grove Weidenfeld, 1989), 366–89.

36. Oberdorfer, *From the Cold War*, 200–1.

37. Ibid., 196.

38. U.S. Memorandum of Conversation, Reagan-Gorbachev Final Conversation, October 12, 1986, 3:25–4:30 and 5:30 – 6:50 P.M., United States Department of State, October 16, 1986, reproduced as Document 15 in *The Reykjavik File: Previously Secret U.S. and Soviet Documents on the 1986 Reagan-Gorbachev Summit*, National Security Archive Electronic Briefing Book No. 203, posted October 13, 2006, ed. Dr. Svetlana Savranskaya and Thomas Blanton, 9, 11, http://www.gwu.edu/~nsarchiv/NSAEBB203/index.htm. The U.S. and Soviet accounts of these crucial meetings largely align. The main difference is that the Soviet transcript takes the form of a dialogue, recreating the words of the participants, whereas the U.S. memorandum generally summarizes or paraphrases the exchanges.

Some early accounts argue that Reagan was confused about the meaning of the different categories of weapons, and that he likely did not truly mean to offer total nuclear abolition. See, for example, Bob Schieffer and Gary Paul Gates, *The Acting President: Ronald Reagan and the Supporting Players Who Helped Him Create the Illusion That Held America Spellbound* (New York: Dutton, 1989), 282. But the emphasis on reducing ballistic missiles, as noted, followed customary U.S. logic. Reagan's proposal for nuclear abolition was reported consistently by all witnesses, and recent scholars have viewed it in light of his increasingly frequent public statements to the same effect, not as a lapse in concentration.

39. U.S. Memorandum, 12; Russian Transcript of Reagan-Gorbachev Reykjavik Talks: Part 4, 12 October 1986 (afternoon), published in FBIS-USR-93–121, September 20, 1993, reproduced as Document 16 in *Reykjavik File*, 7.

40. U.S. Memorandum, 12, 13; Russian Transcript, 7.

41. Russian Transcript, 8; U.S. Memorandum, 15.

42. Russian Transcript, 8.

43. Oberdorfer, *From the Cold War*, 209.

44. This was recalled by Donald Regan, who was with Reagan in the car. John Newhouse, *War and Peace in the Nuclear Age* (New York: Knopf, 1989), 397.

45. Oberdorfer, *From the Cold War*, 183.

46. Shultz, *Turmoil and Triumph*, 777.

47. Morris, *Dutch*, 599. These quotations are from a 1995 interview that Morris conducted with Hermannsson.

48. Garthoff, *Great Transition*, 525.

49. Strobe Talbott, *Master of the Game: Paul Nitze and the Nuclear Peace* (New York: Knopf, 1988), 330.

50. Ibid., 334; Frances FitzGerald, *Way Out There in the Blue: Reagan, Star Wars, and the End of the Cold War* (New York: Simon and Schuster, 2000), 397–400.

51. Shultz, *Turmoil and Triumph*, 989.

52. FitzGerald, *Way Out There*, 425.

53. Garthoff, *Great Transition*, 305.

54. Shultz, *Turmoil and Triumph*, 723.

55. Ibid., 890.

56. Lou Cannon, *President Reagan: The Role of a Lifetime* (New York: PublicAffairs, 2000), 695; John F. Kennedy, "Remarks in the Rudolf Wilde Platz, Berlin," June 26, 1963; Gerhard Peters and John T. Woolley, *The American Presidency Project*, http://www.presidency.ucsb.edu/ws/index.php?pid=9307.

57. The USSR had to destroy about 1,500 warheads, the United States, 350. Shultz, *Turmoil and Triumph*, 1006.

58. James Mann, *The Rebellion of Ronald Reagan: A History of the End of the Cold War* (New York: Viking, 2009), 275–76.

59. Brown, *Gorbachev Factor*, 238.

60. Leffler, *For the Soul of Mankind*, 400 (quoting Oberdorfer).

61. Talbott, *Master of the Game*, 363–64.

62. Newhouse, *War and Peace in the Nuclear Age*, 401.

63. Shultz, *Turmoil and Triumph*, 1085.

64. Garthoff, *Great Transition*, 344.

65. Hoffman, *Dead Hand*, 312.

66. Garthoff, *Great Transition*, 351.

67. Ronald Reagan, "Remarks and a Question-and-Answer Session with the Students and Faculty at Moscow State University," May 31, 1988. Gerhard Peters and John T. Woolley, *The American Presidency Project*, http://www.presidency.ucsb.edu/ws/index.php?pid=35897.

68. Shultz, *Turmoil and Triumph*, 1105.

69. Leffler, *For the Soul of Mankind*, 419–20. On the numbers of political prisoners, many of whom Gorbachev had released by this time, see ibid., 463. Amnesty International expressed concern as of 1986 that the true numbers were bigger. Ibid., 544n25.

70. Garthoff, *Great Transition*, 366.

71. Evangelista, *Unarmed Forces*, 316.

72. Garthoff, *Great Transition*, 388–89.

73. Ibid., 411–13.

74. Ibid., 420.

75. See Robert D. English, *Russia and the Idea of the West: Gorbachev, Intellectuals and the End of the Cold War* (New York: Columbia University Press, 2000).

76. See Richard Ned Lebow and Janice Gross Stein, "Reagan and the Russians," *Atlantic Monthly* 273 (February 1994): 35–37 and Mark Harrison, "A No-Longer-Useful Lie," *Hoover Digest*, January 21, 2009, http://www.hoover.org/publications/hoover-digest/article/5466.

77. Richard Pipes, *Vixi: Memoirs of a Non-Belonger* (New Haven, CT: Yale University Press, 2003), 210.

13. The Election of Willie Horton

1. See Jack W. Germond and Jules Witcover, *Whose Broad Stripes and Bright Stars? The Trivial Pursuit of the Presidency, 1988* (New York: Warner, 1989) for a detailed account. The Dukakis campaign later fired Donna Brazile, its deputy national field director, after she, in frustration at what she considered a double standard for Democrats and Republicans, urged reporters to investigate rumors that George Bush kept a mistress. "Dukakis Aide Resigns Over Remark on Bush," *New York Times*, October 21, 1988.

2. They were Bruce Babbitt, Joseph Biden, Dukakis, Richard Gephardt, Albert Gore, Jesse Jackson, and Paul Simon.

3. Germond and Witcover, *Whose Broad Stripes*, 310.

4. Roger Simon, "The Killer and the Candidate: How Willie Horton and George Bush Rewrote the Rules of Political Advertising," *Regardie's Magazine* 11, no. 2 (October 1990): 80–93.

5. Richard Stengel, "The Man Behind the Message," *Time*, August 22, 1988.

6. Robert Justin Goldstein, *Burning the Flag: The Great 1989–1990 American Flag Desecration Controversy* (Kent, OH: The Kent State University Press, 1996), 74.

7. Anthony Lewis, "Abroad at Home: Willie Horton Redux," *New York Times*, February 26, 2000.

8. Sidney Blumenthal, *Pledging Allegiance: The Last Campaign of the Cold War* (New York: HarperCollins, 1992), 296.

9. Kathleen Hall Jamieson, *Dirty Politics: Deception, Distraction, and Democracy* (New York: Oxford University Press, 1992), 22.

10. Blumenthal, *Pledging Allegiance*, 265.

11. John Brady, *Bad Boy: The Life and Politics of Lee Atwater* (Reading, MA: Addison Wesley, 1997), 182.

12. Elizabeth Drew, *Election Journal: Political Events of 1987–1988* (New York: William Morrow, 1989), 332. The group, for which Floyd Brown worked, was called the National Security Political Action Committee; it had a subgroup called Americans for Bush.

13. Brady, *Bad Boy*, 208.

14. Maureen Dowd, "Bush Paints Rival as Elitist, with 'Harvard Yard' Views," *New York Times*, June 10, 1988.

15. Blumenthal, *Pledging Allegiance*, 264.

16. Robin Toner, "Bush, in Enemy Waters, Says Rival Hindered Cleanup of Boston Harbor," *New York Times*, September 2, 1988; Philip Shabecoff, "Conservationists to Back Dukakis," *New York Times*, September 14, 1988; Robin Toner, "Dukakis Asserts Foe Somersaults on Environment," *New York Times*, September 18, 1988; Charles M. Haar, "Mr. Bush Sinks the Truth in Boston Harbor," *New York Times*, October 18, 1988.

17. Adam Clymer, "Democrats Use Humor and Scorn in Mounting Attack Against Bush," *New York Times*, July 20, 1988.

18. Walter V. Robinson, "Dukakis Sweeps to the Nomination; Jackson's Forces Make It Unanimous," *Boston Globe*, July 21, 1988.

19. Michael S. Dukakis, "'A New Era of Greatness for America': Address Accepting the Presidential Nomination at the Democratic National Convention in Atlanta," July 21, 1988, http://www.presidency.ucsb.edu/ws/index.php?pid=25961#axzz1KenoPhoo. Unless noted otherwise, subsequent references to presidential statements and nominating convention speeches are to this same online archive.

20. Blumenthal, *Pledging Allegiance*, 285.

21. Margaret Carlson, "A Tale of Two Childhoods," *Time*, June 20, 1988. The Bush camp also may have hoped to link Dukakis with mental illness through family history or association. Stelian Dukakis, the candidate's dead brother, had been unwell emotionally. Dukakis was first elected governor in 1974. After losing his reelection bid in 1978, he came back to regain the office in 1982.

22. Germond and Witcover, *Whose Broad Stripes*, 361.

23. Drew, in *Election Journal* (334), makes a connection between Dukakis's comment about corruption and Reagan's statement. Only minutes afterward, Reagan said "I don't think I should have said what I said," but he also maintained "that the medical history of a President is something that people have a right to know." Andrew Rosenthal, "Dukakis Releases Medical Details to Stop Rumors on Mental Health," *New York Times*, August 4, 1988.

24. Germond and Witcover, *Whose Broad Stripes*, 390; Blumenthal, *Pledging Allegiance*, 274.

25. Drew, *Election Journal*, 345.

26. George Bush, "Address Accepting the Presidential Nomination at the Republican National Convention in New Orleans," August 18, 1988, Gerhard Peters and John T. Woolley, *The American Presidency Project*, http://www.presidency.ucsb.edu/ws/index.php?pid=25955.

27. Blumenthal, *Pledging Allegiance*, 270.

28. Goldstein, *Burning the Flag*, 75, 76. No such photographs existed, and Mrs. Duka-kis responded simply, "It's outrageous. It did not happen." Drew, *Election Journal*, 252; Germond and Witcover, *Whose Broad Stripes*, 402. The story was ludicrous on its face; the candidate's wife had never been a radical.

29. Bush, "Address Accepting the Presidential Nomination."

30. Blumenthal, *Pledging Allegiance*, 303.

31. Ibid., 307–8.

32. Ibid., 313, 315.

33. Thomas Geoghegan, *Which Side Are You On? Trying to Be for Labor When It's Flat on Its Back* (New York: Plume, 1992), 281.

34. The woman was Donna Fournier Cuomo. It was never clear if Horton had liter-ally taken a hand in killing her brother. The political action committee sponsoring the tour was called the Committee for the Presidency, and it put up $2 million for this pur-pose. Jamieson, *Dirty Politics*, 22.

35. Ibid., 17–21, 34.

36. Brady, *Bad Boy*, 189.

37. Jamieson, *Dirty Politics*, 35.

38. For figures, see the results of the postelection Gallup Polls, at http://www.gallup.com/poll/9463/election-polls-vote-groups-19841988.aspx, and the *New York Times* survey of party preferences, published November 5, 1988, available at http://election.nytimes.com/2008/results/president/national-exit-polls.html.

39. Drew, *Election Journal*, 323.

40. Brady, *Bad Boy*, 217–18.

41. Karl Gerard Brandt, *Ronald Reagan and the House Democrats: Gridlock, Partisan-ship, and the Fiscal Crisis* (Columbia: University of Missouri Press, 2009), 126–29; Ju-lian E. Zelizer, *On Capitol Hill: The Struggle to Reform Congress and Its Consequences, 1948–2000* (Cambridge: Cambridge University Press, 2004), 215.

42. John M. Barry, *The Ambition and the Power* (New York: Viking, 1989), 6.

43. Zelizer, *On Capitol Hill*, 241, 242.

44. Don Phillips, "Top Wright Aide Quits Over Criminal Record," *Washington Post*, May 12, 1989; Robin Toner, "Wright Aide Quits Amid Furor on '73 Crime," *New York Times*, May 12, 1989. Mack's personal history was not unknown in Washington, but Small's decision to tell her story brought it a far wider airing.

45. Michael Oreskes, "The No. 3 Democrat," *New York Times*, May 27, 1989. Coelho's activities are detailed in Brooks Jackson, *Honest Graft: Big Money and the American Politi-cal Process*, rev. ed. (Washington, DC: Farragut, 1990).

46. This account is given in Barry, *Ambition and the Power*, 707, 744. According to Barry, the story may have been inspired by a February 1989 raid by Washington, DC, police of a gay prostitution ring that had implicated several Reagan and Bush adminis-tration officials. The insinuations against Foley also played on memories of scandals in 1973 and 1980 relating, respectively, to sexual affairs that Representatives Gerry Studds (Democrat of Massachusetts) and Daniel Crane (Republican of Illinois) had had with teenage male House pages.

47. Brady, *Bad Boy*, 241–43, 247.

48. Maureen Dowd, "After Budget Deal's Failure, President Treads Carefully," *New York Times*, October 27, 1990.

49. Herbert S. Parmet, *George Bush: The Life of a Lone Star Yankee* (New York: Scribner, 1997), 470.

50. David T. Courtwright, *No Right Turn: Conservative Politics in a Liberal America* (Cambridge, MA: Harvard University Press, 2010), 207–8.

51. In 1991, after the former Ku Klux Klan leader David Duke attracted national attention with a second-place finish, running as a Republican, in the Louisiana governor's primary election (thus qualifying for the final run-off election), the political calculus surrounding this issue shifted, and Bush signed a law little different than the one he had vetoed. Parmet, *George Bush*, 499.

52. Ibid., 424–25; Courtwright, *No Right Turn*, 209.

53. George Bush, "Address to the Nation on the National Drug Control Strategy," September 5, 1989, http://www.presidency.ucsb.edu/ws/?pid=17472.

54. Courtwright, *No Right Turn*, 205.

55. Goldstein, *Burning the Flag*, 72–73, 105–12 (quotation on 109).

56. Ibid., 153.

57. Ibid., 121.

14. The Free World

1. Charles Krauthammer, "The Reagan Doctrine," *Time*, April 1, 1985.

2. Stanley Karnow, *In Our Image: America's Empire in the Philippines* (New York: Ballantine, 1989), 366.

3. George P. Shultz, *Turmoil and Triumph: My Years as Secretary of State* (New York: Scribner's, 1993), 628, 617.

4. A new National Security Study Directive was adopted in January, 1985, calling Marcos both "part of the problem" and "part of the solution" in the Philippines. Walden Bello, *U.S. Sponsored Low-Intensity Conflict in the Philippines* (Food First Development Report No. 2) (San Francisco, CA: Institute for Food and Development Policy, 1987), 58.

5. Karnow, *In Our Image*, 414.

6. Alfred W. McCoy, *Policing America's Empire: The United States, the Philippines, and the Rise of the Surveillance State* (Madison: University of Wisconsin Press, 2009), 440; Karnow, *In Our Image*, 433.

7. Han Sung-Joo, "South Korea in 1987: The Politics of Democratization," *Asian Survey* 28, no. 1 (January 1988): 52–61; George Katsiaficas, *Asia's Unknown Uprisings Volume 1: South Korean Social Movements in the 20th Century* (Oakland, CA: PM Press, 2012), chapters 9–10. Kim Dae Jung was elected president in 1997 and brought momentous social and political reform to the ROK (without disturbing the U.S. military presence).

8. Raymond L. Garthoff, *The Great Transition: American-Soviet Relations and the End of the Cold War* (Washington, DC: Brookings Institution, 1994), 636.

9. See, for example, the editorial "Hailing the Butchers of Beijing," *New York Times*, December 12, 1989. Scowcroft, along with Deputy Secretary of State Lawrence Eagleburger, made a second trip to Beijing in December. Subsequently, their secret June visit became known. Garthoff, *Great Transition*, 643.

10. Tony Smith, *America's Mission: The United States and the Worldwide Struggle for Democracy in the Twentieth Century* (Princeton, NJ: Princeton University Press, 1994), 293, 290.

11. See the documents and commentary in Padraic Kenney, ed., *1989: Democratic Revolutions at the Cold War's End* (Boston: Bedford/St. Martin's, 2010), 100–121.

12. William M. LeoGrande, *Our Own Backyard: The United States in Central America, 1977–1992* (Chapel Hill: University of North Carolina Press, 1998), 507–8.

13. Ibid., 522.

14. Chamorro received 54.7 percent of the vote, Ortega 40.8 percent. Ibid., 561.

15. LeoGrande, *Our Own Backyard*, 574. The killers also murdered a housekeeper and her daughter on the university's premises. In 1992, two Salvadoran officers, including Colonel Guillermo Benavides, who ordered the murders, were convicted in El Salvador and sentenced to thirty years in prison. Those who did the actual killing went free. Ibid., 576.

16. Christian Smith, *Resisting Reagan: The U.S. Central America Peace Movement* (Chicago: University of Chicago Press, 1996), 287, 301, 309.

17. LeoGrande, *Our Own Backyard*, 585.

18. See John Dinges, *Our Man in Panama: The Shrewd Rise and Brutal Fall of Manuel Noriega* (New York: Random House, 1990) and Frederick Kempe, *Divorcing the Dictator: America's Bungled Affair with Noriega* (New York: G. P. Putnam's Sons, 1990).

19. Shultz, *Turmoil and Triumph*, 1073.

20. Brian R. Hamnett, *A Concise History of Mexico*, 2nd ed. (Cambridge: Cambridge University Press, 2006), 273; Andrew Reding, "How to Steal an Election: Mexico, 1988," *Mother Jones*, November 1988. The outgoing president in 1988, Miguel de la Madrid of the Partido Revolucionario Institucional, later admitted the fraud in his memoir. Ginger Thompson, "Ex-President in Mexico Casts New Light on Rigged 1988 Election," *New York Times*, March 9, 2004.

21. This information was reported to me by a former U.S. Air Force helicopter pilot who took part in the invasion.

22. William Branigin, "50 Kilos of Cocaine Turn Out to Be Tamales," *Washington Post*, January 23, 1990.

23. Robert Pear with James Brooke, "Rightists in U.S. Aid Mozambique Rebels," *New York Times*, May 22, 1988; E. A. Wayne, "Mozambique Rebels Deny Charges of Civilian Abuses," *Christian Science Monitor*, April 25, 1988.

24. James Scott, *Deciding to Intervene: The Reagan Doctrine and American Foreign Policy* (Durham, NC: Duke University Press, 1996), 207; Sean Gervasi and Sybil Wong, "The Reagan Doctrine and the Destabilization of Southern Africa," in *Western State Terrorism*, ed. Alexander George (New York: Routledge, Chapman and Hall, 1991), 245.

25. Nelson Mandela, *Long Walk to Freedom: The Autobiography of Nelson Mandela* (Boston: Little, Brown, 1994), 508.

26. Odd Arne Westad, *The Global Cold War: Third World Interventions and the Making of Our Times* (Cambridge: Cambridge University Press, 2007), 391.

27. David E. Hoffman, *The Dead Hand: The Untold Story of the Cold War Arms Race and Its Dangerous Legacy* (New York: Doubleday, 2009), 313, 315.

28. Michael R. Beschloss and Strobe Talbott, *At the Highest Levels: The Inside Story of the End of the Cold War* (Boston: Little, Brown, 1993), 4.

29. George Bush and Brent Scowcroft, *A World Transformed* (New York: Knopf, 1998), 4.

30. Beschloss and Talbott, *At the Highest Levels*, 87, 92.

31. This quotation comes from a February 1989 report of the International Department of the CPSU Central Committee. Jacques Levesque, "The Emancipation of Eastern Europe," in *Ending the Cold War: Interpretations, Causation, and the Study of International Relations*, ed. Richard K. Herrmann and Richard Ned Lebow (New York: Palgrave Macmillan, 2004), 111.

32. According to the Polish leader, Myaczyslaw Rakowski, Gorbachev merely inquired "what is going on." Vladislav M. Zubok, *A Failed Empire: The Soviet Union in the Cold War from Stalin to Gorbachev* (Chapel Hill: University of North Carolina Press, 2009), 323.

33. For a vivid account, see Timothy Garton Ash, *The Magic Lantern: The Revolution of '89 Witnessed in Warsaw, Budapest, Berlin and Prague* (New York: Random House, 1990).

34. Address by His Excellency Vaclav Havel, President of the Czechoslovak Socialist Republic (House of Representatives), February 21, 1990, http://thomas.loc.gov/cgi-bin/query/F?r101:5:./temp/~r101d1aP0P:e0:.

35. In general, see Philip Zelikow and Condoleezza Rice, *Germany Unified and Europe Transformed: A Study in Statecraft* (Cambridge, MA: Harvard University Press, 1995).

36. Mary Elise Sarotte, *1989: The Struggle to Create Post–Cold War Europe* (Princeton, NJ: Princeton University Press, 2009), 205.

37. Zubok, *Failed Empire*, 319.

38. Beschloss and Talbott, *At the Highest Levels*, 132, 81.

39. Bill Keller, "Gorbachev, in Finland, Disavows Any Right of Regional Intervention," *New York Times*, October 26, 1989.

40. Sarotte, *1989*, 42–43, 45.

41. Ibid., 110–15, 180–86.

42. Ibid., 128.

43. Beschloss and Talbott, *At the Highest Levels*, 176.

44. See Mark R. Beissinger, "The Intersection of Ethnic Nationalism and People Power Tactics in the Baltic States, 1987–91," in *Civil Resistance and Power Politics: The Experience of Non-Violent Action from Gandhi to the Present*, ed. Adam Roberts and Timothy Garton Ash (New York: Oxford University Press, 2009), 231–46.

45. Beschloss and Talbott, *At the Highest Levels*, 205.

46. Sarotte, *1989*, 158.

47. The pointlessness of violence became clear in January 1991, when Soviet troops shot and killed fifteen Lithuanian protesters in an effort to retake government buildings. Other violence followed in smaller incidents in Lithuania and elsewhere. Gorbachev claimed that military commanders had given the order to use deadly force without his authorization. He himself condemned the violence, amid an international outcry, and the departure of the Baltic republics from the Soviet Union was only a matter of time. Bush and Scowcroft, *A World Transformed*, 496–97, 513.

48. Melvyn P. Leffler, *For the Soul of Mankind: The United States, the Soviet Union, and the Cold War* (New York: Hill and Wang, 2007), 450.

49. Andrew Bacevich, *The New American Militarism: How Americans Are Seduced by War* (New York: Oxford University Press, 2005), 44, 192.

50. Robert Gates, who moved from the NSC to the CIA in late 1979, and later became Casey's chief deputy, stated in his memoir—and Brzezinski later confirmed in an interview with a French newspaper—that U.S. aid began six months before the Soviet invasion. Brzezinski stated that, in undertaking this policy, the Carter administration "knowingly increased the probability" of the invasion. Robert M. Gates, *From the Shadows: The Ultimate Insider's Story of Five Presidents and How They Won the Cold War* (New York: Simon and Schuster, 1996), 146–49; "The CIA's Intervention in Afghanistan: Interview with Zbigniew Brzezinski, Jimmy Carter's National Security Advisor," *Le Nouvel Observateur*, January 15–21, 1998, posted in English at http://www.globalresearch.ca/articles/BRZ110A.html. See John Prados, "Notes on the CIA's Secret War in Afghanistan," *Journal of American History* 89, no. 2 (September 2002): 467.

51. Steve Coll, *Ghost Wars: The Secret History of the CIA, Afghanistan, and bin Laden from the Soviet Invasion to September 10, 2001* (New York: Penguin, 2005), 102. According to Westad, Brzezinski already had forged this agreement before Carter left office. Westad, *Global Cold War*, 329.

52. Coll, *Ghost Wars*, 62.

53. Ibid., 125; Garthoff, *Great Transition*, 712. Reagan did not sign a new finding. Instead, he authorized these new methods in National Security Decision Directive 166.

54. Alan J. Kuperman, "The Stinger Missile and U.S. Intervention in Afghanistan," *Political Science Quarterly* 114, no. 2 (Summer 1999): 219–63, gives a thorough evaluation of the Stinger's effectiveness.

55. Robert Dreyfuss, *Devil's Game: How the United States Helped Unleash Fundamentalist Islam* (New York: Metropolitan Books, 2005), 291.

56. Coll, *Ghost Wars*, 155.

57. Leffler, *For the Soul of Mankind*, 404.

58. Coll, *Ghost Wars*, 158.

59. Ibid., 176–77, 194.

60. Ibid., 217.

61. Efraim Karsh, *The Iran–Iraq War, 1980–1988* (Oxford: Osprey Publishing, 2002), gives a minimum figure of two hundred thousand Iraqi deaths. The numbers of Iranian deaths are a matter of greater dispute.

62. Robert Fisk, *The Great War for Civilization: The Conquest of the Middle East* (New York: Knopf, 2005), 220.

63. See Karsh, *Iran–Iraq War*, 50–51, 57–59 on the tanker war.

64. Robert Fisk, *Great War for Civilization*, 267. See John Barry and Roger Charles, "Sea of Lies," *Newsweek*, July 13, 1992, for a highly critical account of U.S. government efforts to cover up the truth regarding the incident. In 1996, the U.S. and Iranian governments reached a legal settlement, according to which the United States agreed to pay a total of $61.8 million, or a bit more than $213,000 per passenger on IR655 killed. But the United States refused to admit legal culpability or apologize to Iran.

65. "U.S. Embassy Baghdad to Washington (Saddam's message of friendship to George Bush) [*declassified 1998*]," July 25, 1990, www.margaretthatcher.org/document/110705.

66. Flora Lewis, "Between-Lines Disaster," *New York Times*, September 19, 1990.

67. "Questions and Answers," *New York Times*, August 6, 1990.

68. Michael Kelly, *Martyrs' Day: Chronicle of a Small War* (New York: Random House, 1993), 6.

69. Fisk, *Great War for Civilization*, 597. Schwarzkopf (son of a U.S. general who had helped overthrow the democratic government of Iran in 1953 and replace it with the shah's regime) may have been referring to the notorious case of Kitty Genovese, a (young) woman who was raped and murdered in New York City in 1964 while (according to urban legend) her neighbors listened and took no action.

70. Anthony Swofford, *Jarhead: A Marine's Chronicle of the Gulf War and Other Battles* (New York: Pocket, 2005), 11.

71. Hoffman, *Dead Hand*, 352.

72. Beschloss and Talbott, *At the Highest Levels*, 277–78.

73. Francis Fukuyama, "The End of History?" *National Interest*, no. 16 (Summer 1989): 3–18.

74. Charles Krauthammer, "The Unipolar Moment," *Foreign Affairs* 70, no. 1 (Winter 1990/1991): 23–33.

75. Paul Kennedy, *The Rise and Fall of the Great Powers: Economic Change and Military Conflict from 1500 to 2000* (New York: Random House, 1987).

76. Swofford, *Jarhead*, 18.

15. Top of the Heap

1. Kim Phillips, "Lotteryville, USA" (1995), in *Commodify Your Dissent: Salvos from The Baffler*, ed. Thomas Frank and Matt Weiland (New York: Norton, 1997), 237.

2. The lyrics "top of the heap" are from "Theme to *New York, New York*," included in Frank Sinatra, *Trilogy* (1980), Warner Bros. B000002KDK, CD, 1990.

3. Judith Stein, *Pivotal Decade: How the United States Traded Factories for Finance in the Seventies* (New Haven, CT: Yale University Press, 2010) makes the case for the 1970s.

4. Avi Feller and Chad Stone, Center on Budget and Policy Priorities, "Top 1 Percent of Americans Reaped Two-Thirds of Income Gains in Last Economic Expansion," September 9, 2009, 1 (Figure 1), 3 (Figure 3), http://www.cbpp.org .

5. The bottom income quintile's average after-tax income was $14,800 in both 1980 and 1990. The second quintile's average rose 3 percent, from $29,800 to $30,700; the third (or middle) quintile's average rose 5.6 percent, from $42,600 to $45,000. The top 1 percent's average was $339,200 in 1980 and $586,000 in 1990. See "Number of Households, Average Income and Income Shares, and Income Category Minimums for All Households, by Household Income Category, 1979–2007," among the tables linked to Congressional Budget Office, *Average Federal Income Taxes by Income Group*, www.cbo .gov/sites/default/files/cbofiles/attachments/all_tables2010.pdf.

6. The income share of the top 1 percent rose from 9 percent in 1970 to 10 percent in 1980 (a 10 percent increase) and then to 14.3 percent in 1990 (a 43 percent increase from the 1980 figure). The income share of the top 0.01 percent rose from 1 percent in 1970 to 1.3 percent in 1980 (a 30 percent increase) and then to 2.3 percent in 1990 (a decennial increase of 76.9 percent). The figures for income share were calculated by Thomas Piketty and Emmanuel Saez and are available at http://elsa.berkeley.edu/~saez/

TabFig2007.xls. On earnings in the 1970s, see Lawrence F. Katz and Kevin M. Murphy, "Changes in Relative Wages, 1963–1987: Supply and Demand Factors," *Quarterly Journal of Economics* 107, no. 1 (February 1992): 41.

7. The Fair Labor Standards Act of 1938 created a federal minimum wage for the first time. Before the 1980s, the longest it had gone unchanged was six years—from 1950 to 1956. "Federal Minimum Wage Rates Under the Fair labor Standards Act," http://www.dol.gov/whd/minwage/chart.htm. See John Bound and Richard B. Freeman, "What Went Wrong? The Erosion of Relative Earnings and Employment Among Young Black Men in the 1980s," *Quarterly Journal of Economics* 107, no. 1 (February 1992): 217.

8. Juliet B. Schor, *The Overworked American: The Unexpected Decline of Leisure* (New York: Basic Books, 1993), 30.

9. David O. Beim, "It's All About Debt," *Forbes.com*, March 19, 2009, http://www.forbes.com/2009/03/19/household-debt-gdp-market-beim.html. Also see the chart reproduced in Laura Conaway, "Household Debt Vs. GDP," *Planet Money Blog*, February 27, 2009, http://www.npr.org/blogs/money/2009/02/household_debt_vs_gdp.html, and Reuven Glick and Kevin J. Lansing, "U.S. Household Deleveraging and Future Consumption Growth," *FRBSF* [*Federal Reserve Bank of San Francisco*] *Economic Letter*, No. 2009-16, May 15, 2009, http://www.frbsf.org/publications/economics/letter/2009/el2009-16.pdf.

10. Kevin Phillips, *The Politics of Rich and Poor: Wealth and the American Electorate in the Reagan Aftermath* (New York: Random House, 1990), 80.

11. The proportion of those whose incomes exceeded this threshold was higher before 1983. The income limit for Social Security taxation was $25,900 in 1980 and $51,300 in 1990. Kevin Whitman and Dave Shoffner, *The Evolution of Social Security's Taxable Minimum*, U.S. Social Security Administration, Office of Retirement and Disability Policy, Policy Brief No. 2011-02 (September 2011), http://www.socialsecurity.gov/policy/docs/policybriefs/pb2011-02.html.

12. These growth numbers are derived from the U.S. Department of Commerce, Bureau of Economic Analysis, in Table 1.1.3, "Real Gross Domestic Product, Quantity Indexes," within National Income and Product Tables, Section 1—Domestic Product and Income, http://www.bea.gov/itable/index.cfm. I calculated the percentage increases by noting the differences between the inflation-adjusted measures of GDP at decennial intervals.

13. John W. Sloan, *The Reagan Effect: Economics and Presidential Leadership* (Lawrence: University Press of Kansas, 1999), 236.

14. For figures on the federal government's taxing and spending, see Table 1.2, "Summary of Receipts, Outlays, and Surpluses or Deficits as Percentages of GDP: 1930–2017," in the U.S. Office of Management and Budget's Historical Tables, http://www.whitehouse.gov/omb/budget/Historicals. For the overall tax burden of government, see the figures calculated by the Tax Policy Center, run jointly by the Urban Institute and the Brookings Institution and presented in "Federal, State and Local Government Current Receipts and Expenditures: 1929–2010," http://www.taxpolicycenter.org/taxfacts/listdocs.cfm?topic3id=21&topic2id=20.

15. The nation's debt had stood at 28.2 percent of GDP at the end of 1970. Congressional Budget Office, *Historical Data on the Federal Debt*, August 5, 2010, http://www.cbo.gov/publication/21728 (data in spreadsheet file linked to this page).

16. Sloan, *Reagan Effect*, 233.

17. This data is from the tables gathered in Barry Hirsch and David Macpherson, "*U.S. Historical Tables*: Union Membership, Coverage, Density, and Employment, 1973–2010," within "Unionstats.com: Union Membership and Coverage Database from the CPS [Current Population Survey]," http://unionstats.gsu.edu.

18. Sloan, *Reagan Effect*, 236.

19. Carolyn Friday and Joshua Hammer, "'Now They're Just Rich,'" *Newsweek*, November 13, 1989; David E. Sanger, "Worried About Reaction in U.S., Japanese Assess Investment Policy," *New York Times*, November 24, 1989; Phillips, *Politics of Rich and Poor*, 140.

20. Phillips, *Politics of Rich and Poor*, 123.

21. Michael Lewis, *Liar's Poker: Rising Through the Wreckage on Wall Street* (New York: Norton, 1989), 171.

22. Greta R. Krippner, *Capitalizing on Crisis: The Political Origins of the Rise of Finance* (Cambridge, MA: Harvard University Press, 2011), 33 (Figure 3).

23. Hirsch and Macpherson, "Union Membership, Coverage, Density, and Employment."

24. Thomas Piketty and Emmanuel Saez, "Income Inequality in the United States, 1913–1998," *Quarterly Journal of Economics* 108, no. 1 (February 2003): 3. Piketty expands greatly on these data and their implications in Thomas Piketty, *Capital in the Twenty-First Century* (Cambridge, MA: Belknap Press of Harvard University Press, 2014).

25. These figures, compiled by the Economic Policy Institute, compare the average total compensation of CEOs in 350 large publicly traded companies to the average total compensation (including benefits) of the approximately 80 percent of U.S. workers classified by the authors as nonsupervisory. These ratios are lower than some found elsewhere. Lawrence Michel, Jared Bernstein, and Heidi Shierholz, *The State of Working America 2008/2009* (Economic Policy Institute; Ithaca, NY: ILR Press, 2009), 221 (Figure 3AE).

26. Connie Bruck, *The Predator's Ball: The Inside Story of Drexel Burnham and the Rise of the Junk Bond Raiders* (New York: Penguin, 1989), 135.

27. Ibid., 197, 230.

28. James B. Stewart, *Den of Thieves* (New York: Simon and Schuster Paperbacks, 1992), 500–3.

29. Andrei Shleifer and Robert W. Vishny, "The Takeover Wave of the 1980s," *Science*, New Series 249, no. 4970 (August 17, 1990): 745–49; Bengt Holmstrom and Steven N. Kaplan, "Corporate Governance and Merger Activity in the United States: Making Sense of the 1980s and 1990s," *Journal of Economic Perspectives* 15, no. 2 (Spring 2001): 121–44; Sanjai Bhagat, Andrei Shleifer, Robert W. Vishny, Gregg Jarrel, and Lawrence Summers, "Hostile Takeovers in the 1980s: The Return to Corporate Specialization," *Brookings Papers on Economic Activity: Microeconomics* 1990 (1990): 1–84. Some qualifications of this positive evaluation can be found in Andrei Shleifer and Lawrence H. Summers, "Breach of Trust in Hostile Takeovers," in *Corporate Takeovers: Causes and Consequences*, ed. Alan J. Auerbach (Chicago: University of Chicago Press, 1988), 33–67. The broad outlines of the changing shape and scope of American business firms can be followed in Gerald F. Davis, Kristina A. Diekmann, and Catherine H. Tinsley, "The Decline and Fall of the Conglomerate Firm in the 1980s: The Deinstitutionalization of

an Organizational Form," *American Sociological Review* 59, no. 4 (August 1994): 547–70, and Naomi R. Lamoreaux, Daniel M. G. Raff, and Peter Temin, "Beyond Markets and Hierarchies: Toward a New Synthesis of American Business History," *American Historical Review* 108, no. 2 (April 2003): 404–33.

30. Gerald F. Davis, *Managed by the Markets: How Finance Reshaped America* (New York: Oxford University Press, 2009), 90–91.

31. Alfred D. Chandler, Jr. with Takashi Hikino and Andrew von Nordenflycht, *Inventing the Electronic Century: The Epic Story 'of the Consumer Electronics and Computer Industries* (New York: The Free Press, 2001), 141.

32. Ibid., 139.

33. Stephen Manes and Paul Andrews, *Gates: How Microsoft's Mogul Reinvented an Industry—and Made Himself the Richest Man in America* (New York: Doubleday, 1993), 446.

34. Nelson Lichtenstein, *The Retail Revolution: How Wal-Mart Created a Brave New World of Business* (New York: Picador, 2010), 42, 201.

35. Ibid., 55.

36. Ibid., 122, 170–71.

37. Maury Klein, *The Change Makers: From Carnegie to Gates, How the Great Entrepreneurs Transformed Ideas Into Industries* (New York: Times Books, 2003), 214.

38. Lichtenstein, *Retail Revolution*, 269.

39. Marc Levinson, *The Box: How the Shipping Container Made the World Smaller and the World Economy Bigger* (Princeton, NJ: Princeton University Press, 2006).

40. Lichtenstein, *Retail Revolution*, 201, 203.

41. Levinson, *Box*, 265.

42. Walter LaFeber, *Michael Jordan and the New Global Capitalism* (New York: Norton, 2002), 54.

43. Ibid., 16.

44. Ibid., 90–91.

45. Krippner, *Capitalizing on Crisis*, 31 (Figure 1).

46. Andrew Hacker, *Money: Who Has How Much and Why* (New York: Scribner, 1997), 188.

47. Ibid., 187.

48. Linda Greenhouse, "Supreme Court, 5-4, Narrowing Roe v. Wade, Upholds Sharp State Limits on Abortions," *New York Times*, July 4, 1989; Al Kamen, "Supreme Court Restricts Right to Abortion, Giving States Wide Latitude for Regulation," *Washington Post*, July 4, 1989.

49. Megan Rosenfeld, "Across the Nation, Reactions Divided on Court's Abortion Ruling," *Washington Post*, July 4, 1989.

50. Dan Balz, "Grass Roots: New Turf for Abortion-Rights Forces," *Washington Post*, July 22, 1989; Dan Balz, "NOW Calls for Expanded Bill of Rights, New Party," *Washington Post*, July 24, 1989.

51. Bush's son, George W. Bush, restored the family honor by defeating Richards when she ran for reelection in 1994. The rest, of course, is history.

52. Celia Morris, *Storming the Statehouse: Running for Governor with Ann Richards and Dianne Feinstein* (New York: Charles Scribner's Sons, 1992), 39, 72–77, 101–2.

53. Richards got 24 percent of Republican women's votes and 58.5 percent of independent women's votes. Independent men gave Williams 59.7 percent of their votes,

but only 18.6 percent of male Democrats crossed over to vote for him. Sue Tolleson-Rinehart and Jeanie R. Stanley, *Claytie and the Lady: Ann Richards, Gender, and Politics in Texas* (Austin: University of Texas Press, 1994), 109 (Table 5.1). The total vote was 49.6 percent for Richards to 47.1 percent for Williams. Ibid., 59.

54. Ibid., 69, 98–99.

55. Morris, *Storming the Statehouse*, 161.

56. Ibid., 174.

57. See Susan Welch and Jon Hibbing, "Financial Conditions, Gender and Voting in American National Elections," *Journal of Politics* 54, no. 1 (February 1992): 197–213; Carole Kennedy Chaney, R. Michael Alvarez, and Jonathan Nagler, "Explaining the Gender Gap in U.S. Presidential Elections, 1980–1992," *Political Research Quarterly* 51, no. 2 (June 1998): 311–39; Laura R. Winsky Mattei and Franco Mattei, "If Men Stayed Home . . . : The Gender Gap in Recent Congressional Elections," *Political Research Quarterly* 51, no. 2 (June 1998): 411–36.

58. William Kristol and Robert Kagan, "Toward a Neo-Reaganite Foreign Policy," *Foreign Affairs* 75, no. 4 (July–August 1996): 23.

59. Ronald Reagan, "Farewell Address to the Nation," January 11, 1989. Gerhard Peters and John T. Woolley, *The American Presidency Project*, http://www.presidency.ucsb.edu/ws/?pid=29650.

60. Ronald Reagan, *An American Life: The Autobiography* (New York: Simon and Schuster, 1990).

61. David T. Courtwright, *No Right Turn: Conservative Politics in a Liberal America* (Cambridge, MA: Harvard University Press, 2010), 150.

62. Herbert S. Parmet, *George Bush: The Life of a Lone Star Yankee* (New York: Scribner, 1997), 394–96, 439–40.

63. Tom Wolfe, *The Bonfire of the Vanities* (New York: Farrar, Straus & Giroux, 1987); Phillips, *Politics of Rich and Poor*.

64. Peggy Noonan, *When Character Was King: A Story of Ronald Reagan* (New York: Viking, 2001), 248, 249.

65. Reagan, *American Life*, 478.

66. The Commission on the Truth for El Salvador received its mandate from the United Nations in 1992. Its report, *From Madness to Hope: The 12-Year War in El Salvador*, is available on the website of the United States Institute of Peace, http://www.usip.org/files/file/ElSalvador-Report.pdf. Also see Charles D. Brocket, "El Salvador: The Long Journey from Violence to Reconciliation," *Latin American Research Review* 29, no. 3 (1994): 174–87. Similarly, in 1996, a United Nations–brokered set of peace accords ended Guatemala's civil conflict and established a Commission for Historical Clarification, whose report, *Guatemala: Memory of Silence*, concluded that government forces committed 93 percent of atrocities in the country during the period considered. The report is available at the web site of Yale University's Genocide Studies Program, http://shr.aaas.org/guatemala/ceh/report/english/toc.html.

Index

247, 248; and China, 263–64; as CIA director, 36; and civil rights legislation, 259, 349n51; and the culture wars, 257–60 (see also Bush, George H. W.: and the 1988 presidential campaign); Democratic fear of, 266; and the fall of the Soviet Union, 269–74; fiscal policy, 257–58; and Gorbachev, 3, 225, 269; governing approach, 257–58; and Iran-Contra, 182, 184–85, 190, 195–96, 198, 242, 248, 335n14; and the Iran hostage crisis, 305n57; and the minimum wage, 281; and Panama, 267–68; and the Persian Gulf and Middle East, 274, 276, 277–79; and the Philippines, 83, 262; and Reagan's economic policy, 34; and the Republican attack on Foley, 257; and the savings-and-loan crisis, 205; and South Africa, 268, 269; Soviet policy, 224, 225, 269
Bush, George W. (son), 62, 356n51
Bush, Neil, 294
business, 41, 43–46, 62, 95, 125–26, 285–89. See also banking industry; deregulation; Wall Street
Butch Cassidy and the Sundance Kid (1969 film), 237
Byrd, Robert, 49
Byrne, Jane, 142

Cabey, Darrell, 152
California: 1990 gubernatorial race, 292; anti-discrimination laws, 12, 213; immigrants in, 81, 159; JBS in, 12; policing in, 157–58; and presidential campaigns, 19, 171, 254; Proposition 13 (property tax bill), 20; Reagan as governor of, 13–14. See also Los Angeles; San Francisco; and specific individuals
Canada, 40–41
Cannon, Lou, 8, 49–50, 202, 334n2, 337n35
capital gains tax, 20, 44, 61–62, 255
capitalism: in China, 263; Reaganist belief in virtues of, 1, 125, 207, 223; as social norm, 3. See also business; Wall Street; wealthy, the
Cárdenas, Cuauhtémoc, 267
Caribbean basin, 101–2. See also Central America; Cuba; Grenada
Carranza, Nicolas (Col.), 105
Carson, Johnny, 121
Carter, Billy, 19
Carter, Jimmy: 1976 campaign and election, 16, 174; 1980 campaign, 11, 21–29, 99–100, 173, 174, 305n58, 63; and Central America, 39, 77, 79; character, 7, 19–20; domestic policies, 25–26, 43; economic policy, 16–18, 20, 29, 35, 44, 85, 303n23); foreign policy, 19, 36, 274, 314n61 (see also Carter, Jimmy: and the Soviet Union); and human rights, 71, 82; inauguration, 47, 110; and the Iran hostage crisis, 18, 114; on Marcos, 83; military

spending/buildup under, 19, 26, 39–40, 54, 67, 68–69, 303n30, 307n32; and nuclear nonproliferation, 27, 110; presidency, 16–20; social skills, 49; and the Soviet Union, 18–19, 27, 36, 68–69, 274
Casey, William ("Bill"): and anti-Soviet policy, 36–37, 72; as campaign manager, 21; and Central America policy, 78, 82, 165; credibility of, 165; foreign policy and Reagan's relationship with, 70, 82; on the Grenada invasion's message, 115; and Iran-Contra operations, 182, 184, 185, 192, 195–97; and the Iran hostage crisis, 305n57; and the Lebanon war, 187, 336n27; and the national security adviser vacancy, 113; and North, 182
Catholics, 16, 28, 173–74
CBO. See Congressional Budget Office
CDF. See Conservative Democratic Forum
Celeste, Richard, 205
Center for Creative Non-Violence (CCNV), 146
Central America: American missionaries in, 39, 73–74, 79; Reagan policy in, 39, 66, 72–73, 76–83, 101–6, 238, 265–66, 296–97 (see also Iran-Contra scandal); refugees/immigrants from, 80–81, 158. See also Latin America; and specific countries
Central Intelligence Agency (CIA): and the Afghan mujahideen, 275, 276; agents killed in bombing of U.S. embassy in Beirut, 111; and arms sales to Iran, 191, 198 (see also Iran-Contra scandal); and Nicaragua, 106, 165–66, 266; personnel spying for the USSR, 228; and secret Contra funding/operations, 106, 184–86, 195 (see also Iran-Contra scandal); Soviet analysis audited, 36. See also Casey, William
Central Park jogger, 155–56
CEO pay, 284, 355n25
Challenger disaster, 201
Chamorro, Violeta, 266, 350n14
Chapman, Tracy, 160
Chariots of Fire (1981 film), 119
Charles, Ray, 172
Chen, Vincent, 151–52
Cheney, Richard ("Dick"), 62
Chernenko, Konstantin, 117, 225
Chernobyl nuclear disaster, 229–30
Chicago, 141, 142–43, 149–50
children: advertising aimed at, 45; and AIDS, 133, 212; busing of, 8; crack epidemic and, 124; drug education, 122, 267; homeless children, 144, 146; predation and violence against, 131, 139, 147–48, 260, 327n37; programs for needy children, 60, 91–93, 95, 143–44, 310n51, 316n29; Quayle interviewed by, 250. See also Pledge of Allegiance
Chile, 74, 264–65

176–77 (*see also* Southern Democrats); conservative publications, 72, 127–28 (*see also specific publications*); conservatives as percentage of population, 4, 300n7; crisis of legitimacy, 202–3; cultural split, 2, 128 (*see also* culture; hedonism; traditional values); and the culture wars, 259–60; détente opposed, 15, 35–40; economic conservatism, 85, 88–89 (*see also* economic policy); and economic inequality, 280–82; gay conservatives, 128–29; and hedonism, 3, 129–30; outraged by Reagan tax hikes, 95; and patriotism, 10, 292 (*see also* patriotism and national pride); post-1990 relationship to Reaganism, 292; public debate framed by, 4–5; public dissatisfaction with, 201–2; and racial equality, 7, 8 (*see also* civil rights; race and racial [in]equality); and the Reagan legacy, 293; Reagan reluctant to be called conservative, 22; rightward tide hailed, 40–41; and the Third World, 72–73; voluntarism preferred over government, 251. *See also* neoconservatives; Reaganism; Republican Party; *and specific individuals, organizations, issues, and topics*

Contras. *See* Iran-Contra scandal; Nicaragua

Coolidge, Calvin, 23, 174

corruption: in Congress, 204–5, 206–7, 255–56; in the Reagan administration, 6–7, 164–65, 177, 205–6, 294, 331n8; and the savings-and-loan crisis, 202, 204–5, 339n11; on Wall Street, 202, 207–9, 284–85

COS (Conservative Opportunity Society), 255

Cosby, Bill, and *The Cosby Show*, 141–42, 288

Costa Rica, 265

Country (1984 film), 147

Courtwright, David T., 294, 299n3

CPD. *See* Committee on the Present Danger

crack cocaine, 122–24. *See also* drugs.

crime: crack and, 123; fear of, 139, 148–49; gangsta rap and, 157; murder for shoes, 288; police powers broadened, 124; prison construction, 5, 259; race and, 149–58, 327n40, 328n43, 328–29n62; sodomy as, 133; war on, 5, 124; Willie Horton case, 245–46, 250, 253–54. *See also* gangs; drugs

criminal justice system: and African Americans and the poor, 7, 151, 154–55, 157–58; defendants' rights, 148–49; drug war and police powers, 124; growth of, 5; incarceration rates, 5, 124, 149

Crist, David, 111

Crocker, Chester, 268

Crouch, Stanley, 144, 288

Crowe, William (Adm.), 262

Cuba: 1984 Summer Olympics boycotted, 169; and Angola, 38, 73; blockade suggested, 24; Cuban refugees, 80, 158; and Grenada, 102,

114–15; Haig on, 79; and the Nicaraguan Contras, 77; and terrorism, 71

culture: Carter on materialism, 19–20; culture wars, 241, 257–60; drugs and, 121–24 (*see also* drugs); glitz, 210; of greed, 125, 209 (*see also* corruption); hedonism vs. traditionalism, 2, 119–20, 292, 296, 299n3 (*see also* hedonism; traditional values); and homosexuality (*see* homosexuality); liberal trend among general population, 299n3, 300n7; music, 99, 136–38, 144, 156–57, 160; Olliemania, 218–19; postmodernism, 134–36; rap/hip-hop culture, 156–57; Reaganism's influence on, 2, 3; rising black middle class, 141–42; Wall Street culture, 125–26, 208 (*see also* Wall Street); wealth/luxury emphasized, 119–21; yuppie culture, 126–27. *See also* fear; patriotism and national pride; race and racial (in)equality

Curran, James, 131

Czechoslovakia, 270–71

Daily Oklahoman, 93

D'Amato, Alfonse, 207

Daniloff, Nicholas, 228, 230

Darman, Richard, 32, 52, 162

Dart, Justin, 32

Dartmouth Review, 127

D'Aubuisson, Roberto, 73

Davies, Gareth, 95

Davis, Mike, 159

Day After, The (ABC, 1983), 116

Deaver, Michael, 6, 51–52, 89, 113, 183, 205

de Borchgrave, Arnaud, 72

debt, federal, 283, 354n14. *See also* deficits, federal

debt, household, 281–82

deconstructionism, 134

deficits, federal: under Carter, 18; Deficit Reduction Act (1984), 164; Gramm-Rudman law and, 178, 258, 333n58; Reagan budgets and tax cuts and, 55–56, 60, 62–63, 282–83. *See also* debt, federal

deindustrialization. *See* manufacturing sector

de Klerk, F. W., 269

DeLillo, Don, 134–35

democracy, spread of, 261–69, 278. *See also* Warsaw Pact nations

Democratic Party: and the 1982 budget, 56–57, 58; and the 1990 budget, 258; and the 1980 election, 28–30; and the 1982 midterm elections, 96–98; and the 1984 presidential campaign and election, 166–69, 171–72, 174–77 (*see also* Mondale, Walter); and the 1986 midterm elections, 201; and the 1988 presidential campaign and election, 242–43, 248–49, 254–55, 346nn1,2 (*see also* Dukakis, Michael); and African American voters,

Organization of Petroleum Exporting Countries (OPEC), 16, 17, 302n16
organized labor: 1981–82 recession and, 87–88; and Democratic campaigns, 252–53; FIRE sector's unionization rate, 284; influence of, 41; and Mondale, 171; power eroded, 86–87, 88; strikes, 85–87; as target of Reagan administration, 44; unemployment a concern for, 17; union jobs lost, 283 (*see also* manufacturing sector); Wal-Mart and, 287
Ornstein, Norman, 97, 317n54
Ortega, Daniel, 194, 265, 350n14. *See also* Nicaragua
Owen, Robert, 186

Packwood, Bob, 96
Paine, Thomas, 2, 5, 23, 295
Pakistan, 274, 276
Palestine Liberation Organization (PLO), 66, 76
Palestinians, 19, 71, 75, 187–88
Palme, Olof, and the Palme Commission, 227, 343n18
Panama, 14, 267–68
Pan American Airlines Flight 103, 193
PATCO (Professional Air Traffic Controllers Organization), 85–87
patriotism and national pride: 1988 presidential campaign and, 247, 250–51, 253 (*see also* Pledge of Allegiance); American flag, 251, 259–60, 348n28; conservatism and, 10, 292; Dukakis, the Pledge of Allegiance bill, and the 1988 election, 244–46; Reagan and, 4, 10, 26, 161–62, 169–70, 172, 201, 295; Vietnam War's impact on, 4, 14
peaceful coexistence principle, 237–38
Pennsylvania, 19, 28, 168
Pentagon. *See* military, U.S.
People Like Us (Moyers; CBS, 1982), 94
Perelman, Richard, 285
Perle, Richard, 35–37, 68, 104
Perpich, Rudy, 87
Persian Gulf, 274, 276–78. *See also* Middle East; *and specific countries*
personal attacks, as political tactic, 255–57, 348n46. *See also* Bork, Robert; Dukakis, Michael
Petrov, Stanislav (Lt. Col., USSR), 113
Philippines, 82–83, 163, 261–63, 314n61, 349n4
Phillips, Kevin, 295
Pickens, T. Boone, 125
Pickering, Thomas, 105
Piketty, Thomas, 284
Pinochet, Augosto, 74, 264–65
Pipes, Richard, 36, 67, 70–71, 72, 239
Pledge of Allegiance, 244–45, 250, 253. *See also* elections: 1988 presidential campaign and election

Plunkitt, George Washington, 204
Podhoretz, Norman, 36–37
Poindexter, John, 191–98, 219–20, 334–35n7
Poland, 269–70, 351n32
police, 5, 124, 148–49, 151, 154–55, 157–58
political appointees, ideology of, 40–41
political protest: AIDS activism, 214–15; antinuclear protests, 27, 110; anti-Reagan protests, 92, 163; gay rights movement, 214, 341n40; and political repression, 266; Tiananmen Square, 264; UC-Berkeley student rally, 14
Politics of Rich and Poor, The (Phillips), 295
poor, the: and crack cocaine, 123–24; growing income inequality, 281; increased imprisonment of, 5; lack of compassion for, 5–6, 60, 85, 92, 94–95, 140, 297, 325–26n16, 326n23; Paine's sympathy for, 5; poverty rate, 85, 143; race and poverty, 142–45; Reaganism's negative impact on, 7, 294–95; spending cuts' impact on programs for, 59–60, 65, 85, 91–93, 94, 95, 310n51
pork-barrel projects, 59
postmodernism, 134–36
Postol, Theodore, 319n23
Powell, Colin (Gen.), 192
Powell, Lewis, Jr. (Justice), 222
Prince, 136, 137
prisons, 5, 259. *See also* incarceration rates
Professional Air Traffic Controllers Organization (PATCO), 85–87
property taxes, 17, 20
PTL Club, The, 210–11
Public Enemy (PE; rap group), 144, 156–57
public housing, 142–43
Purple Rain (Prince album/movie, 1984), 137

Qaddafi, Moammar, 74, 192, 193
Quayle, J. Danforth ("Dan"), 96, 249–50, 251
Quilt (AIDS Quilt), 214–15

Rabin, Yitzhak, 190–91
race and racial (in)equality, 42; and the 1984 presidential election, 170–71; and the 1988 presidential election, 243, 247, 253–55 (*see also* Horton, Willie); poverty and, 142–45; race and the Democratic Party, 174–75, 333n43; racial fear and tension, 139–40, 149–58; Reagan and Reaganism's racial stance, 7–9, 24–25, 140, 301n17; and Reagan's judicial appointees, 178; white opposition to antidiscriminatory laws, 7–8, 12–13, 15, 16; white racism, 147, 175. *See also* African Americans; civil rights
Rachel and Her Children (Kozol), 146
Rafsanjani, Ali, 187
Raines, Howell, 94
Rand, Ayn, 32

wealthy, the (*continued*)
campaign, 252, 255; celebration of wealth, 202; CEO pay, 281, 355n25; concentration of wealth, 280–81; exploitation of, 6; ostentatious lifestyle of, 47–48, 120–21, 205, 210; and the Republican Party, 174; tax cuts aimed at, 32, 53, 61, 63, 255, 281; unfitness for leadership, 295; wealth gospel, 210. *See also* Wall Street; *and specific individuals*
Webster v. Reproductive Health Services (1989), 290
Wedtech scandal, 206
Weicker, Lowell, 96
Weidenbaum, Murray, 55
Weinberger, Caspar ("Cap"): about, 103–4; and Iran-Contra operations, 184, 189, 190, 192, 195–96, 198; and the military budget, 54; military strategic goals, 68, 69; military strategy goals, 318n9; Miller's criticism of, 95; and the national security adviser vacancy, 113; on Reagan and terrorism, 188–89; and SDI, 234; and Shultz, 103–4; on the U.S. presence in Beirut, 114
Weir, Benjamin, Rev., 190, 339n81
Welch, Jack, 285
Weld, William, 206
welfare: benefits cut to working poor, 59–60, 94, 310n51; budget cuts to, 59–60, 95, 98, 162; negative perceptions of, 8, 143–44, 325–26n16, 326n23; Reagan's views on, 8–9, 12, 65, 172, 172; school lunch program as, 92, 93; and single parenthood, 143–44. *See also* Aid to Families with Dependent Children; food stamps; Medicaid
Westad, Odd Arne, 269
West Germany: Berlin Wall, 67, 235, 272; and German unification, 271–72; missile deployment in, 67–68; Reagan's visit to Bitburg military cemetery, 179–80; Red Army faction, 71; West Berlin nightclub bombing, 193
Weyrich, Paul, 256
White, Byron (Justice), 133
White, Robert, 79
White House: "donations" to redecorate, 48; Michael Jackson's visit to, 137–38; Reagan's staff, 50–52, 113–14. *See also* Reagan administration
White Noise (DeLillo), 134–35
whites: and the 1988 presidential election, 243; death rate, for young males, 327n40; incarceration rates, 328n43; opposition to antidiscriminatory laws, 7–8, 12–13, 15, 16; percentage of, in New York City, 328n46;

race and the Democratic Party, 174–75, 333n43); racism and white backlash, 7–8, 12–13, 16, 147, 175, 327n36 (*see also* race and racial [in]equality)
white-supremacist movement, 147, 327n36
Whitten, Jamie, 79
Wick, Charles Z., 32, 47
Wigton, Martin, 208
Will, George, 32
Willders, James, 97
Williams, Clayton, 291, 356–57n53
Williams, Vanessa, 161
Wills, Garry, 37, 103
Wilson, Charles ("Charlie"), 59, 79
Wilson, Pete, 292
Wilson, Woodrow, 6, 300n12
Wirth, Timothy, 164, 206–7
Wirthlin, Richard, 23
Wisconsin, 96, 159
Wolfe, Tom, 125
Wolfowitz, Paul, 262
women, 48; and the abortion issue, 290 (*see also* abortion); African American women, 143–44; churchwomen murdered in El Salvador, 39, 79; clothing, 119–20; equal rights, 15, 22, 342–43n66; feminism and postmodernism, 135; first vice presidential candidate, 168–69; gay women, 214; judicial appointees, 178–79 (*see also* O'Connor, Sandra Day); rap music's misogyny toward, 144, 157; Reagan's attitude regarding, 15; single parents, 142, 143–44; women voters, 28, 174, 254, 290–92, 356n53; in the workforce, 281, 289–90. *See also specific individuals*
Wonder, Stevie, 163
Woodward, Bob, 115, 336n27
working class, 93, 281–82. *See also* manufacturing sector; organized labor; unemployment
Wright, Jim (Speaker of the House): and the 1982 budget, 56, 58; bills pushed through House, 203; downfall, 255–57; on H. Baker as chief of staff, 217; and the Nicaraguan peace agreement, 265; on Reagan's veracity, 203–4; and the savings-and-loan crisis, 204–5
Wyman, Jane, 302n14
Yakovlev, Aleksander, 233
Young Americans for Freedom, 46, 73
yuppies, 126–27

Zablocki, Clement, 103
Zia ul-Haq, 274, 276
Zimbalist, Efrem, Jr., 47